Young America
1830-1840

Young America
1830-1840

BY

ROBERT E. RIEGEL

UNIVERSITY OF OKLAHOMA PRESS

NORMAN

BY ROBERT E. RIEGEL

The Story of the Western Railroads (New York, 1926)

America Moves West (New York, 1930; revised edition, 1947)

United States of America (with Helen Haugh) (New York, 1947)

Young America, 1830–1840 (Norman, 1949)

EDITOR OF

An Introduction to the Social Sciences (2 vols., New York, 1941)

TO *Florence*

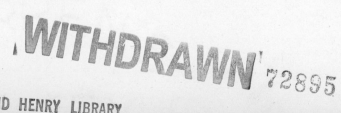

Preface

THE DECADE of 1830–40 has long been a relatively unknown period
in American history, even though its obvious importance as a transi-
tional period has struck many eyes. Recent publications have dispelled some of the ignorance, but much remains to be done. The
present book has been in progress for a good many years as an effort
to present a cross-view of a civilization which has had vital influence
in producing the modern America. Political events have been practically excluded, since the age of Jackson has been presented ex-
haustively by various other persons. The effort has been to present a
comprehensive view of how people earned their livings, how they
amused themselves, and what were their thoughts and their ideals.
All quotations are contemporary in origin, and are designed to give
the attitudes of the people of that day in their own words.

Mention cannot be made of the many people to whom in one way
or another I am indebted for contributions to this work. No one but
an author can realize the indebtedness which is inevitable for any
book. I would like, however, to express my special appreciation to
Merle Curti, not only for his specific suggestions in a field in which
he is thoroughly at home, but even more for the encouragement he
has provided. Needless to say, he cannot be blamed for any errors.

ROBERT E. RIEGEL

Hanover, New Hampshire
August 22, 1949

Contents

PART IV : AT PLAY

Illustrations

Young America
1830-1840

PART I : AMERICANS

1. A Changing World

THE FUTURE pressed heavily on each American of the eighteen thirties. For him there was no question that this was "the crisis age of the world."[1] Civilization was shaping before his very eyes. The day of the cocked hat, of monarchial governments, of the spinning wheel, and of horse-drawn carriages was being pushed into the discard. In its place was appearing the day of pantaloons and spittoons, of the factory and steam locomotive, and of the triumph of democracy. Today was the day of decision, which should lead to a rosier tomorrow.

Few doubted that the future would be better than the past. "Progress" was in the air, and change meant "improvement." To the average American, today was better than any day of the past. Was not the steamboat better than the sailing ship, the textile machine than the land loom, Christianity than paganism, democracy than monarchy? And the future would surpass the present. A young and vigorous nation could have no misgivings that the future belonged to the energetic and forward-looking. God would not permit his chosen people to go anywhere but upward and onward.

But time pressed. Speed was essential. The world might well be reconstructed within a generation if every man did his best—and God had so ordered human affairs that the pursuit of enlightened self-interest was also the pursuit of general human betterment. An intense sense of urgency obsessed men's minds, and they worked morning, noon, and night to free slaves, reform drunkards, or lay railroad tracks. They gulped their food and hurried from place to place as though the world would collapse if they neglected the real

[1] Quoted in G. H. Barnes and D. L. Dumond (eds.), *Letters of Theodore Dwight Weld, Angelina Grimké Weld and Sarah Grimké 1822–1844* (2 vols., New York, D. Appleton-Century Company, 1934), II, 337.

5

business of life for more than ten minutes at a time. As one French-man commented: "A man builds a house in which to spend his old age, and he sells it before the roof is on; he plants a garden, and lets it just as the trees are coming into bearing; he brings a field into tillage, and leaves other men to gather the crops."[2]

A young nation blessed with millions of acres of virgin land and comparable amounts of other resources, with immense distances to be conquered, may be excused for giving preference to the material aspects of life. This frame of mind was obvious to every visitor. "Compared with the same classes in England," said one of them, "one cannot but be struck with a certain resolute and obtrusive cupid-ity of gain, and a laxity of principle as to the means of acquiring it." He then added: "The only restraint upon these men is the law, and he is evidently considered the most skillful in his vocation who con-trives to overreach his neighbor, without incurring its penalties."[3]

Wealth was not only a very pleasant possession but the most usual criterion of social importance in a new and amorphous nation, where other lines of demarcation were often either blurred or non-existent. To some extent a man possessed prestige by his job, whether it was senior senator from Massachusetts or stage driver on the Na-tional Road, and to some extent socially acceptable occupations were distinguished by titles—as captains, judges, or senators—for there was actually a plethora of such designations in spite of a theoretical democratic abhorrence of titles. And yet the acquisition of wealth was for most people the favored way to improve their standing in society.

Wealth was the common ideal, but up to the moment there was little concentration of wealth as compared with conditions a century later; possibly this lack of concentration was the condition that was necessary for a continuation of the respect given material possessions. Rich men such as Astor and Girard had no fortunes comparable with those of a later Rockefeller and Ford. In fact, there was common

[2] Alexis de Tocqueville, *Democracy in America* (2 vols., Cambridge, Mass., Sever and Francis, 1863), II, 164.

[3] T. Hamilton, *Men and Manners in America* (Philadelphia, Carey, Lea and Blanchard, 1833), 74.

insistence that enormous private wealth was inconsistent with a true republicanism. Wealth was a goal—the prize for being smarter, more ambitious, and more diligent than a neighbor. The prizes were at the moment moderate and did little to disturb a rough equality that was greater than was ever to exist later. And wealth, once obtained, was not hoarded: "The Americans, although highly acquisitive, are not sordid as a nation. They expend their wealth freely, and where the object meets with their approbation, they are even munificent in their donations."[4]

But not for every American was the making of money simple. The United States was above all a nation of small farmers, and farming was not an occupation that embraced fundamental changes rapidly or in which large fortunes were easily attainable. While the average farmer subscribed thoroughly to the idea of progress, and was certain of the ultimate high destiny of the United States, he often clung tenaciously to what he considered the tried and true methods of his father and grandfather. He tended to view changes with a somewhat suspicious eye—an attitude that was not without justification as he saw new and complicated machinery, such as the reaper, fall to pieces, and attractively advertised new crops, such as silk, push some of his neighbors into bankruptcy.

Farming tended to be conservative, but even here there was change and movement. Novel ideas of crop rotation, fertilizer, new crops, land drainage, farm machinery, and scientific stock breeding were in the air. Well-to-do farmers reported their experiments—at least the successful ones—to the rapidly growing farm journals, and the editors of these same journals banged away month after month at the same ideas. The lessons were driven home in a practical way at the increasingly popular agricultural fairs, where popeyed farmers goggled at fat steers, powerful horses, and big ears of corn, while their wives exclaimed admiringly over new quilt patterns and jars of homemade jelly.

For many farmers the movement of the day was an actual physical transplanting. Hard-bitten Yankees sought the more fer-

[4] George Combe, *Notes on the United States of North America* (2 vols., Philadelphia, Carey and Hart, 1841), I, 333.

tile acres of the upper Mississippi Valley. Southern planters deserted worn-out eastern lands for the greater opportunity beyond the mountains. And along with the farmers went the center of gravity of farming. Cotton, wheat, corn, tobacco, and sheep were among the products which also migrated to the West. Both farming and the farmer were on the move.

But many a farm boy was dissatisfied with the moderate returns that he might expect from following in the footsteps of his father. Many looked toward manufacturing, commerce, or transportation to provide the main opportunities for the wealth which would make them outstanding. And since occupations were not as specialized as they were later to become, a man might try several fields in his search for fame and fortune. "An American takes up, leaves, goes back to ten occupations in his life; he is constantly changing his domicile and is continually forming new enterprises," said the young Tocqueville, and added, "Less than any other man in the world does he fear to compromise an acquired fortune, because he knows with what facility he can gain a new one."[5]

Americans were proud of their busy factories, whether the textile mills of Lowell, the shoe factories of Brockton, the pottery works at Trenton, or the iron mills at Richmond. Here was a new declaration of independence, this time from subservience to English factories, for evidence was being amassed that American freemen could out-compete the servile labor of Europe. And along with the factory came the rise of the corporation, the expansion of banking, and an increasing importance for stock exchanges. The United States could no longer be neglected as an important modern industrial nation. More large businesses, of course, meant a trend toward monopoly, and Americans had always objected to monopoly and special privilege, but in spite of that drawback it was hard for a patriotic citizen to fail to thrill to the industrial giants who testified to the initiative and energy of American citizens.

Factories meant wage labor, and it was in this field that difficulties began to appear. Americans much preferred to own their own

[5] Quoted in G. W. Pierson, *Tocqueville and Beaumont in America* (New York, Oxford University Press, 1938), 130.

8

farms or shops or mills than to work for wages, with the result that mill owners had to search frantically for a labor supply. Improved machinery decreased, but did not solve, their problem. Immigrants were seized avidly for industries that could use them, but unfortunately a German or Irish peasant farmer often failed to be satisfactory in a factory, particularly when any skill was needed. New England mills sent their agents through back-country New England to lure girls with the bait of high wages. Children were often coerced by pressure on their parents.

Not everyone greeted the growing factories with pleasure. Sorrow and anger filled the hearts of the old-fashioned artisans who had been looking forward to some day being masters of their own small shops. Now they were hard put even to make their livings, for how could a hand weaver compete with a textile mill full of machinery run by young girls? How could a shoemaker compete with a shoe factory? How could printers hold out against a steam press operated by women? The reaction of the skilled was the formation of unions to try to hold back the tide, and labor unions had their first important American development during the eighteen thirties. From the skilled artisans the idea spread to the factory workers, and soon a rash of strikes swept over the face of industry. Traditional American opportunity apparently did not satisfy everyone. Certain men presumably accepted the conclusion that owning their own businesses was a remote possibility and that they had most to gain by uniting with their fellow workers for higher wages. The future was taking form.

Factory production changed vitally the activities and the appearance of the American home. The rough homespun clothes of the past retreated before their manufactured counterparts until even the farming family in the remotest back country had mill cloth for at least its church-attending suits and dresses. While tailoring and dressmaking did not seem suitable occupations for a factory, the making of cloth, hats, shoes, furniture, and tools increasingly left the home. More and more the average family filled its desires by visiting a store—whether the rich city emporium of gas lights and plate-glass windows or the dirty and cluttered general store of the country. And store goods meant that the farmer needed a surplus to trade for desired products. More and more he began to specialize in a single cash crop rather than to try to be self-sufficient, and this specialization in turn inspired him to read his farm journals more avidly to find ways in which his production might be increased.

Factories meant more trade, and together they expanded the towns and cities, which seemed the very acme of rush, bustle, and modernity. The marveling farmer and his wife gaped in astonished admiration at the hurrying crowds, the omnibuses, the palatial homes, the glittering stores, the saloons, theaters, and hotels. Here and there they could see the very latest of modern improvements—garbage collection instead of pigs, sewage pipe, waterworks, coal stoves, gas lights, and even furnaces, inside toilets and bathtubs. Of course such new-fangled gadgets were still rare, but the country visitor could marvel at the wonders of his age as he visited the Fairmount Park waterworks at Philadelphia, saw the gas lights at the Park Theater in New York, or used the modern bathing facilities at the Tremont House in Boston. Going back home to his tallow candles, his open fireplace, and his backhouse, he could regale his neighbors with marvelous tales of the almost incredible luxury which was possible in the modern world.

The show places of the nation were the public buildings and monuments. Everyone who had the opportunity admired the Capitol at Washington, the rising Bunker Hill Monument, the important banks, theaters, city halls, and churches. The old-fashioned Georgian architecture seemed too simple and plain for these up-and-coming people, but there was too little time and energy to develop a new and distinctive American architecture, so they dug back into antiquity and revived Greek and Roman forms, thereby establishing a classical tradition for public buildings which has seemed almost impossible to overcome. Even the Washington Monument was planned originally with a ring of small columns at its base, while banks in particular seemed to fancy themselves as Greek temples, even when the cold weather necessitated a chimney protruding from the flat roof.

While buildings were becoming more ornate, clothes were becoming more sober, particularly for the men. This was the Jacksonian era, when the common man was coming into his own—and the common man and his wife needed utilitarian clothes for the hard work of life. Significant of the changing times was the acceptance by the well-to-do and well-born of the costume of the working people. Knee breeches, buckles, silk stockings, cocked hat, and ruffles at breast and wrists gave way to pantaloons, coat, and waistcoat. For the ladies, colonial silks and powdered hair were supplanted by somewhat more utilitarian costumes. Only a few elderly conservatives continued to cling to the dress of their fathers and grandfathers.

The very heart of the modern, forward-looking improvements of the eighteen thirties were the newer forms of transportation—improved roads, canals, steamboats, and above all the railroad. Little argument was needed to convince people that future national prosperity depended primarily upon the moving of people and goods cheaply and rapidly over the vast country. Roads were being macadamized, which means that gravel roads were being built. Canals were constructed in amazing profusion and projected in reckless numbers. Wild-eyed enthusiasts even talked of the day when a series of canals would span the continent from the Atlantic to the Pacific. Steamboats jammed the wharves of New York, Albany, Louisville, St. Louis, New Orleans, and other river towns. By the end of the decade steam had been applied to trans-Atlantic service; even though the heydey of the clipper was still in the future, many progressive people realized that the death knell of the sailing vessel had been sounded.

Newest and most admired of the transportation improvements was the railroad, which was greeted by enthusiasm not far short of hysterical. When the first dirt was thrown for the earliest standard commercial road, the Baltimore and Ohio, the novelty of the event did not prevent its celebration with magnificent gusto. Over fifty thousand people lined the streets of Baltimore on July 4, 1828, to cheer what *Niles Register* called "The most splendid civic procession, perhaps, ever exhibited in America."[6] Members of Congress and of the legislature, the mayor and city council, Revolutionary soldiers, cavalry units, farmers and barbers, carpenters and stone cutters, cordwainers and hatters, coopers and turners, school chil-

[6] *Niles Register* (Baltimore), Vol. XXXIV (July 5, 1828), 297.

dren, and benevolent societies, with placards and floats, made the occasion memorable.

The central figure of the Baltimore celebration was the venerable and respected Charles Carroll of Carrollton, last surviving signer of the Declaration of Independence. Carroll was duly impressed by the honor accorded him, and stated: "I consider this among the most important acts of my life, second only to my signing of the Declaration of Independence," and then upon second thought added, "if even it be second to that."[7] On this same day the President of the United States, John Quincy Adams, laid aside his coat to throw the first dirt for the Chesapeake and Ohio Canal, but time was to show that he had backed the wrong horse.

Railroads came of age with startling rapidity. When the first passengers on the Baltimore and Ohio in 1829 exclaimed in wonder at the pleasures of following a horse on such a smooth road, they had not the least idea of what the next ten years were to hold in store. Steam locomotives puffing over thousands of miles of iron track and hauling cars which contained even parlors and bedrooms could hardly have been predicted except by the most unrealistic of dreamers. By 1840 there was little doubt that the railroad was to be the prime land carrier of the future.

Vast economic changes loomed impressively in people's minds, but they represented only a part of the fascinating story of a changing America. To outsiders the United States appeared materialistic, but no American was willing to admit that his country was in any respect the inferior of a decadent Europe. True, he boasted of the new railroads and mills and the rapid street travel in New York. But he also boasted of the writings of Washington Irving, the paintings of Washington Allston, the operations of Valentine Mott, and the sermons of Lyman Beecher. Mention any field you liked, whether sculpture or the study of the digestive tract, the New World was willing to match the best that the Old World had to offer.

While American bombastic claims to universal superiority need a large amount of contraction to come within the realm of the prob-

[7] Quoted in M. Reizenstein, *The Economic History of the Baltimore and Ohio Railroad 1827–1853* (Baltimore, Johns Hopkins Press, 1897), 20.

able, the actual accomplishments of Americans were greater than might have been expected. Workers in abstract science, such as Benjamin Silliman, were few, while scientific books and magazines were not first rate. But in two lines of scientific endeavor the Americans made notable contributions. The first was in the collection and classification of the new animals, plants, and minerals of the New World. Men such as Say and Audubon are still given credit for their pioneer work, while a long series of western explorations and eastern geological surveys provided a vast amount of information about the nation. The second contribution was in the realm of practical inventions, for the American was ingenious. A flood of inventions ranging from the reaping machine to the flying machine, from the standardized plow to the revolver, from rubber vulcanization to the collar button, gave the lie to the prediction made early in the decade that the patent office might as well close for lack of business.

The best-occupied field of science was medicine, but the practitioners were for the most part not overly impressive, even to the most patriotic Americans. Medical systems were still copied slavishly from Europe. Bloodletting and calomel remained the average doctor's stand-bys. Useful innovations, such as vaccination, were largely brought from Europe. Epidemics continued to sweep the country, leaving the medical profession in complete bafflement. Hospitals were little more than breeding grounds for disease as long as germs and antiseptics remained completely unknown. The one field of medicine of which Americans really were proud was surgery, in which they felt no one would ever exceed the proficiency of a Warren of Boston or a Mott of New York. In actual fact such men were clever, but modern surgery can hardly be said to have begun before the use of antiseptics and before the introduction of anesthetics; only an unknown Georgia doctor was ingenious enough to make practical use of an anesthetic before 1840.

Medicine may have been in general conservative and stodgy, but that did not mean that it was not bombarded from all sides with new ideas which a certain number of people thought would revolutionize the practice of medicine in accordance with new and modern ideas. Homeopathy was a European-born attack on the old calomel-bleeding routine. Thomsonian medicine—largely a steam bath and herb affair—was a native product. The doctor-author Oliver Wendell Holmes labored to show that puerperal (child-bed) fever was contagious. Dentistry made valiant efforts to obtain professional training and recognition. Phrenology, European born, attracted a wide American following, including many eminent doctors. Hypnotism was widely advertised, but in general was viewed askance by the medical profession; in spite of this skepticism, important discoveries were made by Americans. Sylvester Graham made outstanding contributions to the public-health movement, even though he is remembered today only for a kind of bread of which he had no knowledge. An American was the first doctor in the world to write a book on birth control—probably the most important book of its kind ever published. Altogether, the American medical scene could hardly be considered completely static.

The American also liked to boast of his accomplishments in more purely esthetic fields. In architecture and sculpture, American enthusiasm for Greece in her struggle for independence had brought a bursting revival of interest in classic forms. Greek temples rose overnight in the orderly dignity of Philadelphia, in the wilds of Indiana, and on the rolling plantation land of Virginia. Classical subjects became common in sculpture and in painting, with even the reintroduction of the nude female figure, to the shocked horror of the more conservative citizenry. Actually the American's taste was fairly primitive, with the greatest appreciation for a painting that was either impressively large or else depicted with photographic fidelity someone he knew—preferably himself. Admiration of size produced the diorama, often thousands of feet of painting, as of a whole river. Size combined with portraiture might result in a magnificent display of the founding fathers or of Washington and his officers. Pictures of this type might be satisfying to painter and viewer, but ordinarily they were not economically profitable, and since even a painter had to eat, the average artist used his talents to produce hundreds of portraits. Here and there an iconoclast willing to starve in a garret turned out landscapes, for the Hudson River School was starting work, but men of this kind were exceptions.

The artistic field in which Americans felt the most confidence was literature, for a host of eminent men were following the lead of the dean of American letters, Washington Irving. Contemporary favor went in part to such writers as Simms and Sigourney, over whom the future literary historian was to raise his eyebrows, but no period can be dismissed lightly which includes such names as Longfellow, Lowell, Whittier, Holmes, Poe, and Hawthorne. The first volume of Bancroft's monumental history appeared, and Prescott was at work. Magazines, newspapers, and books flowed from the presses in a never ending profusion. Horace Greeley began his newspaper career, and Benjamin Day opened the age of the cheap and sensational daily paper. The *Southern Literary Messenger* and Hall's *Western Monthly Magazine* gave notice that by no means all significant literary endeavor was monopolized by the Northeast.

Even in music and drama, America was by no means sterile. Musical composition tended to limit itself to patriotic songs and hymns, but larger aspirations existed, so that even a first native opera could be unveiled to an admiring public. Likewise there were American playwrights and American actors, and yet music and the drama were largely in foreign hands, partly because of the lack of American talent and partly because of the absence of international copyright restrictions. Truth to tell, America was not yet ready for outstanding work in music and drama. The best type of accomplishment was that of Lowell Mason, who trained music teachers and who introduced music into the Boston schools.

Literature, art, the sciences, and, in fact, even the earning of money seemed to Americans to have no significance unless geared to a belief in God and a future life. A useful life in this world should mean a happy hereafter, and how could one feel assured that true merit would have its just reward in the present life unless a loving God ran a well-ordered universe and looked out for his own? The United States was deeply and sincerely religious. The wave of agnosticism, free thinking, and deism of the Revolutionary period and the early Republic had given way to a thoroughgoing and all-embracing piety which seems exaggeratedly mawkish to the modern investigator, particularly as he reads the intimate family letters of the day. A mother writes: "O my dear son, be prudent, be wise, meek, modest, humble; remember that life is uncertain, and that those only are safe, truly honorable, or really happy, who have laid up treasure in heaven. Make it your first, your great concern, to be reconciled to God."[8]

Religious homilies did not imply any lessening of attention to more immediately practical matters. After Mother Weld gives her other-worldly advice, she follows it, in the best canons of the period, by urging son Theodore to pick the occupation from which he could obtain the greatest financial remuneration. These two bits of advice were felt to be in no sense clashing. Religion and business were two separate and independent matters. Business ethics were not the province of the church. One made money to the glory of God, and the possession of wealth indicated, all other things being equal, that God had smiled upon man's efforts.

The religion which was so central to American thought was above all Protestant, in spite of the increasing flood of Roman Catholic immigrants, particularly Irish. To a large part of American Protestants, Catholicism was no better than paganism—in fact, it might be worse, since a void was relatively easier to fill. For them it was equally commendable to fight the Pope or the Devil, and many seemed to fail to distinguish between the two.

The efforts of aggressively minded Protestants might have been more successful if they could have agreed on the exact doctrines they were supporting. Actually, the United States was the happy hunting ground of Protestant sects. Many of them had sought asylum in the United States, but others were indigenous, since as long as men read the Bible for themselves and were advised to follow their own consciences, there were inevitable differences of opinion. Even the peaceful Quakers argued vigorously over a split in the church, while fragments of other sects seemed continually to be coming loose. Most intriguing of the new sects was the Mormon, led by Joseph Smith, Jr., but it was only symptomatic. From time to time efforts were made to reunite all Protestants, but for most people this end could only be attained properly by persuading other

8 Barnes, *Weld Letters*, I, 5.

16

people to renounce their own beliefs in favor of the "truth." Alexander Campbell had tried to persuade Christians to unite in a simpler and "purer" set of doctrines, but by the eighteen thirties there was no question that what he had produced was one more sect.

Religion was not vague and remote, but of immediate and vital importance, for men felt that God watched them every second with a searching eye, rewarding and punishing, advising and interfering. Man searched his conscience and pored over the words of Holy Writ to make sure he was not offending a God who not only was loving but also could be terrible in His justice. The family Bible was read assiduously, and was accepted as literally true, word for word. Careful reading brought much speculation about the more mystic and abstruse sections. William Miller, for example, derived from these portions the exact date for the end of the world and the second coming of Christ; thousands of Americans believed his word and prepared themselves for being snatched up to Heaven in the near future.

Christians emphatically considered themselves their brothers' keepers, with the sacred duty to convert those less knowing than themselves to proper ideas of piety and morality. And again a sense of urgency spurred them on, for perfection seemed very close. Tract societies flooded the country with religious literature. Sunday schools flourished. Sunday-observance groups protested vigorously the secularizing of the Sabbath, particularly the Sunday carrying of the mail. But, above all, missionaries, both home and foreign, carried the Word of God and salvation to the more benighted parts of the world. As they proclaimed, "the field is ripe for the harvest," and Christian diligence would bring the conversion of the world within a generation.

The reforming impulse, backed by strong religious convictions, swept into all sorts of movements for social improvement. Attention went to paupers, deaf and dumb, orphans, blind, and insane at a time when any attention meant a definite improvement over conditions in the past. Two important prison societies, inspired by religious impulses, gave a significant push toward modern penology, even though the two groups disputed each other vigorously. Prostitution became a matter of social concern, with the reform societies usually reaching back to the Bible for the title Magdalen. Programs for the aid of the Negro found religious support, whether to return the slaves to Africa or to give them freedom within the United States; the antislavery movement was manned in significant part by ministers.

No reform movement was better advertised than that for temperance, which tended more and more to be converted into a prohibition drive. Something of a climax came late in the decade with the Washingtonian movement, by and for drunkards. And if liquor were bad, why not also tobacco, tea, coffee, and indeed anything which diverted men's minds from the eternal truths? Sternly conscientious men and women waged crusades against tobacco, the theater, novels, or any human foible which seemed to them to waste time which had better be spent to the glory of the Lord. The eighteen thirties loom large among the periods in which a multiplicity of reform movements buffeted the common man from every side. Moral earnestness and a thorough belief in the perfectibility of man were linked with the unshakable conviction that American civilization was the best the world had ever seen, and would be completely perfect if only it corrected the few flaws that the reformer sought to remedy.

Not least of American beliefs was the unhesitating conviction that the American form of government was the best in the world. American democracy was the final and perfect government, which meant to a religious and reforming America that God had taken a direct hand in human affairs to create a model for the rest of the world to follow. "No one who admits the intervention of a special providence in the affairs of nations," and the author was emphatically of this mind, "can hesitate to believe, that the statesmen and heroes of the revolution were raised up by the God of heaven, for the important and definite purpose of achieving the independence of America . . . and of presenting to the monarchical governments in the eastern hemisphere, the example of a government, founded upon the principles of civil and religious liberty."[9] The greatest

[9] C. A. Goodrich, *Lives of the Signers of the Declaration of Independence* (New York, Jonathan Leavitt, 1829), 3.

celebrations of this liberty came upon Independence Day, when parades, oratory, toasts, and fireworks held the right of way, but any day was a proper occasion for making the eagle scream.

Most men agreed that a democracy could function properly only with an educated citizenry, but at this point money-making and patriotism collided, for more education meant greater investments in schools and teachers rather than in mills and railroads. The result was somewhat less education than the flamboyant speeches led one to expect; nevertheless, progress was respectable. Common-school education at public expense, the first real development of the high school, and the first normal school for the training of teachers were among the ideas pushed into practice by such men as Horace Mann and Henry Barnard. New subjects for the schools ranged from music to manual training. Specialized academic work was introduced in such diverse fields as dentistry and agriculture. New colleges, such as New York University, improved the opportunities for higher education, while Oberlin made the startling innovation of permitting women and Negroes to join white men in the search for the B. A. In adult education, the lyceum did a splendid piece of work.

The government of which Americans were so proud was a government of limited powers, for Americans had a strong theoretical regard for personal independence and individual initiative. Most people nodded their heads at Jefferson's dictum that "that government is best that governs least." The doctrines of Adam Smith, Ricardo, the Mills, and the other English economists were accepted by most people as self-evident truths. Theoretically the government confined its attention to such matters as preserving order, insuring defense, enforcing contracts, and establishing a sound currency.

Free competition was a golden theory which was by no means always achieved in practice. Americans were gregarious and tended to gather into groups, whether to build a railroad or to crusade against the use of coffee. Sometimes the group was little more than a mob celebrating an election, rioting against working conditions, breaking up a theater, or burning a convent. More usually it was orderly, and convened to construct a constitution and elect officers.

The next step frequently was to call for government action, as to raise the tariff, create easy money, prevent steamboat accidents, end lotteries, give easier land terms, remove the Indians, lessen hours of labor, or prohibit liquor. Somehow the general theory of a limited government was lost to view when any group found an object which it considered of vital importance. In general, the government should remain out of the private lives of its citizens, but in this particular case .... "Rugged individualism" was combined with a tendency to work in groups and call for governmental action in a way that is utterly confusing to the observer.

Since American democracy was the highest form of human government, the United States was considered the ideal of the oppressed people of the world—and that meant all people beyond the boundaries of the United States. America was the shining example of a free people living under an enlightened constitution, and anyone failing to recognize this obvious fact must either be living in besotted ignorance or belong to the outmoded monarchial forces which sought to oppress the common man. Under such circumstances, the United States had a high duty to mankind. "Ours is considered as the final trial. If free institutions cannot exist and flourish and prove permanent, and be the channel of immeasurable good to the inhabitants of these States, where shall the philanthropist hope to find human nature that is qualified to enjoy and perpetuate them? Not on this earth."[10] The apparent questioning pessimism of this statement is only rhetorical, and should not be taken seriously; the author had no real doubt that the institutions of the United States would flourish and become a model for the rest of the world.

American democracy, American Protestant Christianity, and other American ways of life were the hope of the world. And following Biblical injunctions, Americans could not justify themselves in sitting back smugly and waiting for the rest of the world to catch up. They felt the call to crusade positively and aggressively to carry the good news to the ends of the earth. But Satan at times was so strongly entrenched that the good news had to be crammed down

[10] *The Biblical Repository* (Andover), Vol. VIII, 1st series (October, 1836), 257.

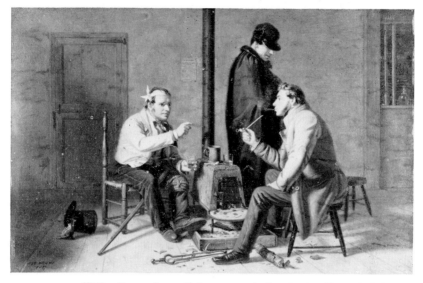

"The Long Story," from a painting by William S. Mount

In the collection of The Corcoran Gallery of Art

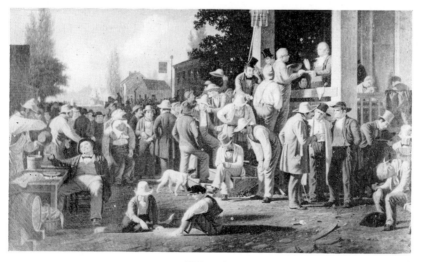

"The County Election," from a painting
by George Caleb Bingham

Courtesy of the Boatmen's National Bank of St. Louis

unwilling throats. Closest at hand was the American Indian, who frequently was so benighted that he not only refused to accept Christ, but even objected to such obvious trappings of civilization as pantaloons and only one wife. Even church and state combined could not change his mind. Such obduracy brought the inevitable conclusion that God must have meant that the Indians should be removed from their ancestral lands to make way for the white farmers who believed in God and democracy. Further afield, American missionaries journeyed to the far places of the earth with the blessings, if not always with the firm financial support, of the entire nation. They were unshakable in the belief that American civilization should replace the pagan and "uncivilized" practices of such regions as China and India. Apparently they never had an inkling that they were dealing with cultures that were older and better established than their own.

Most spectacular and historically of the greatest importance of the expressions of militant Christian democracy was the growing feeling that the United States was destined inevitably to expand to the Pacific, with extensions north and south—a feeling which later bore the name of "manifest destiny." Senator Benton asked modestly that along the Rockies "the western limit of this republic should be drawn, and the statue of the fabled god Terminus should be raised upon its highest peak,"[11] but in time he became more demanding, while others were at least equally aggressive. Tucker of Virginia orated that settlement "Marches on, with the increasing rapidity of a fire, and nothing will stop it until it reaches the shores of the Pacific,"[12] an event which he estimated conservatively would take place in 1872. A better-known American, Fenimore Cooper, prophesied that the United States "will sweep its coasts of every hostile hold; that Bermuda, and all such places, will come into the possession of the Americans in the course of the next half century."[13] Certainly Americans of the eighteen thirties were not modest in their expecta-

[11] Quoted in F. J. Turner, *Rise of the New West 1819–1829* (New York, Harper and Brothers, 1906), 131.

[12] *Register of Debates*, 18 Cong., 2 sess., I, 37.

[13] J. F. Cooper, *Notions of the Americans* (2 vols., Philadelphia, Carey, Lea and Carey, 1828), II, 87–88.

tions, and yet future events often exceeded their wildest dreams. Few guessed territorial expansion with sufficient liberality, and no one came even close in his estimates of population growth.

America was loud and boastful. By common repute the Kentuckians were the cream of the braggarts, but certainly the rest of the United States was not far in arrears. But might not Americans be talking so loudly in order to shout down the doubts that lingered in the backs of their minds? In many ways the United States was exhibiting the traits of adolescence. It was self-conscious of its incipient industrialism, its religious and artistic and governmental strivings, in somewhat the same way that the adolescent is conscious of his lengthening arms and legs and the beginning of his beard. Also, like the adolescent, it boasted altogether too loudly of its own superiorities, with now and then its voice cracking to a very feeble treble. It took bitterly to heart the criticism of a Mrs. Trollope or a Charles Dickens—criticism that a century later would have been overlooked. Was it not possible that somewhere deep in American consciousness was the unpleasant feeling that maybe the United States did not have the final word in everything—that possibly Europe had certain superiorities of her own?

Psychological subleties do not, however, change the great central facts. The United States of the eighteen thirties was a bustling and kaleidescopic community, giving evidence of the nature and greatness of its future. Social thinking and nonmaterial culture were changing somewhat more slowly than material conditions, but everywhere there was life and movement. The developments of the next century were becoming visible to the far-sighted. And above all, Americans had unquestioning confidence in the future. The next century was to be a period of American greatness, when the United States was to become the dominant nation, and when all the peoples of the world would try to copy its superior institutions. Truly the United States was youthful, but with a robust energy, confidence, and enthusiasm which were being translated rapidly into very real accomplishments.

2. The People

ADOLESCENT AMERICA with its roseate dreams of grandeur was basically English in blood and institutions. Even though rabid patriots twisted the lion's tail regularly and joyously, they also listened respectfully to English politicians, reformers, writers, and divines. American magazines reprinted English stories, American doctors looked toward England with awe, and American theaters presented English plays and starred English actors.

The United States was historically a cultural offshoot of England, but New York was by no means a suburb of London, or Boston an infant Manchester. The New World was different from the Old, and not primarily because of the pressure of nationalistic fervor. Physical features were different, and non-English stocks contributed parts of their cultures. Not only was the United States distinct from England, but also the United States itself had no uniformity. The Yankee farmer and the southern planter both traced their heritage to the tight little isle, but no one confused the two.

New Englanders were the most stereotyped of all Americans, and the usual portrait was not favorable: "One meets in them much to approve, little to admire, and nothing to love. . . . Nature, in framing a Yankee, seems to have given him double brains, and half heart."[1] The Yankee appeared most frequently to the rest of the country as a solemn and sanctimonious hustler, frequently a peripatetic peddler who from the pack on his back sold all kinds of gimcracks, including clocks that would not run, wooden nutmegs, and sanded sugar. His reputation included credit for being the sharpest trader on the continent.

In truth, New England soil and climate were not favorable for

[1] Hamilton, *Men and Manners*, 126–27.

the expansive jollity and carefree existence that comes from warm weather and deep, rich soil. Almost inevitably the New Englander was long and lean, laconic, strict, and religious; he did not spoil his children by sparing the rod in spite of being zealous for them, giving them the best education that could be obtained in the United States. The New Englander was an introvert, with a morbid curiosity about the progress of his soul. Voluminous and self-revealing diaries and involved theological disputations were more to his taste than novels and horse races. The Calvinism of the Puritan fathers throve on New England air.

But New Englanders were by no means completely self-contained. For men not ordinarily loquacious, their sermons and their town meetings could run to prodigious lengths, while their urge toward literary self-expression gave a distinctly New England complexion to the "golden age of American letters." Their searchings of their own consciences did not prevent them from keeping a sharp eye on the actions of others, for the Yankee emphatically insisted that he was his brother's keeper. He embarked on many far-flung crusades to bring truth and morality to the less enlightened portions of the world. Missionary societies and all kinds of reform movements looked north for much of their support, both in dollars and in men, for a good religious New Englander such as William Lloyd Garrison was a promising candidate for martyrdom.

New England was a diversified area, with small farms, sheep raising, lumbering, fishing, shipping, and manufacturing all important, and all revolving around the hub of Boston. New England even had a frontier of its own, where men were carving new farms from the wilderness. But even with this diversity, New England lagged in population growth. Foreign additions were offset by a falling birth rate and by a vast trek to the West—a movement that was not always popular in Yankeeland. New Englanders followed the sun through central and western New York, leaving a trail of baked beans and brown bread as far west as Wisconsin and Iowa. Other energetic Yankees pursued wealth and fame as merchants in New Orleans, as college presidents in South Carolina, or as lawyers in Missouri, thus making vital contributions to American professional intelligence. As different men as Stephen A. Douglas and Joseph Smith, Jr., were both born in Vermont.

The Middle states boasted the main metropolitan centers, for here were America's two largest cities, New York and Philadelphia, with pretensions toward dominating both ocean shipping and interior trade toward the West. Between the cities lay important industrial areas. In their hinterlands lay some of America's richest farming land—the Hudson and Mohawk valleys to the north, and the valleys of the Delaware, Susquehanna, and Schuylkill farther south. That American population should tend to concentrate in this region could be no surprise to anyone.

The bustling diversity of the Middle states, together with their shipping facilities, brought the greatest variety of population. German and Irish immigrants landed increasingly at New York, where many of the Irish congregated in the growing slums. Along the Hudson were significant remnants of the old Dutch patroons, who now were waging a losing battle to retain the land tenures of an earlier day. In the Mohawk Valley were the remains of an older German migration, now being submerged by a flood of new migrants, particularly Yankees from New England.

In eastern Pennsylvania and extending south into Maryland were the orderly, well-cultivated fields, the bulging barns, and the beautifully tended houses of the Pennsylvania Germans. Slow, stolid, and conservative, these people retained a vulgarized German language, hexing and good-luck symbols, and an abiding suspicion of such new-fangled ideas as education at public expense. On the other hand, however, no one questioned their industry, their frugality, their honesty, or their hospitality. Their prosperity was based on good soil, but only as it received hard labor and shrewd management. In mingled respect and exasperation comes the comment that the Pennsylvania German was "in business matters more than a match for the keenest Yankee."[2]

South of the Mason-Dixon line, shipping and manufacturing became somewhat less important, even though cities like Baltimore,

[2] T. J. McCornack (ed.), *Memoirs of Gustave Koerner* (2 vols., Cedar Rapids, Iowa, Torch Press, 1909), I, 322.

Richmond, Lynchburg, and Charleston would have objected to that statement, pointing to iron mills, textile factories, tobacco manufactures, and other evidences of industrialization. In spite of these pretensions, the fact remained that Virginia, the Carolinas, and Georgia were above all cotton and slave states, with cotton now dominant over such earlier staples as tobacco and rice. One-crop farming was bringing evidences of soil exhaustion in spite of a slight renaissance with the increasing use of fertilizers. Far to the south, much of Georgia and Florida represented a frontier area from which the Indians had not yet been removed.

Since the South had few large cities and a slave economy, it attracted few immigrants, with the result that society was more static and better ordered than farther north. At the top of the social pyramid were the few important white planters, with broad acres and many slaves. Below them came merchants, manufacturers, and farmers, until at the bottom were the Negroes, who performed a large part of the manual labor. Actually only a comparatively few whites had any important number of slaves. The small independent farmer might have one or two who worked side by side with him in the fields. The shiftless "cracker" of the pine flats or the mountain white with his Elizabethan culture had none.

For almost every Southerner life was less arduous and more haphazard than for his northern counterpart. The longer growing seasons brought less pressure, the more moderate climate necessitated less tightly built houses, while the heat sapped energy. Every visitor commented on the poorer roads, the more ramshackle houses, and the slothful habits, even while he was enjoying the greater leisure and the more open-handed hospitality of the South.

Into this Anglo-Saxon America was coming an ever increasing flow of foreign born to change perceptibly the racial composition of the United States—for half of the new arrivals were Irish and one-third were German. Irish pigs and potatoes had fallen upon evil times, while the Germans were experiencing the sad aftermath of an unsuccessful revolution. What could be more reasonable than to come to a new world where everyone was free and where the streets were said to be paved with gold? The number of arrivals declined when the panic of 1837 brought the sad realization that the supposed gold was no more than gilt.

Paddy would never have been able to leave County Killarney had not the harassed government and landowners been willing to give him a boost, and the ship companies to offer him special rates. But with these aids Paddy could come to America in magnificent numbers.

> *Wid my bundle on my shoulder,*
> *Faith! there's no man could be boulder;*
> *I'm lavin' dear old Ireland without warnin'*
> *For I lately took the notion,*
> *For to cross the briny ocean,*
> *And I shtart for Philadelphia in the mornin'.*[3]

Irishmen were fascinated by the rumors of fifty cents a day paid for unskilled labor, and thousands swung picks and wielded shovels on the Baltimore and Ohio Railroad, the Pennsylvania System, and other public improvements. Others seeped into the factory towns such as Lowell and Fall River to do common labor. Still others undercut the Negroes for the unskilled jobs in the cities, even though the Negroes were held to be more trustworthy. As house servants, the Irish were reputed to be cheap, but uncouth, independent, cantankerous, and slow to learn. Sympathy was expressed for the unfortunate persons who could not obtain good servants but had to take "the low Irish; and everyone knows what kind of servants they commonly are."[4] When the Irish went west, they seldom reverted to the farming from which they had escaped, but gravitated to unskilled labor on the canals and railroads.

In good times Paddy might exult in his fifty cents a day, with even free whiskey. But he soon discovered that prices kept step with wages, and that in bad times he might receive no more than his board.

[3] Quoted in W. F. Adams, *Ireland and Irish Immigration to the New World from 1815 to the Famine* (New Haven, Yale University Press, 1932), 128.

[4] H. Martineau, *Society in America* (2 vols., London, Saunders and Otley, 1837), II, 249.

If married, he took boarders, so that a shack fourteen by ten might house a family on the first floor and half a dozen boarders in the attic; chickens under the porch and a pig under the bed added to the confusion. Negro slaves were often better treated, since they represented an investment, while a dead Irishman could be replaced by a live one at no cost to the employer.

The city slums were crowded by the Irish, who consumed prodigious quantities of bad liquor, entered enthusiastically the frequent brawls and riots, and furnished more than their fair share of criminals and paupers. Moreover, the Irish were politically minded; they participated in elections whole-heartedly and controlled city machines like Tammany. In religion they were Catholic, with a resultant multiplying of Catholic churches. In consequence, native-born Americans from New York to Michigan and from Maine to Georgia anathematized the Irish as low, illiterate, boisterous, uncouth, and generally undesirable, with some suspicion that the Pope was sending them to pave the way for papal control of the New World.

Compared with the Irish, the Germans were relatively acceptable since they were more literate, cleaner, less cantankerous, and less apt to congregate riotously in the cities. Most persons considered them sober, stolid, unimaginative, and somewhat credulous. They worked hard, with even the women laboring in the fields. Their land was cultivated intensively, and their barns were kept in excellent condition. While they clung somewhat to European customs, some of which, such as the Continental Sabbath, seemed objectionable, they did not find excessive difficulty in translating Schmidt to Smith or in substituting whiskey for beer.

Germans proved less objectionable partly because a large proportion moved west to farm instead of settling in the eastern cities. Barge after barge of Germans traveled the Erie Canal heading for central New York and as far west as Cleveland and Detroit. Farther south they flooded down the Ohio Valley, with the advance guard reaching St. Louis. Cincinnati became the most German of American cities, with the German language, German papers, German signs, German beer halls, and even German peasant dress of black velvet with red coats. Few Germans went to New England, to the traditional Pennsylvania German area, or to the South, where slave labor closed the door of opportunity. Most of them traveled in parties and settled with their friends in the great and new American West.

Other nationalities appeared only in negligible quantities. A few English laborers were imported for skilled work, while here and there an upper-class Tory decried everything American. Frenchmen and Italians appeared mainly in the cities as hairdressers, barbers, caterers, wig makers, and dancing masters. Swiss were so few as to be curiosities. Scots could now and then be spotted as they wore their traditional Gaelic dress on special occasions. Jews became more numerous after the German anti-Jewish legislation of the mid-thirties, with synagogues dotting the more populous eastern centers. Taken all together, however, these and other groups brought little change to the American racial composition.

Immigration was a matter of pride to most Americans—at least when they made patriotic addresses. Here was a source of much needed labor to promote the future greatness of the United States. But more important, here was proof positive of the attractiveness of free institutions. The inhabitants of a decadent and monarchial Europe were escaping their bonds to the freedom of the New World. And if American institutions were such a powerful magnet, would not the time soon come when the European masses would arise and adopt the ways of America?

In spite of the glowing panegyrics of Independence Day orators, the ideal of the United States as an asylum for the oppressed peoples of the world was put to a severe strain by the actual arrival of large numbers of strange-appearing newcomers. The migrants frequently arrived ragged, penniless, and half-starved. Crowded shamefully on the way over, they became an easy prey to disease, and literally starved if the ship were delayed. Arriving at New York, their favorite port of entry, they were jammed into the quarantine station on Staten Island for examination. Conscienceless agents met the ships and fleeced the immigrants of their small funds with the promise of land and jobs that never materialized.

Penniless immigrants naturally gravitated to the city slums, where they could at least talk their own language. Here they worked at whatever jobs presented themselves, usually for meager pay. Poverty and crowded tenements then took their toll in sickness and death, with the men tempted to crime and the women to prostitution. Drunkenness and rioting were undesirable ways of escaping the depressing tedium of ordinary life.

Americans had little objection to the immigrants as labor competition, but here was almost the only bright spot in the picture. The immigrants were different in race, language, habits, and beliefs. They slowed down all reform movements, whether labor organization, public education, Sabbath observance, or temperance. They voted in groups and were held especially easy to delude by the wiles of a spellbinding demagogue. They were Catholic, which most natives found less than a step removed from paganism. They cluttered the almshouses, with various cities reporting over half of their paupers as being foreign-born. Commonly accepted were stories that paupers and criminals were being shipped to the United States as a matter of policy.

Surveying the troubles brought by immigration, many Americans protested loudly the very movement of peoples that seemed so pleasant in moments of patriotic reverie. "All Europe is coming across the ocean; all that part at least who cannot make a living at home; and what shall we do with them? They increase our taxes, eat our bread, and encumber our streets, and not one in twenty is competent to keep himself."[5] But such protests, no matter how bitter, brought little action. No proper inspection excluded the diseased, even though most people thought the cholera epidemic of 1832–33 was immigrant borne. A federal ten-dollar tax was the only result of an effort to make entry more difficult. Several states passed bonding laws in a futile effort to make the shipping companies guarantee that their passengers would not become public charges. A minor crusade to ship undesirables out of the country died in its infancy. As a matter of fact, labor was so badly needed that no movement to limit new arrivals could succeed. Actually the immigrant, with rare exceptions, was given excellent treatment in the United States.

[5] A. Nevins (ed.), *The Diary of Philip Hone, 1828–1851* (2 vols., New York, Dodd, Mead and Company, 1927), I, 209.

A rapidly increasing population seemed to most Americans an unmixed blessing. The factories of the East and the farms of the Middle West clamored unendingly for workers, while west of the Missouri lay fifteen hundred miles of virgin country. Opportunity was immense, with world power the reward for expansion. The only discordant squeak of complaint came from rural New England, which found itself lagging in the general procession.

American population expanded in accordance with the opportunity which was presented. The ten years between 1830 and 1840 saw thirteen million become seventeen million. Quite obviously immigration produced only a small part of the growth. The great bulk was the result of human fertility, for American cradles were never empty. The doubling of American population each generation was much more the result of the American birth rate than of foreign arrivals—and America viewed this magnificent flowering of mankind with deep satisfaction as one more evidence that God was smiling upon the free institutions of the United States.

American pride in its virility in the production of children ran headlong into English population theory—a sorry circumstance as long as the United States remained in intellectual tutelage to English economic and social speculations. The greatest English population theorist, Thomas R. Malthus, had popularized the depressing thought that people multiplied faster than hogs and corn. According to his theory, only wars, disease, and famine could keep human fertility in check, and the kindly humanitarian was but sowing the whirlwind by hastening the fatal day when population would outrun the food supply.

Many Americans gulped the Malthus draught of hemlock without even a chaser, just as they bolted English classical economic theory. Some, however, sampled the draught and found it unpalatable. Drawing on their knowledge of American growth, they insisted that food production actually increased more rapidly than babies. They insisted that under free institutions all people, no matter how numerous, would be happy and prosperous. God's divine order, as exemplified in America, would not permit starvation for true believers.

31

Americans who brushed Malthus aside put their trust in God to regulate population, even though they added the pious hope that human beings would exercise moderate self-restraint. The most eminent American economist, H. C. Carey, wrote: "We may safely trust that population will limit itself, and that the wisdom of the arrangements of the Deity, in regard to man, will be as evident as it is in every other part of the creation."[6] Carey believed that fertility decreased as intelligence increased, and that population was like economic endeavor in being self-regulating.

A few Americans showed such little confidence in divine law that they distrusted the willingness of God to intervene to limit the number of babies. They held that if parents desired fewer children, they had to take matters in their own hands. Robert Dale Owen and Dr. Charles Knowlton braved the wrath of the conservative majority by writing descriptions of contraceptives. Dr. Knowlton's book was the first of its kind ever written by a doctor, and became the most influential book of the sort ever to be printed. The almost universal overt reaction of the American public toward controlling births was horror and disgust—and yet the birth rate dropped, particularly between 1840 and 1850. The suspicion arises that many men were willing to practice in private what they anathematized in public.

America of the thirties had infinite variety. The scions of old, landed families brushed shoulders with the freshest Mick just landed from the old country. Hard-bitten New Englanders, as closed and cold as their granite hills, looked askance at the genial horse-racing and whiskey-drinking southern gentry. The vast, unpopulated western plains contrasted startlingly with the densely packed slums of New York and Boston. The rocky soil of New England resembled neither the red hills of Pennsylvania nor the lowlands of the Carolinas, while the sandy coast of New Jersey had nothing in common with the ranges of the Appalachians.

Underlying this obvious variety was a vital sense of unity. No

[6] H. C. Carey, *Essay on the Rate of Wages* (Philadelphia, Carey, Lea and Blanchard, 1835), 243.

one could deny that the United States had emerged from the troubled times of the Revolutionary period with a feeling of commonness of purpose and high destiny. People might vary in individual traits, and they might compete vigorously for personal advantages, but such divisions and conflicts meant as little as the eddies of a mighty river. Utter conviction existed that, no matter how the current swirled, the stream was headed for the ocean of world power and pre-eminence. American political, economic, and social institutions were accepted as the best ever devised by man. The future was to be the era of American greatness.

3. Eastern Cities

A YOUNG, BOOMING NATION was inordinately proud of its mushrooming cities, which showed in concentrated form the energy of the new republic. The new buildings rising on every hand, the crowded streets, the busy stores, the congested water fronts, and the flood of immigrants and other travelers, all gave visual proof of a magnificent surge of life—a surge which surely would carry the United States to a position of dominance in the coming years.

The greatest metropolis of the New World was New York City, with its magnificent harbor which reputedly could hold the entire ocean shipping of the world. The busy wharves were lined with sailing ships which had called at such distant ports as Canton and Calcutta, and late in the decade by the new and exciting steamships. Equally important, Erie Canal barges and luxurious river steamboats poured goods and passengers from upstate and from the West.

New York had no doubt of the glory of its future. While only one-third of Manhattan had been occupied, the entire island and fourteen miles of Brooklyn had been platted into streets. The strident voice of the land speculator was clearly audible over the surrounding din, and every resident with a few surplus dollars took a flyer in real estate. Even the most stupid could see population increasing day by day; the 200,000 of 1830 expanded by one-half in the succeeding decade. Prevailing optimism permitted no question of the greatness and prosperity to come.

New York was a city of amazing contrasts. At the foot of the island the walks, shrubbery, and trees of the Battery provided a pleasing contrast to the paved wastes farther north. Castle Garden was connected with the Battery by a bridge. The lower part of the city was a maze of stores, warehouses, offices, and slums. Residential areas were farther north, as at Washington Square. But the striking feature was that an old warehouse might stand side by side with a mansion, that a miserable tenement might be within stone's throw of a splendid building such as the City Hall or the Astor House. Rapid and unplanned growth mixed together the most incongruous structures.

The better New York homes were ordinarily made of brick, although a scattering were of stone or wood. A typical house might have something like a twenty-five-foot front and a forty-five-foot depth. Marble steps, a silver-plated doorknob, and green shutters gave it an attractive appearance, which might then be marred by clotheslines on the roof and by the hovel next door. Here and there were more imposing homes, which were rumored to have cost as much as $30,000 and to rent for as much as $5,000 a year. Here was the height of urban luxury in living quarters.

At the other end of the living scale were the crowded, unsanitary firetraps that congested such areas as the Five Points. Cow Bay Court, for example, thirty feet wide and one hundred feet deep, was lined with five-story tenements dubbed with such names as Jacob's Ladder, Brickbat Mansion, and Gates of Hell. An old brewery was labeled Den of Forty Thieves, while a narrow passage beside it was not unduly complimented by being called Murderer's Alley. A recent investigator insists that during the eighteen forties the brewery held about one thousand inmates, largely Irish and Negro, and averaged a murder a night. Davy Crockett told of four families living in an attic, with their quarters separated by charcoal lines; he remarked that the arrangement worked fairly well until one of the families began to take boarders.

The great thoroughfare of New York was Broadway, paved with stone and edged with a badly broken sidewalk. A straggling line of "stunted and miserable-looking poplars"[1] gave a slight touch of the rural. Along lower Broadway were shops which were often resplendent with gas lights and plate-glass windows. A sprinkling of wooden posts supported awnings. Most of the hotels fronted

[1] Hamilton, *Men and Manners*, 24.

Broadway. Farther uptown the street generally was lined with houses.

While Broadway was the show street of the metropolis, it left much to be desired. One visitor commented rather bitterly: "Broadway is, I suppose, named from scriptural allusions; and you cannot walk over the half of it, without a conviction that it leads to death, and worse."[2] Broadway, like other streets, constituted a real adventure for the pedestrian. He tripped over the rough sidewalks and stumbled over the bad pavement. He waded through filth. He was solicited by prostitutes and by runners for gambling halls and brothels. He might be attacked by gangs of rowdies and could not expect aid from the police, who clung cautiously to their wooden boxes and stoves; rumor had it that a bribe was necessary to persuade a policeman to arrest a thief.

Among the more obvious hurdles that confronted the New York pedestrian were the various animals running wild in the streets. Hordes of pigs functioned as scavengers, paying but little attention to their human rivals for street room. Stepping off a sidewalk on a sleeping pig had obvious hazards. Thousands of dogs assisted the pigs in rooting through the trash and garbage on the streets. Now and then groups of dog killers roamed the streets splattering gore here and there to the horror of the more squeamish of the pedestrians, but apparently producing little effect in their efforts to decrease the canine population. Cattle were driven through the streets to the slaughterhouses. Now and then they got loose, and as late as 1844 an enraged bull gored a man walking on Hester Street near the Bowery.

The streets were made particularly dangerous by the roving gangs of toughs who were practically uninfluenced by the police. Five Points had such pleasant little groups as the Forty Thieves, Shirt Tails, and Plug Uglies; the last, who wore plug hats filled with wool and leather, which they pulled over their ears as a sort of helmet, were noted for their brutality. The East River area had such gangs as the Buckaroos, Hookers, Daybreak Boys, and Swamp Angels, while the Chrystie, Forsyth, and Elizabeth street region

[2] S. P. Holbrook, *Sketches, by a Traveller* (Boston, Carter and Hendee, 1830), 88.

The Croton Dam, New York State

The Park and City Hall, New York City
From an engraving by J. Archer
after W. H. Bartlett, *ca.* 1830

had the notorious Slaughter House gang. Local bullies lined up their gangs in bloody group warfare. Bricks and stones furnished long-distance weapons. Upon closer contact, clubs and bottles and brass knuckles were brought into play, as well as ingenious variations of biting, eye-gouging, kicking, and stamping. From time to time the rowdies showed their high spirits by beating up innocent bystanders or by utterly meaningless riots during which they threw lime and flour, broke windows, tipped over wagons, demolished fences, and manhandled watchmen.

The gangs were only evidences of the crowding and filth of the city. A lack of education and of parks, together with improper housing, pushed boys and girls into the streets at an early age. The boys often became gangsters, beggars, thieves, chimney sweeps, or pimps. The girls became beggars, flower girls, or prostitutes. Apparently the average girl had her first illicit sex experience at the age of eleven or twelve, and the path to prostitution was simple, if not always rosy. The disease, crime, and vice that began in the slums then spread to the more prosperous parts of the city. Still New York remained the metropolis of the nation, the show place of the continent.

In complete contrast to New York was America's second city, Philadelphia. Philadelphia was well planned, orderly, and quiet. Its regular streets were paved and comparatively clean; they were edged with poplars and paralleled by well-laid brick sidewalks. The stores, each with an awning, were well ordered and well stocked, even though not as resplendent as those of New York. Philadelphia had its slums, but the Irish hovels at Kensington were more or less invisible to the average visitor. Most streets were lined with pleasant brick houses, each with its white marble steps, its iron railing, and its brass knob; a basement which rose above sidewalk level provided not only for storage, as of coal and wood, but also space for the kitchen. Fashionable streets such as Mulberry, Chestnut, and Walnut contained the finer homes. Everything was well tended and scrupulously clean, for the widely admired city waterworks permitted the daily scrubbing of steps and sidewalks by the industrious Philadelphia housewives.

Philadelphia's Quaker calm, broken only by the bustle of Market Street, led many visitors to conclude that Philadelphia was unprogressive and stupid—"a city of mediocrity."[3] The charge was not fair, as any Philadelphian would have insisted, providing he felt any necessity of replying to such a ridiculous charge. The intellectual quality of the city was high. Scientifically, Philadelphia could claim to be the most important American center, with the most learned of scientific societies. Artistically, the city did not lag, and was particularly proud of its public buildings, such as the Doric portico of the Bank of the United States and the Ionic entrance to the Bank of Pennsylvania. From the standpoint of the patriotic, it was the site of Independence Hall, even though that historic building had fallen into serious decay. As a progressive American city, it could point with justifiable pride to its many factories, its two wooden bridges spanning the Schuylkill, the modern waterworks at Fairmount Park, and its excellent markets. In no way—except in population—was it willing to accept second place to any other American city.

Third and most worried of American cities in 1830 was Baltimore, which agonized as she lost ground steadily in terms of population. By 1840 she had been overtaken by Boston and New Orleans in spite of tremendous and somewhat despairing efforts that included the beginnings of the Baltimore and Ohio Railroad. Baltimore possessed a reasonable harbor, but other harbors were better. She had a fair claim to western business, but other cities were superior. Hence, while Baltimore attracted a moderate amount of business and a few immigrants, she found herself continually slipping in the race for commercial dominance. The Baltimorean could and did take great pride in the attractiveness of his streets, of his monuments, of his public buildings; the Catholic cathedral was unusually impressive, for Baltimore was the greatest American center of Catholicism. The Baltimorean also felt assured that his male friends were intelligent and witty, and that his female friends were the acme of beauty and charm. Social life in Baltimore was entirely delightful and satisfying.

The one great urban center of New England was Boston, with some hundred thousand residents in 1840. Bostonians were not unduly modest concerning their virtues; one presumably disgruntled commentator wrote sarcastically that "many people, especially Bos-

[3] Hamilton, *Men and Manners*, 183.

tonians, find it the finest city in the United States."[4] The average Bostonian, however, felt that the cultural superiority of Boston was so obvious that no person of even moderate intelligence could fail to recognize the fact. This calm assumption of outstanding excellence infuriated many visitors, and even irritated other New Englanders who actually looked to Boston for leadership. One New Hampshire resident remarked bitterly: "It seems as though your Bay folks thought all sense and knowledge belonged to them."[5]

No matter how irritated the visitor, he had to admit that Boston was an attractive city with its many prosperous-looking granite and brick buildings and its universal white Venetian blinds. While the streets were narrow and winding, they were comparatively clean. The town centered on the Common, which was enclosed by a handsome iron fence and edged by some of the finer residences of the city; Beacon Hill was impressive. The main business thoroughfare, Washington Street, was lined with clean and well-stocked stores. The harbor was crowded with ships to a maximum of five hundred at a time.

The visitor to Boston could hardly avoid being hauled to survey the many Colonial and Revolutionary remains of the Bay area, but his guide tended to stress modern improvements. Impossible to miss was the new Tremont House on Beacon Street—a pretentious three-story hostelry made impressive by its portico and fluted columns, and containing 180 elegant rooms replete with the latest modern conveniences. Other sources of Bostonian pride included the Athenaeum, the Massachusetts General Hospital, and the unfinished shaft of the Bunker Hill Monument. If the visitor did not balk by this time, he was encouraged to attend one of the three theaters or to worship at one of the fifty churches.

The political capital of the nation was a young dream city with vast aspirations expressed by magnificent distances, but marked more obviously and immediately by a straggling of brick and frame houses and taverns, and bottomless streets. "Everybody knows that Washington has a Capitol; but the misfortune is that the Capitol wants a

[4] *A Trip to the Prairies and in the Interior of North America, 1837–1838. Travel Notes of Count Francesco Arese*, trans. by A. Evans (New York, Harbor Press, 1934), 199.

[5] N. Hale, *Notes Made During an Excursion to the Highlands of New Hampshire and Lake Winnipiseogee* (Andover, Flagg, Gould and Newman, 1833), 43.

city. There it stands, reminding you of a general without an army, only surrounded and followed by a parcel of ragged little dirty boys; for such is the appearance of the dirty, straggling, ill-built houses which lie at the foot of it."[6] Many people felt that the tone of society corresponded to the city's physical appearance. "It is the City of Selfishness. It is a den of thieves," wrote Samuel Gridley Howe, who added, "It is the place where wicked men most do congregate, and it is the more intolerable because they are generally the *ablest* rogues in the country."[7]

Adverse criticisms of Washington were not universal, since many people thought the city a pleasant place. They insisted that the architecture was impressive and that unfinished buildings spread over vast distances merely presaged a magnificent tomorrow. True, most of the streets were impassable much of the time, but they were all wide, while Pennsylvania Avenue was paved. More important, they pointed out that society was interestingly mixed, including such widely different men as Daniel Webster and Davy Crockett, while the foreign legations gave a distinctly unusual touch of the exotic. Nowhere else in America was there such variety, and nowhere else in America could one find men who made pleasure their business.

Washington was a man's town. While some members of Congress brought their families for the sessions, most came alone and lived in boardinghouses that were known more for their democracy than for their comfort. Men dominated all government activities and even social life, which tended to be formalized. "God help the woman who must live in Washington!" wrote Peggy Eaton or her literary ghost. "If they go there of their own free will and choice so much the worse for them; but if the lines have fallen to them by Providence to be natives or residents, they require the sympathy of the civilized world."[8] Certainly Peggy should have known, since she created more excitement in Washington than anyone short of the President.

[6] Capt. Marryat, *A Diary in America with Remarks on Its Institutions* (New York, D. Appleton and Company, 1839), 89.

[7] L. E. Richards (ed.), *Letters and Jouurnals of Samuel Gridley Howe* (2 vols., Boston, Dana Estes and Company, 1906–1909), II, 196.

[8] *The Autobiography of Peggy Eaton* (New York, Charles Scribner's Sons, 1932), 209–10.

Charleston was the most important city south of Washington, but definitely sliding downhill. Even in population its thirty thousand of 1830 decreased a trifle during the succeeding decade. The Charleston harbor was satisfactory, but communication toward the west left much to be desired. The more energetic of Charleston merchants and planters viewed the situation with deep-seated alarm, and tried frantically to buttress the foundations of Charleston's prosperity. Their plans for canals and then for railroads were hopeful, but the actual results attracted but little additional western business. Charleston retained an aura of wealth and importance—"a little gone down in the world, yet remembering still its former dignity."[9]

Charleston drowsed in the sun, lazy but hospitable. The luxuriant vegetation took the curse from the sandy, unpaved streets, and provided a charming setting for the brick public buildings and for the wooden houses with their commodious verandas and green Venetian blinds. Flocks of buzzards wheeled over the city to act as scavengers, but did not prevent a high morbidity rate. Although a majority of Charleston residents were Negroes, the tone of society was set by a handful of well-to-do planters, who were considered the most cultured group in the Old South. The Charleston planting aristocracy was in many ways like the charming houses its members occupied; the superstructure was beautifully finished and decorated, but the foundation was rotting.

Hundreds of other smaller American cities either flourished or wasted away. Some were old and some were new; but each boasted proudly of its public buildings, its comfortable houses, its promising industries, and its potential roads, canals, and railroads. Each was inhabited by optimistic Americans who looked to the future with confidence—a confidence that was not always justified. Whatever American failings were, living in the past was not one of them.

Two other cities, on the border between East and West, had unusual promise for the future. Both Buffalo and Pittsburgh had rosy dreams of tomorrow. Younger of the two, and hence cruder and more boisterous, was Buffalo. No more than a small village in 1830, it swelled to a population of twenty thousand within the next decade.

[9] F. A. Kemble, *Records of Later Life* (New York, Henry Holt and Company, 1882), 123.

Standing astride the junction of the Erie Canal with Lake Erie, its prosperity seemed assured for all time to come.

Buffalo was a boom town, with land speculation ever present. Few could resist the urge to dabble in town lots, when quite obviously many lots doubled in price within five years. Along the wide streets, which were expected to be eternally adequate, blossomed new buildings which seemed to rise overnight. In keeping with the grandiose dreams appeared a new theater, reputed to have cost $40,-000, which was nearly as large as the famous Park Theater in New York City. Big, ramshackle wooden hotels were so crowded that men bedded in the halls and women slept five or six to a room. The streets were jammed with not only local residents but immigrants, land speculators, fugitives to and from Canada, runaway slaves and their pursuing masters, drunken Indians, and merchants. At night the drunken roisterers made the streets unsafe for a lady alone.

Pittsburgh had for a generation considered itself the "gateway to the West" and now was buttressing its claim by an elaborate system of canals, inclined planes, and railroads to the East. Now it was daily being transformed into the "Birmingham of America" as it developed its manufacturing of iron, glass, ships, engines, liquor, and other products. The official population of slightly less than twenty thousand seemed a gross underenumeration as men rushed in the staccato emphasis of business. Pittsburgh citizens seemed in a perpetual hurry, with regret at leaving their businesses long enough to snatch the necessary sleep and three meals a day.

Pittsburgh was an extremely attractive city for the businessman in search of profits, but it was extraordinarily unpleasant for the traveler looking for beauty and comfort. The city was compact and dirty. The streets were badly paved and the houses dingy. No traveler failed to note the "voluminous column of smoke, which mounted slowly, but majestically, into the regions of attenuated air."[10]

American cities felt little responsibility to protect or amuse their citizens. Taxpayers, who ordinarily were the only voters, refused to burden themselves with those whom they considered improvident or stupid; they insisted with noble gestures that giving a man some-

[10] F. Hall, *Letters from the East and from the West* (Washington, F. Taylor and W. M. Morrison, 1840), 49.

thing he had not earned only sapped his initiative and independence.

The larger city made futile gestures at keeping order by means of a police force, or rather patrol guards, who actually were careful to sidestep trouble. The smaller town had one or two constables. Petty crime and hoodlumism were rampant, and more serious disorders were not unusual. Unescorted ladies hesitated to appear on the streets at night, and even the supposed stronger sex used discretion. The larger the town the worse the conditions, since the criminal could escape detection more easily.

Streets usually remained in a state of nature, and were practically impassable after a heavy rain. One traveler reported about Vicksburg, "I found the streets absolutely choked with mud—Trade at a standstill,"[11] and Vicksburg was not unique. The larger cities tried feebly to pave their more important throughfares, ordinarily by gravel, which graded from larger rocks on the bottom to sand on the top. In theory such a street packed to a smooth surface. In practice it became rutted and washboardy. Asphaltum was rare and expensive, so that the little brought from Switzerland late in the decade was used only for sidewalks. Flagstones, bricks, and wooden blocks were tried here and there.

American streets were the permanent repositories for discarded furniture, old boxes, dead cats, garbage, and trash, into which sifted the inevitable dirt, straw, and horse manure. A good fall of snow brought a really nauseous mixture everywhere except in Philadelphia, which was one of the few cities to remove snow. Garbage collection, begun on a limited scale in New York in 1821, remained a rare and radical innovation. Most cities, such as Baltimore, Philadelphia, Cincinnati, Albany, and Boston relied on hordes of porkers. In New York they roamed Wall Street and Broadway at will—

> *A question 'tis, and mooted strong*
> *Between the citizens and swine,*
> *To which the streets do most belong,*
> *Of this most glorious city.*[12]

[11] Quoted in T. D. Clark, *A Pioneer Southern Railroad from New Orleans to Cairo* (Chapel Hill, University of North Carolina Press, 1936), 22.

[12] *Constellation* (New York), June 4, 1831, II, 228.

An effort to clear New York streets of pigs in 1830 was foiled by a mob which maltreated the collectors and stopped the project for a generation. Very possibly the mob was right. Mrs. Trollope at Cincinnati insisted that "though it is not very agreeable to live surrounded by herds of these unsavory animals, it is well they are so numerous . . . for without them the streets would soon be choked up with all sorts of substances, in every stage of decomposition."[13]

Street travel was becoming a real problem as the cities grew, so that walking from home to work was not always possible. The better-to-do could often afford their own carriages or hire a private coach or hack. The law of supply and demand apparently did not work satisfactorily with hacks, for as early as the eighteen thirties New York licensed them, provided public stands, and set maximum prices. As poorer people could not afford such luxury, by 1830 New York had an omnibus line up Broadway, and the next year Philadelphia opened a similar line. The omnibus had two long seats facing each other the length of the vehicle, and could seat between twelve and twenty passengers. The door and stairs were in the rear. Rival lines fought energetically for business, with the drivers whipping up their horses to pick up waiting passengers. The result was much cursing and jolting, with danger to the riders and to other users of the street. By 1834 the Broadway Coach Line was operating coaches at seven-minute intervals from 7:00 A.M. to 7:00 P.M., and then more infrequently until service stopped at 10:00 P.M. Late theatergoers were expected to be those with money to afford private carriages, and not workmen who had to start their labors at sunrise.

The railroad with its steam locomotive opened new vistas for rapid street travel, except that locomotives frightened the horses, and most people drove horses. Various cities, such as Philadelphia and New Orleans, prohibited steam locomotives within their city limits, thereby holding back all railroad development. First and most famous of the street railways was the New York and Harlaem, chartered in December, 1831. Speculative New Yorkers oversubscribed the stock on the day the books were opened. They realized that half the line would serve only scattered farms, but they main-

---

[13] A. B. Hart (ed.), *American History Told by Contemporaries* (4 vols., New York, The Macmillan Company, 1901), III, 521.

Utica, New York, 1838
From an engraving by R. Brandard after W. H. Bartlett

State Street, Boston, 1837
From an engraving by S. Lacey after W. H. Bartlett

tained that until the city expanded farther, profits might come from excursions, and that very possibly artisans would find profit in living on the Harlem River and sending their products to the city. The directors' opening excursion came in 1832, and within half a dozen years the line was opened south to Walker Street and north to the Harlem River. The main terminal was at the present Madison Square, and shops at the present Grand Central Terminal. Steam was used north of Madison Square, but horses to the south. The first cars were three omnibuses joined together, with the driver perched on top.

Not all New Yorkers exulted over the new railway. Property owners said it hurt property values. The locomotives frightened horses, while even without the locomotive the cars further conjested the streets. Moreover, cars of excursionists were driven rapidly, with frequent accidents. The peak seemed to be reached in 1843 when a car of pleasure seekers ran over an eleven-year-old girl, cutting off her legs. A mob threw stones at the cars and were only prevented from tearing up the track by the arrival of the police.

The city at night was a place of stygian darkness alleviated here and there by the pin pricks of flickering oil lamps or by modestly lighted windows. Since householders went to bed early and street lights burned out, the early hours of the morning were ordinarily pitch black. Whale oil was the preferred fuel, but poor people had to be satisfied with lard lamps or tallow candles.

The great modern improvement was the introduction of gas made from coal. Conservatives held that the new gas was "as ignitable as gunpowder"[14] and that the refuse from its manufacture would pollute the rivers; the objections were valid, but did not deter the progressive. By 1830 the cities of Boston, New York, and Baltimore had gas available, while Philadelphia joined the list during the decade.

Gas lights were used early in the museums as one of their many novelties. Theaters soon discovered that they made the first really effective footlights. The newer hotels naturally fell in line, as did

---

[14] Quoted in W. Kaempffert, *A Popular History of American Invention* (2 vols., New York, Charles Scribner's Sons, 1924), I, 554.

the more up-to-date stores. Attractive display advertising could be done with gas; one traveler reported he saw many "handsome figures," including "one in form of a harp."[15] Street gas lights dispelled more gloom than had their oil predecessors, even though town fathers were frugal and kept the lamps dark whenever the calendar indicated a moon.

Illuminating gas entered private homes slowly. It stank and it might explode. Only here and there was it available through pipes, and then two or more competing companies might tear up the same streets. More frequently it was bought in copper or iron vessels, and the supply might come to an end in the middle of a dinner or a cotillion. Moreover, it was so expensive as to be out of the reach of any one not well to do. In consequence, many people felt that gas was "illy calculated for the ordinary uses of a family."[16]

Natural gas was a cheap alternative for the manufactured product, but its only known source was western New York. There it was used in Fredonia, and some was piped to a lighthouse in Lake Erie, but larger ideas of taking it to Albany and New York were never realized. A few imaginative souls speculated about distilling a gas from the Seneca oil (petroleum) of western Pennsylvania and using it to light Pittsburgh, but conservative people of property held the idea to be chimerical.

No trouble oppressed the city more than the recurring fires. No hour seemed to pass during which fire companies were not rushing down the streets—and the fire might be anything from the burning of weeds in a vacant lot to a huge holocaust that destroyed acres of stores and houses and injured hundreds of people. The threat of fire hung as an immediate red menace over every property holder, and dozens of large cities such as New York, Baltimore, Mobile, Charleston, and Buffalo had their worst fears realized. This hazard was inevitable with the flimsily constructed wooden buildings, candles, oil lamps, and fireplaces, not to mention the hints given about people who had overinsured their property or insurance com-

[15] Bernard, Duke of Saxe-Weimar Eisenach, *Travels through North America* (2 vols., Philadelphia, Carey, Lea and Carey, 1828), I, 121.

[16] Nevins, *Hone Diary*, I, 233.

panies that thought a moderate-sized fire on uninsured property would be good for business.

Most spectacular of the fires of the eighteen thirties was the one that started on Merchant Street, New York, on the evening of December 16, 1835. With the zero temperature much of the available water was frozen, and the fire soon got out of control. Fire companies from as far away as New Haven and Philadelphia did yeoman service, but could not stop the desolation of fifty acres of the commercial heart of the city, with the destruction of a reputed 674 buildings having a value of $18,000,000.

Fires were destructive, but American energy and optimism left no doubt that work would start at once on a newer and better city. In New York, ten insurance companies became insolvent, but other companies loaned them the necessary funds to prevent their collapse. Companies of soldiers and private citizens patrolled the streets to prevent looting. Within three days a committee of businessmen was planning reconstruction, including buildings that would burn less easily. Within a year the entire burned area had been rebuilt—reputedly better than before.

Fire fighting was the job of unpaid volunteers except in the one city of Boston, but there seemed no lack of volunteers, whether for the bucket brigade of a small village or the more elaborate equipment of New York City. What vigorous young man could resist the lure of a red flannel shirt, a fireman's hat, and a broad leather belt with trumpet attached? And particularly when he rushed down the street followed by the curious, to become the center of the excited mob that always surrounded a fire? Maybe he might even rush into a burning building and save some fair damsel from the all-devouring flames.

The firehouses naturally became centers of interest for small boys who worshiped their heroes, while the heroes in turn responded by swaggering and recounting their remarkable exploits—deeds that lost nothing in the telling. Many fire companies became gangs of toughs much more interested in defeating rival gangs in personal encounters than in fighting fires. The step to political action was small. Legendary figures soon appeared, like Mose Humphreys of New York, who was said to have used a wagon tongue and a flagstone in fights, to have uprooted and waved an oak tree, to have carried a streetcar with the horses dangling, to have blown vessels back down the East River, and to have jumped across the Hudson. The lesser emulators of Mose were hardly ideal influences on the small boys of the city, but the proper corrective of a paid department was far in the future for most cities.

Although firemen received no regular pay, they did obtain donations from householders, merchants, and insurance companies. Presumably any property owner realized that the quenching of a fire depended on a diligence that might be encouraged by reasonable payments. Similarly, most property owners saw the value of buying tickets to the charity balls that the firemen held. Now and then the city made contributions. Such payments provided fire-fighting equipment. How much stuck to the palms of the smoke-eaters remains uncertain.

The most-prized piece of fire-fighting equipment was a gleaming engine, with its fresh paint, its polished metal, and its well-oiled leather. The power was entirely that of men. Men drew the engine to the fire. Men worked the long handles on each side of the engine to draw water from river, well, lake, or hydrant and cast it on the building. When the water supply was at a distance, two or more engines were hitched together, and the water pumped from one box to the next until it reached the fire. The hose was of leather fastened by rivets, with a screw connection each fifty feet. Some companies specialized only in hose or in ladders; the hooked ladder had been invented, but was not in common use.

A fire was spotted either by a private citizen or by a town watchman, whereupon a city or church bell—and possibly all bells—sounded the alarm. The volunteers rushed to their respective stations and hastily donned their regalia. Then ensued a mad rush to be the first company at the fire and gain the favored spot. Often an advance guard was sent to occupy the place of honor—with resulting clashes between similar groups.

Meantime the various fire companies were galloping toward the scene of action. "At the head of the procession came a runner blowing a horn with a deep unearthly sound, next a long team of men (for no horses are employed) drawing a strong rope to which the ponderous engine was attached with a large bell at the top, ringing all the way; next followed a mob, some with torches, others shouting loudly; and before they were half out of hearing, another engine follows with a like escort."[17] Sometimes the engines were dragged down the sidewalks, to the imminent danger of all pedestrians, and always a mob of small boys followed in the wake of the procession.

Once arrived at the fire, the first company got the favored place where the greatest display was possible. If two or more companies arrived simultaneously, their members battled for the right of precedence while the fire blazed unmolested, for the honor of the living was more important than the fate of the burning. If two or more companies connected their hose, more attention was paid to "washing" the rival than to fighting the fire—that is, to pump water faster than the men of the next engine could handle it.

A burning building actually saved by the fire companies was a rarity. Even when the companies fought the fire and not each other, the difficulties were almost insuperable. Often water was not readily available and had to be pumped long distances. In cold weather the fire hydrants froze. All pressure was man-made and too weak, even when the hose was carried up a ladder. The best the fire fighters could do was to save neighboring buildings. Frequently they dynamited threatened structures, and even then did not always prevent the fire from spreading. Little wonder that the fires of the thirties were frequently destructive.

The difficulties of fire fighting underlined the lack of adequate supplies of water in most American cities. Historically water was a matter of individual initiative. If a man had no spring and no nearby stream, he dug a well. With growing cities, individual wells were a somewhat difficult problem. Private companies dug wells, established reservoirs, and laid pipes which at first were wooden with iron joints but by the eighteen thirties were all iron. If population was too sparse to make pipes profitable, the water was sold from door to door out of wooden tubs. The result was that running water was a rare luxury. Only the more pretentious hotels had inside toilets.

[17] C. Lyell, *Travels in North America, in the Years 1841–42* (New York, Wiley and Putnam, 1845), 61.

Inadequate and expensive water inspired various cities to go into the water business. Philadelphia opened the first important city waterworks in 1822 at the staggering cost of over $400,000. A dam on the Schuylkill provided a water drop to run three wheels which pumped the water into a reservoir some ninety feet higher than the city. From this reservoir iron pipes supplied homes and fire hydrants throughout the city. Every visitor to Philadelphia visited Fairmount Park to see the waterworks, noted with pleasure the clean steps and sidewalks throughout the city as the housewives plied broom and leather hose, and noted the few disastrous fires. Most exciting of all, the visitor was informed that by 1840 the city, including liberties (suburbs), had over two thousand private baths; their exact nature remains a little speculative since the cost was fixed at about $3.50 a bath.

Other cities followed Philadelphia by either buying out private companies or constructing plants of their own. Soon such metropolitan centers as Pittsburgh, Cincinnati, Wilmington, St. Louis, and New Orleans were distributing water from their own reservoirs. Of course, in every case it was untreated river water that was being used, which certainly had some relation to the various epidemics that swept the United States.

Of the larger cities, Boston and New York had the poorest water supplies of the eighteen thirties, even though both had municipal systems. Boston kept talking of tapping the Charles River, but took no positive action. New York was more aggressive. After a referendum of 1835, work was begun the next year to bring the water of the Croton River to the city. By June, 1842, water flowed into a reservoir at Yorkville to the accompaniment of a celebration which included the governor of the state. All the following summer New York streets were a maze of ditches, pipes, hose, prospective water hydrants, and fountains. By fall the system could be opened with parades, fireworks, dinners, and speeches. A fountain in City Hall Park co-operated by throwing water one hundred feet into the air.

The American city of the thirties was essentially an overgrown small town. While more people meant that there could be larger city halls, more elaborate hotels, more ornate theaters, more varied stores, and more resplendent parties, the result was little more than the small town raised to the nth degree. People lived much as they had in the small village except that they jostled other people more frequently. The impersonality of the modern city had not even been conceived, for people knew each other and their affairs intimately. The newspapers found little reason for printing the tittle-tattle about the great and near-great when such gossip was common conversation.

Even though cities were only big villages, they gave unmistakable clues to a future that was to be altogether different. Growth like that of Jack's fabulous beanstalk was fast bringing the day when a city resident would no longer know his neighbor, when he would live in an apartment rather than in a separate house, and when he could no longer walk to his work. Even now better street transportation was in the making; more adequate water supplies, garbage disposal, and better lighting were on their way. More efficient policing, better sanitation, and more parks and amusements were dimly visible.

For the small town, the pressure of public opinion was an effective control, but for the large city, that control was much feebler, and more drastic action was necessary. Gangsters, gamblers, holdup men, prostitutes, arsonists, and others of the socially undesirable felt little control within the city unless that control was exercised by a blue-coated figure swinging a club. Increasingly the cities were accepting more social responsibility—all the way from licensing hacks and providing parks and water to city planning. The progress which most people desired and expected could apparently arrive only through the ever expanding activities of the government.

4. The West

THE UNITED STATES of the eighteen thirties looked west rather than east. Its small concern with the affairs of Europe rested less on the width of the Atlantic than on the vast, unsettled wilderness that beckoned toward the west. An empire lay ready for the taking, and the dominant noises of the growing nation were the creak of wagon axles and of oar sweeps. Nothing was more typically American than the hegira of farmers looking for new, cheap, fertile land; beside this exodus, the trickle of men seeking the growing factories of the cities was trivial. A nation was on the march.

The westward-moving throng was composed above all of native Americans seeking their fortunes. "It's only Americans . . . who can have the courage to submit themselves to such miseries and who know how to buy prosperity at such a price."[1] These migrants were not philosophers in search of freedom or solitude. They were hopeful Americans looking for wealth and the trappings of prosperity which they had admired in the East. As soon as possible they built impressive houses, published books and newspapers, constructed roads and churches, argued politics and world affairs, and attended theaters. Their wives desired passionately ingrain carpets, solid silver, and the latest Parisian styles.

The frontier was not a safety valve to release the pressure of industrial discontent during periods of depression. Men went west in good times rather than in bad, since travel and a new farm required capital which was unavailable in a depression. They migrated from eastern farms rather than from eastern factories, since a factory operative could seldom imagine himself as a successful frontier farmer. In fact, even the seaboard farmer seldom went to

[1] Pierson, *Tocqueville*, 249.

the rawest frontier, not being equipped by either training or mental outlook to explore, fight Indians, build log cabins, and plow virgin soil. Normally he sought a community where the first rigors of the frontier had passed, and where life had more of a normal pattern. The corollary was that the extreme edge of the frontier was occupied by men from neighboring regions and not from the East.

Western population clustered on the rivers, particularly along the Ohio and its tributaries, but also on others from the Illinois to the Chattahoochee. During the eighteen thirties population spread like ink on a blotter, but never passed the great bend of the Missouri. The older states of the Ohio Valley were the great centers of population, with three of them—Ohio, Kentucky, and Tennessee—included in the ten most populous American states of 1840. A host of bustling cities and thousands of prosperous farms gave evidence that much of the area could not truthfully be called frontier.

"Queen of the West" and the greatest Ohio Valley city was Cincinnati, seventh American city in 1830 and sixth ten years later. Its clean although unlighted streets, its trees, its flowers, and its attractive houses pleased visitors, who further admired "the appearance of commercial activity."[2] Manufacturing was a source of particular pride, especially the efficient pork-packing industry which was responsible for the city's pseudonym of "Porkopolis." As a visitor said, "The harbour was crowded with boats, the wharfs covered with merchandise, the streets thronged with people. The indications of wealth, of business, and refinement, were too striking to pass unobserved, by one who reflected how recently the forest frowned upon this spot."[3]

Cincinnati was the cultural center of the West, and quite properly proud of its four daily and six weekly newspapers, its magazines, and its book publishing. Its museums, scientific societies, libraries, theaters, medical colleges, and hospitals were sources of profound satisfaction. Charitable and religious societies such as the American Sunday School Union had their western headquarters in Cincinnati. Dozens of lawyers and doctors, with even a few professional writers and painters, made the city outstanding.

[2] Lyell, *Travels*, II, 38.
[3] J. Hall, *Letters from the West* (London, 1828), 158.

The populating of the Ohio Valley meant that more and more of the new migrants went farther north or farther south. Following the Erie Canal, thousands of homeseekers were entering northern Ohio, Indiana, and Illinois, occupying Michigan, and even spreading into the new territories of Wisconsin and Iowa. Cleveland, Toledo, Detroit, Chicago, and other towns boomed vigorously, while for each successful settlement dozens advertised pretensions which were never realized. Alton, Illinois, platted the neighboring bluffs for a city of fifty thousand; the sixteen miles between Peru and Ottawa was planned as one continuous city; Grand Rapids lots sold for fifty dollars a front foot. Many an Allegan or New Buffalo had hopes of becoming the outstanding western metropolis.

Michigan was the greatest mecca of the Northwest, as thousands of New Englanders and New Yorkers sang "Yea, yea, yea, to Michigania"[4] on their way to fortune. Detroit was the bustling center of the new territory, and as a typical noisy, dirty, and confused frontier town with large hopes that had not been transformed into reality, justified comments ranging from enthusiastic admiration to the ill-tempered accusation that *"physically, morally and intellectually* Detroit is the meanest and the vilest spot upon creation's surface."[5]

The settlement of Michigan brought into dispute the area around Toledo, which was claimed by Michigan under the Ordinance of 1787 and by Ohio under her constitution. Both sides breathed bloodthirsty threats and raised militia for "defense." Ohio had the larger resources, but as one Michigan editor said, "Will the people of Michigan surrender their just claim to the disputed strip? . . . Never."[6] Ultimately the federal government intervened and gave Ohio her desires; after all, Ohio had more electoral votes than Michigan. Michigan was "compensated" by the northern peninsula and was admitted as a state in 1837 under circumstances of doubtful legality.

Central and northern Illinois boomed mightily as settlers in

---

[4] Quoted in D. A. Dondore, "Points of Contact Between History and Literature in the Mississippi Valley," in *Mississippi Valley Historical Review,* Vol XI (September, 1924), 229.

[5] J. T. Smith, *Journal in America 1837–1838* (Metuchen, N. J., 1925), 37.

[6] *Niles Gazette and Advertiser* (Niles, Mich.), March 19, 1836.

great numbers entered the treeless prairie country and gave a preview of the later troubles of settlement west of the Missouri. More immediately exciting was the lead boom which centered at Galena and stretched north into Wisconsin. Here went the adventurous and footloose, with Galena jammed with miners, storekeepers, gamblers, and prostitutes. Business flourished. One visitor estimated that Galena, with a population of about one thousand, exported seven million pounds of lead in a single year.

The wonder city of Illinois was Chicago, which at the opening of the decade was no more than a small abandoned stockade, half a dozen cabins, monotony, peace, and sand. Then came the commissioners of the Illinois and Michigan Canal, who platted the city, gave it a name, and started selling lots. Speculators descended on Chicago in an avalanche, with all of them soon becoming rich—that is, rich theoretically as land values soared. Rumors circulated of profits of 100 per cent in a couple of months, or of a plot bought for $5,000 which was soon resold for $80,000. By 1834 the two thousand optimistic Chicagoans had provided building lots for 300,-000, and the town was crowded with immigrants, speculators, and Indians. Apparently the only nonspeculator was the Indian.

By the time of the collapse following the panic of 1837, Chicago had collected some six thousand inhabitants, together with the necessary stores, taverns, theaters, and churches. It boasted of various mills and factories, public schools, printing presses, reading rooms, three daily papers, several stage lines, and more or less regular steamboat service—although of course no canal. Even casual visitors echoed the belief of local residents that "Chicago is destined to become a great city."[7]

On the fringes of the northwest frontier lay Iowa and Wisconsin. When Wisconsin became a territory in 1836, the metropolis of Milwaukee could boast only four hundred settlers, including seven young ladies with a real scarcity value; the state capital of Madison represented a geographical compromise between the claims of the lead-mining and lake areas. As for Iowa, the first settlers arrived after the defeat of Black Hawk, and settled along the Mississippi; the first territorial capital was Iowa City.

[7] Evans, *Trip by Arese*, 173.

South of the Ohio River, Kentucky and Tennessee considered themselves as rather elderly and dignified states, with cities such as Louisville, Lexington, and Nashville proclaiming themselves the equals of their older seaboard rivals. Western Tennessee was just being settled, however; Memphis, the first important river town south of St. Louis, was booming mightily, and aristocratic planters drank their mint juleps alongside of Indians, explorers, traders, prostitutes, and gamblers, in true western style. Still farther south the great flow of population was into western Georgia, Alabama, Mississippi, Louisiana, Arkansas, and even Texas. Nightly the glowing pin pricks of myriad campfires gave token of the magnificent growth of the Deep South.

Southern culture was different from northern, and not only because the planters were bringing Negro coffles to work the cotton and sugar plantations. Rivers were slow and deep, so that there was less power and less need for cities. Indians were more numerous and more dangerous. Roads were poorer, taverns worse, houses more dilapidated, and towns shabbier.

Laws seemed to be enforced more leniently in the South than in the North. In many places it was bad manners, not to say dangerous, to be inquisitive about the former home, occupation, and name of a new friend. For some reason western Georgia was particularly noted as a gathering place for the vicious and the criminal, while of the Mississippi towns, Natchez had the top reputation as the resort of the underworld. Gamblers and prostitutes lined the streets with saloons, gambling halls, and brothels, and the visitor was warned not to walk the streets at night alone.

The bottleneck of the two-thirds of the continent drained by the Mississippi was New Orleans, which rivaled New York as a port. The 46,000 residents of New Orleans in 1830 more than doubled within the next decade as settlement flowed into the Mississippi Valley. Business was good and becoming better. Hundreds of wholesalers and retailers profited from the business coming down the river and from foreign ports. At the wharves, river steamboats jostled sailing vessels from all over the world. Taverns, cabarets, gambling halls, saloons, and brothels catered to the visiting sailors when pay burned their pockets. The future of New Orleans seemed boundless.

Water was the key to the prosperity of New Orleans, but water brought troubles as well as advantages. The river spread mud far into the Gulf, increasing navigation difficulties; plans to improve the channel never seemed to reach fruition. Much of the land was so swampy that it was rumored that coffins had to be weighted. Drainage plans continued to remain in the discussion stage. The lack of stones meant no street paving; the sidewalks were brick. Swamps attracted mosquitoes and mosquitoes brought yellow fever, which helped give New Orleans the reputation of the sickliest city in the United States. Well-to-do citizens left the city during the summer; those who remained helped to fill the cemeteries.

New Orleans seemed an exotic city to New England visitors, particularly as they roamed the French quarter and heard French spoken on the streets. The American section on the other side of Canal Street was somewhat cleaner and more progressive, but the French area was more exciting. Then, too, New Orleans was heavily Catholic, with an impressive cathedral. The people were hospitable and the women beautiful, with particular masculine interest going to the Creole and Quadroon girls. Visitors expressed doubts about the virtue of the lush Creole beauties, but such suspicions seemed to be based more on rumor than on experience. Many New Orleans citizens were comparatively leisured, for the bulk of the hard labor was performed by the Negroes and the Irish. Balls were many and elaborate, and the theaters, both French and American, were among the best in the West. The great day of shopping and entertainment was Sunday, and visitors may have overstressed the excitement and pleasure because such joys were tinged in their minds with the wickedness of Sabbath-breaking.

Across the Mississippi, both Arkansas and Missouri were booming, with populations increasing in the neighborhood of 200 per cent. Arkansas attained statehood; its capital and largest town was Little Rock, which counted some two thousand residents. Missouri seemed particularly attractive to German migrants, even though such new arrivals tended to be unhappy in a slave economy.

The unrivaled metropolis of the trans-Mississippi country was St. Louis, which almost tripled during the decade. St. Louis was an old city which had seen three flags. Lying at the confluence of the Missouri and the Mississippi, it was confident of the greatness of its future, and laughed with scorn at the pretensions of the raw and upstart settlement of Chicago. St. Louis was the distributing point for most of the business of the Far West, and trappers, traders, Indians, and explorers jostled the river men on the streets, giving the city its distinctively frontier appearance.

St. Louis naturally leaned on the river, which the main street followed, and along which steamboats were lined two and three deep. The commercial area was badly drained and filthy, swarming with millions of flies. The older sections exhibited narrow streets with many French and Spanish buildings, but the newer American areas had broader streets and newer buildings, including a large theater of which the city was inordinately proud. A Cathedral, a Catholic university, and a Convent of the Sacred Heart attested the number of Catholic residents.

The westward surge of white farmers kept alive the perennial problem of the Indian, but now for the first time there was developed a "permanent" solution—or at least an answer that men really believed would last for all time. With the complete white occupation of all the country east of the Mississippi, obviously the Indians had to be moved, and the Indian promised land should be the immense wilderness west of the Missouri—an area labeled by the school geographies as the "Great American Desert." Here was a country which the whites would "never" want and in which the Indians might pitch their tepees and hunt the buffalo for time everlasting. Wilderness and Indians seemed as fit companions as ham and eggs, or hog and hominy. Bringing them together seemed a fine and philanthropic solution to Easterners whose distant and hazy view now tended toward tolerance and sympathy.

The new policy developed slowly, but was stated clearly as early as 1825. All eastern tribes were to be given land west of the Mississippi—"*a permanent* home, and which shall, under the most solemn guarantee of the United States, be, and remain, theirs forever."[8] Here was the theme song, but there was incidental music. Western tribes must be nudged aside to make room for the newcomers. A commissioner of Indian affairs—in the War Department —was given supervision of the Indians. A strict law was expected to hold entrants to the Indian country to a minimum. A new and special force of dragoons was to help the army police the border. Forts were placed strategically from Lake Superior to Texas, and a road to connect them was surveyed, even though never built.

The permanent frontier was successful if one limits his reading to the laws and to Presidential reports. In sober fact, however, eastern Indians greeted the nice plans with anything but enthusiasm, expressing unexpected devotion to the lands of their fathers, their cornfields, and hunting grounds. Frequent bloodshed was necessary to "persuade" these tribes of their best interests. Moreover, the western tribes resented the new arrivals vigorously, while white settlers, explorers, and traders laughed at the one man per mile that the army had for the patrol of the frontier.

The northern tribes which required the most drastic persuasion were the Sac and Fox, whose ancestral homes were in Illinois along the lower Rock River. Illegal white entries to the Indian country were met by equally illegal Indian opposition, since the reds had promised to go west. When the aged Black Hawk ordered the whites to leave, the frontier took fright, and the governor of Illinois demanded the removal of the Indians "*dead* or *alive*," adding that he did not want "to injure those unfortunate deluded Savages, if they will let us alone."[9] This statement might have produced loud, ironical merriment from the Indians if they had heard it. Federal troops chased the natives across the river.

In the spring of 1832, Black Hawk with five hundred warriors and their families returned to Illinois and started up the Rock River with rather vague plans. The frontier was panicked, and both militia and regulars took the field; even the West Point cadet corps started west under Scott. Black Hawk apparently was surprised and

[8] *Statutes at Large*, VII, 311.

[9] E. B. Greene and C. W. Alvord (eds.), *The Governors' Letter Books 1818–1834* (Collections of the Illinois State Historical Library, Vol. 4, Executive Series, Vol. 1, Illinois State Historical Library, Springfield, 1909), 166.

alarmed by all the furor, but when he tried to surrender, his flag of truce was fired upon. He then determined to sell his life dearly, so when the whites neared a prepared ambush, the Indians charged, singing their death songs. To the utter astonishment of the Indians, the white troops turned and ran, carrying home stories of thousands of well-armed and ferocious savages under the Napoleonic direction of Black Hawk. As for Black Hawk, the victory turned his head and he began to ravage white settlements.

Indian victories were short lived as more troops gathered, and soon Black Hawk retreated up the Rock, through the lake region near present Madison, Wisconsin, and down the Wisconsin River. The Indian braves fought rear-guard actions to protect the women and children, who were reduced to eating horse flesh, roots, and herbs. The white volunteers plodded and grumbled, for instead of glory and booty they found only hardships in the chase after an elusive foe. The only important action came when a white detachment blundered upon a party of women and children floating down the Wisconsin, and had the fun of shooting at them from the river bank. When Black Hawk reached the Mississippi, he tried again to surrender, and again his white flag was fired upon. Of the 1,000 Indians whom he had led across the river, about 150 returned to Iowa. In time Black Hawk was captured and the Indians ceded land west of the Mississippi; within a decade Iowa was freed of all Indian claims.

Black Hawk was taken East after his capture, and visited Baltimore, Washington—where he was pardoned by the President— Philadelphia, and New York—where he saw a balloon ascension. Big crowds attested the attractiveness of Black Hawk's press notices, but actually he was a great disappointment, being an elderly man who was anything but ferocious in appearance. His own possibly apocryphal statement of his point of view was terse: "Rock River was a beautiful country. I loved my towns, my cornfields, and the home of my people. I fought for it. It is now yours. Keep it as we did."[10]

[10] Quoted in C. Cole, *I Am A Man* (Iowa City, State Historical Society of Iowa, 1938), 269.

Indian troubles of the Northwest were minor when compared with the major tragedies of the South. Here the Five Civilized Tribes—Choctaw, Chickasaw, Creek, Cherokee, and Seminole—numbered sixty thousand and held eighteen million acres from which they declined to move until the pressure was overwhelming. The shameful story of their ejection followed a definite pattern. Acquisitive white settlers and miners flooded the Indian country, demoralizing the Indians and putting pressure on eastern governments to legalize their aggressions. The federal government under Jackson was delighted to co-operate, but ordinarily was unsuccessful. Then impatient state governments jumped the gun and annexed Indian land, whereupon the federal government, instead of penalizing the illegal state actions, redoubled its efforts to buy the land. Fraud, bribery, and force obtained treaties which the army then enforced.

The effects of white treatment on the southern Indians were pitiful. Their high civilizations were ruined, and their property and improvements were lost. Herded by the army like cattle, they were shipped to the West with little more than the clothes on their backs. They were cheated unmercifully by the merchants and captains with whom they dealt. Food ran low, with the result that sickness and famine took frightful toll.

The suffering of the Indians was but a part of the story. The disorganization of the southern frontier was inevitable, while political and constitutional morals suffered. The states violated federal laws with impunity, and in fact forced the federal government to produce a spurious legality after the fact. Furthermore, both the states and the federal executive flouted the opinions of the Supreme Court.

Three Indian cases reached the Supreme Court. In the first, the Court ordered the state of Georgia to appear before it concerning a state sentence of hanging for an Indian who had killed another Indian. Georgia refused. The Indian was hanged. In the second, the Court refused to act because it held the Cherokee a "domestic, dependent" nation which had no recourse to the Court. In the third, the Court held unconstitutional a Georgia law under which two missionaries to the Cherokee were held in jail. Actually, the men remained in jail until pardoned by the governor, while

President Jackson is reputed to have remarked: "John Marshall has made his decision—now let him enforce it!" Understandable is the Indian reaction that he could not expect justice from white governments and courts.

While the Cherokee, Creek, Chickasaw, and Choctaw provided constitutional and humanitarian problems, they never presented the organized armed resistance of the Seminole of Florida. The Seminole had been forced into a removal treaty, but then took fright and fled to the swamps during the winter of 1835–36. During the following years the United States was treated to the unedifying spectacle of the might of the American Army trying unsuccessfully to capture a few poverty-stricken and poorly armed natives. A succession of American generals floundered over the countryside with little success except through treachery. The Florida legislature provided Cuban bloodhounds that only sat and howled.

The last battle of the "Seminole War" came in 1842, by which time some three thousand Indians had been removed. The removals had cost about $7,000 an Indian plus the life of one white soldier for each two Indians transported, plus the damages to individual Floridians. And in the process the Indians had either been killed or completely impoverished. Maybe the Seminole had the last word in that possibly five hundred remained permanently in Florida.

Removal of the Indians west of the Mississippi by no means ended their troubles, since inevitably they arrived destitute and demoralized. Their survival depended upon government handouts, and dishonest contractors prevented them from receiving more than a spoiled fraction of what Congress had voted them. Consider for example one Captain Armstrong, who arrived in the Indian country with a large and demanding family, debts of $20,000, and a salary of $1,500; after a few years of comfortable living he was able to pay off his debts and show a surplus of $40,000. Hundreds of such cases were collected by Major Ethan Allen, but his report was discovered conveniently "mislaid" when it might have harmed some of the higher officials.

An additional trouble was that the Plains Indians, particularly the Osage, objected vigorously to being pushed aside by the new arrivals. New forts and more troops were needed, and several expeditions, such as that of General Atkinson and Colonel Dodge in 1835, delimited land holdings and forced back the western tribes. Western settlers liked the forts and troops, partly for protection but even more because of the purchases which provided one of the few cash incomes of the West. The troops were of course also charged with the duty of keeping unauthorized whites out of the Indian country, but for some reason failed ignominiously to eject the traders with their demoralizing stocks of whiskey.

Ultimately the Indians made their own treaties with neighboring tribes, reconstituted their governments, and established schools, churches, and newspapers. Their powers of survival and adaptation were little short of miraculous, even though in the process they lost much of their distinctive cultures. At a later date an Indian commissioner was to wonder in print why they had ever been known as "civilized."

Americans in general approved the governmental Indian policy, holding it the kindest possible method of acquiring the land which God had manifestly designed for white use. A minority, however, was very scathing in its criticisms. When a man maintained that "The Indians in due course must either become civilized or be shot,"[11] he generally preferred the shooting. On the other hand, many people found their religious and moral sympathies engaged; some of these thought the Indians to be descended from the lost tribes of Israel, while others had donated money for Indian schools and missions.

Men sympathizing with the Indians liked to contrast the attitude toward Indian independence with the universal sympathy given to foreign efforts at liberation, and particularly those of the Poles and the Greeks. Such comparisons were especially frequent during the Seminole War, which never was popular. "How did Christian nations Applaud the Poles when they manifested a spirit of resistance to the dictates of an autocrat! And now, when this in-

[11] E. Bandel, *Frontier Life in the Army, 1854–1861*, Vol. II of *Southwest Historical Series*, ed. by R. P. Bieber (Glendale, Calif., A. H. Clark Company, 1932), 252.

effectual resistance has brought upon a part of them the sentence of expatriation, how are our sympathies excited in their behalf! But, when we are endeavoring to transplant a whole nation, and leave them no alternative except death, who pities the red man?"[12] A New York newspaper excoriated a war in which "success wins no honor, and defeat hardly brings with it disgrace."[13]

The reaction of the Indian was seldom recorded—for obvious reasons. Here are the comments of an Indian chief living near Buffalo in 1839: "Here we are, surrounded by white men, who found their prosperity on individual property in the soil, and yet they prohibit us, as a tribe, from dividing our own lands among ourselves, and laying the foundation of our own improvement. Not only so, but when we, as individuals, acquire their knowledge, and adopt their manners, they still prohibit us from owning individual property in the soil, either of our own lands or of theirs. In such circumstances, our advance in civilization is impossible. Our people associate only with the outcasts and lowest of the whites, because all others exclude us from participation equally in their rights and in their society. We adopt their vices, because an insurmountable barrier is placed between us and their virtues. We become miserable, degraded, extinct."[14]

Indian travails might have been more bearable if they had not been largely in vain. The idea of a permanent frontier had hardly been imbedded in the popular mind before it ceased to exist as the Great Plains proved no barrier to white ambition. The "eternal" promises of the United States proved no more than scraps of paper within the very generation they were made. And yet the American government should be debited with poor prophecy rather than with Machiavellian duplicity. Also it should be credited with a plan that did not include the direct exploitation or enslavement of the natives. The American occupation of a continent was not a pretty story for adolescent girls, but it was a child's fairy tale in comparison with the later Belgian rape of the Congo.

As the Indians were pushed farther and farther west, they could

[12] *Eighth Annual Report of the American Peace Society* (Hartford, 1836), 5.
[13] *Morning Courier and New-York Enquirer* (New York), August 28, 1837.
[14] Combe, *Notes*, II, 85.

be viewed more tolerantly and with more intellectual curiosity than when they had been an immediate menace. Magazines and travel books described Indian life. Indian biographies and historical works appeared. Anthropological researches included the work of Albert Gallatin and Henry Schoolcraft, who were both present at the first meeting of the American Ethnological Society in 1842. In general such accounts were sympathetic, with many a protest at the "farce"[15] of Indian treaties, and the proposing of agreements "fairly and honorably made."[16] Sometimes the writer became entirely eulogistic, reviving the old concept of the noble savage—that their lives "should illustrate the true constitution of man."[17]

But Americans wanted to see as well as read about Indians. George Catlin capitalized this interest by painting hundreds of Indian pictures and then exhibiting them in the East and in Europe. Indian delegations to the East were always surrounded by popeyed crowds. Each museum had its Indian exhibits, while the American Museum of New York had real Indian braves and women who did native songs and dances, elected a chief, smoked the pipe of peace, fought mock battles, and otherwise illustrated Indian customs. Apparently the greatest disillusionment came when the spectator discovered that the Indians' skins were not a nice bright copper color but "were dark, almost like those of mulattoes."[18]

The Indians also entered belles-lettres in force, so that an author was practically a literary eccentric if he did not introduce Indians into his novels, poetry, or plays. On the border line between fact and fancy was the Indian horror-thriller, which occupied the place later to be held by the dime novel. One prize effort was set during the Black Hawk War, and bore the following descriptive title: *Narrative of the Capture and Providential Escape of Misses Frances and Elmira Hall Two Respectable Young Women (Sisters) of*

[15] Col. Baillie, "An Englishman's Pocket Note-Book in 1828," in *Magazine of American History*, Vol. XIX (April, 1888), 332.

[16] *Report of the American Board of Commissioners for Foreign Missions*, 17th Annual Report (Boston, 1826), 48.

[17] B. B. Thatcher, *Indian Biography* (2 vols., New York, Harper and Bros., 1836), I, Preface.

[18] Alexis de Tocqueville, *Memoir, Letters and Remains* (2 vols., Boston, Ticknor and Fields, 1862), I, 141.

*the Ages of 16 and 18 who were Taken Prisoners by the Savages at
a Frontier Settlement, near Indian Creek, in May last, when Fifteen of the Inhabitants Fell Victims to the Bloody Tomahawk and
Scalping Knife: among whom were the Parents of the Unfortunate
Females* (1832). Little imagination is needed to picture the adventures of these two innocent maidens, on the threshold of life, their
honor at the mercy of bloodthirsty and merciless savages.

For two centuries the conflict between red and white had been
an ever present design on the fringe of the fabric of white civilization. During the eighteen thirties that design had been eliminated
from the region east of the Mississippi. The country east of the
Father of Waters had finally been made secure against all rival
claimants, whether European or American. The Indian problem
had not disappeared, but its location had changed; the strong continued to acquire that which the weak could not hold. Only a few
moralists and idealists among the stronger group sympathized with
the pleas for "justice" by the weaker.

While the thirties did not see completion of the occupation of
the land east of the Mississippi, the future was clear. Less attractive
and less available land would soon have its quota of hopeful immigrants. At the same time, the older areas would furnish many of the
migrants to Texas and Oregon and California, to the gold and silver
mines of the mountains, to the farms of the Great Plains, for each
frontier drew heavily from the last frontier, with Easterners and
Europeans following along in the rear. Migration humped forward
like an earthworm and did not do handsprings like an acrobat.

Increasing population soon meant that American life became
moderately uniform from the Atlantic to the great bend of the Missouri, and a man might feel equally at home in Galesburg, Illinois,
or in Passaic, New Jersey. With great rapidity the wilderness was
transformed into farms and cities, with stockyards, grocery stores,
theaters, churches, and saloons. Men desired to live like other men,
only more impressively—better jobs for themselves, better homes
for their wives, and better education for their children. No one
boasted of being a frontiersman. The hope was to attain more rapidly in the West the goals which seemed most attractive in the East.

66

5. Beyond the Frontier

WEST of the great bend of the Missouri lay an immense wilderness sprinkled thinly with red aborigines. Near the edge of white settlement were the refugees from the East. Some were making noble efforts to reconstruct their badly damaged civilizations, but others had given up the struggle and lived in filth, depending on small game and white charity; their main borrowings from a superior white civilization were liquor, gunpowder, and syphilis.

Farther west were the seminomadic tribes of the Plains, whose economy was based on the buffalo. These men were hardy, brave, and good fighters; they considered war and horse stealing the most honorable activities of man. They were also devoted to their families, loved jokes, and could be exceedingly garrulous upon occasion; in fact, they bore little resemblance to the gloomy and taciturn Indians of fiction. Their contacts with the whites were ordinarily limited to periodic meetings with traders, trappers, travelers, explorers, and army men, but many had never seen a white; even missionaries and the army had not reached them.

The Indian's first white contact was with the fur trader or trapper, who commonly was in advance of even the government explorer. Theoretically the fur trade was controlled by stringent federal laws, but actually the pitifully small western army could make only the feeblest pretense of patrolling the wilderness. Unlicensed traders abounded. Foreigners seeped across the border. Competition was of the rugged variety, with fraud and violence washed down by violent draughts of the worst whiskey.

The most important of the fur-trading companies was the American Fur Company, the creation of John Jacob Astor. But Astor was getting old, and retired in 1834; within another decade he was so senile that he was described with "the saliva dropping from his mouth, and a servant behind him to guide the victuals which he was eating, and to watch him as an infant is watched."[1] The American Fur Company dominated both the Great Lakes region and the Missouri Valley. Its trading methods did not exclude price cutting, fraud, robbery, Indian incitation, and sales of whiskey. It justified its whiskey sales—at thirty-two dollars a quart—not only on competitive grounds but to prevent the Indian from interrupting his fur gathering to go East to get drunk.

The American's great competitor in the mountains was the Rocky Mountain Fur Company, a rapidly fluctuating group which included such outstanding men as Jedediah Smith and Jim Bridger; when it was dissolved in 1834, many of its members went to work for the American. West of the mountains the Hudson's Bay Company monopolized the Oregon country. Directed by the impressive John McLoughlin, "king of old Oregon," its business dealings were fair and it sold no liquor. McLoughlin himself lived in feudal splendor in a great baronial hall opposite the present city of Portland. His wide-flung fields, gardens, vineyards, and orchards provided the means for his open-handed hospitality which extended even to the missionaries and settlers who presaged the end of his rule.

The fur business had a strongly foreign complexion. Trading goods were frequently English, and the top fur market was London. Traders and trappers were often French, Spanish, English, or Scotch. French terminology was usual, as the *burgeois* who commanded a fort or the *mangeur de lard* who did unskilled labor. Practically all business was done on credit, with the beaver skin the standard of value. Operations were extremely hazardous, with returns ranging from a large fortune to bankruptcy and death.

The white trapper was the true heir of the Boone tradition. Typically clad in a highly decorated mixture of Indian and white garments, he was gaunt and silent, with a penchant for dry humor and practical jokes. Best known in time was Jim Bridger, with the tall tales he told around the campfire—of an eight-hour echo that

[1] Nevins, *Hone Diary*, II, 717,

permitted a man to be his own alarm clock; of petrified trees, bark, birds, and even songs; of a stream running so fast that it got warm on the bottom; of a telescopic glass mountain that made an elk ten miles distant seem close enough to shoot.

The fur business had its great American outfitting center at St. Louis, but did most of the trading in dozens of wilderness forts which ranged from rude log cabins to the pretentious establishments of Fort Laramie and Bent's Fort. The large fort was a rectangle of pickets or adobe, and its two-story towers at diagonal corners were arranged for both musket and cannon fire. Inside were the necessary houses, storerooms, and repair facilities. Such a fort, properly manned, was impregnable to Indian attack. Life in the fort was ordinarily dull, especially during the isolation of a long winter.

An alternative to the fort was the yearly rendezvous, held usually in the vicinity of southwestern Wyoming. To some designated valley with good water and grass would come the Indians and trappers with their pelts, and the traders with their goods. Trading was done leisurely while the trappers indulged in a spree of feasting, wrestling, drinking, and gambling. When the furs were gone, the traders sold on credit to be sure of next year's business.

Thus the fur trade provided the main contact between Indian and white. The whites received not only furs, but geographical knowledge, costumes, ways of life, and even wives. The Indians received mainly whiskey, knives, and gunpowder, all of which led to trouble. Commerce between the two races led not always to friendly understanding, but frequently to bitter disagreement and conflict which laid the foundation for the frictions which were to bring plentiful employment for the army before the Indians were finally beaten into submission.

The army upon which frontier peace largely depended was always inadequate. Seldom did the western force number as many as two thousand—not an impressive number to patrol half a continent, even though it was possibly one-third of the entire United States Army. Some six hundred dragoons, operating either on foot or on horseback, were the only men particularly trained for work in the

West, and their short enlistments and Republican sentiments were not conducive to proper discipline and precision.

The soldier stationed in the West spent most of his time in a fort much like the fur-trading post. Here he experienced the daily and monotonous routine of roll call, mess, guard duty, foraging, cutting wood and hay, and construction work. His life was little more exciting than farming, and in fact the soldier often did some farming. The soldier's food was poor, with heavy emphasis on watery soup, and his five dollars a month hardly permitted extravagent supplementary rations from the post sutler. After 1832 most of his money was spent for liquor, since in that year the War Department was converted to temperance and stopped liquor rations.

To make the poor food and monotony more unbearable, there were added frequent and severe punishments for breaking the simplest of the complicated rules for soldierly behavior. A missing button might bring confinement on a reduced diet or extra guard duty in the sun while carrying a log. More severe infractions evoked the "cat"—an unpleasant feline of nine thongs of eighteen inches each, knotted each inch, and attached to a short handle. The miscreant was stripped to the waist and tied to the flagpole, with the drummers taking turns with the cat. The soldier's answer when conditions became unbearable was to desert; in the one year 1830 there were some 1,250 desertions from an army of about 6,000.

The monotony of fort life might be broken by reading, games, horse races, hunting, or fishing. Married officers immersed themselves in visiting, teas, dinners, and dances, but all were made uncomfortable by worry over precedence due to rank. Amateur theatricals were a possibility, but since actresses were considered immoral, the men sacrificed their whiskers, borrowed their wives' clothes, and spoke the female roles in deep bass voices.

Among the diversions should be included any trip away from the fort, and consequently explorations and Indian outbreaks were viewed with considerable enthusiasm. Most exciting was the tour designed to overawe the Indians—an optimistic aim when the smallness of the force was considered; conferences, speech making, and present giving were among the pleasant activities. Now and then the army was used to capture an Indian thief or murderer, which necessitated major diplomatic genius if an entire tribe were not to be sent on the warpath. The effectiveness of such army functions has been questioned, but no doubt exists that any trip away from the fort was a boon for the soldier.

Across the Indian country stretched three main routes to the Pacific Coast. Most northerly was the path of Lewis and Clark up the Missouri, across the mountains, and down the Columbia. Steamboats were possible over part of this route, and in 1832 the *Yellowstone* reached Fort Union at the mouth of the Yellowstone. The country directly west from the Great Lakes to the Missouri, long well known by the trappers, was explored more formally by I. N. Nicollet, who included in his party the young and enthusiastic John Charles Frémont. The source of the Mississippi in Lake Itasca was finally identified in 1832 by Henry Schoolcraft.

The second route followed the Platte River, and crossed the mountains by way of South Pass. West of the main ranges of the Rockies the Oregon-bound traveler struggled through the rugged and desolate country of the Snake River. The California-bound traveler plodded through long desert wastes and then scaled the snow-capped ranges of the high Sierras. In either case the hardest part of the trip came when men and animals were badly worn, when wagons were falling to pieces, and when an early snowfall might mean complete disaster.

The third route followed the Arkansas River and then the Cimarron—or more circuitously by Bent's Fort and Raton Pass— to Santa Fé. From Santa Fé the traveler descended the Río Grande to El Paso, cut overland to the Gila, followed the Gila to the Colorado, and then passed through the desert country of southern California. A more direct route from Santa Fé was opened in the thirties, but was too arduous for all except the most energetic of migrants.

Plains travelers during the thirties were mainly traders, trappers, missionaries, explorers, and adventurers; not until the end of the decade did the farmer appear for the long trip to the Pacific Coast. Most usual jumping-off place was Independence, Missouri, where the traveler made last-minute preparations while he waited for the grass to become green and the ground firm. Since most of the men were professionals, they planned on the least possible supplies, expecting to round out their diet with game, particularly buffalo. They traveled generally in parties for protection against the Indians and against the obvious physical hazards.

A day's travel for the experienced trader might be thirty to forty miles, but when conditions really became bad, that distance might be cut in half, while it was not unknown to take a day to cross an overflowed stream or to haul wagons up and down a rocky crag. The professional ordinarily traveled seven days a week, but the amateur preferred to devote Sunday to rest, repairs, and needed religious consolation. Everyone stopped at the larger forts to replenish supplies, repair wagons, and rest the stock and the men.

The life of an overland traveler was largely dull and monotonous routine. On the average day he was up at dawn, ate breakfast, harnessed his team, and started walking. The day was broken only by a midmorning rest, lunch, and a midafternoon stop. Camp was pitched before dark to make sure that there was water, grass, and wood or buffalo chips. Wagons were arranged in a protective circle, the stock turned loose to graze, and a guard set. Day after day the routine continued. Day after day men plodded endless miles in the scorching heat of the sun, enveloped in dust and maddened by inadequate water.

Uncomfortable monotony had as its undertone a perpetual nagging worry over water supplies, grass, game, storms, and Indians. Men were bitten by snakes, kicked by mules, and clawed by bears. They were blown up by defective guns, rolled upon by horses, and fell into ravines or otherwise damaged themselves. An unchanging diet brought scurvy and dysentery, while other ailments ranged from stomach-ache to tuberculosis. All medication was simple, but surgery was also brutal; amputation of an arm with a butcher knife and meat saw, the patient fortified only by a pint of whiskey taken internally, made such troubles as missing a ford seem downright pleasant in retrospect.

An endless succession of travelers, suffering from inadequate food and water, were inspired to keep their weary legs moving only by the basic urge for survival. Even experienced trappers were not immune—as the seven members of the Pattie party on the Gila in 1825. Late in March, while they were away from the river, Indians stole their horses and left them without food or water. The warm blood of an antelope quenched their worst thirst, and then they surprised some Indians and appropriated their food and water. By April 8 all the food was gone, whereupon James Ohio Pattie recorded: "And so having nothing to eat, we felt the less need of water."[2] On the twelfth the party got back to the Gila; the next day they killed a raven, which in time was followed by a buzzard and then another buzzard. At this point Pattie's father became too weak to walk, but he was revived by eating a stray dog, and by May 1 the entire party was back in Santa Fé.

Western Indians were normally friendly and hospitable, but the wary traveler did not depend on this attitude. Certain groups might be on the warpath, while young men won their spurs as warriors by stealing horses or taking scalps—of course with no personal ill will toward the victim. Furthermore, the Indian exacted personal vengeance when he or his family or friends had been injured, and he was not careful to punish the white who had inflicted the original damage.

Indian outrages were also often inspired directly or indirectly by white actions. When a trader cheated his Indian customer unmercifully and gave him bad whiskey with a kick like a Missouri mule and a morning-after hangover, brotherly peace was not encouraged. When a Westerner now and then shot a random Indian for sport or on the theory that the only good Indian was a dead one or just on general suspicion, cordial interracial relations were not furthered. When a white man with a grievance visited his vengeance on the wrong man, or when the army showed the same lack of discrimination, the result could hardly be anything but trouble.

Most Plains conflicts were comparatively small encounters, usually between a few individuals. The Indians seldom operated in large parties, and in any case they would only have been committing suicide by attacking a large fort or a well-armed party. Some of the brushes seem little more than accidental, involving misunderstanding on both sides. Seldom were many killed, since the marksman-

<hr>

[2] T. Flint (ed.), *The Personal Narrative of James O. Pattie of Kentucky*, ed. by M. M. Quaife (Chicago, Lakeside Press, 1930), 104.

ship of the pioneer was not nearly so good as later stories would have it. Both sides performed feats of heroism and both sides engaged in acts of savagery, including the mutilation of the dead.

Most picturesque of western plains travels were the annual trading caravans to Santa Fé, in Mexican territory. Loading their wagons at Independence, the merchants drove their mules by way of the Arkansas and the Cimarron to Santa Fé, with some of them continuing south of the Río Grande or west to the Pacific. Goods were usually nonperishable items such as textiles and hardware, with comparatively large value in small bulk. The most valuable might be concealed from the customs inspector, but frequently an arrangement could be made which was profitable to everyone except the Mexican government. Returning to the United States before snowfall, the traders brought money, bullion, horses, mules, and beaver skins.

The most exciting moment of the trip was the entrance to Santa Fé, even though the town was but a cluster of adobe houses and contained only some three thousand people. The teamsters rose early on the morning of the entry, washed and shaved for the first time on the trip, donned their best clothes, and spruced up their wagons. Then they roared into town with the best burst of speed the mules could muster, and came to a stop with the screeching application of brakes—all of which attracted a crowd of the citizens, who had been waiting all spring for this moment.

The significance of the Santa Fé trade did not depend entirely on its value, which was seldom as much as a quarter of a million dollars in any one year. The rough and ready teamsters found the Mexican government weak and the region attractive. They sampled with enthusiasm the *tortillas, atoles, fijoles,* and chili. They got tipsy on Spanish wine. They yelled themselves hoarse at cockfights. They were impressed by the exotic buildings, the Catholic ritual, and the Spanish speech. They gaped at the *caballeros* with their high-brimmed *sombreros,* their ornamental jackets, their pantaloons split and laced from knee to ankle, their colorful sashes, and their blankets of varied utility. They ogled the dusky, black-haired beauties, each with her high comb, her plentiful jewelry, and her huge *rebozo* (scarf). Rumor had it that Santa Fé girls were not unapproachable, but this report may have arisen from their shocking habit—from the American point of view—of smoking many black cigarets. Actually the traders' favors were bestowed largely on the numerous ladies of professional easy virtue. All told, Santa Fé was an exciting place to American traders, who transmitted their enthusiasms to their friends farther east. Dirt and disease seemed small matters, particularly when viewed through the haze of two thousand miles.

Far away on the fringes of American territory lay a crescent of foreign possessions—Texas, New Mexico (including Arizona), California, and Oregon (including present Washington). All but Oregon were Mexican, and Oregon was claimed by both England and the United States. Theoretically such regions should have been of little interest to Americans, particularly to American farmers, who had unnumbered millions of unoccupied acres within their own country. And yet the land-hungry were casting covetous glances toward these far places. The golden haze of distance made fields look greener.

Most accessible was the Mexican state of Texas, with its warm and fertile Gulf Coast. Covered wagons lumbered southwest with hopeful cotton planters. Nominally the new residents became good Catholics and patriotic Mexicans, but actually they all looked forward to the day when Texas would be added to the Union. The South and the West were particularly enthusiastic, and when Northerners expressed hostility to the expansion of slave territory, the *Western Monthly Review* suggested balancing Texas with Canada, with the possible addition of Cuba and further parts of Mexico. When Mexican papers protested such plans rather bitterly, many Americans seemed surprised.

The American government was by no means blind to the wishes of its migrating citizens. President Adams tried unsuccessfully to purchase Texas. Upon the accession of the more vigorous Jackson, annexation seemed to many a matter of days, or at the most, of weeks. Unfortunately, Jackson attempted to buy Texas through that swashbuckling and ineffective diplomat, Anthony Butler, and failed ignominiously.

The Mexican reaction to United States aggression was a belated and futile effort to limit American immigration, to encourage other settlers, to limit slavery, to make all trade go to Mexico, and to strengthen military garrisons. The only visible result was to irritate American settlers and increase their dislike of Mexicans. Most Americans saw the Mexicans as stupid, brutal, treacherous, and superstitious, while the Mexicans responded by holding the Yankees lawless, arrogant, impolite, grasping, ambitious, and untrustworthy. Differences of race, language, and legal and political backgrounds did not help matters, while the thin cloak of an all-pervading Catholicism did not hide basic religious differences.

Santa Anna gained ascendancy in Mexico in 1832, and Texans placed unwarranted confidence in his expressed intention of favoring them. Actually conditions became worse, especially after Santa Anna became dictator in 1834. The following year General Martín Perfecto de Cos started to invade Texas, and Texas replied with a provisional government and an army that stopped Cos at Bexar. Santa Anna and the main army started to advance in 1836, whereupon Texas proclaimed its independence.

Texan revolutionists counted not unnaturally on American sympathy and aid. Public meetings throughout the United States lauded the revolt and sent men and supplies. Border authorities winked at neutrality violations as a flood of men and materials flowed across the Louisiana border. President Jackson followed closely the operations of the Texan army under the command of his good friend Sam Houston. An American army under the ubiquitous Edmund Gaines was placed on the border, ready for any eventuality.

The enthusiastic chorus of expansionists did not succeed in blotting out the discordant note of many Americans who objected vigorously to the "eternal disgrace"[3] of annexing Texas. Benjamin Lundy wrote "that the immediate cause and the leading object of this contest originated in a settled design, among the slave-holders of this country . . . to wrest the large and valuable territory of Texas from the Mexican Republic, in order to re-establish the SYSTEM OF SLAVERY; to open a vast and profitable SLAVE-MARKET therein; and, ultimately, to annex it to the United States."[4] This

[3] Martineau, *Society*, I, 323.
[4] B. Lundy, *The War in Texas* (Philadelphia, 1836), 3.

The St. Louis river front in 1840, with the Market
House and City Hall in the foreground, from a
lithograph by J. C. Wild

Fort Snelling, Minnesota

slavery-plot theory, as accepted by Adams and others, later delayed the annexation of Texas.

The initial victories in the struggle went to the Mexicans, and Houston retreated steadily, much to the disgust of his contemporaries. Finally he was almost forced into an engagement in which his men charged with the battle cry "Remember the Alamo!" Soon American papers could print the "Glorious News from Texas."[5] Texan independence was assured. Immediately the new republic claimed the territory to the Río Grande and asked for annexation. Then came the great surprise. Jackson turned cool and only after delays received the Texas minister. Annexation failed in Congress, and Texas was left to enjoy an independence that she had probably never really desired. The Lundy argument had done its work.

Texan independence was not a period of complete joy. How to raise money baffled the most astute Texan intellects; foreign loans were difficult with the precarious state of Texan sovereignty, while the plentiful Texan land had little immediate cash value. Relations with Mexico brought invasion and counterinvasion, with no credit to either side. Indian relations remained unsatisfactory in spite of the Texas Rangers. On the other hand, a political and legal system was established and roads and education supported. By the end of the thirties most people felt that Texas was only marking time until its eventual annexation by the United States, for clearly the urge toward American expansion was increasing.

In the Far Northwest the imperialist order of trader, missionary, and settler was followed. The thirties were the missionary period. At the beginning of the decade the vast region north of California and west of the Rockies was labeled "Oregon," and held in joint occupation by England and the United States. Actually early American trading ventures had been replaced by the Hudson's Bay Company, which boasted a monopoly. Governor Simpson of "the great company" could contend that "as regards formidable opposition I feel perfectly at ease."[6] With this remark Simpson placed himself in the van of the world's poorer prophets.

[5] *Galena Advertiser* (Galena, Ill.), May 21, 1836.
[6] M. S. Sullivan, *The Travels of Jedediah Smith* (Santa Ana, Calif., 1934), 150.

Most energetic of Oregon enthusiasts was a serious New England pedagogue, Hall J. Kelley. Nearsighted, earnest, religious, humorless, and diffident, he was so nervous that at times he lost the power of speech, and so sensitive that he was often considered insane. He informed Congress and the rest of the world that Oregon was the modern world's garden of Eden, and planned a magnificent settlement which ultimately boiled down to a handful of followers who soon deserted. Kelley himself made the trip to Oregon, but was robbed en route, and then suffered the final ignomiñy of being considered a horse thief by Chief Factor John McLoughlin of the post at Vancouver. Returning home by boat, Kelley was broken in both health and spirits, but continued to write of Oregon, even though at times extremely vituperatively and incoherently. While his claim that "the colonization of Oregon was both conceived and achieved by me"[7] was untenable, he did increase the interest in Oregon notably.

Kelley's greatest disciple was Nathaniel Wyeth, a practical Yankee businessman who had attained a competence in the ice business. Wyeth and like-minded friends gathered every Saturday night to plan a grandiose Oregon trading and fishing venture. They designed a unique frontier costume, built two amphibious monsters they called "Nat-wye-thiums," and practiced wilderness life on an island in Boston harbor. Impatient at Kelley's delay, they ultimately left Boston without him. While most of the men in time deserted and the special equipment proved worthless, Wyeth himself reached Oregon. Later (1834–35) he made a second trip, during which he founded Fort Hall, which he named for the master.

Kelley and Wyeth inspired interest in Oregon, but the real spark was furnished by four Indians who visited St. Louis to see white civilization. Advertised in the religious press as wanting Christianity, they aroused great furor, since pagans almost never desired to leave their wallowings. First to answer the supposed call was a Methodist party headed by Jason Lee in 1834. The group was received kindly by McLoughlin, and followed his advice to stay in the Willamette Valley. There they found the adult Indians "com-

[7] F. W. Powell (ed.), *Hall J. Kelley on Oregon* (Princeton, Princeton University Press, 1932), 135.

paratively hopeless"[8] and worked with the children and the whites
—something of a let-down from the original plans.

More missionaries soon arrived under the auspices of the American Board, mainly Presbyterian and Congregational. The American Board's first and reluctant appointment was Reverend Samuel Parker, elderly, sickly, and inexperienced; his one qualification was his enthusiasm for converting a world "white for the harvest,"[9] and apparently even his zeal had limitations, for he missed the annual trading caravan across the plains in 1834. Joined by the not-too-well Dr. Marcus Whitman, he finally made the trip to Oregon in 1835, but at the Green River, Whitman turned back to get further help, while Parker continued to Vancouver and then home by ship; the result was no missionary work.

The help Dr. Whitman obtained was partly a bride and partly the young married couple the Reverend and Mrs. H. H. Spalding. The trip west in 1836 was difficult, and frayed tempers were not improved by Spalding's jealous and critical nature. A main mission station was established near the present Walla Walla, and smaller stations were added as new missionaries arrived. The results proved disappointing, with conversions infrequent. The Indians were suspicious and sullen, showing no enthusiasm either for the white man's God or the white man's pants. And then the missionaries hardly were good models of Christian forgiveness and brotherly love, since they bickered continually. Before many years the missions were all closed—the Whitman establishment by force of an Indian massacre.

The Catholics also did work in Oregon, and had somewhat better success among both Indians and whites. Even McLoughlin himself joined the Catholic church, to the great distress of the Protestants. Best known of the Catholic workers was Pierre Jean De Smet, who arrived in 1840.

The missionaries were important, but not in converting Indians. Their glowing letters home and their appeals for funds increased the interest in Oregon. Congressmen began to talk more vigorously

[8] Quoted in G. W. Fuller, *The Inland Empire of the Pacific Northwest* (3 vols., Spokane, H. G. Linderman, 1928), II, 5.

[9] A. B. and D. P. Hulbert (eds.), *The Oregon Crusade* (Denver, Stewart Commission of Colorado College and Denver Public Library, 1934), 212.

of holding the country, and farmers considered the long trip to the Willamette Valley. When the first farmers actually moved in 1839, they naturally found the missions a center of American interest. While in 1840 the remoteness of Oregon kept the American influx small, the direction of the wind had become evident.

California was one more exhibition in the story of the endless ambitions of the American nation. American trappers from time to time crossed the Sierras, and sometimes settled permanently. American ships traded for hides and tallow, with now and then a sailor deciding to remain in the golden California climate. Travelers and merchants appeared periodically, with some staying permanently. Thomas O. Larkin became the outstanding Monterey merchant, and in time American consul. Johann August Sutter, a Swiss by birth, established his magnificent and semifeudal estate of New Helvetia, which was the first California stop for travelers from the East, and a center of American influence. By 1840 even the van of the American farming frontier had reached California.

The Mexican government of California was presented with the same problems as that of Texas, even though on a smaller scale, and vacillated in the same way between encouraging and discouraging American migrants. The power of Mexican control, however, was even less in California than in Texas. The great cultural centers of the missions lost importance with secularization laws. Garrisons became more and more anemic, while a series of revolts lessened Mexican power. Dissatisfied native Californians were often joined by Americans, as when the abortive revolution of 1836 was supported by Isaac Graham and his followers. Revolutionary plottings were common among the Americans, and seemed to center around the person of Larkin.

Even more ominous to the Mexican control of California was the attitude of the United States government. President Jackson made unsuccessful overtures for purchase, and official government representatives talked of revolution. Army explorers overstepped national boundaries to take a look. Navy officials dropped in now and then. Most illuminating was Commodore Jones' seizure of Monterey in 1842 on the erroneous assumption that war with Mexico had begun. Informed of his error, he returned the city with apologies, but no power of clairvoyance was needed to conclude that the United States had a special interest in California.

The United States of the eighteen thirties was laying the groundwork for magnificent expansion in the next decade, and yet probably the average American citizen had only the vaguest ideas of anything west of the Missouri, and only a half-formed opinion that some day the United States would continue its expansion. Possibly he now and then read a newspaper item or magazine article, heard a lecture by a returned missionary, or received rumors of random discussion in Congress.

If Americans had been vitally interested in the Far West, they would have devoured eagerly any books they could have found on the subject, but actually the number of such books was small and their circulations were not great. The truth was that Americans were above all concerned with themselves. The travel literature which they seized avidly was the book written by a foreign visitor to American shores. Americans read such books with an eagerness that was almost morbid. They wanted to read about themselves, and they were interested only in praise. Any hint of criticism produced deeply hurt feelings which were expressed in bitter diatribes against the authors.

Expansion was then not a top subject of interest in the thirties, and yet the trend was so clear that dozens of men made prophetic utterances on the subject. The progression of trappers, merchants, missionaries, and farmers pointed the way to eventual American control of at least Texas and the Pacific Coast. So far as men thought of the matter, they accepted the proposition that Providence had intended that these areas some day be covered by the superior American type of civilization. Few had any idea that the Great American Desert (Great Plains) would be occupied by white farmers, but many assumed that the nation would expand to the Pacific Ocean in the not distant future.

PART II : AT WORK

6. The Farm

THE LANGUAGE of adolescent America was that of the farm. Most men were farmers, and the least common denominator of conversation was the weather, the price of corn, the possibilities of the mangel-worzel, and the profits from shorthorn cattle. Whether men tilled the rocky hills of New Hampshire or the fertile river bottoms of Alabama, the red soil of Pennsylvania or the vast plains of Texas, they had a common meeting ground in their universal concern over farming.

Even city dwellers were acutely conscious of the surrounding countryside. Many of them had been farm boys, either at home or abroad, and nearly all were dependent on the farmers' business, since towns were the centers where farmers sold their products and bought their supplies. Manufacturing depended heavily on the farmer demand, and transportation was of farm products; both were but the lace fringes that decorated a predominantly agricultural dress.

Diversified farming was the American rule, with the usual farmer providing most of his own food and clothes, and trading his surplus—frequently by barter—for the remaining necessities and a few luxuries. Vermont and Missouri farmers saw eye to eye because they used similar methods to raise similar crops. Specialization was the rule with only a few crops such as tobacco, cotton, and rice.

The farmer's investment was small since his buildings were cheap, his machinery simple and inexpensive, and his land low in price. A small investment and relative self-sufficiency made the farmer less dependent on banks and on markets than his grandson was to be, and in consequence his discontent in time of depression was less vociferous. While he had the normal agricultural suspicion of the city man, particularly of the banker, he developed no crusades comparable to the later Granger and Populist movements.

The farmer worked long and hard and took his pleasures crudely and roughly. His native intelligence was adequate, but his formal education was slight, even in favored New England; frequently he was illiterate. He worked on his father's farm from the time he could toddle until he came of age; then he married, produced a large family because the Lord willed, and worked both himself and his family without mercy. For him a wife was a necessity, and so he generally remarried if his wife succumbed to excessive cooking, cleaning, gardening, and childbearing. A vigorous man might wear out several wives before he found one to survive him—and she in turn usually remarried, for an unattached woman had even more insoluble problems than an unattached man.

The farmer's tools and methods were generally those of his father, of his grandfather, and of countless generations in the past. The iron plow was the one universally accepted improvement, although a few skeptics had misgivings that it was a device of the Devil and poisoned the soil. Farms were untidy in comparison with those of contemporary Europe, and not tilled intensively. Livestock was inferior, fruit dubious, and vegetables scarce. Diet was limited and unhealthful. Everywhere there were flies and vermin— trials sent by the Lord. Sewage polluted the wells and rivers from which drinking water was obtained. Disease was common, and was but little alleviated by the doctors, even if they could be obtained upon short notice.

Farm life may have been uncomfortable from the standpoint of a later century, but men could not miss what they had no knowledge of. The farmer was proud of his position as a freeborn American citizen with the right of suffrage. He was an independent husbandman, owning his own land unburdened with a mortgage in at least three-quarters of the cases. He looked down with a deep conviction of superiority upon the "servile" populations of Europe.

Farm tenancy and farm labor were both rare. One curious feudal survival came to light in the thirties, in the Hudson Valley, when the heirs of Stephen Van Rensselaer tried to collect past rents and precipitated a "rent war." Ordinarily a tenant paid his rent in grain

—one-third to one-half of his crop, depending on the owner's advances of seeds and tools. Farm labor was scarce and hence received about a dollar a day, which was high for the time. Even these wages were not sufficient to deter men from trying to become independent farmers, or even farm tenants or industrial laborers.

An average American farm contained somewhere between 80 and 160 acres. The land seldom was valued at more than $50 an acre, while poorer land and virgin prairie commanded no more than $1.50, and Texas land went begging at 10 cents. Eastern prices reflected the plethora of rich western land, and one Indiana farmer pointed the obvious moral: "If you intend to compete with the prairie farmer, who cultivates land of surpassing fertility at a cost of only a few shillings an acre for the purchase, you must break down your rail-roads and fill up your canals, or else we can deliver wheat at your own doors for 50 cents a bushel."[1]

Western land was cheap, but not free. Theoretically government land sold at auction for a minimum of $1.25 an acre, even though the West pleaded persistently for a lower price and for prior rights for the settler who had arrived before the survey. Actually the government was in the process of acceding to western demands by aiding the squatter—first by a series of limited pre-emption laws and then by a general Pre-emption Act in 1841. But even without governmental action very few original settlers lost their lands. Groups of them banded together to "adopt *such measures* as *may* be *necessary* effectively to secure each other in our just claims."[2] These rather vague "measures" included whipping, and tar and feathers—rather convincing arguments to the outsider not to bid land away from some worthy settler. An incidental effect of the claims' clubs was that the average auction prices were very little higher than the legal minimum.

The West also opposed land speculation bitterly, but in their diatribes they were referring only to the eastern speculator. Many a frontiersman realized that great profits were more likely from an

[1] H. A. Kellar, *Solon Robinson* (2 vols., Indianapolis, Indiana Historical Bureau, 1936), I, 360–61.

[2] *Ibid.*, I, 70.

increase in land values than from farming, and planned to sell out to later arrivals. Sometimes he was lucky. More frequently he received little more than enough for a moderate binge before he started for a new frontier. Pioneering was a gamble, and once a frontiersman always a frontiersman.

Frontier farming was no poor man's paradise. The trip west, land, buildings, fences, tools, seed, farm animals, and a year's supplies cost an average family an estimated $2,500, while better land and living quarters were more expensive. Even the young couple squatting on an unsurveyed forty acres, going barefoot, and living on corn bread and sowbelly, needed money. Many a young man worked on his father's farm in the East until he attained his majority, and then labored in the West until he had sufficient savings to get the girl of his choice and settle the western farm he had selected. Migrating families were financed, usually inadequately, by their savings, the sale of their eastern possessions, and loans from relatives and friends. They could be bankrupted by drought, flood, sickness, or economic depression.

Western settlement started with the construction of a temporary shelter and the clearing of wooded land; brush was grubbed out, small trees cut and burned, and larger trees girdled. Prairie settlement avoided the necessity of clearing, but required a heavier plow and three to seven yoke of oxen to break the tough sod. In any case the first year's crop was ordinarily poor—say fifteen bushels of corn or ten of wheat to the acre. Fields were enclosed with eight- or nine-rail wooden fences, since no substitute for the wooden fence had as yet been found.

The first permanent western homes were always log cabins. Cracks were chinked with moss or twigs or homemade mortar. The roof was held in place by saplings fastened with wooden pegs. The floor was mother earth, or sometimes log halves, called "puncheons." Furnishings were simple and homemade, except that here and there was a beautiful chest of drawers or a bureau or a piano or other heirloom which had been brought at tremendous cost and against the advice of all Westerners. A few simple cooking utensils, a little cutlery, a minimum of bedding, and a few tools completed the equipment of the house.

A western farm was not a show place. Always the family was trying to make its fortune on the least possible investment. The house was overcrowded and the equipment poor. Farm tools were simple. Cows, chickens, and pigs were scrawny and tough. Fruit trees were untended. While an ambitious family had a garden, other families existed all year on corn bread and salt pork.

Improvements came with the years. The fields were better cultivated and more productive. Machinery increased in amount and complexity, and sometimes blooded stock was added. The garden was larger, and the orchards better tended. The house became clapboard or even brick, although all too frequently it remained without trees, flowers, or grass. Furniture and clothes showed the influence of the local artisan and the factory. Often, however, it was a later purchaser who enjoyed these improvements, since the original owner might long since have departed to try his fortunes on a newer frontier.

The breaking of millions of virgin western acres brought home to many eastern farmers the sad realization that their own lands were losing fertility. Most alarmed were Virginia farmers, who had long been witnessing a decline in productivity, but farmers in other areas were also worried. The single-crop system of the South did the greatest damage, but even in the Middle and Northern states the results of improper rotation and inadequate fertilization were becoming apparent.

Crop rotation was no new idea. Indeed it had long been practiced to some extent in the Middle and Northern states. Even here, however, the agricultural magazines and progressive farmers found conditions far from ideal. In the South and the West, conditions were worse. The southern planter resisted tenaciously any efforts to diversify southern agriculture, contending that thereby his labor force would become ineffective. The western farmer could not be bothered by such new-fangled ideas as long as his land remained fresh and rich.

Fertilization was also propagandized vigorously by the more progressive, but against the stolid inertia of most husbandmen, who refused even to bother with available animal manures and decayed vegetation. There were even stories of farmers who found barnyard manure so much in the way that they moved their barns. Yet the reformers remained active. During the decade mineral and chemical fertilizers, particularly lime and plaster, were introduced. Distinctively American was Edmund Ruffin's support of marl (common fossil shells) to restore the fertility of his native Virginia.

Drainage was practiced but little. Only rarely did it seem profitable to a farmer to drain a swamp when so much cheap land was available. Subsurface drainage by tiles was not introduced to the United States until the late thirties. Here and there efforts were made to restrain the streams, as through the construction of levees on the Mississippi.

The United States was pre-eminently a grain country—corn and wheat, but also rye, barley, and oats. Corn was grown on practically every farm, and fed by the farmer to both his stock and his family, with most Westerners and Southerners expressing a preference for corn meal over wheat flour. Since there was no important national market for corn, the price jumped erratically from as high as one dollar to as low as ten cents a bushel during the depression. Part of the corn was changed in form so that it could be poured down American throats with explosive effects.

Wheat was the great money crop of the West and of certain eastern areas such as parts of Virginia and the Genesee Valley of New York. A price of two dollars a bushel before the depression was very profitable. The great milling centers were Richmond and Rochester, and a modern flour mill was one of the mechanical wonders which excited the awed admiration of every visitor. A revolving screw pushed the grain to the top of the building, from which point gravity carried it through all of the various processes until it emerged as barrels of flour.

Tobacco had deserted the Tidewater for the Piedmont of North Carolina and Virginia, and had even crossed the mountains into Kentucky and Tennessee. Southeastern Pennsylvania contained no more than a few experimental growers. The male cheek usually bulged with a cud of Kentucky tobacco, even though the famous "Honeydew" was Virginian. The discriminating pipe smoker favored Virginia tobacco, but might add Louisiana perique or Kentucky Burley (from 1838). Richmond had the country's largest tobacco market, with the growers complaining of the usual five-cent price. Lynchburg was the great manufacturing center.

Minor crops were numerous. Hemp produced bags, cotton bales, and cordage. Flax was utilized by thousands of housewives for linsey-woolsey. Rice came largely from the lowlands of South Carolina, and was extremely prodigal of Negro labor even after the improved threshing mill of 1832. Cane sugar was practically a Louisiana monopoly, with New Orleans the great market. Planters protested vigorously at the low tariff of 1832 which they held responsible for the usual price of about six cents. Experiments with sugar beets were not successful, but many families used maple sugar.

The northern or western farmer ordinarily had a garden, primarily for his own use. If he lived near a city, he might sell his surplus to provide a welcome increase of cash income. The South had fewer gardens, and the traveler complained that he was seldom able to obtain fresh vegetables except at New Orleans.

The markets of a city like Philadelphia made the housewife's eyes shine and her husband's mouth water. Such vegetables as potatoes, sweet corn, onions, peas, and beets were present in great profusion, even though novelties such as turnips, rutabaga, mangel-worzel, and Jerusalem artichokes were missing because they were considered fit only for cattle. Butter, eggs, flowers, and fruit were displayed on snowy napkins. Even such exotic foreign products as oranges, lemons, and pineapples could now and then be seen.

Most common of American fruits were apples and peaches, but plums, pears, and cherries also appeared on the market. Smaller fruits such as strawberries and currants were uncultivated and inferior, being picked by children when they had no more important chores. Many Americans hoped that the plentiful grapes would produce an important wine industry, but most people continued to prefer foreign wines like Madeira and port. Here and there Americans tried unsuccessfully to grow dates, nectarines, and olives.

The great current farm mania was silk, which thousands of farmers, even as far north as Maine, welcomed with open arms. The agricultural journals sang its praises and several were devoted ex-

clusively to the subject. A Long Island nursery made a fortune selling mulberry trees at two to five dollars each. One gentleman appeared in Washington clad in a suit made of silk grown and manufactured on his farm. Two Frenchmen established a silk-spinning
factory in Philadelphia, and as a bit of advertising donated a domestic silk flag to the House of Representatives, where it was draped
over the portrait of Lafayette. The boom collapsed late in the decade, and mulberry trees which had sold readily at five dollars went
begging at one cent.

Agricultural experimentation was largely the work of gentlemen
farmers, who farmed for pleasure rather than profit; best known
was Dr. David Hosack, a retired New York physician who had an
estate at Hyde Park. Various nurseries and seed houses experimented commercially, not only with food plants, but also with ornamental trees and shrubs and flowers. Most popular flowers were
roses and dahlias, of which hundreds of varieties were offered for
sale.

Every farmer except the cotton specialist kept one or more cows
to furnish milk and butter for his family; in the West they were
belled and allowed to forage for themselves. Most cattle were hy-
brid and uncertain in breed, neither beautiful nor very productive.
A cow following its own dietary preferences or subsisting on city
garbage gave poor milk, which was often diluted before marketing,
while butter was not good and steaks were tough. Most western
steers were salted for marketing, but a few were driven over the
National Road to be fattened in Pennsylvania. Poor stock meant
low prices. A cow could frequently be bought for ten dollars, while
the well-known Brighton, Massachusetts, market averaged only
thirty dollars apiece for beef cattle in 1836, when prices were comparatively high.

Scrawny and disreputable cattle did not satisfy the more progressive farmers, who were importing various blooded stock such
as Hereford, Holstein, and Jersey. The greatest enthusiasm was
reserved for the Durham Shorthorn, which shamed the domestic
scrubs all over the country, particularly in Kentucky. Even a little
Shorthorn blood might shoot the price of a cow up to one hundred

Mowing with cradle scythes, the usual method in the 1830's

Courtesy of the International Harvester Company

Cyrus H. McCormick's first mechanical reaper, 1831

Courtesy of the International Harvester Company

dollars, while a purebred cow with calf might bring one thousand dollars or more. Little wonder that the more modern farmer greeted blooded stock with high hopes.

Most ubiquitous of American animals was the hog, which the traveler found picking the garbage on Wall Street, absorbing the refuse on a southern plantation, or roaming the forest in the West —"root hog or die." Pork was the basic food of the eastern farmer, of the southern slave, and of the frontiersman—not to mention every other class of the population, and after the United States had eaten its fill, there remained a surplus for export.

Most American hogs were thin, scrawny, and muscular—well able to take care of themselves. In the West they were often shot like other wild game. As in the case of cattle, inferior animals brought inferior prices, and hogs averaged less than six dollars each at the Brighton market in 1836. As with cattle, also, many farmers realized the virtues of blooded stock, and such varieties as the Irish Grazier and Poland China were imported. The greatest enthusiasm, however, was reserved for the Berkshire, which swept the country even to the more remote reaches of the frontier.

Western hogs invaded eastern markets even more than did western cattle. Thousands were driven East each year, while greater numbers were salted and packed. The "porkopolis" of America was Cincinnati, with such towns as Chicago only minor competitors. "The pork aristocracy of Cincinnati does not mean those innumerable pigs which walk at large about the streets, as if they owned the town, but a class of rich merchants, who have made their fortunes by killing annually, salting, and exporting, about 200,000 swine."[3]

Pork packing exhibited modern division of labor and utilization of by-products. Each pig was driven into a small pen, knocked on the head with an iron mace, its throat slit, the carcass dipped in boiling water, the bristles removed, and stretchers fixed between the legs; then it was hoisted on a hook and disemboweled. The entire process was completed within three and one-half minutes from the last grunt. After cooling, the hog was cut into pieces, placed in barrels with brine—two hundred pounds to a barrel—and was ready for shipment. By-products included glue from hooves, dye from

[3] Lyell, *Travels 1841–42*, II, 61.

blood, brushes from hair, and fertilizer from offal. The price of pork for most of the decade was some three to four cents a pound on the hoof and six to seven cents when packed.

The sheep industry was booming, spurred by the high wool prices which topped fifty cents a pound. Northern New England was the heart of the sheep country, with the woolies outnumbering their human rivals for living space; the ratio in Vermont was almost six to one. By the end of the decade there was visible a definite trend for sheep to follow the frontier west. An ordinary sheep could be bought for from one to three dollars, and sheep growers were turning to blooded stock, particularly the Merino. Merino wool was not only heavier per sheep, but enough better that it commanded a premium. The result was that a first-class Merino might sell for one hundred dollars or more, while a ram might bring one thousand.

In a horse-and-buggy age not only the farmer but many a city dweller had one or more horses. A good nag could always be bought for $100, but special stock such as the excellent Morgan horses of Vermont brought more. If a man wanted to impress his neighbors or go into racing, he might well buy one of the Arabian horses introduced early in the decade by Henry Clay and others and probably bred in Kentucky. With such ambition, $1,000 was a moderate price, and the sky was the limit. A man more interested in stamina than in beauty or speed might stick to mules, at somewhere between $80 and $150; and again he probably bought from Kentucky. A good jack brought much higher prices—"Warrior" may be said to have hit the jackpot at $5,000. Even more enduring, and certainly cheaper, were the widely used oxen which could be obtained at $40 to $80 a yoke.

Animal breeding was not a profession, but rather a trade learned by observation, tradition, and instruction. There were only a few trained veterinarians, mostly English; the first had come to the United States as recently as 1810. The average animal doctor was frequently illiterate and often incompetent. A veterinary hospital was so rare as to be startling news.

The scarcity of farm labor encouraged the farmer to replace human hands with mechanical gadgets, of which there were great numbers in the market. Unfortunately, many of the machines were costly, complicated, inefficient, and subject to breakdowns. Usually the farmer could not get replacement parts and did not have the mechanical knowledge to make necessary repairs. Then too many farmers were conservatively suspicious of such new-fangled contraptions. In fact, even the nonfarmer felt a trifle shocked when the hens were "thrust aside from the uses of creation"[4] by an incubator, called an "Eccaleobian."

Tools and machines offered anything the farmer could imagine, whether a sausage filler or a carriage lifter, a lactometer or a stump puller. Almost no farm process was immune from man's ingenuity, as the advertisements of mowers, harrows, shellers, cultivators, drills, and other devices illustrated. Even the ancient and honorable wooden plow was modernized, streamlined, glorified—and then made extinct. The great plow maker was Jethro Wood, who manufactured a cast-iron plow in three interchangeable parts. And when the iron plow proved ineffective in the thick, rich loam of the prairies, two Illinois blacksmiths arrived independently and almost simultaneously at the idea of using steel, and only a short time later another ingenious Illinois citizen invented the self-scouring plow.

Best advertised historically of the new farm machines was the reaper, designed to replace the cradle scythe, which itself was fairly young. Many inventors tried their hands at mechanical reapers only to have them collapse disastrously in practical trials. Success finally came to Cyrus McCormick, who proudly demonstrated his invention in the Shenandoah Valley in 1831. Quite surprisingly, in view of his later business acumen, McCormick forgot to patent his reaper for some years and did not start commercial production until 1840. In the meantime an ingenious Cincinnatian, Obed Hussey by name, invented and patented (1833) a machine of his own, so that during the thirties the Hussey reaper was the only one on the market.

Another arduous farm job was threshing, and again a machine was offered for the work. During the twenties various rather crude English threshers were presented to the American farmer, but by

[4] L. M. Child, *Letters from New York Second Series* (New York, C. S. Francis and Company, 1845), 110.

the thirties improved American machines were available. Greatest popularity went to the combined thresher and fan mill of H. A. and J. A. Pitts of Winthrop, Maine—a machine that could be run by either horse or steam power. While the thresher was immediately popular and widely used, the reaper was introduced more slowly, and a combined reaper and thresher invented in 1836 was not considered successful.

Agricultural improvements were propagandized continuously and effectively by a multitude of farm papers, which month after month hammered at the use of fertilizer, machinery, crop rotation, new crops, and similar matters. After the death of the famous *American Farmer* early in the decade, the best of the farm journals was probably Edmund Ruffin's *Farmers' Register*. Every editor apparently considered himself as an evangel of progress on the American farm.

This period was before the day when government felt any great and direct responsibility to help farmers. Of course the government was concerned with tariffs, road building, and similar matters, but the farmer was expected to grow, finance, and market his own crop. A few states went as far as bounties on specific crops, or monetary aid to agricultural societies, while the federal government embraced a limited free-seed program because of the crop failures of 1837 and 1838.

The farmers' own efforts at improvement came mainly in the agricultural societies. At the beginning of the decade the prevailing type was the Berkshire plan club, with its annual fair that featured prayers, addresses, singing, plowing matches, a ball, and prizes for the best exhibits. By the end of the decade, however, such societies were declining in importance—partly because the states were withdrawing aid.

The new and growing type of agricultural society was the county or state group, which sometimes published a journal. The high point of the society's year was the annual fair, toward which many a farm family looked hopefully as its big outing. The town in which the fair was held was jammed, while crowds milled about the exhibits, the gambling games, and the shacks offering a variety of food and drinks. The main exhibits were cattle, grain, fruit, farm machinery, home products, and at times manufactured products. Prizes were awarded for the best stock, the most grain per acre, and similar superior achievements. The women's section contained displays of everything from cakes and jellies to quilts and diapers. Dances, speeches, pulling matches, and other entertainment broke the round of sight-seeing.

An agricultural fair permitted the farmer to see with his own eyes the good Berkshire hogs, shorthorn cattle, improved cereals, and threshing machines. Also he could gather with other farmers and discuss the best fertilizer for corn and the comparative advantages of Holstein and Devon cattle. His wife could exchange her pet grape-jelly recipe for some one else's hint on hemstitching, and could obtain news of the latest addition to the family down the road. These fairs and the societies that sponsored them performed effective service in spreading knowledge of agricultural innovations and improvements.

Thoughtful farmers were worried over the lack of dignity and prestige of their work. Farm boys and girls tended to move to the cities, not entirely because the potential rewards were greater. While the farmer seldom was distinguished by great wealth, he also lacked the prestige that comes from special training, professional pride, and a distinctive code of ethics. By common belief, anyone could be a farmer. The farmer might be lauded as the member of a vital group, but he was never honored as an individual. To meet this situation, farmers talked of professional agricultural schools, but the best they obtained were infrequent series of lectures, as at Transylvania at Lexington, Kentucky; the first chair of agricultural chemistry was not established until 1847—and then at Yale. Professional standards and prestige were to be cultivated by a national society established at Washington in 1841, but the organization soon died of financial malnutrition.

Farming was clearly declining in relative importance during the eighteen thirties. While one could still say that most Americans were no farther than a generation from the farm, the time gap was increasing rapidly. More and more city dwellers knew nothing of farming. They accepted food rather casually, like air and water, and kept their eyes on factories, railroads, banks, and other profit-making enterprises that seemed to offer greater opportunities.

Quite naturally the farmer made efforts to retain the prestige which was slipping from his grasp. Since money seemed the goal, the farmer tried to make his share of it, and making money depended on the growing of more crops that could be sold for cash. The old self-sufficient farm worked by hand labor tended to give way to the mechanized farm with a larger investment in land, buildings, machinery, and blooded stock, with more specialization in a single crop, and with larger purchases of food, clothing, and furniture. The transition was still in the embryo stage, but its existence was evident to the discerning men of the period. Another generation and it would become obvious even to the dim-witted.

7. The Plantation

SOUTH of Mason and Dixon's line King Cotton wielded a despotic scepter. The South had deserted the varied production of the North and West to bow before the demanding monarch. Along with cotton went Negro slavery, which pinned the badge of degradation on manual labor, thereby discouraging both the foreign and the native born. Immigrants did not go to the South, while poorer whites were driven back into the hill country by the economic competition of the white planter and by the force of social disapproval. Farms grew larger and accumulated "in the hands of the few, to the exclusion of the many,"[1] who thereupon sought new opportunity in the West or retrogressed to abject poverty and ignorance.

The rosy tradition of a lost civilization now pictures the plantation as thousands of fertile acres, in the midst of which loomed an impressive white-pillared and galleried mansion, flanked by commodious barns and wide-flung slave quarters; the whites sat on the broad veranda sipping mint juleps while the murmur of rich Negro voices and the strumming of guitars stole through the warm, fragrant evening stillness. In sober fact such plantations were rare. The usual house was small and unadorned, and there was a sprinkling of log cabins. The great majority of southern whites owned very few slaves or none at all. The ruling planter class was always numerically small.

The cultivation of cotton was comparatively simple; otherwise slave labor would have been impractical. The old stalks were turned over in the field and the cotton planted in rows with a seeder. Culti-

[1] *Farmers' Register* (1838), VI, 458, quoted in U. B. Phillips, "Plantations with Slave Labor and Free," in *American Historical Review*, Vol. XXX (July 1925), 747.

vation was usually by hand, although sometimes by horse hoe. The ripe cotton was picked by both men and women, each with a bag tied to his waist, and a good farm produced about a bale an acre, although the average was much less. Large plantations did their own ginning, but smaller growers gave part of their crop for the services of commercial mills. The better mills had steam power, but horse and water was more usual. Cotton bales ran four to five hundred pounds, occasionally including stray bits of iron and other weighty impurities. The cotton seed was sometimes pressed for its oil, to be used particularly in paint; at other times it was sold for fertilizer or even just discarded.

Cotton marketing was largely a function of the city merchant. The large planter shipped directly to his factor on the coast, while the small grower sold to his local merchant, who in turn shipped to the coast. Most of the important factors were located in Charleston, Savannah, Mobile, and New Orleans, with those of New Orleans the most important. These factors either sold to the agents of northern and English manufacturers or else themselves acted as agents for such concerns.

The cotton planter very seldom saw any actual cash. The small grower received credit on the books of his local merchant, and often remained in debt from year to year. The larger planter might be paid in sixty- or ninety-day drafts which he discounted at his bank and which were then collected in New York or London. In many cases, however, he left the payments with his factor, who also acted as his purchasing agent. When he found, as was often the case, that his new crop barely settled his past debts, he excoriated the "tribute" he paid the North in commissions on purchases and sales, bank charges, costs of manufactured goods and food, and shipping charges.

Southern prosperity was the Siamese twin of cotton prices, and the planter watched the price of cotton more closely than he did his own ever expanding family. Luckily for him, the booming expansion of cotton mills more than matched his doubling and quadrupling of production, so that a price of fifteen cents in the middle of the decade brought rumors of 35 per cent profits for Alabama growers. But then came the depression, with prices dropping to six

The Death Chamber

Butchering methods of the period

Cutting and Packing

cents, the lowest before the Civil War, and unprofitable to many planters.

Planters harassed by flunctuating prices could still view the future with hope, but the approach of land exhaustion was an unalleviated tragedy. The usual cotton farmer was as much a waster of natural resources as a forest fire or a flood. He might produce cotton on the same land year after year for a generation or more, with no more fertilization than the occasional application of cotton seed. The inevitable result was declining production, whereupon the planter either went broke or moved west—to Alabama, to Mississippi, or even to Texas.

Expanding cotton production meant an increasing demand for labor, with slavery becoming ever more firmly imbedded in southern society. Prices of slaves rose steadily, so that a good field hand who could have been obtained for five hundred dollars in 1830 sold for over twice that amount seven years later, while well-trained house servants and artisans sometimes commanded over two thousand dollars. Prices quite naturally fluctuated with health, age, sex, and reputation; for instance, a scarred back denoted insubordination and brought down the price. A woman was cheaper than a man; like a cow, she brought a higher price if she had one or more children. Mixed blood did not affect the price, but a very light Negro was difficult to sell in most places.

The buying and selling of human beings was always a distasteful business, to Southerners as well as to Northerners. Men and women were inspected like cattle, except that sometimes an intimate examination, as of a female, might take place in a side room. Southern opinion approved the kind master who sold only through necessity and was careful not to disorganize families, but public opinion alone could not eliminate the cruel and vicious owners. All too common was the advertisement: "FOR SALE, A NEGRO WOMAN, with one or more children, to suit the purchaser."[2] To the South, the slave dealer was viewed with dislike and was something of a social outcast, with the result that many dealers posed as planters.

[2] *Virginia Herald*, February 7, 1835, quoted in F. Bancroft, *Slave-Trading in the Old South* (Baltimore, J. H. Furst Company, 1931), 27.

Particularly distasteful was the slave trade of Washington, D. C.—the capital of a nation dedicated to freedom and the dignity and rights of the common man. Many a visitor viewed with shocked horror the plethora of public auctions, the existence of slave pens, the use of public jails as slave quarters, and the strings of shackled slaves being marched past the Capitol. Slave firms such as Franklin and Armfield, or Washington Robley, were a stench in the nostrils of thousands of men and women who considered themselves anything but ardent abolitionists.

The great slave trade was from East to West, with possibly 200,000 Negroes being transplanted between 1830 and 1840. Virginia and South Carolina were the great senders and Mississippi the great receiver. Professional dealers toured the East collecting their purchases in either private or public jails. They sometimes shipped their human merchandise by water down the Ohio or through the Gulf, but more frequently made the slave furnish his own power by land. The overland "coffle" traveled some twenty-five miles a day and camped at night. Upon arrival in the West, the slaves were auctioned at the more important towns. Most dealers treated their slaves moderately well, since they recognized the higher prices paid for cheerful, healthy, well-clothed men and women, but there were always a few dealers who expressed their sadistic natures regardless of economic motivation. Slaves were the most profitable crop on many a worn-out plantation, and some owners were accused of breeding slaves like cattle. That white owners gave the process of procreation their personal assistance for the profits to be obtained from mulatto sons and daughters, as was sometimes charged, seems highly unlikely, while the necessity of encouraging slaves to have more children seems nonexistent. On the other hand, however, the purchasers of slaves undoubtedly gave consideration to female generative power in making their selections.

The attitude of the South toward the Negro was generally incomprehensible to the North. What the North saw was the Negro doing slave labor, being considered inferior as a race, and being feared as a group. What it seldom saw was the liking and respect between individual members of the two races. Negroes cooked and served the food, suckled the babies, and took care of the small children. A personal slave often slept in the same room with his master or mistress, to whom he was bound by the closest ties of affection. Even closer relations between the two races were evidenced by the number of mulatto children. The North never quite comprehended how one can dislike a group and still like individual members of it.

Southern thought was obsessed by the danger of a slave revolt, since Negroes not far removed from savagery were in a majority in many areas. Only one disturbance of the thirties might conceivably be magnified to such stature. Nat Turner was a Virginia slave who had been given special privileges because of his physical weakness. His followers, who credited him with divine attributes, broke loose in August, 1831, killing and destroying; whether they had been incited directly by Nat is uncertain. Whites immediately gathered and hunted the participants. Nat himself was tried and hanged.

The Nat Turner outbreak was suppressed easily, but it gave point to people's worst fears. The result was increased severity to the Negro, and more elaborate protective measures, including curfew laws and armed guards. Any disturbance—even a fire—was announced by a bell, whereupon all the women dressed and the men collected their firearms for an emergency. This state of tension was fed by a series of rumored slave revolts, often imaginary.

Most picturesque of the potential insurrections was credited to the bandit Murrell, whose widespread organization specialized in holdups, counterfeiting, and slave stealing. The generally accepted story was of a widespread slave revolt which was to cover the entire South from Maryland to Mississippi, and to occur late in 1835. The whole tale seems somewhat fantastic, even when buttressed by the supposed confessions of a member of the gang. At any rate the insurrection never materialized.

The condition of the slave was a matter of the widest difference of opinion. Commentators represented a wide range of vigorous preconceptions, and never saw more than comparatively few of the millions of slaves who worked under all sorts of conditions and under all kinds of masters. Many eye-witnesses pictured the slave as well treated, not worked too hard, and happy—in fact, better off and more contented than the laborers of the North. Other equally competent witnesses described bad conditions, cruelty, and prevailing discontent. The truth is probably not an average of the two extremes, but more likely a statement broad enough to include many variations.

Slave quarters were ordinarily the crudest of log cabins or shacks clustered in back of the manor house, although the better plantation sometimes boasted small whitewashed frame cabins with plank floors. Dirt floors, overcrowding, and lack of proper sanitation were prevalent. Food was cooked over an open fireplace in the most primitive of utensils. Furniture was homemade, unattractive, and scanty, with beds built into the wall. Both sexes slept in the same room except on the few plantations using the dormitory plan, and bedclothes were limited to a periodic issue of blankets. The simple and cheap clothes were made on the plantation, although the cloth was often bought outside. Shoes were for cold weather only; they were plain and cheap, the same for men and women, and were repaired on the plantation.

Food was simple and coarse, but ordinarily ample and healthful. The staples were a peck of corn meal and three or four pounds of pork a week, with a reasonable amount of molasses; the slave did his own cooking. Vegetables such as potatoes (usually sweet), peas, cabbage, turnips, squash, onions, and green corn were issued in season at some places. Brown sugar, coffee, rice, poultry, fish, wheat flour, and rye flour were luxuries. Plantations using the task system often allowed their slaves to raise poultry, eggs, and garden stuff for the town market; sometimes the slave had to pay for his time.

Most slaves were field hands who worked at hoeing, picking, and other gang labor under the constant supervision that was both a legal and an economic necessity. House servants were picked for their intelligence and adaptability, and the large plantation would have cooks, housemaids, nurses, gardeners, firemen, wood cutters, cobblers, coopers, and dressmakers. In the towns could be found slaves trained as mechanics, draymen, hostlers, blacksmiths, carpenters, and wheelwrights.

A slave was a costly investment, which repaid not only adequate food and clothes, but reasonable medical care. Every master found profit in keeping a supply of medicines—castor oil, quinine, laudanum, paregoric, epsom salts, vermifuge, liniments, and patent medicines—and a doctor was called for serious illness or accident. Nearly every plantation set aside a cabin for sick slaves, and some had regular hospitals. Maternity cases were given lighter field work, with usually a month or six weeks of rest at parturition.

Plantation medical care was better in theory than in fact. Masters with no medical training made many sad mistakes. Rural doctors were none too good at their best, and they were seldom at their best with Negro patients. Furthermore, many a master was tempted to try to squeeze a little extra work out of each slave. A pregnant woman might be given only a week or two for the delivery and recovery, with resulting high child and maternal mortality. A slave woman might easily have a record of a dozen miscarriages and twice that many live births, of which only half would pass childhood.

Negro sex life was highly irregular. Marriage or divorce was at the will of the master, who seldom interfered unless a marriage included a Negro from another estate. A Negro girl usually became a mother by the age of fifteen, although not necessarily by virtue of a regular husband. Crowded living quarters and the readjustments necessitated by slave sales tended to make sex relations temporary and unsatisfactory. Then, too, the Negro girl sometimes found that she might obtain preferential treatment by bestowing her favors on the overseer or on the planter or his son. Such "bestowal" might of course be only a polite legal fiction, since there could be no such thing as rape of a slave.

White-black sex relations, usually involving a white man and a black woman, were tolerated but not approved. Some Southerners contended that these relationships insured the purity of white women—a justification used for white prostitution elsewhere. In some parts of the Southwest a well-to-do white bachelor customarily had a colored mistress until his marriage; such liaisons were known but never mentioned by the white girls. Ordinarily both Negro and white man favored a mulatto girl over a full blood—"twenty-six black girls not make mulatto yellow girl"[3] said the Negro song—but a man might change his luck with a real black girl.

[3] F. A. Kemble, *Journal of a Residence on a Georgia Plantation in 1838–1839* (New York, Harper and Brothers, 1863), 219.

A small planter was his own slave driver, but the large plantation had an overseer, who was usually assisted by Negro drivers.
The overseer managed the farm, taking complete control when the
owner was absent—and many farms had absentee owners. He al-
loted tasks, meted out punishments, and in general acted as God.
The slave might appeal his decision, but the appeal was ordinarily
fruitless. A good overseer was difficult to obtain despite high wages,
and not primarily because the work was hard. Slave-driving was
considered a degrading occupation, and hence lacked social position.
Owners and merchants, the only comparable classes, would associate neither with the overseer nor with his family.

Slave discipline was administered through rewards and punishments. Good work brought tobacco, special food, privileges to fish
or to cultivate a garden, and presents at Christmas. Poor work, indolence, insolence, drinking, or disobedience usually brought whipping, since jail meant only the gift of idleness. The ultimate possibility was sale of the culprit. Whippings seldom exceeded thirty
lashes lest a large investment be injured at least temporarily, but
even thirty lashes by a rawhide whip or thin paddle caused a great
deal of distress. Some whippings had little purpose except to provide pleasure for perverts, as when a woman for some minor offense would be lashed by her wrists to a tree until her feet barely
touched the ground, her dress either pulled down to her waist or
thrown over her head, and then beaten until she was bathed in
blood. A titillating refinement was to have a husband or lover do
the beating. The more squeamish owner might hire his whippings
done by the town, which also furnished stocks, and did branding
and ear cropping.

The slave had little legal protection. Unusual cruelty or murder carried penalties which were seldom applied, while even lynching ordinarily went unpunished. The slave could not sue or be sued,
marry legally, hold property, or leave a will. He could not testify
in court against a white man, although another Negro or a white
could testify against him. He could be convicted and punished for
a crime, and he could be sold. Usually he needed a pass to leave the
plantation or to appear in a town at night. Freedom was difficult to
obtain in many states even if a master wanted to grant it.

Negro education was illegal, but religion was approved. Education was generally felt to bring discontent and the desire for freedom, although some masters felt different and flouted the law. Religion, on the other hand, was expected to give an emotional release even as it taught humility and obedience. White churches provided seats in the rear for Negroes, while Negro churches included plantation chapels. The Baptist and Methodist churches appealed particularly to the Negroes. Camp meetings were very popular and noisy, leading some masters to suspect that a slave might get too much even of religion.

Outside of religion and sex, the pleasures of the Negro were few. On Sunday he could visit, sleep, hunt, or fish. A barbecue was a big event, and marriage was celebrated even though the ceremony had no legal significance. But in spite of hardships, the Negro continued to laugh, to dance, to sing, and to play the banjo. Poetry and music appeared spontaneously, and even the whites would gather on the piazza to hear the strumming of the banjo and the lilting Negro voices as they floated through the warm dusk. Rhythm was often more important than the exact words of a song:

> *Jenny shake her toe at me,*
> *Jenny gone away;*
> *Jenny shake her toe at me,*
> *Jenny gone away.*
> *Hurrah! Miss Susy, oh!*
> *Jenny gone away.*
> *Hurrah! Miss Susy, oh!*
> *Jenny gone away.*[4]

Needy slaveowners sometimes rented out their slaves for work on other farms, on railroads and canals and roads, in cotton factories, iron mills, and mines, or as waiters, mechanics, nurses, cooks, or servants in homes and hotels. Some of the girls became prostitutes. Negroes filled satisfactorily such skilled jobs as carpenter, blacksmith, cooper, and factory hand. Most renters were hard masters, but sometimes the Negro was better off and took pride in his value.

[4] *Ibid.,* 128.

A few Negroes bought their own services and hired themselves out, even though this procedure was illegal in most areas.

Southern papers were filled with the traditional, standardized cut of a Negro with a bundle that indicated a runaway slave. The fleeing Negro was motivated ordinarily by a temporary desire to visit a distant family, to escape a hated overseer, to enjoy a vacation, or merely to see the country. Many a master did not advertise for the eloping slave, realizing that in all probability the fugitive was remaining near home and would soon return to take his inevitable whipping.

Only a few Negroes ran away of their own volition to escape the degradation of the slave status. Two classes of people encouraged the desire for freedom. One was the professional crook who enticed the slave away and then returned him for the reward. The other was the ardent abolitionist, cocksure and self-righteous, who was certain that slavery was wicked, and who was willing to sabotage it even at great personal inconvenience. Such bigots were popular in neither North nor South, and always teetered on the brink of lynching.

Slavery may well have injured the whites more than it did the blacks. The young lady who disrobed in the presence of her coachman was expressing forcefully the belief that the Negro was a lower order of creature which was scarcely human; the uncontrolled authority all too frequently produced pride, intolerance, and cruelty. An illiterate and superstitious black population was not fertile ground for the flowering of an educated, intelligent, and sensitive white population—southern theory to the contrary notwithstanding. Newspapers, books, colleges, museums, and art could hardly flourish in a region where their patrons were only a handful of the wealthy. True, white women of the better class remained chaste and ornamental, but only at the cost of personal vigor and well-balanced emotional lives, and in turn encouraged their menfolk to seek more robust pleasures elsewhere.

Slavery had possibly its worst effect in making manual labor menial and demeaning. Both Negro and white tried to avoid it as much as possible. "The whites stand with their hands in their breeches pockets, and the blacks are helping them do nothing.

Fences are down, doors are ajar, filth is in the streets, foul odours in the air, confusion and neglect are everywhere. Go into a house late at night, they are all lounging about, too lazy to go to bed; go in the morning, they are all yawning in bed, too lazy to get up. No one has his prescribed duties—the master scolds and drives, the slave dawdles and shirks; and if anything *must* be done, it takes one white longer to hunt up two negroes and force them to do it than it would take one uncorrupted Saxon to finish it alone."[5]

The problems of Negro slavery were by no means solved when the Negro was freed. Free Negroes, both North and South, lived under great handicaps which were only partly legal, while even completely Negro communities were never quite successful. One wonders not so much why many people expected slavery to last indefinitely, as how those at the other extreme of thought expected Negroes to adapt themselves successfully to sudden freedom.

Freedom in the South was extremely difficult to obtain and then hedged by restrictions, for slaveholders feared the influence of successful freedom. In fact, even freedom itself was difficult to maintain before skeptical white officers, who resolved all doubts in favor of slave status. The free Negro was barred from meetings, public schools, and voting. His occupations and his ownership of property were limited. Upon the least possible pretext he was arrested and punished severely. He received separate and inferior accommodations in rooming houses, churches, theaters, and railroad cars. His wife could not sit down as long as a white lady was in the same room, and he and his wife were always called by their first names. To the credit of the free Negroes, some of them succeeded in becoming educated and in living comfortably. New Orleans probably had the most successful free Negro community in the South; an observer of 1836 estimated that 855 free Negroes had two and one-half million dollars' worth of property, including 620 slaves.

The northern free Negro was but little better off than his southern brother, except in rural regions where his numbers were inconsiderable. He was generally barred from white hotels, restaurants,

[5] Richards, *Howe*, II, 110–11.

theaters, and lectures, although he appeared in abolition and other reform movements. He ordinarily was given separate and inferior schools, since black-white education was greeted with hostility that sometimes took the form of mob action. The opening of Oberlin to the Negro was viewed with general distaste. The Negro was ordinarily excluded from the polls, even when no legal obstacle existed. In most churches he was forced to sit in the rear or in the balcony.

Economically, the northern free Negro was faced by almost insuperable obstacles. Most trades and professions were closed to him; consequently he appeared frequently as a common unskilled laborer or as a house servant. Even here he might be displaced by Irish competition. As a result his contributions to pauperism and criminality were high. These conditions derived from the general hostility of all white labor, which agreed with most Southerners in considering the Negro a member of an inferior race—"a link as it were between man and the brutes."[6]

Hostility to the Negro at times took the good old American form of mob violence. Philadelphia had several race riots; for example, the one of 1832 in which a white mob ravaged the Negro district, battering down doors, breaking windows, and beating Negroes until dispersed by the police; a little later a Negro man, partner in a mixed marriage, had his head held under a pump for half an hour immediately after the ceremony. Other communities similarly mistreated Negroes for real or fancied wrongs. A Negro academy near Norwich, Connecticut, was attacked by a mob in 1835 and destroyed.

Most famous anti-Negro riot of the period involved the school of one Prudence Crandall, a Quaker of Canterbury, Connecticut. Miss Crandall operated a girls' school to which she admitted Negroes, with the result that the white pupils withdrew. Miss Crandall was persistent, and advertised her school as a Negro school, flouting the boycott of the town. Her students were arrested as vagrants, and she herself was arrested and fined. When this conviction was reversed upon appeal, a crowd of townspeople took matters into their own hands, attacked the school, and put it out of business.

In spite of restrictions and discrimination, a few of the northern

6 Hamilton, *Men and Manners*, 55.

free Negroes attained a measure of prosperity. Some ran successful businesses and others became skilled artisans. In many places they held property, and there was talk of better education and even of a Negro college. A weekly newspaper, *The Colored American*, was published for a time. Several conventions considered long-run plans for the race. General opposition was expressed to the movement to Liberia, but favor greeted the idea of migration to some part of the West—a proposal which, needless to say, was never translated into action.

The importance of the free Negro was not great, except that his difficulties in adjusting himself to a white civilization should have given the abolitionists cause for considerable concern. If a few thousand Negroes experienced tremendous troubles because of white prejudice, the adjustment of millions of blacks to freedom should certainly have appeared as a perilous project. Slavery was not a problem to be solved satisfactorily by a simple and doctrinaire answer.

8. Business

AMERICA was money mad, "devoured by the thirst for riches."[1]
Wealth was the visible evidence of success and the symbol
of eminence in a society where a virgin continent gave
even the poorest farmer's son a fair start in his chase after
the all-important dollar. Wherever men gathered, the conversation
concerned crops, land speculation, canals, cotton mills, or banks,
and not paintings, literature, or philosophy. Great riches were the
goal that lay closest to the hearts of men.

The mad rush for wealth trampled and mutilated the finer
codes of business ethics, for the goal seemed more important than
the means of its attainment. The pursuit of gain was a catch-as-catch-
can game, with no holds barred. Perhaps a nation established by
revolution and existing on land wrenched by force from the natives
could hardly have been expected to possess the nicest of ethical
standards as it continued to expand. Certainly the shrewd driving
of hard bargains, which at times could hardly be distinguished from
fraud, was considered the best possible evidence of superior intelligence.

In getting rich, Americans were not violent partisans of any one
brand of abstract economic theory. Like the drunkard, they could
take their principles or leave them alone. Writers, with some exceptions, accepted classical *laissez-faire* doctrines. Practical men of affairs sometimes gave lip service to the same theories, but not to the
extent of allowing ideas to interfere with their desires. Americans
felt close to their government, and welcomed enthusiastically government spending for railroads, roads, prisons, almshouses, or other
objects they considered desirable or necessary. Americans even accepted such government activities as the regulation of railroad rates

[1] Pierson, *Tocqueville*, 71.

and hack fares and the supervision of steamboat safety, although with a certain amount of bitterness on the part of the men being regulated.

English *laissez-faire* theory by no means always suited American conditions, and that fact was nowhere better illustrated than with the tariff. England could contemplate free trade as a benefit to her well-established and efficient manufacturing plants, but America had only infant factories that clamored for protection, while certain farming groups, such as New England wool growers and Louisiana sugar planters, craved similar help. Such people argued plausibly that more factories meant more markets for farmers and more self-sufficiency in war. Naturally they did not stress personal profits, nor did they mention who would pay the bill.

A high tariff was hotly opposed by several groups who felt they would be injured. Any Southerner realized that a tariff would raise the price of the cloth and machinery that he bought and would not help the price of the cotton that he sold. Shippers feared a decline of foreign trade. Skilled laborers forsaw a rise in living costs. Bitter invective greeted these "laws for the promotion of smuggling, multiplication of crimes, severity and frequency of punishments, and the entailment of pauperism on posterity."[2]

The tariff of 1828 had been passed by southern votes, on the assurance that there would be included "such ingredients in the chalice as would poison the monster."[3] The poison turned out to be a tonic, and northern industrialists clamored for still higher rates, while Southerners wept for the Constitution and the Union, and talked of secession. A modified tariff of 1832 failed to produce peace and concord. South Carolina "nullified" the act and provided "protection" against northern invasion. Jackson strengthened Fort Moultrie and sent General Scott to the scene of the trouble. While the immediate crisis was averted by the Clay compromise tariff of 1833, the obviously increasing divergence between North and South might well have given lovers of the Union excellent cause for alarm.

The demand for a higher tariff was an outward sign of growing

[2] Hale, *Notes*, 45.
[3] Quoted in Turner, *New West*, 319.

industrialization. The bone and flesh of American economic life remained the farm and the plantation, but the heart that pumped the hot blood of economic activity was composed of mercantile houses, banks, canals, and mills. Here was the throbbing pulsation of feverish activity, and here lay the peak rewards for young men of energy and ambition. Here was the future.

Industrialization brought possibilities of a greater concentration of wealth than had ever existed in the past. The wealth itself inspired feelings of intense pride, but its concentration was not such a happy event. Many a Jeremiah feared that the United States "shall soon add one more to the catalogue of nations, whom aristocracy has blasted, and whom inequality of wealth, has precipitated from a comparatively prosperous situation to the lowest grade of degradation and misery."[4]

The great objections were not so much to the accumulations of a Girard or an Astor as to the inheritance of wealth, and to the chartered, monopolistic company. The building of an individual fortune was after all only the goal to which all men aspired. The criticism came when this wealth descended to children and grandchildren, for equality of economic opportunity was an ideal dear to American hearts. When Governor Gilmer of Georgia intoned in 1830, "We have no such class as the poor,"[5] he was not denying the obvious existence of poverty, but rather asserting that poor people had no class consciousness—that each poor man aspired some day to become rich.

Even more hostility went to the "chartered monopoly," which somehow seemed cruelly impersonal and despotic. These corporations were, first of all, banks, which in some mysterious way made money difficult for the poor man to obtain, but included also such concerns as canals, railroads, insurance companies, and water companies. "There can be no doubt that all chartered monopolies are infringements on the rights of the citizen, however we may be disposed to accede to their usefulness."[6] Such objections were impotent in the face of the need for larger aggregations of capital than could

[4] *Mechanics' Free Press*, August 9, 1828, quoted in J. R. Commons, and others, *A Documentary History of American Industrial Society* (10 vols., Cleveland, A. H. Clark Company, 1910–11), V, 125.

[5] Quoted in E. M. Coulter, *A Short History of Georgia* (Chapel Hill, University of North Carolina Press, 1933), 254.

be supplied by any one man. Even in the thirties the practice of chartering each corporation by special act of the legislature was giving way to the simpler general incorporation acts, which were to become universal within a generation.

Concentrations of wealth were as yet only isolated rocks projecting from a sea of small enterprise. The tailor dickered with his customer over the price of a coat, the shoemaker over that of a pair of shoes. The horse trader, the slave dealer, the tobacco buyer, and the cattle dealer arrived at prices through individual haggling. The result was the comparatively free working of supply and demand.

Prices in general followed the fluctuations of supply and demand, but that did not mean that all marketing was as simple as selling a dozen eggs to the next-door neighbor. A path was not always beaten to the door of the best maker of mousetraps; frequently the maker had to seek his customers. Marketing might be an extremely complex system.

A retail store ordinarily bought from a jobber, who in turn had bought from a wholesaler or commission merchant, although there were many variations in this line of events. The jobber usually stocked a wide variety of commodities, but now and then specialized, as in shoes, hats, or hardware. The wholesaler specialized more frequently, as in textiles or hardware, but he never limited his sales territory, and sometimes also sold directly to the consumer. He did much of his business on book credit.

Commission merchants were more numerous than wholesalers, and acted as agents rather than owning anything outright. Such a man's prime function was to sell the goods for which he was agent, and he charged ordinarily a fee of 5 per cent on foreign goods and 2.5 per cent on domestic. In addition he might do purchasing, make collections, provide for storage and insurance, handle bills of exchange, and even advance funds to his principal—of course for a commission in each case.

At the other end of the process, the large planter usually patronized a commission merchant. The small farmer, however, swapped

[6] *Mechanics' Free Press*, July 10, 1830, quoted in Commons, *Documentary History*, V, 118.

his surplus at the local store, and the storekeeper then sold to a wholesaler or traded through a commission merchant. The cattleman sold to a local butcher or to a packing house. The factory owner might work through either a wholesaler or a commission merchant.

One method of distribution peculiar to the period was the use of auctions in which the retailer might buy domestic or foreign products, but generally bought imports. Practically all such business was done in New York, which in the peak year of 1836 sold $53,000,000 worth of goods by auction. Irritated middlemen petitioned Congress for restrictions, but their anger cooled as the business declined.

The retail merchant, whether in town or country, ordinarily stocked anything and everything—cloth and stationery, hardware and liquor, musical instruments, tobacco, and medicine. His goods were jammed into one or two rooms, with no apparent arrangement. He made no real effort to sell goods, but allowed the customer to buy them—at his own risk. A few select city stores stocked only a single product, such as coffins, men's clothes, hardware, dry goods, flour and feed, baked goods, fruit, or oysters.

The store was taken to the customer in the rural regions by the peripatetic peddler. The peddler carried his goods on his back, or on a horse, or in a wagon. His stock was usually obtained on credit in Connecticut, and emphasized the cheap and gaudy articles which were considered most attractive to the South and West. It included a plentiful supply of "Yankee notions" produced by the Nutmeg State—tortoise-shell combs, rings, bracelets, pencil cases, penknives, scissors, steel purses, silver thimbles, and gold and silver spectacles in shagreen cases—the "gold" and "silver" were of course transparent fictions. Other items might be rouge papers, essences and oils, soaps, pomatum, sewing materials, playing cards, picture bricks and puzzles for the children, hats, footwear, clocks, firearms, furniture, books, matches, and suspenders. Cases existed where the peddler even stocked washing machines, spinning wheels, cabinet organs, winnowing machines, and wagons.

The peddler was a sanctimonious hustler, with a twinkle in his eye, and a head full of good stories. Day after day he plodded over bad roads or no roads at all, eating and sleeping as opportunity offered. He judged his smartness by the amount of his sales, and took

"Greenwood," near St. Francisville, Louisiana, built in 1830

"Oak Alley," near Valerie, Louisiana, built in 1836

Courtesy of Wayne Andrews

Courtesy of Wayne Andrews

pride in disposing of shoddy jewelry, wooden nutmegs, charcoal for indigo, soapstone for soap, and clocks that would not run. Had he not himself been cheated by the supply house? Often told was the story of the peddler who sold wooden clocks that would not run, and then returned to replace them, at a slight additional cost, with other clocks that likewise would not run. Sharp dealing brought much back-country hostility to the Yankee, and many a Southerner asked naïvely whether there were no gentlemen in New England.

The peddler was guilty of sharp practices, but much of his merchandise was well worth the price, particularly for an isolated family that could get to a store only with great difficulty. Even with poor merchandise, the hard-working wife or daughter could feel the thrill of possessing some long-felt necessity or desirable frivolity—at least for the short time before it went to pieces. The peddler praised the personal appearance and character of his customer outrageously, which in itself was a service of real worth to the harassed wife who had not been complimented since her marriage. Moreover, he gave a tiny glimpse of the outside metropolitan world, and acted as a clearing house for local and national gossip, thus giving the isolated farm family a real feeling of connection with the rest of the nation and the world.

America's natural resources laid the broad base for American economic expansion. Most obvious was the rich American land, but almost equally evident were the vast forests, which had withstood nobly the combined onslaughts of the pioneer farmer and the lumberman. Wood was the almost universal building material, even in the cities, and wood heated homes, furnished mill power, and even ran the locomotive and steamship. A few householders experimented with coal, but most people were skeptical of the black rock, which reputedly had unhealthy fumes and required new grates and a new technique for the fire tender. Only the most venturesome were willing to try the new fuel in place of the tried and true wood.

Although coal was frequently viewed askance, its use was increasing. The greatest soft-coal center was coming to be western Pennsylvania, which was wresting supremacy from Virginia. Pittsburgh smoke was even then proverbial, with cinders falling like hail

and "smog" making the air opaque. Pittsburgh residents were reported to marvel at the whiteness of the snow outside the city.

Hard coal was the monopoly of eastern Pennsylvania, with the
outstanding producer the Lehigh Coal Company, centering its operations at Mauch Chunk. The coal came from open pits, where it
was loosened by gunpowder and shoveled into the cars of a primitive
railroad that coasted to the river bank. There it was loaded on barges
by means of an iron chute which was also a grate, so that the dust fell
into the river. Apparently it was not further cleaned or graded.
Flotillas of barges, two abreast, then transported it to Philadelphia.

In addition to coal, Americans mined only iron, lead, and gold
in significant amounts; metals such as tin, zinc, and copper were
largely imported. American lead came either from Missouri or from
the Illinois-Wisconsin area, and was used mainly for shot, although
it entered pewter and other alloys. Mined and smelted by the crudest
of methods, it was then heated and run through a sieve in the top
of a tower, falling into water. Later it was graded and rubbed, but
the resulting shot was so irregular that it needed thick wrappings to
make it stick in a gun.

The lead bonanza of the thirties was in the regions of Galena,
Illinois, and Mineral Point, Wisconsin, and produced such boom
towns as New Diggings, Hard Scrabble, Coon Branch, and Fair
Play. Opportunity beckoned the footloose, who needed no more
capital than a pick, a shovel, and a strong back. The first arrivals,
with their simple rules concerning claims, were soon joined by a
flood of gamblers, prostitutes, saloonkeepers and thieves, who trans-
muted lead into headaches. Towns blossomed boisterously overnight, prices soared fantastically, and women commanded a scarcity
value.

The other big mining rush was for that perennially seductive
metal, gold. Until 1828, North Carolina produced almost all the
American gold, but in that year began a series of gold strikes which
ultimately covered most of the South, especially Georgia. Thousands of miners rushed madly from one strike to another in the
eternal quest for easy money, which usually went to the merchant,
with the miner failing to make ordinary day wages. All mining was
of the placer variety, with pans and simple rockers. The entire south-

ern output averaged possibly one million dollars a year, but was sufficient to inspire two new mints. Probably the most important feature of the gold discoveries was that they were on Indian land— but that story has already been told.

Lead and gold produced feverish excitement, but iron reigned supreme in dollars and cents. In iron production, Pittsburgh was far in the lead, with Richmond a poor second, and other communities far in the rear. Pittsburgh iron produced machines ranging from cotton looms and platform scales to nail, pin, and horseshoe machines. It made all kinds of hardware, and was twisted into ornately decorative railings, lamps, vases, and garden furniture. Since steel remained expensive, the comparatively brittle cast iron could not be used for large construction, as of buildings.

The great manufacturing center for cutlery, tinware, bone combs, buttons, and other small objects was Connecticut. Here was produced the cheap jewelry that became even cheaper with the introduction of electroplating in the early eighteen forties. Here were outfitted most of the peddlers. Best known of the Connecticut products were clocks, especially those made by Seth Thomas and Chauncy Jerome. It was Jerome who was responsible for the brass clock, which was made by mass production methods to sell for less than ten dollars, and which not only pushed the wooden clock off American mantles, but invaded the rest of the world.

Yankee ingenuity also revolutionized the small-arms industry. Percussion firing cast the old flintlock into the discard during the early thirties, but there remained an insistent demand for a gun which could fire several shots without reloading. Additional barrels were awkwardly bulky, while several shots in the same barrel tended to explode simultaneously, with more damage to the marksman than to the target. The right answer was found by the youthful Samuel Colt, who whittled a model wooden revolver while on a sailing trip to Calcutta.

Colt's first guns were spectacular failures. Of the two which were financed by his father, one would not fire and the other exploded. Colt repaired his fortunes by touring the country giving "educational" talks and exhibitions concerned with the effects of nitrous oxide. With his earnings he had several repeating rifles made, and with these guns he toured Europe trying unsuccessfully to interest men of capital. Returning to the United States in 1836, he obtained American patents, chartered a company, and started production at Paterson on a plan which included interchangeable parts and an assembly line. But now he could not find purchasers. Intensive lobbying brought army and navy tests, but the services held the new guns overly complicated and dangerous. Samuel then hawked his wares in the streets, but could not sell enough to avoid bankruptcy in 1843. Not until after the Mexican War did success finally come to him.

A predominantly agricultural United States contained a surprising number and variety of factories, which made everything from ships to candles and from mattresses to the new sulphur matches. Sawmills, tanneries, and grist mills flourished by the hundred, while distilleries were only slightly less numerous than drunkards. Massachusetts had its carpets, New Jersey its silk, Rhode Island its lace, the Ohio Valley its rope, Philadelphia and New York their pianos, Delaware its Du Pont powder, Trenton its pottery, Boston its ice, and Danbury its straw and felt hats.

The one industry most obviously missing was the manufacture of clothing, for the housewife, the seamstress, and the tailor had as yet no machine competition. Dressmaking was regarded as such a fitting occupation for widows and spinsters that when Walter Hunt of New York invented a sewing machine in 1832, he refused to market it lest seamstresses be deprived of their livings.

Shoemaking was just on the point of becoming completely industrialized for mass production. Traditionally, shoes had been made by individual shoemakers, and the first change was the organization of a company to take orders and make shipments. Thus, while Lynn, Massachusetts, was the greatest center for the making of women's and children's shoes, each shoemaker worked in his own little shed. When the factory received an order, each man was allotted a number of shoes to make. When they were finished, they were all assembled at the factory and packed—ordinarily in barrels without distinguishing between rights and lefts. The Lynn Quakers made over one million pairs of shoes each year under this system, and were comparatively wealthy; between periods of shoemaking, they farmed or fished. However, this system proved transient, because even during the thirties machinery was being introduced that in the long run brought all shoemaking under the factory roof.

Fifteen hundred printing offices catered to the insatiable American demand for self-expression by issuing a torrent of newspapers, magazines, pamphlets, and books. Typesetting was still a hand job, but the steam press was speeding the actual printing, while the rotary steam press was just around the corner. The immense plant of Gales and Seaton boasted of turning out five hundred sheets of Congressional debate per hour; apparently no one questioned the value of the words thus immortalized.

No novelty was more significant for the future than rubber, even though the existing rubber was little more than a scientific toy. Men allowed their imaginations full rein and coated not only such obvious objects as shoes, clothes, traveling bags, and fire hose, but also flasks and cushions and even ships. A tablecloth would be advertised as impervious to water, soft and pliable as velvet, and more beautiful than oilcloth. Actually, such an article was usually treated with rubber dissolved in turpentine and lampblack, and would melt in summer and crack in winter. A few people had reservations about the effects of rubber used on shoes—might it not make the feet puny, for had not the Lord provided rain to get the feet wet?

Charles Goodyear speculated somewhat idly about rubber, until he had a chance in debtor's prison in 1834 to work himself into near mania on the subject. Then followed a long series of unsuccessful experiments and bankrupt factories. Final success came through a lucky accident which involved dropping on his wife's red-hot stove a lump of rubber he had been boiling in sulphur. The resulting vulcanization laid the basis for the rubber industry, although the process was not patented until 1844, and Goodyear himself continued to live on charity.

The colossus of American manufacturing was the textile industry, which emitted a steady stream of cotton sheeting, shirting, and drilling, woolen cassimeres, satinettes, blankets, and broadcloth. Cotton cloth was highly profitable, particularly with the new printing machinery, which permitted six colors by 1845. American cloth was increasingly dominating the American market and being exported as far as South America and the Far East. Textile production was the thermometer showing the manufacturing health of the United States.

Every part of the Union could boast of textile mills, but New England claimed two-thirds of the output and of the hundred thousand workers. The South, spurred by the enthusiastic William Gregg of South Carolina, was trying to bring the factory to the cotton field, but its most flourishing center of Richmond was outclassed by half a dozen New England cities. In fact, Lowell, Massachusetts, was the manufacturing capital of the United States. Nothing more than a tiny agricultural hamlet in 1820, it collected seventeen thousand citizens by the time it attained the status of a city sixteen years later. The textile mills which dominated the city produced a predominantly feminine town, since women did practically all the mill work except supervising, cleaning the cotton, and the heavy manual labor.

Textile mills were largely the creatures of shipping profits, especially those of Boston. As business boomed, new firms entered the field, while old ones plowed their profits back into the business. The million-dollar corporation became common. Most important was a group of Boston capitalists, who soon had control over 20 per cent of American spindles, together with railroads and insurance companies. Their large-scale operations permitted a rough specialization among the various controlled mills, an exchange of patents, and a "stabilization" of prices.

Most Americans were pleased with the expansion of manufacturing and the increasing use of machinery. Labor was scarce, prices were rising, and goods were in great demand. Many private societies used their funds to encourage mechanical inventions. Groups like the Franklin Institute of Philadelphia held annual exhibitions and dangled rich prizes before the eyes of impoverished inventors. The occasional man who wept at the prospect of unemployed seamstresses suffering from machine competition, or who insisted that only hand labor made a people strong and self-reliant, was a rarity. The majority greeted each new factory with enthusiasm.

Expanding industries should have run headlong into the traditional American hostility toward monopoly. Textile manufacturing exhibited definite trends in this direction, while the salt producers of western Virginia not only fixed prices but restricted and allocated production. Curiously enough, however, little opposition was expressed. Most Americans viewed with pleasure the growth of large industries as an indication of American energy and superiority; the diatribes against monopoly were saved for the banks and the various utilities.

Growing factories forecast the decline of the home manufacturing which had been characteristic of previous generations. Factory cloth, with its printed designs, seemed much more exciting than drab homespun. The result was less work for mother and more for father, who had to provide the necessary cash. The farmer was increasingly interested in crops that gave him dollars, and less concerned with self-sufficiency. The resulting specialization increased average incomes but also increased mutual interdependence, so that depressions became more severe.

Expanding American business strained the existing money and credit. The old-fashioned farmer had been content with a little periodic barter, such as wheat for salt, but his grandson wanted store shoes, an iron plow, and a flute, whether or not he had the necessary goods to give for them. And when he wanted chewing tobacco, he found that corn or potatoes or lead was not convenient change. Increasing consumer demands opened the way for stores, mills, mines, canals, and railways, all of which needed capital. The result was that men used various stratagems to cause two dollars to appear where only one existed in fact.

Monetary troubles began with the gold and silver coins which were the basic currency of the country. The United States was theoretically bimetallic, but actually the two metals never circulated at the same time. The fifteen-to-one ratio of the early thirties undervalued gold, which then went into the family sock, the melting pot, and international trade. A new ratio of sixteen to one in 1834 undervalued silver, with the result that a few gold coins reappeared while all silver vanished—not a notable improvement. The consequence was that people used any money available, including foreign coins, particularly Mexican dollars.

The obvious substitute for metal coins was paper money, which was issued in notes as small as twelve and one-half cents. Anyone could issue paper money, and there seemed always plenty of people sufficiently credulous to accept even the poorest issues. In fact, the demand for money was so great that at times people even used money they knew to be fraudulent or forged. The trouble was that there was not sufficient money; the peak of banknote circulation in 1837 was only about ten dollars per capita. Honest and conservative Americans warned foreign travelers never to accept notes on a remote bank or from a stranger. Bulky manuals listed the common forgeries and noted current discounts, while brokers devoted their lives to exchanging money. The unscrupulous employer or trader could increase his profits by speculating in doubtful banknotes.

The general public was divided in opinion about paper money. Businessmen frequently had bank investments and favored note issues, provided the notes remained stable in value. A few speculators greeted poor banknotes with enthusiasm, since they gave profit opportunities for the knowing trader. Workmen were most impressed by the bad notes they sometimes received, and held the theory that bankers in some mysterious way created money for their own advantage and other people's loss—a theory that had some justification. Farmers were divided in their opinions. On the one hand, they were sufficiently conservative to prefer the feel of "hard" money to that of the crispest paper; but on the other hand, they liked the easier loans and rising prices that came from plentiful paper money—all things considered, banknotes were to be preferred.

Paper money was but one small part of the morass of debt in which the United States was mired. The farmer owed the village storekeeper and the local moneylender. The merchant owed the wholesaler or commission merchant, who in turn owed the bank. The exporter or importer was in debt abroad, usually to English merchants. State governments owed money both at home and abroad. The United States as a whole was a debtor country, with much of its capital coming from abroad; even the United States Bank was financed in part from England.

Lending agencies were varied. A farmer or businessman might approach a relative or friend, and unhappy was the man who had too great confidence in his friends' integrity and business ability.

Some men specialized in loans, as the western broker who acted for eastern investors. Funds were supplied by insurance companies— fire and marine, but not life. A large industry might sell its bonds and stock publicly, but some of the most profitable, like the New England textile mills, might confine their offerings to friends and to friends of friends. The New York Stock Exchange flourished, with frequent half-million-dollar days. Speculative favorites were such transportation companies as the Delaware and Hudson and the Harlem Railroad, and trading ethics did not outlaw the fleecing of unwary sheep.

The most important sources of funds were the banks, which ranged from the two New York financial giants which each could claim a capital of over $5,000,000 to the feeblest of rural saddlebag banks. In most of the United States a bank claiming resources of $100,000 was considered large, and even this figure was very possibly a figment of the imagination. The claimed assets were probably little more than promises of stockholders to contribute at some unspecified future date.

The average bank was above all a paper-money machine, issuing its notes as fast as the community would absorb them, and praying that people would not ask for their redemption. A demand for the redemption of one-half, or even one-quarter, of its notes would have forced the average bank to close its doors. Banks also took deposits, paying as high as 6 per cent interest; a few were mutual savings banks.

American banking was decentralized and relatively uncontrolled. A banker felt no more public responsibility than a farmer or storekeeper. Let the user beware. Most banks were unincorporated, and the only moderately effective inspection was in Connecticut. The one real banking combination was the Suffolk System of Massachusetts, in which country banks kept deposits in the Suffolk Bank of Boston to maintain all notes of member banks near par.

The top of the American banking system was theoretically the Second Bank of the United States, but while it acted as fiscal agent of the federal government, it exercised practically none of the other usual functions of a central bank. Its one attempt at regulation consisted of sporadic efforts to scare the country banks into keeping proper reserves for their banknotes by now and then presenting large numbers of such notes for redemption. Actions of this kind were hailed with approval by the more conservative businessmen, but were greeted with loud yells of distress by the banks and their clients, while all debtors deplored the deflationary results. And even this slight control disappeared as a result of the fight with Jackson and the virtual death of the bank.

Banking was the one business which could literally make its own money, and then loan it at 15 per cent, 20 per cent, or more, with customers clamoring for the privilege of borrowing. No wonder that each prospective bank was deluged with hopeful stockholders who wanted to turn the flow of wealth in their direction. Banks doubled in number and still the demand came for more sources of credit. Eight states listened to the pleas of their citizens and went into the banking business; the resulting institutions seem to have averaged neither better nor worse than the private companies.

More banks, more loans, and more paper money brought the inevitable forward surge of prices which was interrupted only temporarily by a recession engineered by Nicholas Biddle to demonstrate what would happen if the United States Bank disappeared. Public and private debts mushroomed mightily, except for the federal government, which actually showed a surplus. More people had more money than ever before. The capitalist built a new factory and purchased more machinery; the farmer built a new home and bought machinery and blooded stock; the speculator acquired stocks, bonds, land, and townsites; the railroad promoter started thousands of miles of new construction. Prosperity seemed permanent, and there was common agreement that this idyllic condition was the inevitable product of democratic institutions as applied by a young, industrious, and intelligent nation. Only a few conservative Jeremiahs shook their heads forebodingly as both prices and debts skyrocketed.

The balloon of overinflated credit collapsed with a tremendous bang that rocked society to its core. The trouble started in Europe, especially in England, which was the source of much American investment. When English bankers became conservative and contracted American loans, the whole shaky financial edifice began to topple. President Jackson's specie circular hastened the climax by creating more western demands for nonexistent specie, but that was not the basic difficulty.

The pessimists proved to be correct. In March, 1837, Philip Hone noted in his diary: "A number of failures have taken place to-day, only the forerunners of greater disaster. The names are not worth recording, for such events will soon cease to be worthy of remark."[7] Prices fell, orders dropped off, building slumped, and businesses failed. Everyone wanted specie. Banknotes were accepted only grudgingly and at a heavy discount. On May 9 a run on the New York banks produced riots in which women were trampled underfoot. The next day all New York banks suspended specie payment, and another day saw the Philadelphia and Baltimore banks take like action.

The crash of the spring of 1837 was followed by a false dawn of recovery. Prices rose slightly, and the New York and Philadelphia banks resumed specie payments. But then came an even more resounding crash in 1839, with prices plummeting. All banks but those of New England and New York again suspended specie payments, while about one-fourth of them closed their doors permanently. Even the United States Bank (now a Pennsylvania concern) went bankrupt in 1841, but Jackson's pleasure must have been marred by the nearing induction of a Whig president.

A few philosophic Americans found desirable the closing of unsound banks, but the majority opinion was the other way. Much American money became worthless as banks refused to accept even their own notes; a well-supplied traveler might find himself penniless. Loans were contracted and businesses throughout the nation went bankrupt, with the owner losing his factory, his farm, or his store. Business activity slowed, values collapsed, and everyone felt poverty stricken. Farmers stopped buying stock and machinery, manufacturers left their new factories uncompleted, and railroads ended in the middle of fields. Only the old-fashioned, self-sufficient farmer could laugh at the antics of a money economy as he went to the local store to trade his surplus for the few articles that he wanted.

One outstanding result of the depression was the evaporation

[7] Nevins, *Hone Diary*, I, 250.

of huge loads of debt through bankruptcy—always by state law, since there was no federal enactment. As a contemporary stated: "Some debts paid by the Bankrupt law, many by going to Texas. By both combined the greater part of the heavy debts have been settled."[8] State governments also slid from under the debts they had created for roads, canals, railroads, and banks. After a few feeble and conscientious flutterings, many exercised their sovereignty by stopping service on some $100,000,000 worth of debts. Some of these debts were repudiated outright—an action that later was to be recalled by foreign debtors when the shoe was on the other foot.

The federal government began to show a deficit as tariff and land receipts dropped. The policy of distributing federal funds as "loans" to the states was stopped, even though the "loans" were not recalled. When banks holding government funds began to close, the government realized that something had to be done, but President Van Buren also recognized that as the political successor of Andrew Jackson, he could hardly re-establish a national bank. After considerable turmoil, he finally obtained an Independent Treasury plan, which became law shortly before he left office.

In accordance with immemorial custom, the American electorate blamed the existing administration for its trouble and was not at all impressed by Democratic pleas that the depression was not their baby, but of foreign parentage. Thus the people's favor went to the Whigs, who insisted that the whole trouble was caused by Democratic incompetence. "The popular belief . . . among us and which is encouraged by the party now [1840] about to come into power, is, that the fall of prices was not necessary, and the leaders have pledged themselves to manage the banks & the currency, as far as they have influence and control, in a way to restore former prices."[9]

The incoming Whigs found themselves on no bed of roses. They got rid of the Independent Treasury as an evidence of "Van Burenism," but then unanimity came to an end. Twice Congress passed a national-bank bill and twice Tyler vetoed it. Tyler proposed a modi-

---

[8] Quoted in J. S. Bassett, *The Southern Plantation Overseer as Revealed in His Letters* (Northampton, Smith College, 1925), 168.

[9] K. W. Porter, *The Jacksons and the Lees* (2 vols., Cambridge, Harvard University Press, 1937), II, 1417–18.

fied Independent Treasury scheme, but Congress was adamant. Meantime federal money was kept in state banks until the revival of the Independent Treasury in 1846.

The eighteen thirties illustrated all the worst aspects of a free economic system. Optimism, speculation and overborrowing inspired a rapid rise in prices which ended in a panic, with the slackening of business activities, a fall in prices, and large-scale unemployment. The results were not as cataclysmic as a century later only because of the large number of farmers who were relatively unaffected. Even if a farmer went bankrupt, he might still hope some day to go west and start again. His reaction was not an immediate and overwhelming demand that government change the rules of the economic game.

In a larger sense, the depression was only a brief interruption in the magnificent expansion in which Americans were engaged. For the moment business was bad, but Americans were thoroughly imbued with the notion of the rich destiny of the nation. They did not turn to the government to provide them security against all of the hazards of life, but continued to feel confidence in their own ability to win individual successes. American expansion was stopped temporarily, but no one doubted that before long it would again pick up speed on the road to a bright and rosy future.

9. The Wage Earner

AMERICA was a golden land of opportunity for the wage earner. Expanding industries and public improvements produced the high wages that permitted the workmen to sport "sleek coats, glossy hats, gay watch-guards, and doe-skin gloves!"[1] Not that everyone was uniformly well-to-do, for some industries were badly paid and some hand trades such as weaving were dying; but it was only during a depression period that a man might moan that "it is altogether more difficult for the common laborer to maintain the same social position now than it was fifty years ago."[2] The more usual comment was amazement at how much better the American workman lived than his European contemporary.

Not only was labor well paid, "but it is held in honour."[3] In fact, the claim was made that "there is no more honorable character ... than that of the independent American Mechanic."[4] Such a statement involved a trifle of wishful thinking, when account is taken of merchants and professional men, but the fact remained that the American workingmen could maintain their confidence, their self-respect, and their optimism.

From the modern standpoint, labor conditions were bad. A few employers were tenderly paternal to their employees, providing houses, parks, libraries, and medical care, and settling quarrels, guarding morals, and selling provisions. The employer's usual point of view, however, was that labor was a commodity to be bought

[1] Martineau, *Society*, II, 63.
[2] *Boston Quarterly Review*, July, 1840, 380, quoted in N. Ware, *The Industrial Worker 1840-1860* (New York, Houghton Mifflin Company, 1924), 20.
[3] Quoted in Hart, *History by Contemporaries*, III, 524.
[4] *Albany Working Man's Advocate*, quoted in *Arkansas Advocate*, August 8, 1831.

as cheaply as possible, used hard, and then discarded when its efficiency declined—after which, as a property owner, he objected to taking care of the poor at public expense. Black lists eliminated the troublesome workers. An injury or sickness was the hard luck of the workman unless a miracle occurred and he received damages under the common law.

Other bad conditions—from the modern standpoint—were prevalent. The working day was accepted as from sun to sun, but was often longer; throughout the year it averaged a good twelve hours. Most factories and shops were firetraps, with improper lighting and the most primitive sanitation. No safety devices were provided against dangerous machinery, or for such hazards as flying lint or filings. Fraudulent employment agencies were common.

But the contrast with modern conditions is not pertinent. Independent farmers and businessmen of the eighteen thirties worked just as long and just as hard, and often under identical conditions. Workingmen in other parts of the world labored in the same way, and for smaller wages. The American worker could well feel complacent that he was in a relatively fine position.

The aristocrat of labor was the skilled craftsman—carpenter, cooper, cordwainer, tailor, printer, jeweler, apothecary, blacksmith, plasterer, bricklayer, and cabinetmaker. Such an artisan could command two to three dollars a day, excellent pay in view of a minimum of a dollar and a half a week for room and board. The novice entered such an occupation through an apprenticeship, which varied in length with the occupation. When an apprentice ran away, there was usually only a nominal effort to apprehend him—"One Cent Reward & No Charges Paid."[5] Sometimes apprentices were used by employers as cheap unskilled labor, whereupon the journeymen might try to stop the practice.

White-collar workers, such as salesmen and clerks, might receive as little as six hundred dollars a year, which was less than the income of a fully employed artisan. The lowness of the wage reflected the overstocking of the market by ambitious (or lazy) boys who preferred writing letters and keeping books to wielding pick

[5] New York *Morning Chronicle*, September 30, 1831.

and shovel. With the depression, many clerks were paid appreciably less than porters in the same business.

The great mass of pick-and-shovel labor received commonly seventy-five cents a day, plus possibly a few jiggers of whiskey. Crowded in dirty hovels, with a bad diet which included much inferior whiskey, they were riddled with sickness and plagued with immorality. A special type of labor was the seaman, whose ten dollars a month and keep corresponded to payments on land, and was sufficient to attract English sailors, even though American ships carried somewhat fewer men per ton of freight. Unskilled factory labor was paid at the same rate as other unskilled labor but of course smiths, dyers, pattern engravers, bronze molders, and other skilled workers received much more.

The bottom of the masculine social working scale was the domestic servant, even though he was in great demand. Most Americans considered domestic service demeaning and not a job for a vigorous male. This attitude, together with the shortage of such workers, brought an independence of manner which at times approached outright truculence. Many stories were told of American servants. One tale was of a new servant who, when told by his mistress to wait a few minutes before serving lemonade, answered "all right" and sat down between two guests. The president of Harvard University reputedly had a servant who was also a major of cavalry in the militia. On muster day the servant donned his uniform and sat at the head of the table, with the president on his right, after which he took off his uniform and served tea to the president's guests.

When male labor was insufficient, employers turned to women and children in spite of current prejudices, particularly the prejudice against women's working outside the home. Theoretically a girl helped her mother until her marriage, and then kept house and reared children of her own. Certainly a wife with small children had no time for outside employment, but by no means every woman belonged in this classification. A widow or a spinster—either waiting for marriage or having given up hope—had no desire to starve even if she had no man to support her.

A manless woman traditionally lived with her relatives, took in

Merchants Exchange, Philadelphia;
William Strickland, architect, 1834–36

"Bargaining for a Horse," from a painting by
William S. Mount

sewing, opened a boardinghouse, did general housework, or became a prostitute. Which option was the least inspiring is an open question. Living with relatives was seldom good for self-respect, and often there were no relatives with a spare bedroom and charity in their souls. Keeping a boardinghouse was not an easy or always pleasant occupation. Household work was paid fairly well, but was unattractive because of the long hours, hard labor, personal servility, and lack of social prestige; housewives generally proved undesirable employers. A seamstress or milliner might work a fourteen or fifteen hour day, with her housework in addition, and still earn little over two dollars a week. Industrial homework, such as crocheting lace or binding shoes, sometimes earned less than ten cents a day, and was not stimulating employment, even though the women thereby "preserve themselves against those temptations which beset worthy females unblessed with wealth."[6] Maybe the prostitute had made the wise choice, for her work was no harder and her pay more. Abortions were no more painful than the headaches, vertigo, menstrual irregularity, and hysteria that afflicted her more moral sisters.

The occupations open to women during the eighteen thirties included certain business and industrial occupations, although the list was limited. Professional and managerial jobs were out of the question, as beyond the weaker feminine intellect. Clerkships in either stores or business offices were thought to contaminate the more delicate feminine sensibilities, while nursing would violate a woman's modesty and innocence. Even teaching was difficult, with the presence of big boys in every class. Thus the industries open for women were primarily the making of textiles, boots and shoes, hats, carpets, cigar and other tobacco products, printing, and making smaller metal objects. Men argued, sometimes apparently against the facts, that such industries had formerly been in the home and hence were best fitted for female labor. They did not mention that they were also only slightly skilled and were poorly paid.

The greatest opportunity for the working girl was in the expanding textile industry, which employed some 40,000 women— possibly one-third of all working women. Lowell, Chicopee, Waltham, and other textile towns were crowded with young ladies drawn

[6] *Niles Register*, Vol. XXXII (June 23, 1827), 276.

from the farms and small towns. These women worked partly from economic necessity, but also to escape farm isolation, to buy more clothes, to send a brother to college, to meet the family mortgage, or to collect a dowry. Almost all were under thirty, and many under twenty, a fact which explains why they looked "healthy, cheerful and moral."[7] Every girl expected to get married eventually and stop work, and the labor turnover of one-third to one-half each year indicated that most of them realized their hopes.

Working conditions in the mills were quite satisfactory and pay was high. True, the hours were from 5:00 A.M. to 7:00 P.M. in the summer, with two half-hours for meals, and working hours averaged over seventy a week through the year, but that was no more than working at home and the work was not as hard. True, the mills were gloomy, with whale-oil lamps used only when absolutely necessary. True, also, they lacked sanitation, and had only ladders for fire escapes. And yet, by comparison with farm homes, they could hardly be called objectionable. The discipline was lenient, with visiting back and forth, and now and then rest periods which could be used for shopping. The pay was often above $3.00 a week, which was excellent with board and room at $1.25.

Conditions might be distressing if the girl antagonized the overseer, who had despotic powers. He might fine or discharge the girl if she whispered, or attended dances, or because he did not like the color of her hair. Once discharged, she might as well go home to her father, because the mills collaborated in a black list. Even in this extremity, however, she was probably at least no worse off than if she had never worked.

All unmarried persons lived in company boardinghouses—of course, with the sexes segregated. A small room might hold as many as six girls in three double beds, and was kept clean by the girls. The food, simple but adequate, was served at long tables. While there was the usual amount of minor sickness and of gossiping and bickering, the accommodations were at least as good as those of the average home, and the privacy was not much less.

The mill controlled the private life of each female employee, but not primarily to get more work out of her; the father and

[7] *Ibid.*, Vol. XXXIV (July 5, 1828), 297.

mother would not have permitted their daughter to go to the wicked city otherwise. As for the girl, she was accustomed to supervision and did not protest. Dishonesty, sullenness, idleness, intemperance, theft, gambling, late hours, dancing, or card playing might bring dismissal. The town fathers co-operated, as by excluding a visiting menagerie; combining piety and self-interest, they stopped the girls from spending money outside the local stores. Generally, regulations of this kind met popular approval, even though a few evil-minded snoopers suggested that six girls to a room was demoralizing and that many of the girls, in spite of their modest airs, were no more moral than necessary.

Textile girls were neat, clean, pretty, well dressed, and attractive—no doubt more because of their youth than because of the effects of factory life. Men noted the scarves and shawls, the ringlets, the calico bonnets, and the parasols, as well as the pretty faces. Women stressed more the savings accounts, the workers' homes built from savings, the libraries, evening schools, churches, "improvement groups," and lectures, not to mention the *Lowell Offering*, an employee literary magazine subsidized by management. One can but marvel at the physical stamina of a young lady of 1835 who could work a thirteen-hour day and then dress in her best and trip away to a dull two-hour lecture to improve her mind and bolster her morals.

Many Americans objected to women's working outside the home. The National Trades Convention of 1836 neatly summarized the opposing arguments—one, that such work forced a woman to associate with all kinds of men and learn their rude habits, "thus losing all that sacred influence which is the peculiar prerogative of woman to exercise over man"; two, that her low wages created "a destructive competition with the male."[8] This twofold argument well merits the description of "enlightened self-interest."

Since removing women from all industry was impractical, less sweeping proposals were made. Possibly women should be limited to industries where their moral sensibilities would not be injured, and where incidentally their competition would not be so disastrous, but search failed to locate the proper industries. Possibly women

[8] Commons, *Documentary History*, VI, 251.

should be paid as much as men, which of course would drive women out of industry; this radical proposal was at once labeled as chimerical by the believers in the inevitability of the "law" of supply and demand. A move in the same direction was made by some women who formed unions and even conducted strikes, but their success was negligible as long as the membership of the union was unskilled and could be replaced with ease.

Women's greatest labor competition was children, "who might otherwise, be doing worse than nothing."[9] Child labor was not unusual; the most valuable crop on many a farm was children, and school terms were arranged so as not to interfere with their work. Factories naturally turned to this source, and when the local supply was exhausted, recruited from farther afield. At times whole families were brought to the mill town, and then fired en masse if the father decided one or more of the children should not work.

Child labor was cheap but inefficient. An infant of six was not necessarily a bargain, even if he worked twelve hours a day for fifty cents a week. Many spoiled both their work and their lives. Some, like the nineteen-year-old superintendent of the Pawtucket Thread Company, who had a background of eleven years of work, were successful in industry. More frequently, the best that could be said of the one-third of the cotton-mill employees who were under twelve was that children were better than no labor at all.

Most people were indifferent to child labor. A committee of the Massachusetts legislature in the eighteen twenties dismissed it as inconsequential since only a few children under fourteen were working, and even these worked only a twelve-hour day. But adverse sentiment was growing, with here and there strong opposition raised. "I would lay the most severe restrictions against parents selling their children as slaves to our large manufacturing establishments."[10] In part, such opposition represented fear of labor competition, but more frequently it was part of a drive for the education necessary in a democracy. The Massachusetts law of 1836 prohibited

[9] *Niles Register*, Vol. XXIX (November 19, 1825), 192.

[10] *Boston Courier*, November 4, 1830, quoted in J. R. Commons and Associates, *History of Labour in the United States* (2 vols., New York, Macmillan, 1918), I, 321.

the work of any child under fifteen unless he had attended school for three months of the preceding year. Other states passed similar laws, but before 1840 there was no proper machinery for enforcement.

The rise of the factory was the largest of the detonations that were shaking the ground under the feet of skilled labor. Traditionally, a large job had been turned over to a master workman, who in turn hired journeymen and apprentices. Now the entrepreneur increasingly managed his own production, hiring a master workman only as a sort of straw boss. By employing machinery and subdividing labor he would often eliminate skilled artisans in favor of cheaper, unskilled labor, sometimes women and children.

The new organization of industry undermined the position of many skilled trades. In the past, artisans had joined together in workingmen's associations to encourage technical skill, to comfort the sick, to cherish the widow and orphan, and to drink toasts to "Honesty and industry; the only sure foundation for the prosperity of working-men."[11] Now such associations became obsolete, with a faint odor of moth balls and lavender. Skilled labor was on the defensive and needed a more potent weapon than mutual back-patting.

The new weapon of the artisan was the labor union which was directed more forcefully and directly toward economic ends. With the new unions, skilled craftsmen such as carpenters, cordwainers, and coopers, sought to shore up their slipping power and prestige; organizations of factory workers were fewer and weaker. The usual union was a grouping of the workers of a single skill in one community. Combinations of unions came first in the "city central," an alliance of all unions in one locality. By 1834 there was a General Trades Union, presumably uniting all American labor in effective action, but actually dawdling ineffectively with vaguely general resolutions. The national organization of a single trade came relatively late, with only five such groups in existence by 1836.

The prosperous years of the early thirties were a propitious time for labor to organize and insist on its "rights." But even with business humming and labor in demand, most employers were not

[11] *Niles Register*, Vol. XXXIX (October 23, 1830), 139.

moved to generosity either by resounding resolutions demanding "justice" or by vague threats of future drastic action. Labor found that rapid improvement came only after a "turn-out," and the number of strikes reached flood stage about the middle of the decade. Work stoppages decreased notably with the depression, for with falling pay and increasing unemployment, the worker was more anxious to keep his job than to assert his "rights." In fact, most of the labor unions themselves collapsed.

Strikes were the prerogative of no single group, but were called by carpenters of Boston, printers of Washington, stevedores of New York, or mill girls of Lowell. Most obstreperous were the building trades, where indispensable skills gave a better than average chance for victory. The majority of strikes were aimed at higher wages, and the strikers presented pitiful pictures of starvation pay while the employers implied that every worker was rolling in luxury; which set of "facts" was correct is anyone's guess.

The second most usual objective of strikes was shorter hours, which for the building trades really meant higher pay in the form of overtime during the busy season. The talking point was the ten-hour day, toward which definite advance was made in a series of important strikes. Labor argued that working from dawn to dark was a "grievous and slave like system of labour,"[12] and that a shorter day would not only make the wage earner a better father and citizen, but would actually increase his output by improving his efficiency.

Employers replied that they viewed "with regret the formation of any society that has a tendency to subvert good order, and coerce or molest those who have been industriously pursuing their avocation and honestly maintaining their families."[13] They disavowed any sordid personal interests, but deplored the effects of a ten-hour day on apprentices—"by seducing them from that course of indus-

[12] *Democratic Press*, June 14, 1827, quoted in Commons, *Documentary History*, V, 80.

[13] *Poulson's Daily Advertiser*, June 18, 1827, quoted in A. E. Martin and H. H. Shenk, *Pennsylvania History Told by Contemporaries* (New York, Macmillan Company, 1925), 473–74.

[14] *Columbian Centinel*, April 20, 1825, quoted in Commons, *Documentary History*, VI, 76.

try and economy of time, to which we are anxious to enure them."[14] The results of such idleness on journeymen prone to sport and dissipation were almost too horrible to contemplate. Clearly the ten-hour day was an "evil of foreign growth"[15] and should not be allowed to take root in the favored soil of the New World.

A scattering of strikes were aimed at objects other than wages and hours. The closed shop was not an unknown objective, while one strike involved a jurisdictional dispute between slaters and tin-plate workers. Some were concerned with apprenticeship rules or with the employment of women or of Negroes. An occasional sympathetic strike, general strike, or boycott, even though seldom successful, has interest for the modern student.

Strikes ranged from mild demonstrations to bloody battles. Possibly the girls of Lowell or Chicopee would desert their work, parade with flying banners, listen to a few speeches, and then go back to work; the only result would be the firing of the ringleaders. Generally any strike involving women was quiet and peaceful, for ladies were ladies in 1835. At the other end of the scale were demonstrations in which ships were damaged, looms broken, houses burned, furniture smashed, and heads cracked. Many such a strike might well have been called a riot, for with no organization, poor leadership, defective backing, and vague objectives, the men merely gave way to the urge to smash something.

The great majority of strikes either fizzled ignominiously or were smashed by employers who were superior in wealth and organizing ability. The usual strike was called after a vote of the union membership, and financed as long as possible by union funds. The employer always insisted that the demands were unreasonable and that meeting them would bring bankruptcy, after which he hired strikebreakers, whom the strikers picketed. Police and private guards might have the virtue of inspiring violence which would justify state troops; arrests were frequent, but the charges might be dropped if the men went back to work. Eventually the strike was broken and the strikers returned to work—except the leaders, who were black-listed by an employers' association.

American courts gave no help to labor during the eighteen

[15] *Ibid.,* 77.

thirties. Judges were well aware that the common law prohibited combination and conspiracy in restraint of trade, and most of them seemed to feel that the law of supply and demand was also in legal force. They had doubts whether any strike could be legal, or, indeed, any labor union. They regularly prescribed penalties for workers who combined to coerce others, whether employers or fellow workmen. When strikers were freed, it was more frequently by the mercy of the jury than by the tolerance of the judge. Of course, the courts insisted that "the law will as soon punish any unlawful combination of the employers, as of their journeymen,"[16] but illegal acts of employers seemed difficult to find. In one case which involved the combination of employers to produce lower wages, the judge felt that they were only restoring the "natural level" of pay.

Most publicized of court cases concerning labor was the trial of New York journeymen tailors who struck against wage decreases in 1836. Twenty men were hauled into court and fined the rather intimidating total of $1,150, whereupon a "coffin handbill" appeared in the city: "A deadly blow has been struck at your *Liberty*! The prize for which your fathers fought has been robbed from you! The freemen of the North are now on a level with the slaves of the South! With no other privilege than laboring, that drones may fatten on your life-blood!"[17]

Not so well advertised, but much more important, was the case of certain Boston shoemakers (Commonwealth *v.* Hunt). When the decision was appealed to the Supreme Judicial Court, Judge Shaw in 1842 clearly upheld the right of workers to form unions and to strike for higher wages provided they committed no illegal acts. Judge Shaw's decision was in time accepted generally, but his implication that a closed shop was legal was not always upheld in later decisions.

Labor also promoted at times "co-operatives" or "labour" stores. Most of these stores were established to hurt the business of an employer during a strike, but the "labour stores" of Cincinnati and Philadelphia in 1828 had more basic aims. The former was run by Josiah Warren, who has been called the first American Communist.

[16] Commons, *Documentary History*, IV, 268.
[17] Quoted in Nevins, *Hone Diary*, I, 211–12.

The Keel-boat

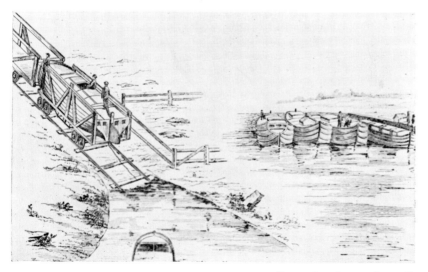

Portaging barges by rail

In stores of this kind all articles were priced according to the labor involved, and the purchase was made with a "labour note" which could be used only to buy other goods. In practice, money was also used, and the experiment did not long endure.

Workmen anxious to improve their status were often impatient at the slowness of economic action, and hence looked with favor on the political maneuvering that was so dear to the normal American heart. The first Working Men's party was born at Philadelphia in 1828, and evanescently held the city balance of power. Its strategic position soon disappeared as professional politicians discounted its strength and stole its issues; and it shortly succumbed to the prevailing infant mortality. Its main panaceas were free public education, no banks or other monopolies, no lotteries, no forced militia service, and no imprisonment for debt.

Most interesting of the numerous labor parties was the New York Workingmen's party. Its early boss was Thomas Skidmore, a versatile reformer whose main ideas were dubbed "agrarianism." A Skidmore pamphlet of 1829 was very informative even if one read only the title: *The Rights of Man to Property! Being a Proposition to Make it Equal among the Adults of the Present Generation; and to Provide for Its Equal Transmission to Every Individual of Each Succeeding Generation, on Arriving at the Age of Maturity.*[18] Such a utopian plan did not represent the average worker, and Skidmore was soon ejected from the party.

Control of the New York labor party passed from Skidmore to a remarkable English-born group of "free enquirers," notably Evans, Owen, and Wright. George Henry Evans was intrigued by the Skidmore ideas, but was willing to settle for a homestead law; he edited the *Workingmen's Advocate*, official organ of the movement. Robert Dale Owen was the cosmopolitan and versatile son of Robert Owen. His favorite plan was to remove all children from their homes at the age of two, and to put them in government boardinghouses which would provide equality in dress, food, education, and opportunity, thus producing real democracy.

Best but not most favorably known of "free enquirers" was

[18] New York, 1829.

Frances (Fanny) Wright. Fanny was tall, slender and graceful; her features were classically regular, her curly chestnut hair was closely bobbed, and her eyes were an earnest and intent blue. Fanny's mind was strong and logical, but unblessed with humor, and she hated to admit error in even the most extreme positions to which her logic carried her. She battled for political and social equality for everyone, regardless of sex or race. She cast doubts on the literal inspiration of the Bible. Worst of all, she wanted more sex freedom outside of wedlock and a relaxation of the marriage tie.

Frances Wright inspired more invective than anyone else but Andrew Jackson. Whether writing, lecturing, or laboring for her ideal Negro community, she was the recipient of harsh and malicious diatribes. She was depicted as "the Red Harlot of Infidelity . . . madly and triumphantly stalking over the city,"[19] convincing Americans "that *religion* is a cheat, *chastity* a dream, and all who adhere to the pure precept of the gospel of our Saviour, fools!"[20] The press jeered: "To hear blasphemy in religion and jacobinism in politics uttered by a great awkward *bungle* of womanhood, somewhere about six feet in longitude, with a face like a Fury, and her hair cropped like a convict, is a little too bad."[21] Fanny was actually a very attractive woman, with an unusually strong belief in the immediate perfectibility of human nature, but her ideas, like those of her friends, were clearly out of line with current American thought, and the result was a black eye for the American workingman in politics, even though the "free enquirers" were soon eliminated from control.

The whole political labor movement was foredoomed to failure as long as industrial labor was such a small part of the American scene. In fact, the few temporary successes of labor parties were actually harmful, since they encouraged labor to devote part of its feeble strength to the impossible, rather than to the building and strengthening of unions.

The intellectuals served as a catalyst to crystallize the ideas of the rank and file of workers. Basic was the conviction that labor was

[19] *Morning Courier*, June 10, 1830.
[20] Saxe-Weimar, *Travels*, I, 42, footnote by translator.
[21] *Morning Courier*, October 19, 1836.

the source of all wealth: "Do not all the streams of wealth which flow in every direction and are emptied into and absorbed by the coffers of the unproductive, exclusively take their rise in the bones, marrow, and muscles of the industrious classes?"[22] Since property was thus the result of group labor, its possession by individuals should be permitted only if it were used properly for the employment of labor.

At one distant day—if labor philosophers were to be believed—there was real freedom and equality. But conditions had deteriorated until now "There appears to exist two distinct classes, the rich and the poor; the oppressor and the oppressed; those who live by their own labour, and they that live by the labour of others."[23] Worst of all, the rich were becoming richer as chartered monopolies clutched the throat of American production. Banks were particularly vicious because they created wealth without labor and thus levied tribute on the industrious.

Machinery and the factory system attracted frequent criticisms, for machinery displaced skilled workers with spineless wage slaves. "To look at the pale and dirty, and spiritless beings, as they pour out of the factory to their hurried meals at the sound of a bell; and, although inhumanly stinted as to time, to see the lazy motion of their jaded limbs, and the motionless expression of their woe-begone countenances, must give a pang to the feeling heart which can never be forgotten."[24] And then, saddest of all, the increased production brought no greater return to labor, even "at the present period, when wealth is so easily and abundantly created that the markets of the world are overflowing with it."[25]

Increasing production was held to help only the rich, who lived in ever more luxurious idleness, while workers were paid the least that would keep body and soul together for future exploitation. The

[22] *Mechanics' Free Press*, October 25, 1828, quoted in Commons, *Documentary History*, V, 85.

[23] *Mechanics' Free Press*, June 5, 1830, quoted in Commons, *History of Labour*, I, 193.

[24] Address of National Trades' Union, 1834, quoted in Commons, *History of Labour*, I, 320.

[25] *Mechanics' Free Press*, October 25, 1828, quoted in Commons, *Documentary History*, V, 86.

worker could not get justice in the courts, which were controlled by the well-to-do. His time was taken by the militia system, while the rich man could hire a substitute. He could be thrown into jail for debt, but he could not collect his wages from a bankrupt company. His meager earnings brought an uncomfortable home and poor food, and he could not afford education for his children, which meant that inequality would be hereditary.

Proposals to remedy this impressive list of presumed injustices were remarkably mild. Such radical ideas as Skidmore's agrarianism were rejected by laborers who hoped some day to have property of their own. Most favored were preference of wages in bankruptcy, no imprisonment for debt, a changed militia system, the end of lotteries, improved courts, simpler laws, and smaller bonds for public officers. Great approval greeted free public education which would open at least partially the door of opportunity to less favored boys and girls. Labor insisted that a properly working democracy needed an educated electorate, which could be produced only with government aid.

Labor was enthusiastic about giving the public domain outright to settlers, or at least leasing it in perpetuity without cost. More Westerners meant less competition for eastern jobs and a greater market for eastern products. Possibly unemployed eastern labor might take up western land, but up to this time the costs had been prohibitive. The merchant Henry Lee wrote in 1844 that "the low prices of land and the disposition of the manual laboring classes to emigrate to the new states, the moment employment slackens, is a check to the fall of wages nowhere else existing."[26] This theory was later accepted by many people, but it ran counter to all labor statements and all evidence, including the rapid fall of wages then occurring.

Labor, like every other group, was sure that its own best interests were the best interests of everyone. "If the mass of the people were enabled by their labour to procure for themselves and families a full and abundant supply of the comforts and conveniences of life, the consumption of articles, particularly of dwellings, furniture and clothing, would amount to at least twice the quantity it does at pres-

[26] Porter, *Jacksons and Lees*, II, 1416.

ent, and of course the demand, by which alone employers are enabled either to subsist or accumulate, would likewise be increased in an equal proportion."[27] The more labor received, the more prosperous everyone would be.

Labor was also like other groups in feeling enthusiasm for the ideal of free competition except as applied to itself. All chartered monopolies should be reduced to competing units. A low tariff was fine since it would produce more price competition and hence lower prices to laboring men as consumers. On the other hand, labor itself should be united in strong unions for the "contest between Money and Labour."[28] Such competitive groups as women, children, and convicted criminals should be restricted or eliminated. Curiously enough, however, immigration received little opposition—possibly because it did not threaten the jobs of the skilled workers who were making the arguments.

Most Americans were farmers who found the labor movement, with its "unnatural and ruinous"[29] conflict between capital and labor, somewhat mystifying. Did not all economic endeavor follow "natural law" and would not the best men win out? Farmers were certainly remote from the idea of economic combination, and saw it only as a detriment, whether promoted by employer or employee. The common reaction of most Americans to unions was the often repeated charge that labor agitators "are chiefly foreigners."[30] And that "combinations among journeymen are usually set on foot by the dissolute, improvident, and therefore restless; and in the outset chiefly sustained by the second and third rate class of hands."[31]

Deeper public thought often brought the conclusion that unions damaged a free society by interfering with individual bargaining

[27] *Mechanics' Free Press*, October 25, 1828, quoted in Commons, *Documentary History*, V, 87.

[28] *The Man*, May 13, 1835, quoted in Commons, *Documentary History*, VI, 94-95.

[29] New York *Review*, Vol. II (January, 1838), 17, quoted in F. L. Mott, *A History of American Magazines 1741–1850* (New York, D. Appleton and Company, 1930), 471.

[30] *Niles Register*, Vol. XXXVI (April 11, 1829), 101.

[31] New York *Journal of Commerce*, June 1, 1833, quoted in Commons, *Documentary History*, V, 210.

for wages. Many changes were rung on this melody. "All combinations to compel others to give a higher price or take a lower one, are not only inexpedient, but at war with the order of things which the Creator has established for the general good, and therefore wicked."[32] A winning strike was also a losing one, for the inevitable higher prices would decrease consumer demand, whereupon men would be thrown out of work and wages would again fall.

Employers felt even more bitter than the general public about unions, and phrased their denunciations accordingly. Any union was held "arbitrary in its measures, mischievous in its effects, subversive of the confidence and good feeling that formerly existed, and equally calculated to destroy the independence of both the master workmen and journeymen in their contracts and private relations."[33] Labor troubles were inspired by the slothful and envious "aping the degenerate practices of English operatives."[34] The elimination of "supposed grievances" was "arrogantly demanded," even though their granting would lead to idleness, immorality, bankruptcy, and unemployment. Employers of integrity had no option. "We consider it the bounden duty of employers to resist the demands of such combinations"[35] and to preserve the American system by not allowing labor "to make both sides of the bargain."

A vulnerable point of the labor movement was its attracting of the intellectual radicals—"the most indolent and most worthless persons, men of no trade or useful occupation."[36] No more insulting epithet could be hurled than "Fanny Wright man." All shades of reformers were dumped into one package, which was labeled with the most objectionable views of each, and then consigned to perdition. "Whenever community of property has been held up by Christian fanatics, and, I believe, also by Mohammedan, community of wives, or promiscuous intercourse of the sexes, was coupled with the fanatical doctrine. We perceive a similar phenomenon in regard to

[32] *Ibid.*, V, 209.

[33] *Pennsylvanian*, March 17, 1836, quoted in Commons, *Documentary History*, VI, 50.

[34] New York *Journal of Commerce*, June 10, 1835, quoted in Commons, *Documentary History*, V, 308.

[35] *Ibid.*

[36] *Ibid.*, June 1, 1833, quoted in Commons, *Documentary History*, V, 190.

modern socialists, at least in the American followers of the English."[37] In this casual fashion Joseph Smith, Matthias, John Humphrey Noyes, and Fanny Wright could be lumped together with Mohammed and accused of doctrines designed to make men into a "herd of sensual and savage beasts."[38]

The general American reaction to labor unions ranged ordinarily from skepticism to outright hostility, which probably had some slowing effects. More important, however, was the depression, which practically annihilated labor organizations. A generation and more were to pass before unions were sufficiently effective to weather a major depression without complete collapse. In the long run, however, the union movement was on the upgrade.

The effectiveness of the labor movement was less significant than its mere existence. Joining a union meant for the average man that he had given up the possibility of promotion through his individual merits, with his own business in the offing. Certainly there would be no advantage in strengthening an organization which one expected later to fight. The growth of a distinct laboring class in American society was loaded with future dynamite, even though the existing climate of opinion was unfavorable. For the time being, the overwhelming majority of Americans continued to believe in a free economic world, with the maximum opportunity for the individual to become rich. The idea of a society in which one class fought another class for the largest possible share of the national income had not as yet emerged.

[37] F. Lieber, *Essays on Property and Labour* (New York, Harper and Brothers, 1841), 164.

[38] *The American Monthly Magazine* (Boston), Vol. II, n.s. (December, 1836), 578.

10. Stagecoach and Steamboat

EXPANDING industrial production was possible only if the resulting textiles and hardware could be exchanged for the farmers' wheat, hogs, and cotton. Specialization in production depended on transportation. As long as hogs were hardly worth the killing in Indiana and beyond the purses of the poor Irish of Boston, as long as corn could profitably be burned as fuel in Illinois, as the Washington ladies lacked ribbons for weeks at a time, as glass became slivers during shipment, as fresh fruit, vegetables, and milk could be carried only to local markets, so long would America's economic potential not be realized.

The demand for the cheap and rapid movement of freight was reinforced by a drive for fast personal travel. Americans were indefatigable travelers. One met New York friends in New Orleans, Philadelphia acquaintances in Green Bay, and St. Louis business associates in Baltimore. Immigrants sought work or land, farmers' sons moved west, rich planters and merchants made the fashionable tour to Niagara and crowded the resorts from White Sulphur Springs to Saratoga, New England girls pursued their fortunes to the mill towns, peddlers infested the back roads, slave dealers scoured the South, traders and explorers crisscrossed the Far West, and the ubiquitous English traveler appeared everywhere. The entire American population seemed on the move.

Desire to move men and goods, when added to a vast country, native inventiveness, and optimism, meant inevitably a whirl of improvement. Visions of canals, steamships, railroads, steam carriages, and locomotives spun dizzily through the American mind, with no limit to speculation. The most unbalanced—or possibly the most prophetic—insisted that "aerial navigation is the next in order, all other means being exhausted."[1] Enthusiasts were impressed with the indisputable fact that air, in contrast to either land or water, existed over every portion of the world and that successful aerial navigation "needs only an immediate appeal, on a sufficiently large scale, to experiment."[2]

The beautiful pipe dreams made the actuality seem peculiarly drab. When John Quincy Adams, president of the United States, traveled from his Massachusetts home to Washington in 1826, the best time he could make was four days; to move this rapidly, he traveled day and night, shuttling from stage to steamboat and back again. Less eminent travelers in more sparsely settled parts of the country obviously did much worse.

Very few American roads had profited by the advances of Telford and Macadam in England and could be called "improved," that is, graveled, with drainage and bridges. These few exceptions were so outstanding that travelers came from far and near to luxuriate in their smoothness. The improved road was normally a private, money-making venture. The states did not seem to find the funds, particularly when railroads and canals beckoned so alluringly. The federal government was chained by the current Constitutional theory that roads could be built only in the territories or when they indisputably were interstate projects.

The one great national artery to feel the pulsing blood of federal money was the National, or Cumberland, Road. In earlier years it had been built between Cumberland and Wheeling, and now it was continued through Ohio and into Indiana before the panic caught it; the completed parts were then given to the states in which they lay. The mountainous sections were most awe inspiring to the traveler as the drivers "crack the whip and rattle down the long declivities much after the manner that we are all heedlessly rattling through the world."[3] While the road was impressive for its day, it hardly rivaled a billiard table. Deep ruts became small rivers in the wet season, and always occasioned a terrific jolting. In fact, travelers

[1] F. Lieber, *The Stranger in America* (Philadelphia, Carey, Lea and Blanchard, 1835), 48.

[2] *American Journal of Science*, Vol. XXV (1834), 25, quoted in Mott, *Magazines*, 468.

[3] Kellar, *Robinson*, I, 273.

complained frequently that the road was "excessively rough or bad."[4]

Travel on the National Road was highly organized. The large stage companies maintained service day and night, summer and winter, in good weather and bad. Horse relays permitted an average speed of ten miles an hour. The ambitious traveler might reach Wheeling in two and one-half days from Baltimore, and Indianapolis in seven days. Really spectacular speeds came with a pony express, in which boys raced relays of horses across the mountains, but the service was a financial failure. Freight was also the practical monopoly of the large companies, but moved much more slowly, since teamsters drove only during the day.

The average American roads could be graded anywhere from bad to terrible, and the only ordinary distinction of the private turnpike was that it charged toll. Between the larger eastern towns double roads existed, which now and then were treated to modest repairs. Farther west and south there was usually only a single track, and no repairs was the rule, with many a road being no more than a horse trail through the forest. Travelers reported with monotonous regularity that "the roads are left when once made to nature alone and are consequently dreadful";[5] or that "no words can describe the horrible condition of the road";[6] or "the most horrible roads ever seen."[7] The only real variation in reports is in their ingenuity and forcefulness.

If any one part of the country merited the accolade of having America's worst roads, it was the South. As one traveler wrote indignantly, they were "positively, comparatively, and superlatively, the *very worst* I have ever travelled."[8] One main road in North Carolina received this description: "The road lay almost the whole way through swamps, and was frequently itself under water. It was made of logs (a corduroy road), and so dreadfully rough and unequal, that the drawing of a coach over it at all seemed perfectly

[4] *Baillie Note Book*, 333.
[5] Smith, *Journal*, 12.
[6] Combe, *Notes*, II, 66.
[7] E. Bigelow, "Letters Written by a Peoria Woman in 1835," in *Journal of the Illinois State Historical Society*, Vol. XXII (July 1929), 336.
[8] Hamilton, *Men and Manners*, 336.

miraculous. I expected every moment that we must be overturned into the marsh, through which we splashed, with hardly any intermission, the whole night long. Their drivers in this part of the country deserve infinite praise both for skill and care; but the roadmakers, I think, are beyond all praise for their noble confidence in what skill and care can accomplish."[9]

Coach travel brought many a feverish headache as the jolting and bumping cracked the passengers' heads against the roof, and few persons took comfort in the suggestion that the lurching might be good for dyspepsia. Rain and mud, however, made just plain jolting seem like a dream of Elysian peace. "For two days and two nights was my body exposed to the thumps of this horrid road, and when I got to Pittsburgh (after having broken down *twice*, and got out *three* times during one night and broken down rail fences to pry the coach out of the mud) my body was a perfect *jelly*—without one sound spot upon it, too *tired* to stand, too *sore* to sit."[10]

The common hazards of travel were met with American inventiveness and rather surprising stoicism. A broken wheel, axle, or harness produced rough and ready repairs; if the break were unmendable, the passengers sat and shivered while the driver went for help. If the coach got stuck in a bog, the male passengers requisitioned a fence rail or sapling to use as a lever. Most rivers were forded. The infrequent bridges were sometimes so rickety that passengers preferred to get out and walk. Ferries were so undependable that the coach might stand for an hour or two while the driver persuaded the ferry operator to interrupt his plowing. When even the maximum ingenuity failed to make the coach move, the party scurried to the nearest cabin to share stoically whatever rough accommodations existed.

In winter, coach travel became definitely worse. Frozen ruts produced greater jars, and the passengers would lean from side to side to prevent the coach from overturning. Snow on the usual single-track road meant that the men got out with shovels to clear a siding. Since a coach was far from airtight, the wind whistled merrily

[9] Kemble, *Later Life*, 112.

[10] "Letters of George Sumner 1837–1849," in *Proceedings of the Massachusetts Historical Society*, Vol. XLVI (1912–13), 342.

through it, inspiring hot soapstones, buffalo robes, shawls, coats, fur caps, and straw on the floor of the coach—all topped off with copious draughts of New England rum. Regardless of preparations, however, sixty or seventy miles of such travel, from before dawn until after dark, was a searching test of fortitude.

Every large town was a center of coaching travel, and might boast a hundred or more coaches per day—which by no means insured punctuality or even transportation. Some lines ran only a few coaches on irregular schedules. None worried about maintaining a schedule within a couple of hours, and sometimes a particular coach never did appear. Certain well-traveled mail lines might be so greatly patronized that the traveler would be forced to twiddle his thumbs for two or three weeks before being able to obtain a seat.

Most travelers did not have the physical stamina to ride both night and day even if such service existed. The result was a scattering of inns, which according to more than one tourist were "receptacles fit only for the animals that frequent them."[11] Usually a coach aimed to stop for the night at a specific inn, but not infrequently the arrival came after 11:00 P.M. and the departure before 5:00 A.M., thus hardly providing a proper night's sleep even if the traveler could overlook the hard, lumpy, vermin-infested beds. The food all too frequently consisted of poor corn bread, rancid bacon, and bitter coffee, with the result that many a traveler carried his own provisions.

The usual coach was built at Concord, New Hampshire, and might cost up to three thousand dollars, which implied size and weight and elaborate decorations, even if not comfort. The supposed seating capacity of a coach was nine, on three seats—one at each end of the coach and facing each other, and the third in the center with a strap for a back rest. If travel were heavy, additional passengers might be packed away, with the surplus overflowing into the driver's seat. The body was swung on leather straps, which by no stretch of the imagination could be mistaken for springs. Leather curtains could be rolled down in bad weather, but actually kept little of the snow, sleet, rain, or wintry winds outside.

The stage driver was lord of all he surveyed and the idol of

[11] *Baillie Note Book*, 332.

every small boy along his route. He was master of magnificent power, and held the lives of his passengers in his hand. Not unnaturally he drove in the grand style, delighting to put on his best speed at the most spectacular and dangerous parts of the road. He entered every town at a gallop, sliding to a stop before the inn with a toot of the horn, a squealing of brakes, and enveloped in a cloud of dust. He felt certain that the honor of the line was in his custody and was willing to show his zeal by racing an opposition driver or bloodying his nose.

Coach travel usually averaged about six miles an hour, but with great possible variations. Under good conditions a coach might double this speed, while under bad conditions it might devote a ten-hour day to plodding over twenty or thirty miles. The usual fare was five cents a mile, but again there were variations. The traveler who really sought comfort might invest in a private coach or carriage, at ten dollars or more a day.

"A stage coach is generally animated, at least after a social dinner has opened the mouths and removed the timidity and restraint of the company."[12] Formality and reserve gave way to a feeling of common purpose and to a joint endurance of common misfortunes. Dignity could hardly be preserved when "without the warning of an instant, we found ourselves, en masse, with broken fragments of the stage, hats and bonnets in a jam, cloaks, coats and pantaloons, fit furniture for a rag-shop—men groaning—women in hysterics—tears running, and blood, too."[13] The occasion of this excitement was the overturning of the coach as it sped downhill, and the writer blamed the accident on the Demon Rum, for a coach driver was reputed never to accept a tip but never to refuse a drink.

Baggage presented a problem that was never solved satisfactorily in the stagecoach. Lacking space inside the coach, it was lashed on the roof, with now and then a metal tag. It was hurled from roof to roof as coaches were changed, and ultimately dropped on the ground with a resounding thud—provided it had not been lost en route. When the traveler recovered his bag, it might be wrenched from his hand by an ambitious porter who immediately set out for a rooming

[12] Hale, *Notes*, 7.
[13] Barnes, *Weld Letters*, I, 59.

house from which he received a commission; frequently both porter and baggage disappeared permanently.

Heavy freight was never carried by coach, but by wagon. The prices were not too high for the cost of the service, but that is the best that can be said. Five or six dollars a hundred pounds from Philadelphia or Baltimore to the Ohio River gave no exorbitant profit to the teamster whose six-horse wagon traveled about twenty miles a day, but it increased prices to fantastic amounts. Farther west, rates might be as much as ten times as great, and hence prohibitive for most articles.

Mail was carried in large part by the stages, although the minimum charge of six cents for one sheet of paper sent less than thirty miles hardly encouraged voluminous correspondence. This charge included collection from the scarce city boxes, but not final delivery. The price increased with size and distance, so that a young migrant to Michigan thought long and hard before he wrote a long letter to his girl in Massachusetts. Newspapers and magazines were given great preference. A newspaper could be sent free to every other American newspaper, which undoubtedly explains why the coaches were filled with papers and why each sheet was loaded with reprinted articles.

The Post Office Department was notoriously lax and inefficient. Contracts were often fraudulent, with the favored company making an impossibly low bid and then having the price raised after the contract had been let. Even the better law of 1836 did not stop the practice. The franking privilege was grossly abused, with congressmen loaning their franks to constituents. Much mail was undelivered—ending either in a vacant pasture or in the new dead-letter office. Deliveries were irregular; New York might receive no Washington mail for several days, St. Louis might receive no mail at all for weeks, and smaller towns were grateful for any mail at any time. Part of the trouble was the bad roads and the bandits, but part was bad political appointments, particularly after the postmaster general was brought into the cabinet in 1829.

Poor service and high rates became all the more exasperating because the recipient paid the postage. A man who had waited weeks for a letter and then paid postage on a small package only to discover it was a circular or tract was hardly in an amiable frame of mind—especially when he felt that the postmaster overcharged him by counting more than the proper number of sheets. The conscientious person wrote only when absolutely necessary, while the unscrupulous added cabalistic messages that could be read at a glance and then the letter refused. A generous correspondent could prepay his letters; this fact was marked on the outside by the postmaster, who by the early forties was using stamps. The first government stamp, however, did not appear until 1847.

An inefficient and expensive governmental postal system attracted private competition. Every traveler was loaded with letters and small parcels. Every city had its "penny post"[14] to deliver letters locally at two cents apiece. Express companies ran regular mail businesses, and only theoretically paid the government the regular postage on their transactions. The government prosecuted a few cases, but encountered vigorous local defense of the private companies.

Ultimately the government bowed to the necessity of cheaper and better service. A law of 1845 fixed rates at five cents a half ounce under three hundred miles, and ten cents otherwise. Local mail was two cents. Pamphlets and magazines had a flat rate. Moreover, mail service was improved and illegal carriers prosecuted. As a result the government monopoly became effective.

The carrying of the mail was profitable for the coaching companies, and it was, moreover, considered an honor since it implied speed. The companies improved their equipment until at times they could average fifteen miles an hour between the larger eastern cities. On special occasions fast riders made even better time. The Presidential message of 1834 was carried to New York in twelve hours, while that of 1837 reached Boston in twenty-four and one-half hours—remarkable times. The only current suggestion for greater speed was that a pneumatic tube be used, with a pumping station every five miles.

Even more important than speed for most traffic was cheapness. The obvious development was to increase the size of wagons and

---

[14] *Early Letters of Mark Hopkins* (New York, John Day Company, 1929), 156.

coaches; the Bordentown transfer had a twelve-horse coach with two levels, which could hold fifty-six passengers. Independent wheel suspension and a lower center of gravity were tried. A few steam-propelled monsters lumbered awkwardly over the roads. But none of these developments proved of permanent importance.

Road improvements inevitably lagged as long as Americans remained certain that water transportation had no peer; at the best, "other forms of transportation may divert passengers and light goods, but the staples must ever go in ships, propelled by wind or steam."[15] The wagon or coach could never rival the boats gliding over the oceans, lakes, and rivers with which the United States was so lavishly supplied. The chief function of the road—as of the canal or the railroad— was to connect navigable bodies of water.

Ocean travel remained generally in the sailing age, with even the heyday of the clipper ship still in the future. The long and honorable American sea tradition had its home in New England, where every boy considered seriously at least one sailing experience before he settled down to farming. Villages such as Duxbury, Dennis, New Bedford, Gloucester, Scituate, and Truro reeked of the sea and not of tourists looking for the picturesque. Such towns furnished the famous shipbuilders and the well-known officers with good old New England names like Elijah Cobb, Ezra Nye, and Job Chase.

Just as New England dominated the building and manning of ocean-going ships, New York and New Orleans dominated the actual shipping. For most of the decade New Orleans was the principal American port. Her wharves were lined with ocean and river vessels, and piled deep with merchandise. Rivermen and ocean tars roistered in the saloons, gambling dives, and brothels. But New Orleans was being challenged by New York, which by 1840 had surged into a leadership that she was not to lose. Hudson River boats, Sound steamers, and ocean-going vessels from all over the world docked at her piers. Foreign arrivals alone totaled some two thousand a year, and included vessels of the greatest shipping lines

[15] H. R. Schoolcraft, *Personal Memoirs of a Residence of Thirty Years with the Indian Tribes on the American Frontier* (Philadelphia, Lippincott, Grambo and Company, 1851), 495.

of the day. Practically all foreign visitors and immigrants arrived at New York.

Foreign trade was profitable, as American wheat, flour, cotton, lumber, and other raw materials were sent abroad to provide the funds for such items as textiles, cutlery, tropical fruits, wines, tea, coffee, cocoa, and sugar. Cairo, Mozambique, Madagascar, and Java were among the far places which dealt with the New England sea captains, who even furnished the Pasha of Egypt with ice. China and India were relatively less important than at an earlier time, but trade was expanding with the Mediterranean countries and with Central and South America. The Spanish West Indies remained closed, but the English West Indies were opened to American ships in 1830. Profits from foreign trade were increasingly being invested in textile mills and in other industries. Minor profits appeared in the form of trinkets, largely Chinese, which littered coastal New England; apparently no sailor returned home without presents for his family and his best girl.

More prosaic than foreign trade was the coastal business, with textiles and salt pork going south, and cotton returning. Sometimes a captain like Job Chase of West Harwich varied his routine by a trip abroad for such exotic products as macaroni, bergamot, and lemons, but such variations were unusual.

Every New England coastal town was the site of fishing, with Marblehead and Gloucester best known. Profits, as in shipping, were shared by captain and crew. The usual fishing was for cod or mackerel, but the spectacular search for the whale received more publicity. The oil hunters ranged the seven seas from the Sandwich Islands to the Azores and Cape Verde. A lookout on the topgallant-mast trees sang out, "Thar she blows," which launched a boat's crew of six men armed with a harpoon attached to eighty fathoms of rope. If the harpooned whale went straight down, the harpoon and rope were lost; if straight up, the boat might be lost; but if the whale were properly behaved, he pulled the boat until he was tired; then he was stabbed in the vitals. The blubber was cut spirally into small pieces and brought aboard to be rendered into sperm oil. The rest of the carcass, except for an occasional steak, was allowed to float away.

The aristocrats of the ocean lanes were the trans-Atlantic packets, particularly those plying between New York and Liverpool. In a day when a 500-ton ship was considered large, the *Montezuma* (1835) went over 1,000. Largest of all was the *Roscius* (1839) with its mainmast towering 160 feet; it was a vessel of the new Dramatic Line, owned by Edward K. Collins, and its captain exhibited his superlative seamanship by waving away tugboats and navigating right up to the dock. These boats were speedy. An ordinary run from New York to Liverpool took about twenty days, while the return trip, in the other direction, against the prevailing winds, consumed about thirty-five. The best record was that of Captain Ezra Nye, who in 1836 sailed his *Independence* eastbound in fourteen and one-half days, and returned in twenty.

Atlantic packets were considered luxurious for the man who could afford $150 for a cabin from Liverpool to New York, even though a recent writer has compared the trip to "a six-weeks sojourn in a dungeon during an earthquake."[16] The fine woodwork, the deep carpets, the gleaming mirrors, and the excellent food compared favorably with the best hotels. The days were spent in reading, walking, chatting, letter writing, cards, and music. The outstanding snakes in this garden of Eden were seasickness and boredom. After five weeks, reading and talking palled, especially when bad weather kept the traveler below decks. Even the best food became monotonous, and a prolonged voyage might mean strict rationing which included a high proportion of tough sea biscuit. And, as always, the steerage passenger suffered bad conditions. His thirty dollars brought him only a bunk in a crowded room, and he furnished his own bedding and food.

The pirate had not yet disappeared. Most famous pirate of his day was one Charles Gibbs, whose hanging on Ellis Island, April 22, 1831, attracted a vast concourse of boatmen. In accordance with the best pirate tradition, he seized the moment before the trap was sprung to plead that others be warned by his fate. The cast of his head was a prize cherished by phrenologists.

A revolution in ocean transportation was forecast by three innovations—steam power, the screw propeller, and the iron ship.

[16] H. C. Kittredge, *Shipmasters of Cape Cod* (Boston, Houghton Mifflin Company, 1935), 101–102.

Steam power was, of course, not new, but its use on the ocean posed difficult problems; wood fires meant wood instead of passengers, while a breakdown of the very fallible machinery in mid-Atlantic was not a pleasant prospect. American ocean steamship business actually started with a rush. New York welcomed its first ocean steamship, the *Sirius*, on April 12, 1838, but the *Great Western* appeared the next day, only to be followed by the *Royal William* in June, the *Liverpool* in November, and the *British Queen* the next July. New York showed its enthusiasm with bands, parades, welcoming committees, toasts, and flocks of visitors.

The newer steamships were larger and faster than the packets. One thousand tons was a large packet but a small steamer, with the *British Queen* over two thousand. The added space meant slightly larger general rooms but it was used chiefly to accommodate more passengers in about the same-sized staterooms—at a slightly higher price. Speed was definitely increased. The poorest times of the new boats were better than the best records of the ships of the Blackball, Dramatic, and other packet lines. Truly a revolution.

Of almost equal potential importance was the idea of the screw propeller—again not new. John Ericsson, a Swedish engineer, hawked a model throughout Europe and then as a last resort came to New York, where he captured the imagination of one Captain Van Cleve. Van Cleve's sloop *Vandalia* was the first commercial boat to be equipped with a screw propeller, but although it ran successfully in November, 1841, the idea was slow to be accepted.

Iron for shipbuilding seemed to most people the first step to the madhouse, but it appealed to certain nonconformists. Reputedly the first iron ship was constructed at Savannah in 1834 by C. B. Lamar, but other men were experimenting about the same time. Popularity was not achieved until steel became cheap a generation later.

American rivers and lakes were crowded with a varied assortment of boats. The homemade canoe jostled the three-decked steamboat, while the western "bullboat" offered startling contrast to the Great Lakes sailing sloop. Two stump pullers—"Uncle Sam's tooth-pullers"—cavorted on the Mississippi. The long, slender keelboat nosed up and down even the smaller western rivers, with its tiny cabin surrounded by a walk for the men to push poles when sailing was impossible and towing unnecessary. Hordes of flatboats descended the Ohio and the Mississippi, with long sweeps for steering and landing. Several flatboats lashed together formed a floating home for an entire community, complete with plows, wagons, hay, cows, children, chickens, and furniture. The women cooked over an open fireplace or knitted industriously while the men whittled, chewed tobacco, and spat into the river.

Rivers were spanned by ferries, sometimes a rope ferry or a canoe, but more frequently one or two scows propelled an inch at a time by a horse turning a crank in the center or walking a treadmill at the edge. Only in New York harbor was there sufficient business to warrant steam ferries.

The acme of transportation was the steamboat, which had behind it a quarter of a century of experience. Its speed, its comfort, and its cheapness clearly outcompeted the stage or the wagon for either passengers or freight. More surprising, it was considered so superior to the infant railroad trains that the suggestion of a railroad alongside a navigable river was held to be ludicrous.

The steamboat appeared wherever there was water enough to take a bath. It traveled not only on such impressive bodies as the Great Lakes, Champlain, George, and Seneca, but on much smaller ponds. Not only the lordly Hudson, Delaware, Ohio, and Mississippi rivers heard the steamboat whistle, but also streams as insignificant as the lowly Piscataqua. Some of the boats made almost incredible runs, as when one ascended the Connecticut as far as Wells River. In general the southern rivers had poorer service than the northern ones because of the sparseness of population and the lack of diversity of production; often the boats were brought from the North after their greatest usefulness had passed.

Most vigorous eastern competition was on the Hudson between New York and Albany. The number of boats increased until over one hundred were in operation in 1840. Times were cut and then were cut again; the *Chief Justice Marshall* made the trip in fourteen and one-half hours during the twenties, but a decade later the *South America* could boast an eight-hour run. Prices were slashed from a profitable five dollars to a paltry fifty cents, with suggestions of carrying passengers for only the cost of their meals. "Uncle Daniel" Drew, "Commodore" Vanderbilt, and their associates fought vigorously with weapons that did not exclude bribery, arson, and murder. Ultimately conditions were so demoralized that a combination bought out Vanderbilt, who moved to the Boston run; whereupon the price rebounded to three dollars.

A traveler leaving New York for Albany was nearly deafened as rival steamboat agents shouted the advantages of the People's, the Eagle, the Union, the North River, and the New York, Albany, and Troy lines. According to the barkers, each ship was just on the point of departure, and each was a luxury liner 150 or 200 or more feet in length. Paper boys increased the din as they hawked the *Standard, Courier and Enquirer, Gazette, Advocate,* or *Temperance Recorder.* Vendors proclaimed the virtues of oranges and other fruit and knicknacks. Porters rushed past, throwing baggage on board. Then came the rush of last-minute passengers, the escape of steam, and the shriek of the boat's whistle.

Once the boat slid from the dock, the traveler caught his breath and looked around. On one of the huge three-deckers he could find two large cabins, each 150 feet long, with luxurious furniture, deep-napped carpets, gleaming mirrors, rich ottomans, silk curtains, and oil paintings. He might purchase liquor or other refreshments, books, maps, and guidebooks. He could get shaved. A spacious diningroom, presided over by the captain, seated three hundred; at night it was used for sleeping, with berths bracketed three high along the walls. While a rare pessimist might sourly describe the boat as "ill constructed & ill arranged,"[17] the vast majority gaped in open-mouthed admiration, and proclaimed that "the steam boat is a great floating hotel."[18]

The majority of steamboats plowed western waters, particularly the Ohio and the Mississippi. New Orleans registered more steamboats than any other American city, and Louisiana registrations were rivaled only by those of New York. In general, the West also built its own boats, with Pittsburgh, Cincinnati, and Louisville the leading cities, in that order. These boats on the average were smaller in

[17] Smith, *Journal,* 10.
[18] Lyell, *Travels 1841-42,* I, 57.

size and shorter in life than those of the East. Whereas the eastern boat could count on ten to fifteen years of active service, the western boat averaged some four or five.

At water level the western boat had machinery, cargo, and "deck passengers," who furnished their own food and bedding, and were supposed to load wood. The second deck contained the dining saloon, with berths for the men, a ladies' cabin, washroom, smoking rooms, and library. The women's quarters were as far as possible from the boilers to give the ladies maximum safety in the not unlikely event of an explosion. The top deck held the officers' quarters, steering apparatus, freight, and additional deck passengers.

The western boat had obvious disadvantages. Even the shallow draft and the busy linesman did not avoid all of the shifting sandbars, while snags and sawyers were perpetual menaces. Passengers were not always the socially elite. Food—poor but abundant—was gulped in a rush, and then the average male picked his teeth with a wooden sliver or a penknife. Washing provisions consisted of one or two dirty basins, plus a common towel, comb, and brush; one New Englander suggested caustically that there would also have been a common toothbrush if anyone would have used it. Professional gamblers and pickpockets infested every ship. Drinking was universal, and everyone was armed with at least a bowie knife. The inevitable Baptist or Methodist minister failed to dam the flow of either profane language or tobacco juice, which laved every available inch. Many women, for understandable reasons, preferred to stay in their cabins.

Most people, however, found a steamboat trip pleasant. Washington Irving noted the beauties of "moonlight—light of fires—chant and chorus of negro boat men—men strolling about docks with cigars—negroes dancing before furnaces—glassy surface of river—undulations made by boat—wavering light of moon & stars."[19] People were sociable, and strangers became bosom friends in a few minutes, even though their heated political arguments sounded ferocious. A race with a rival boat brought everyone on deck to watch and to lay bets on the outcome. Conversation developed the thrilling

[19] *The Western Journals of Washington Irving*, edited by John Francis McDermott (Norman, University of Oklahoma Press, 1944), 71.

storyteller who could fascinate his fellow travelers with such tales as how Lafayette nearly drowned when a boiler of his boat burst.

Steamboat fares were extremely moderate. The trip from New Orleans to St. Louis in the early thirties took some twelve days and cost only twenty-five to thirty dollars, including food, while deck passage could be obtained for from five to eight dollars; the return trip took only half as long, and cost correspondingly less. Prices tended to rise—partly because of a steamboat monopoly like that on the Great Lakes, but also partly because of generally rising prices, improved boats, and increased speed. Whereas the *Paragon* in 1828 had made a record-breaking trip of eighteen days and ten hours, from New Orleans to Louisville, the *Diana* a decade later covered the same stretch of river in five days and twenty-three hours—less than one-third of the earlier time.

Steamboats were so common in the United States that even the conservative navy was willing to try one boat, the *Fulton the Second*, in the thirties, and two more in the early forties. But old navy men were not happy. As one of them said: "When I look at the sail and yards I feel at Home."[20] Apparently the navy was eager to have its men feel at home, for it experimented very little with steam.

Americans loved to boast of the luxury and speed of their steamboats in comparison with European tubs, and many a European admitted the truth of the claim: "The finest ones we have in Europe are much inferior to the smallest, the wretchedest ferry-boat over here."[21] Steamboats were at one and the same time the cheapest, the most pleasant, and the most hazardous means of travel.

Steamboats were unquestionably dangerous. Newspapers were filled with stories of accidents—and grounding on a sandbar was not worth newspaper space. The traveler found his course lined with wrecks, and was informed that each year one in ten boats experienced a major accident, while one in four ultimately ended its life by disaster. The best that the optimist could claim was that "with moderation and care steam boats are not so very dangerous."[22]

[20] M. Armstrong, *Five Generations* (New York, Harper and Brothers, 1930), 297.

[21] Evans, *Trip by Arese*, 1.

[22] *Niles Register*, Vol. XXXII (May 12, 1827), 179.

Major hazards were fires and boiler explosions, although now and then a boat sank after hitting a snag or a sawyer, capsized in a gale, or collided disastrously with another ship. Fire was a nightmare in a wooden ship with an inflammable cargo, and a tiller rope that soon burned; a steel rope was not available until 1841. The *Ben Sherrod,* for example, was racing a rival near Natchez on May 8, 1837, when an overheated engine set fire to the near-by wood supply, which in turn exploded barrels of whiskey, brandy, and gunpowder. Passengers not killed by the blast jumped into the river only to be run down by the following boat, which did not stop. The death toll was about 175. The *Lexington,* en route from New York to Stonington, caught fire January 13, 1840. A cargo of cotton was ignited, the steering rope burned, the engines gave way, and life-boats were swamped in a panicky rush. Men, women, and children jumped from the burning deck to the freezing ocean. Of a passenger list of 150, only 4 persons succeeded in clinging to bales of cotton until they were rescued.

The majority of the really bad accidents, particularly in the West, were boiler explosions. Most horrible was the case of the *Moselle,* a new boat just leaving its Cincinnati dock on April 26, 1838. All four boilers exploded in one tremendous detonation, erupting pieces of boiler, of the ship, and of human bodies all over the area. Many passengers not killed outright were too dazed to save themselves, and the boat sank within fifteen minutes. The fatalities numbered over two hundred, and the entire city of Cincinnati was closed for the funerals.

Accidents were particularly dreadful in that so many were completely unnecessary. Old and faulty boilers, improperly stacked cargo, and inadequate life preservers and lifeboats were clearly avoidable, as were bad navigation, racing, and a drunken captain or crew. Most owners apparently were willing to do nothing more than hold a desultory investigation; possibly there was a perfunctory inquest. The usual owner insisted that the only solution was for the traveler to pick the safer boats. In actual fact, however, the inexpert traveler could not tell that a boat was unsafe until it burned or blew up, which was a trifle late.

Public demand for improvement finally brought the federal

Transporting passengers on the Pennsylvania Canal,
a portion of the trip from Philadelphia to Pittsburgh
over the Allegheny Portage Railroad

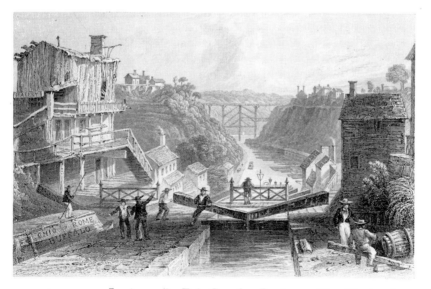

Locks on the Erie Canal at Lockport, New York, 1839
From an engraving by W. Tombleson after W. H. Bartlett

government into action. A law of 1838 required steamship inspection and license, and had specifications concerning steam pressures, lifeboats, fire engine and hose, signal lights, and steering apparatus. Any negligence resulting in the death of a passenger brought ten years for manslaughter, and steam injuries were prima-facie evidence of negligence. The law was one of the many indications that the American people were not blind devotees to the theories of *laissez faire.*

Steamboats were the glorious peak of American transportation in 1830. For freight, they were cheaper than wagons and faster than canal boats. For passengers, they were cheaper and more comfortable than stages and faster and more luxurious than canal boats. Their dominance was limited only by the amount of navigable water. The succeeding ten years decreased the competitive margin of the steamboat, in spite of its improvement. A host of canals cut prices, while the rapidly growing railroad had more flexibility of location and potentially greater speed. The era of the steamboat gave promise of its eventual demise even before it had attained its greatest glory.

11. Canal Barge and Railroad Car

N<small>O SUBJECT</small> aroused more American enthusiasm than transportation. A rash of conventions waxed enthusiastic over river improvements, roads, canals, and railroads. Each town visualized a vast transportational network of which it would be the center. Eastern cities dreamed of a strangle hold on western business, while western cities had visions of dominating the Ohio, the Mississippi, or the Great Lakes.

Early in the decade top priority went to canals, with every town boosting one or more pet projects. Any stranger with whom you drank whiskey at the local bar could discourse learnedly on the best locks or how to get water to a summit level. As early as 1830 at least 10,000 miles of canal were actively projected. The real visionaries topped their plans with a grand national canal, large enough for steamboats, which would link the Hudson, the Great Lakes, the Missouri, and the Columbia, so that a boat could sail from New York to the mouth of the Columbia. A few years later the visionaries filled their dream canals and laid rails without making the dream much less wildly improbable.

A little sober reflection—which few took—would have deflated the rosy hopes of the canal enthusiasts. Although many of the more important projects linked East and West, where was the technical knowledge to leap rivers and mountain ranges? And where was the necessary money? Enthusiasm produced stock subscriptions, but did not provide hard cash. Towns, counties, and states did their limited best, only to flounder in the bog of the depression, with many projects incomplete. The federal government was disappointingly unhelpful, since President Jackson could find few projects that he considered truly interstate.

All canals necessarily connected other bodies of water, and three general types of projects may be distinguished. The simplest was the short canal around some obstacle in a river, and these short canals embroidered dozens of rivers from the Saco to the Tennessee, not omitting such rivulets as the Conestoga. Outstanding was the Welland Canal around Niagara Falls and the Louisville and Portland Canal around the falls of the Ohio at Louisville. Only the teamsters and hotelkeepers objected to these obvious improvements.

A second group of canals connected well-used rivers and lakes, for example, the Hudson and the Delaware, the Schuylkill and the Susquehanna, and the Delaware and the Susquehanna. Most impressive were the western canals connecting the Great Lakes with the Ohio-Mississippi system. Ohio completed one from Cleveland to Portsmouth on the Ohio, and got well started on a line from Cincinnati to Toledo. Indiana connected the Wabash and the Maumee. Illinois talked of linking the Chicago and the Illinois, while Wisconsin likewise had a pet project. South of the Ohio, canals were less successful, partly because of inadequate funds and sparse population, but also because of the frequence of navigable rivers.

The third type of canal was designed to draw western business to some eastern city. The great prototype was the Erie Canal, which after its opening in 1825 had brought an ever increasing flood of business to New York City and encouraged the growth of central and western New York state. The merchants of other seaboard cities chewed their fingernails nervously and lay awake nights trying to discover ways to meet the competition. Their fears became even more oppressive as New York pushed out feeders to its main line, and as the western states provided facilities for Ohio Valley traffic to flow by water to New York.

Practically every seaboard city began canals to tap its back country, with a hopeful eye cocked at western business. Among them were Portland, Boston, Providence, New Haven, New York, Philadelphia, Baltimore, Richmond, Charleston, and Savannah. Most of them were in time thwarted by mountains or lack of funds or both. The really important projects, in addition to the Erie Canal, were those of Philadelphia and Baltimore.

Pennsylvania had long been in the canal business—up the

Schuylkill and across to the Susquehanna—but these small ditches looked pitiful as the Erie Canal took form. Philadelphia merchants became alarmed and gave the state the gentle tap that was all that was necessary. A magnificent dream crystallized into legal authorization of a main canal from Philadelphia to Pittsburgh, with branches from Pittsburgh to Lake Erie, up the Susquehanna to New York state, and up the Delaware. The first and last were completed and the other two well under way before the panic pushed Pennsylvania into temporary bankruptcy.

The main "Pennsylvania System" from Philadelphia to Pittsburgh was opened to the public in the spring of 1834, and was America's greatest mechanical marvel. A railroad spanned the stretch from Philadelphia to Columbia on the Susquehanna, but the grades at each end were so steep that stationary engines hauled the cars up and down. Then came a canal along the Susquehanna and Juniata to Hollidaysburg. The five mountain ridges between Hollidaysburg and Johnstown were surmounted by inclined planes, with the cars pulled up one side of the mountain and lowered down the other by a stationary engine; the intervening valleys were crossed by railroad. West from Johnstown a canal provided still more eyebrow-raising feats of contruction, including a tunnel 2,900 feet long.

The Pennsylvania System attracted the curious from far and near, but its economic effect was disappointing. Rates were only slightly lower than by road, and the speed was little greater. Passengers spent five days on the four hundred miles, while freight dallied twice as long, mostly because of the many transshipments. American ingenuity then provided sectional canal boats, so that each section could be placed on a railroad car, but without producing utopia. Ambitious Philadelphia merchants still ground their teeth in impotent rage as they looked north enviously toward the Erie Canal.

The great Baltimore project was the Chesapeake and Ohio Canal—or, to be more accurate, this waterway had the blessing of Baltimore until Baltimoreans realized they would be only on a branch, at which point they pushed a railroad and refused to aid the canal. The Chesapeake and Ohio was planned to follow the Potomac and then top the mountains to the Ohio by some means never made quite clear. Work was started with a great fanfare on July 4, 1828, in the presence of the President of the United States, the secretaries of treasury, war, and navy, and most of the diplomatic corps. President Adams himself cast aside his coat and threw the first shovel of dirt. Unfortunately, even this good start did not forecast a good ending. Only the eighty-odd miles to Harpers Ferry were completed by 1840, and the final end came at Cumberland in 1850. By this time the canal had clearly been outmoded by the Baltimore and Ohio Railroad.

An American canal was only a four-foot ditch, but its construction demanded ingenuity, since at the outset there were no trained engineers, little labor, and inadequate funds. Blasting with gunpowder was slow and dangerous, the removal of trees a real problem, and work in swamps productive of disease. Locks were difficult to construct even with cement available. The early hydrostatic weight locks were soon replaced by the better steelyards. Tunnels through the mountains and viaducts over the streams required engineering skill, while the inclined planes were excellent examples of ingenuity. Frequently an inadequate supply of water necessitated long feeder channels or an elaborate pumping system.

Traffic on the Erie Canal exemplified the better practices of the day. Freight was accepted by all kinds of boats from the scow to the bull-head, except that steamboats could not be used because of their effect on the banks. Some boats were individually owned and hauled whatever freight was offered; others were run by large companies on regular schedules. Boat crews were rough and tough, apparently loving to fight on any pretext, for example, for the privilege of being first through a lock. Private fist fights might end as free-for-alls, with knives flashing freely, and the watermen roistered in the hundreds of saloons and brothels that lined the bank.

For the passenger, canal travel was above all smooth and leisurely. Few boats exceeded four miles an hour, so that when a traveler tired of reading, chatting, or looking at the scenery, he could walk alongside the boat and stretch his legs. The periodic cry of "low bridge" offered only a pleasing spice of novelty as one ducked to avoid being brained.

Unfortunately for the passenger, a canal boat also had grave disadvantages, many of which resulted from the fact that the boat was small—say, about sixty to seventy feet by fifteen feet—and tried to accommodate as many fares as possible; one hundred or more passengers were not unusual. The deck was therefore cluttered with baggage covered with tarpaulin. The cabin was anything but spacious when quarters for the crew and for the kitchen were cut off the limited space; some saving was possible by curtaining a portion of the main cabin at night for the ladies rather than providing a separate room. A hot, rainy afternoon or evening was a real test of fortitude. Writing, talking, playing backgammon or chess, singing with a flute or violin accompaniment, and violent political arguments were all punctuated by intermittent explosions of tobacco juice. Interruptions of varying enjoyment were provided by thieves, by professional gamblers, and by ministers who took advantage of a congregation that could not escape.

The only really good entertainment was the food, which was served on long wooden trestles, with the captain presiding. Washing facilities were a couple of tin basins and a common towel and comb. Berths were three high along the wall, where they were attached to iron hooks by ropes. A breaking rope was not a serious disaster since the berths were only three feet apart. The size of a bed was ordinarily five and one-half by two feet, which presumably closed canal traffic to the big man. The mattress was thin and the one cover was thinner. All bedclothing was piled in the corner during the day, but that mattered little since it was always filthy. A big crowd exhausted the berths, and men drew lots, with the unluckier ones relegated to the tables, the chairs, or the floor.

Passenger travel needed relays of horses and hence was the prerogative of such lines as the Pilot, Washington, Merchants', Telegraph, Commercial, and Citizens. The all-passenger boat was called a packet, and sped along at five miles an hour, with frequent relays of horses. For its superior accommodations it charged five cents a mile, including food. The line boat took both freight and passengers, was more crowded, less comfortable, and slower—not over three miles an hour; the fare was correspondingly lower—usually one cent a mile without food and two and one-half cents with it. Immigrant families moving west were given special rates, say two and one-half cents a mile without food.

The better canal boat was pulled by three horses which were changed every ten or twelve miles, but even with this equipment few boats could cover more than one hundred miles a day. When two boats met, one slacked its line and the other went over it. When the towpath crossed the canal, the horses were driven under the bridge and then galloped to the other side before the rope tightened. Sometimes a balky horse was pulled into the canal. In the winter the canals were closed; sometimes the water was drained, but more often it was permitted to freeze and thus to furnish a smooth highway for sleighs.

For a brief period many inland "ports" and "havens" flourished from the canal traffic. Farm products, manufactured goods, immigrants, and other travelers crowded the water highways. Transportation costs declined, producing more business and bringing eastern and western prices closer together. Main streets blossomed along the canals, and were lined with saloons, rooming houses, gambling halls, and brothels. The most important news of the year for many a town was the opening of the canal in the spring and the closing of it in the fall.

Canals meant a definite improvement in American transportation, but their defects were almost as apparent as their merits. During the winter they were completely idle. Their locations were determined as much by nature as by man, and they were altogether impossible at many places where they were needed desperately. They were so slow as to be useless for goods that spoiled easily or for which price changes were rapid. Obviously they were not the final word in transportation.

The last word in transportational gadgets was the railroad, which was first conceived as a toll road on which each traveler and farmer would use his own rig. The advantage over an ordinary road was that its smoothness would permit a horse to draw a larger load at a more rapid pace. The railroad's main service was thought to be the connecting of navigable bodies of water; the idea of paralleling a river such as the Hudson or Mississippi was held as chimerical. Nor was the railroad expected to compete effectively with a canal; a parallel route merely meant that the railroad hoped for the crumbs of passengers who liked novelty, and freight when the canal froze.

Every American town wanted railroads, and at least speculated about a spider web of which it was the center. Enthusiasm tended to vary inversely with the excellence of water connections. New York, for example, was much less excited than Boston, which had long wept bitterly at its lack of a good route to the West. By 1841 it completed rail connections to the Hudson opposite Albany, and by the next year seven short lines spanned the miles between Albany and Buffalo. The results were disappointing, for these railroads had varying time systems and track widths; by no stretch of the imagination could they be called satisfactory. No intelligent shipper would desert the Erie Canal and the Hudson River for this complicated and expensive route.

New York and Philadelphia both remained committed to their water routes to the West, although the Erie considered construction. Both cities were interested in small roads to neighboring towns. Their greatest enthusiasm, however, was for two competing roads between the two cities—"the oppressive monopoly of the Camden and Amboy"—and the alternate railroad by way of Trenton and New Brunswick.

Baltimore's one great hope was the Baltimore and Ohio, America's first standard commercial road. A tremendous civic celebration on Independence Day of 1828, when Charles Carroll, the last surviving signer of the Delcaration, threw the first shovelful of dirt, indicated the hopes that were involved. A first section of track was opened in 1829 to travelers who found it "a very pleasant mode of traveling";[1] but frantic efforts took the road no farther than Harpers Ferry by 1840. Richmond dreamed in frustration of a road westward across the mountains. Charleston opened the longest single line of its day, 136 miles to Hamburg on the Savannah River, in 1833, but hopes of further expansion were deferred by the panic.

Eastern railroad construction of the eighteen thirties was magnificent when its difficulties are considered, but disappointing in view of its high hopes. Many eastern cities remained unconnected,

[1] Nevins, *Hone Diary*, I, 21.

A railroad train near Little Falls, New York, 1838
From an engraving by R. Sands after W. H. Bartlett

Smith and Dimon shipyard, from a painting by James Pringle

Courtesy of the New York State Historical Association, Cooperstown, New York

branches and feeders were few, and no good connection to the West had been developed. The greatest possible use of the railroad by a traveler would have been a trip from Boston to the South. He would have started with a railroad to Stonington, Connecticut, a steamer to New York, and another to Jersey, after which a railroad to either Camden or Philadelphia was possible. From Philadelphia he could journey by rail to Baltimore and Washington, but he might prefer steamers on the Delaware and Chesapeake, with a short railroad connection between Newcastle and Frenchtown. A steamship was necessary from Washington to forty miles down the Potomac, from which point a railroad ran to Wilmington, North Carolina. Then came a stage trip to Charleston, after which he might go once more by railroad to the end of the track at Hamburg, opposite Augusta, Georgia.

If eastern railroads were hardly everything that their enthusiastic backers had promised, western railroads were even less satisfactory. The few short lines, largely in the Northwest, frequently ran from nowhere to nowhere, and were so poorly constructed that they soon began to fall to pieces. A traveler of 1845 described the longest Illinois line: "This rail-road . . . is another of the links of that endless chain that was to bind the State in love together, but has bound them in debt forever. It is already so dilapidated that mules have been substituted for locomotives, and as it fails to pay expenses, it must shortly go out of use for want of repairs."[2]

The building of railroads in America during the eighteen thirties should be rated as something near a miracle. With most technical problems unsolved, Americans went ahead blithely and hopefully in a tremendously large country sparsely populated. Whereas European cities were practically within stone's throw of each other, with plentiful traffic waiting for the taking, American cities were small and far apart. A road from New York to Boston would have spanned England from coast to coast, while no project in contemporary Europe was comparable to a railroad from Albany to Buffalo.

Railroads required large investments, for with track building at ten to sixty thousand dollars a mile, one million dollars did not

[2] Kellar, *Robinson*, I, 417.

go far. And where were these millions to come from? Bankers and other conservative men of substance tended to be cautious, even when appeals were made to their local pride; they were quite willing to act as directors, but not usually enthusiastic about large investments. Since railroads generally were corporations, they could appeal to every civic-minded citizen for subscriptions. Names were easy to obtain if no down payments were required, but when the first fine enthusiasm abated and the going became rough, real money was scarce—particularly since stock could ordinarily be bought on the open market for a fraction of the subscription price.

The one resource, when everything else failed, was to call upon the government, and while the federal government under Jackson was generally unresponsive, other governmental units were more amenable to the desires of hopeful voters. A dozen states made surveys, loaned money, bought stock, and even did outright building; sometimes they provided for ultimate government ownership and operation, and always they recognized their power to control rates. Counties, cities, and towns also made their contributions, by the purchase of stock or the giving of rights of way and of depot and wharf facilities.

Investors might well have been exceedingly skeptical in view of the fact that even simple technical matters such as maximum curvatures and grades were still open to dispute. A general opinion existed that no curve should have a radius of over one thousand feet and no grade should rise faster than thirty-five to fifty feet a mile, but there were people who disagreed. Even with these specifications the light equipment got into trouble. Trains would jump the tracks on the curves, engines would have their wheels spin on the grades; where the removal of a steep grade was too expensive, the cars would be hauled up and down by a stationary engine.

Tracks had the dubious benefits of varied guesses. The ordinary plan of the early days was a series of little pits filled with crushed rocks, on which were placed the sleepers and then the rails. Some roads emphasized permanence by planting granite piles on which the rails were pegged; they achieved the desired permanence, but a ride on such a roadbed in a springless coach practically jarred out the passengers' eyeteeth. In the southern swamps the roads were balanced on wooden piles, which at times were elaborated into miles of trestles; such construction produced a resiliency that was sometimes embarrassing when a train would plunge through rotten timbers. One ingenious radical suggested a single overhead track, with the cars suspended in pairs like saddlebags. The experimental period of roadbed making was actually short, with the modern type of roadbed in common use by the end of the decade.

The track itself was far from standardized in either width or composition. Track widths of from three to six feet made impossible any interchange of cars. The earliest tracks were wood, which were soon improved by spiking iron strips along the top. All-iron rails were customary by the end of the decade. Of the eight shapes in common use, the heaviest weighed fifty-four pounds to the yard. Every early railroad planned a double track, but actually only the Baltimore and Ohio attained this goal. Other roads made their beds wide enough for two tracks, but temporarily made shift with spaced sidings. During the early days, when private wagons were permitted, teamsters raced for the sidings and then fought over the right of precedence.

The first motive power was the easily available horse. Here is the primitive Baltimore and Ohio: "The vehicle was of a description somewhat novel. It was, in fact, a wooden house or chamber, somewhat like those used by itinerant showmen in England, and was drawn by a horse at the rate of about four miles an hour. Our progress, therefore, was not rapid, and we were nearly three hours in reaching a place called Ellicott Mills, where we found a wretched breakfast awaiting our arrival."[3] Ingenious Americans soon had other ideas, and tried sails, a treadmill and horse, and a winch worked by men, dogs, or horses. None of these proved satisfactory.

Very early in railroad history, men began to speculate about the possible use of steam power, even though the comments were often neither favorable nor very realistic. The *Illinois Monthly* of October, 1830, was somewhat supercilious: "Even if the art of flying should be invented, who would endure the trouble of wearing a pair of wings and the labor of flapping them, when every gentleman may keep his own 'locomotive' and travel from the Mississippi to

[3] Hamilton, *Men and Manners*, 288.

the Atlantic with no other expenditure than a teakettle of water and a basket of chips!"[4]

The steam locomotive came early, but was often a dubious advantage. A few engines from England were too heavy for American tracks and too expensive for American pocketbooks. The first American-built locomotive, Peter Cooper's "Tom Thumb," was put into service on the Baltimore and Ohio in 1830; it consisted of an upright boiler placed on a flat car, and the story goes that it raced with a horse and lost. Best of the early models was the "De Witt Clinton," built at the famous West Point Foundry for the Mohawk and Hudson, which started to use it in 1831. Weighing six tons and having a horizontal boiler with thirty copper tubes, it had a maximum speed of thirty miles an hour; it remained in service for fourteen years.

Locomotives improved rapidly, with the counterbalancing of wheels, the eight-wheel engine, headlights, equalizing lever, locomotive cabs, steam whistles, and cowcatchers among the improvements. The engines could be heavier as the track became better, and Matthias Baldwin boasted that one of his engines could climb the Philadelphia inclined plane at full speed with a full load. Wood was the almost universal fuel, although some experiments were made with coal under a forced draft. The resulting showers of sparks helped persuade many cities to keep steam engines off their streets.

Early passenger cars were naturally modeled on the stagecoach, even to the use of the roof. One traveler commented: "The carriages we were in held twelve people very uncomfortably."[5] Luckily some of the more ingenious suggestions were never followed—for instance, an extra set of wheels for road travel, large wheels with the axles on the roof, or an engine for each car.

The stagecoach pattern soon gave way to a canal-boat type—an oblong box, with platforms at each end, designed to hold some sixty people. "The windows ... form the walls on each side of the carriage, which looks like a long greenhouse upon wheels; the seats, which each contain two persons (a pretty tight fit, too), are placed down

[4] Mott, *Magazines*, 467.

[5] F. A. Kemble, *Records of a Girlhood* (New York, Henry Holt and Company, 1879), 560.

the whole length of the vehicle, one behind the other, leaving a species of aisle in the middle for the uneasy (a large portion of the traveling community here) to fidget up and down, for the tobacco-chewers to spit in, and for a whole tribe of little itinerant fruit and cake-sellers to rush through, distributing their wares at every place where the train stops."[6]

Democratic Americans disapproved of any special privileges, so each traveler took his chances with a seat and a traveling companion. The only exception was for the weaker and gentler sex, who were sometimes provided with a partitioned part of the coach. Reputedly such a compartment was "carpeted and in every respect beautifully furnished with wide and convenient sofas, dressing table, washstand and other arrangements for the comfort of passengers."[7]

The usual railroad car was no model of luxury. Ventilation was confined to the blasts that came from open doors, since the showers of sparks and soot from the engine soon reduced clothes to dirty sieves if the windows were opened. Heat in the winter came from a red-hot stove that sizzled satisfactorily when it was hit with tobacco juice; the passengers near it roasted, while those at the other end of the car froze. Light was provided by a single oil lamp, and the fore-sighted traveler who wanted to read provided his own illumination. The only specialized equipment was the sleeping car, with bunks in place of seats, and a basin and towel at one end. At first the bedding was provided by the passenger, but in time the railroad supplied it; as on a canal boat or steamboat, covers were dumped on the floor during the day.

Special freight equipment also came slowly—partly because no one expected the railroad to carry much bulky material. The four cars of prize stock hauled to the Syracuse fair in 1841 caused excited comment. Small parcels, however, were early a matter of railroad concern, being put into the care of the conductor—and incidentally no early trainman wore a "servile" uniform. Various men such as William F. Harnden and Alvin Adams saw profit in the business. At first they carried the parcels, then rented space in the baggage car,

---

[6] Kemble, *Later Life*, 105.

[7] Quoted in S. Withington, *The First Twenty Years of Railroads in Connecticut* (New Haven, Yale University Press, 1935), 11–12.

and finally rented complete cars. Both Harnden and Company and Adams and Company were doing prosperous business by 1840. Later they combined as the Adams Express Company.

Mail was a concern of even the first railroads; and in 1833 all railroads were made post roads. This development was not an occasion for universal rejoicing. People complained loudly and bitterly that much mail arrived late or not at all, while even prompt deliveries came no faster than by stage. In time the railroads became more reliable and faster, even saving time by sorting the mail en route.

Travelers often felt that the speed of the new railroads was breath-taking. One, upon riding out of Albany, wrote that he was "hurried along with a rapidity that is inconceivable to one so inexperienced as myself, and in rather less than an hour we reached Schenectady, a distance of sixteen miles."[8] Davy Crockett insisted that "I can only judge of the speed by putting my head out to spit, which I did, and overtook it so quick, that it hit me smack in the face."[9]

Actually the locomotives were disappointingly slow. Schedules assumed with unjustifiable optimism an average speed of some fifteen to twenty miles an hour, but apparently only the Boston and Lowell averaged as much as twenty, which was worth newspaper headlines. Slowness was the result of poor engines and equipment, of the weather, of waiting for passengers, and of stopping when someone wanted a sandwich or a drink. Many people were alarmed at the possibility of greater speeds. *Niles' Register* of 1830 quoted with approval an English comment that "With proper caution this [twenty-two miles an hour] or something a little greater may be attempted, but till we have bones of brass or iron, or better methods of protecting them than we have now, it is preposterous to talk of 50 or 60 miles an hour as a practicable thing."[10]

A railroad was costly to build and expensive to operate, and hauled little freight. The obvious result was high rates—in many places the highest of any form of transportation. Government-set

[8] R. A. Benton (ed.) "A Trip to Niagara in 1835: Miss Caroline Spencer's Journal," in *Magazine of American History*, Vol. XXII (October, 1889), 332.

[9] D. Crockett, *The Autobiography of David Crockett* (New York, Charles Scribner's Sons, 1923), 154.

[10] *Niles Register*, Vol. XXXVII (January 16, 1830), 338.

rates varied from three to six cents a passenger-mile and from seven to ten cents a ton-mile for freight. Five cents was an ordinary passenger rate, with a few rates as low as three cents. Even these charges rarely produced a profit; expanding roads gave an optical illusion of profits by publishing earnings of their best weeks in contrast to their running expenses. With the general depression of the end of the decade, many incomplete roads were not even earning running expenses and necessary repairs.

High costs and low speeds were only part of the drawbacks of train travel. The rumble, the swaying and jolting, the many stops, the fumes, the heat, the hissing of steam, the showers of sparks, the lack of ventilation, the uncomfortable seats, and the all-pervading filth were hardly offset by the possibilities of buying fruit, candy, and other refreshments. Many a traveler complained that "my journeys on it were by far the most fatiguing of any I underwent in the country."[11] The one indisputable advantage was novelty.

Rarely did a railroad trip pass without delay. Hours would be spent waiting for belated travelers or for a connecting train. Other hours might be lost waiting on a siding until a horseback rider could be sent to locate the other train. A locomotive might collapse; if it were not too far from the station, it was pushed back. An engine or car that jumped the tracks might be lifted back by the passengers. Rain, sleet, snow, or grasshoppers slowed or stopped the service. A train might try a grade half a dozen times before conceding defeat, whereupon the passengers headed for the nearest house for the night. Such troubles were accepted philosophically. No one planned within several hours when a train would arrive.

Delays were exasperating, but the many accidents were more serious. Fire was a perpetual menace. Sparks made roof seats untenable, started small blazes in the upholstery and in passengers' clothes if the windows were open, and sometimes ignited the baggage which was ordinarily stacked on a flat car and covered with tarpaulin. The inventors speculated about a smokestack that either bent down to the ground or that passed over all the cars to the end of the train, but no real improvement came until the introduction of coal for fuel.

[11] Martineau, *Society*, II, 8.

More serious accidents came from poor equipment, the lack of signaling devices (limited to a few semaphore towers), or just plain carelessness. Engines exploded, trains collided or ran off the track, wheels and axles broke, bridges collapsed, and cars broke loose. Trains hit cows, horses, pedestrians, sleighs, and carriages. Fortunately, the equipment was light and the speed slow, so fatalities were not very frequent.

The various drawbacks of rail travel, however, limited the enthusiasm of at least a few Americans. Most people recognized what seemed to them the obvious fact that railroads could never compete with navigable waters, but could act only as feeders and connecting links. They agreed that "there is no doubt of the establishment of this means of communication over nearly the whole of the United States, within a few years, as by-ways to the great high-ways which Nature has made to run through this vast country."[12]

Here and there an elderly reactionary rejected railroads completely, protesting violently against their speed and accidents, and connecting them in his mind with other undesirable departures from a more leisurely and courtly age. Philip Hone confided to his diary: "This world is going too fast. Improvements, Politics, Reform, Religion—all fly. Railroads, steamers, packets, race against time and beat it hollow. Flying is dangerous. By and by we shall have balloons and pass over to Europe between sun and sun. Oh, for the good old days of heavy post-coaches and speed at the rate of six miles an hour!"[13]

The reactionaries were more than counterbalanced by the visionary progressives who saw no limits to railroad possibilities. As early as 1829, the year in which the first few miles of railroad were opened in the United States, men had speculated on a railroad to the Mississippi. At a Faneuil Hall meeting of 1837, called to push the Western Railway, Abbott Lawrence was quoted as saying: "Mr. Everett, we shall live to see the banks of the upper Mississippi connected by iron bands with State Street," to which Everett countered: "Don't talk, Sir, of Buffalo: talk of the Falls of St. Anthony and the Council Bluffs."[14] One must remember that when these comments were

[12] *Ibid.*, II, 12.
[13] Nevins, *Hone Diary*, II, 722.

"Beverwyck," the residence of W. P. Van Rensselaer,
Rensselaer, New York; Frederic Diaper, architect, 1839-43

"Andalusia," the residence of Nicholas Biddle
at Andalusia, Pennsylvania; designed by Thomas
V. Walter and Nicholas Biddle, 1834

delivered, neither St. Paul nor Council Bluffs had any white inhabitants.

But the ultimate railroad speculation was even wilder. In 1831 the editor of *Niles' Register* commented sarcastically that "a railroad across the Rocky Mountains may soon enter into the speculations of the enterprising people of the 'far west!' "[15] Within four years Samuel Parker wrote from South Pass: "A railroad might be made from the Atlantic to the Pacific Ocean,"[16] and other men supported this presumably fantastic notion. Oddly enough, many of these people lived to see the completion of such a line.

The truth was that "the American has a perfect passion for railroads."[17] Frequently their passion had no reasonable bounds, for railroads were projected in reckless amounts until their proposed lines laced together the entire United States. And railroads were but typical of the spirit of the American people. "The Americans are impetuous in the way of improvement, and have all the impatience of children about the trying of a new thing, often greatly retarding their own progress by hurrying unduly the completion of their works, or using them in a perilous state of incompleteness."[18] This criticism was well justified, and yet it was completely misleading. The unreasonable American enthusiasm actually produced the things it desired. The impractical idealists were right, and the practical realists were wrong.

[14] P. R. Frothingham, *Edward Everett Orator and Statesman* (Boston, Houghton Mifflin Company, 1925), 141.

[15] *Niles Register*, Vol. XL (June 18, 1831), 285.

[16] A. B. and D. P. Hulbert (eds.), *Marcus Whitman, Crusader* (2 vols., Colorado Springs, Stewart Commission, 1936), I, 101.

[17] M. Chevalier, *Society, Manners and Politics in the United States* (Boston, Weeks, Jordan and Company, 1839), 307.

[18] Kemble, *Later Life*, 104.

PART III : AT HOME

12. Homes and Hotels

AMERICAN LIFE was mobile. Even concerning his home the American felt no permanence. He thought of his house not as a potential ancestral mansion to be cherished and improved from generation to generation, but as the outward sign of his existing wealth and social status. He was always hoping for a more impressive residence that would correspond more satisfactorily with his estimate of his own importance. Moving day (May 1 in New York) found city streets so cluttered with movers and trash that other traffic was almost halted. And houses themselves were evanescent. If they did not burn, they were reconstructed or moved to another site or razed to clear the way for more imposing edifices.

The usual house was the wooden product of the skill of local carpenters unrestrained by an architect. Richer city dwellers could afford brick or stone. A novelty in building materials was concrete, which was praised as "unaffected by the action of the weather."[1] Even more modern were the prefabricated houses ("ready made Houses"[2]) shipped to Texas.

The better city home of brick or stone was at least as standardized as the canal boat. Inevitably narrow and deep to fit the city lot, its long, dark, carpeted halls gave access to the various rooms. On the first floor were living room, dining room, and kitchen, although Philadelphia preferred a basement kitchen. On the second floor were probably a more-used sitting room, a "library" without many books, and a bedroom. The third floor was devoted to bedrooms.

---

[1] University of Michigan, *Regents' Proceedings 1837–1864* (Ann Arbor, University of Michigan, 1915), 138.

[2] E. C. Barker (ed.), *The Austin Papers* (3 vols., Austin, University of Texas, 1927), II, 697.

Servants' quarters were in the attic, and the nursery was in the basement, which was really a half-story.

Just around the corner from the city mansion might be a number of cheap wooden houses of artisans, while within a stone's throw might be the meanest of shacks or tenements. An old brewery might house a hundred families separated only by the flimsiest of wooden partitions. Even a damp and unlighted cellar might be tenanted by dozens of human rats. Such a building might well flare into one great torch or topple of its own weight, burying its unhappy occupants. Public apathy provided an effective block for building restrictions, rent laws, or model housing.

The most magnificent country dwelling was the rambling southern plantation mansion which was just beginning to receive literary glorification. "The rooms are large, and decorated with a profusion of wood work, chiseled into the gorgeous forms of ancient pomp. The doors have large pediments above them, with figures carved upon the entablatures; garlands of roses, as stiff as petrifactions, are moulded, with a formal grace, upon the jambs of the window-frames; and the mantle-pieces are thickly embossed with odd little mythological monsters, as various as the metamorphoses of Ovid. The walls are enriched with a fretted cornice, in the frieze of which cupids, satyrs and fauns are taking hands, and seem to be dancing country-dances through thickets of nondescript vegetables. The fireplaces are noble monuments of ancient hospitality, stately and vast, and on either side of them are deep recesses, surmounted by ornamental arches, and lighted by windows that look out from the gable-ends of the building."[3]

More modest farm homes ranged from the plain and neat New England farmhouse to the western log cabin, which was the most distinctive feature of American architecture. A log cabin was no larger than a fair-sized modern living room, and contained ordinarily a few pegs, rude shelves, simple homemade furniture, beds fastened to the walls, and the necessary utensils. Gentility was guaranteed by muslin curtains and a favorite highboy, rocking chair, or China tea set brought from the East with untold labor. Tacked to

[3] J. P. Kennedy, *Swallow Barn* (2 vols., Philadelphia, Carey and Lea, 1832), I, 257.

the walls were guns, trophies of war, a picture of the President, and a map of the United States, with greasy fingerprints showing the location of the cabin. On the table might be the Bible, Prayer Book, a Milton, a Shakespeare, a religious journal, and the local weekly paper.

The American home—mansion or log cabin—was usually heated by fireplaces. The more modern Franklin wood-burning stove was expensive, and many people believed that it devitalized the air. The very progressive husband bought his wife a kitchen range, which sometimes provided hot water. A few public buildings experimented with central heating, but a basement fireplace with flues to the various rooms permitted most of the heat to escape up the chimney.

Plumbing systems were possible with the new city water systems, but inside running water for bath and toilet was still a luxury for the few. Even a well-to-do bride on her honeymoon found "the luxury of a bath after dancing"[4] worth recording. Most bathing was confined to warm weather, and a stage or canal trip was an olfactory experience, with Americans accused of being the least bathed of any civilized people. Crusaders fought for public baths or portable tubs. Doctors wrote for medical journals on the subject, giving pictures of folding baths with curtains and stoves, for hot or cold baths, steam, or showers.

The busy wife may have kept her house cleaner than her person, but the frequent references to cockroaches, bedbugs, mosquitoes, flies, and other pests produce some doubts. In the South, Negro servants with fans or with cloth-covered frames operated by cords kept the flies off the diners, but elsewhere one fanned with one hand and ate with the other. Spring house cleaning was quite usual, with the wise husband making himself invisible while his wife beat carpets, cleaned stoves, wiped walls and woodwork, washed windows and scrubbed floors. The long-run effects of such efforts, however, were not very successful in the absence of screens and insecticides.

Every house was as highly decorated as the purse of the owner permitted. Although the poorer home might have whitewashed or painted walls, the ideal was rich French wallpaper in gold, silver, velvet, satin, or elaborate pictures, always with a border. Floor cover-

[4] Armstrong, *Five Generations*, 183.

ings might be oilcloth or India matting, but the preference was an ingrain, Venetian, Brussels, or Wilton carpet from wall to wall, reinforced by scatter rugs. Draperies included rich curtains of satin, damask, moreen, or muslin in varied colors, plus elaborate table and piano covers.

The downstairs living room was held inviolate for special guests, weddings, and funerals. Curtains remained drawn to save the carpets, and the only regular visitor was the housewife, who weekly dusted the various curios with which the room was cluttered, and the impressive furniture, which frequently was too uncomfortable for daily use. The rich family gathered regularly in the second-floor sitting room, and the poor family in the kitchen.

Furniture was awe inspiring. Dressers were tremendous, wardrobes had huge cornices, four-posters had gigantic posts; and to these monstrosities the prevailing French influence added gimcracks and furbelows. The beautiful colonial furniture had become a sign of poverty, with Windsor chairs relegated to the kitchen. Duncan Phyfe was the pre-eminent New York cabinetmaker, and outfitted many a drawing room for about one thousand dollars; he had no distinctive style, making what people wanted, and making it well.

Walnut and mahogany were becoming scarce and expensive; hence were being replaced by mahogany veneer and cherry; upholstery was usually mohair. A rosewood piano was many a family's most-prized possession. The rocking chair was distinctively American, and eschewed by the "refined" home as a "lazy and ungraceful indulgence."[5] Most Americans apparently preferred comfort to elegance, and rumor had it that rocking chairs even appeared on the judges' benches.

American high, tall-posted beds were feeling the competition of the low Napoleonic bed, but whether high or low, the posts were weighted with acanthus, laurel, or other traditional designs; headboards and footboards were plain, but surmounted by turned pieces of various designs. The "sleigh-bed" had a roll to the headboard and no posts. Ropes sustained the mattress, with the old-fashioned feather bed resisting nobly the accusations that it was uncomfortable and

[5] H. Martineau, *Retrospect of Western Travel* (2 vols., New York, Saunders and Otley, 1838), I, 72.

unhealthy. Other mattresses might be filled with cotton, hair, straw, husks, or southern moss—the last being extremely lumpy. The most adventurous tried air mattresses from England. A sofa bedstead, a sofa by day and a bed by night, was advertised. Apparently pillow covers were unusual.

Room decorations included frequently an unbeveled glass mirror in a heavy and highly decorated gilt frame; very possibly there were pictures in the upper part of the glass. The cheval glass was attaining popularity; some six feet high, it was attached to feet or posts so that it could be adjusted by the user. Every home had at least one clock, and the mantel clock with brass works was replacing the one with wooden works as well as the old banjo clock. The wealthy had a clock case of alabaster, ebony, or agate, loaded with ormolu decorations.

Other gadgets and knicknacks designed to impress the visitor were almost countless. Small decorative tables, portfolios, bronze busts, cameos, alabaster vases, French porcelain baskets, shell-rock boxes, pincushions, boxes mounted with silver, cigar stands, alabaster candlesticks, and other prized possessions were strewn about the house, especially about the parlor, in studied carelessness and profusion. To impress the intellectual, there were the Bible, one or more gift books bound in silk or velvet, a local newspaper, and a magazine or two, frequently religious in tone. To impress the artistic, there were framed steel or copper engravings, and possibly an original painting.

The important rooms were lighted by oil lamps with cotton wicks, but the common tallow candle, together with the better and more expensive wax candle, still flourished, particularly for bedroom use. Beautiful decorative effects were produced by the many-candled girandole or candelabrum; its base might be marble, or glass, or gilded figures such as Washington, Tecumseh, or Paul and Virginia, while the holders were decorated with glass prisms or "lusters." To light such a contraption, the really modern man eschewed a splinter or spill, and even turned up his nose at the old sulphur match that had to be placed in contact with a small vial of phosphorous; he bought the "locofoco" or "lucifer" in strips, and lit them by friction.

The kitchen was often the most attractive room in the house, being the scene of intense domestic activity, and also the warmest. People were boarding up their fireplaces as the kitchen range increased in popularity. An icebox was the creation of a carpenter, who probably had decided views on the best insulation; late in the decade an icebox might be purchased already built. Other kitchen improvements might become as complicated as a steam dishwashing machine. The well-to-do family with a basement kitchen could boast a dumbwaiter and speaking tube.

The diversified kitchen activities of the old-fashioned home were just beginning to feel outside competition. Spinning, weaving, and sewing were slightly less usual, especially in the cities. Tallow candles and soap still were usually homemade, except for the finer toilet soap. The scouring of iron pots and pans with wood ashes or fine sand was but slightly reduced by the new cookstoves. Cooking had declined a trifle with the rise of the bakery.

Most American china was made in England, even though it was frequently decorated with American scenes, public men, buildings, and events. Most people preferred designs in blue, but brown, pink, green, and plum were also considered good. Lusterware was common. Glassware, both pressed and blown, was made in the United States, and opal glass remained popular for candlesticks, lamps, cups, small plates, and doorknobs.

Cutlery also came largely from England. Knives and forks generally were steel with horn handles, although a really fine carving set might have ivory handles. A knife had a broad blade to help the diner who stuck to a single tool, while the less important fork was generally two-pronged. Spoons might more frequently be made of silver, and the rich man might swank a complete silver set, with hundreds of pieces stamped "C" or "D" in a circle, which corresponded to the later "sterling." Silver church plate, tea sets, soup tureens, pitchers, ladles, sugar tongs, snuffers, and candlesticks were among the luxuries which indicated wealth.

The greatest height of luxurious living was provided by the better American hotels, and their sybaritic charms were aped by the well-to-do. Since there were no apartment houses, the bachelor and the married couple who did not want to keep house patronized the hotels. Viewers-with-alarm wept verbally over the modern wives who were unwilling to make homes of their own.

The first really excellent American hotel was Boston's Tremont House, opened in the fall of 1829. Its white marble elegance dominated Tremont Street, and its superiority was so evident that it disdained even a name plate. The high and spacious rooms were decorated with expensive carved-walnut furniture, deep carpets, and rich curtains. The dozen commodious public rooms, some with marble mosaic floors, were adequate for any possible social event. The main dining room seated two hundred, and there was a room devoted entirely to baggage.

The Tremont's many novelties caused even the blasé traveler to widen his eyes in surprise, and to admit that the hotel "merits its reputation as one of the best in the world."[6] Many of its 170 rooms were single rooms, a unique feature, and each had a lock, with no two the same. Not only did each room have the customary bowl, pitcher, and cake of soap, but also "there is in every chamber a nail-brush and a toothbrush."[7] Even more marvelous, the hotel had eight water closets, eight bathing rooms with running water, and gas lights in the public rooms. "Rotunda men" (bellboys) responded to the bells from the various rooms, and a speaking-tube system permitted the guest to call the clerk and order his carriage without leaving his room. All these luxuries could be obtained, American plan, at two dollars a day.

The Tremont was a shining goal toward which other cities strove, and soon there were rival caravansaries. Travelers spoke well of the Mansion House at Philadelphia, the City Hotel at Baltimore, Gadsby's at Washington, Shepherd's at Utica, the St. Charles or St. Louis Exchange at New Orleans, and others. Most celebrated was the Astor House of New York, which was opened in 1836 on Broadway opposite City Hall Park. It boasted of costing one-third more than the Tremont ($400,000), of two more stories (6), and of over twice as many rooms (390). All the distinctive features of the Tre-

[6] Lyell, *Travels 1841–42*, I, 3.

[7] W. R. Thayer, "Count Arese's Visit to Boston, 1837," in *Proceedings of the Massachusetts Historical Society*, Vol. XLIII (1909–10), 91.

mont were reproduced on a larger scale; for example, seventeen bathrooms, including two showers. The Astor had its own gas plant, and a steam pump to force water to the higher floors. For many years it held undisputed leadership among the nation's hotels.

Large hotels were very similar. Bedrooms varied only in being either single or double. The public rooms always included a lobby, a ladies' parlor, a reading room with papers on high desks, and a dining room; they were decorated with French wallpaper showing hunting, marine, or other scenes. Meals were served at stated hours, with the host presiding. Special parties could use smaller dining rooms, but room service was provided only if the guest were sick. Hot water was brought by the bellboy, and running water above the first floor was provided only by the swank establishments. The usual rate was one dollar a day per person, American plan, but the best hotels doubled that rate. With several rooms and other special services a traveler might push his bill as high as three dollars a day, but more was practically impossible.

Small-town hotels were always inferior. The main room was a combined lobby and bar, with the bar getting the major attention. Its usual decorations were a wooden clock, a map of the United States smudged at the location of the tavern, a lookingglass with comb and brush attached by strings, and several pictures—perhaps a wooden-looking Jackson at New Orleans, Washington gesturing over a scroll of paper, and "General Lafayette in a brown wig and greatcoat, looking like a farmer on a cold day."[8]

The guest was only now and then shown to his room, which ordinarily contained one or two double beds, and in which the only privacy came from paper blinds tacked to the window frames. Bedclothes might be missing, in which case a servant was of more use than the landlord, who was probably busy at the bar. With a full house, the traveler would be asked to share his room, and even his bed. Fleas, mosquitoes, and other vermin seemed inevitable. Washing facilities were a basin and pitcher, or possibly only a rusty tin basin; they might not be in the room, but in the corridor, in the bar, or even outside the hotel.

[8] U. Pope-Hennessy (ed.), *The Aristocratic Journey* (New York, G. P. Putnam's Sons, 1931), 50.

Hotel meals were served at stated hours, as at 7:30, 2:00, and 7:00. The opening of the dining-room doors was the signal for a grand rush, and food was gulped in haste, undeterred by the presence of the landlord at the head of the table. Napkins were generally nonexistent, and the guest was free to use the corner of the tablecloth in case of necessity. The bolting of the food may be excused because of its dirt and grease, but the haste in reaching the table is less understandable. At least there was no tipping.

The smaller hotel was often a private house in which the parlor had been transformed into a bar, and in which the spare bedrooms were used for guests. A bedroom would be decorated with some of the family treasures, such as a framed mirror, or a wood engraving of the Declaration of Independence with facsimile signatures, a portrait of the Empress Josephine, an engraving of father, mother, and child weeping over a tombstone engraved with the names of the departed members of the family. The closet might contain the best clothes of the hostess.

Even the poorest of town accommodations seemed luxurious in retrospect as the traveler entered the log-cabin West. Here each room was filled with all the beds it would contain, and only the most modest maiden lady insisted on a bed to herself. With a large crowd, the latecomers slept on benches, tables, or the floor. If possible, the sexes were segregated; but if the inn were crowded, a room might contain a married couple in one bed, two ladies in a second, and two men in a third. Screens were placed only for the most prudish.

Tales of congested sleeping quarters were legion. One late arrival at an Illinois cabin hotel was escorted through "a large Room where the floor was full of sleeping Women, some of them carelessly covered and exposing their beauty; but my entrance did not in the least interfere with their slumbers."[9] He was ushered into a large room with two occupied double beds and climbed into one of them, only to be kept awake by his bedmate's snores. A later arrival —a Jewish peddler—was bedded on the floor.

Hospitality was primitive at these frontier inns. Decorations were seldom more than newspapers covering the walls. A single

[9] A. P. Hannum (ed.), *A Quaker Forty-Niner* (Philadelphia, University of Pennsylvania Press, 1930), 54–58.

common wash basin might be flanked by an ancient piece of yellow soap and a comb and brush on cords, but seldom by a towel. Frequently the guest washed his hands and face in a near-by stream and wiped with his handkerchief; a full bath was rare, and came only in the summer. Food was limited in variety and swimming in grease. Insufficient silverware forced the guests to use a common spoon, dipping out their sugar and stirring their coffee in rotation. Bedclothes were inadequate and dirty. Vermin were everywhere. Prices were relatively high—50 cents to $1.25 a day, including care of a horse.

If there was no regular tavern, the traveler threw himself on the hospitality of the nearest log-cabin owner. Mother, father, sons, daughters, and guests of both sexes were put to bed in the same room, mostly on the floor, and the inevitable embarrassments were a favorite source of contemporary humor. Only the rare traveler objected to such congestion, and in one case the landlady muttered angrily: "Ugh! great people, truly!—a bed to themselves—the hogs!—they travel together—and they eat together—and they eat enough, too—and yet they can't sleep together!"[10]

Americans had many regrettable habits, but epicureanism was not one of them. They ate only to live. Fenimore Cooper loosed the blast that "The Americans are the grossest feeders of any civilized nation known. As a nation, their food is heavy, coarse, ill prepared and indigestible, while it is taken in the least artificial form that cookery will allow. The predominance of grease in the American kitchen, coupled with the habits of hasty eating and of constant expectoration, are the causes of the diseases of the stomach so common in America."[11]

American food was plentiful—"the Americans have very small churches and exceedingly large markets"[12]—but all too often it was badly cooked and lacked variety, while sometimes it was actually spoiled. Adulteration was present everywhere, with the traditional

[10] C. F. Hoffman, *A Winter in the West* (2 vols., New York, Harper and Brothers, 1835), I, 280.

[11] J. F. Cooper, *The American Democrat* (Cooperstown, H. and E. Phinney, 1838), 156.

[12] F. Lieber, *Stranger*, 139.

wooden nutmegs the least of the trouble. Bakery bread at times contained pulverized stones, bone, plaster of Paris, beans, or peas, with alum to make it white and subcarbonate of soda to conceal the spoiled flour. Tea might include various tree leaves colored with poisonous minerals. Diluted or skimmed milk was given body with rice powder or arrowroot. Even without such adulterants any product might be tainted with the filth occasioned by human carelessness.

Even more distressing, because more easily corrected, was the bad cooking—"if the devil send cooks to any part of the world, it is to the United States."[13] Completely unforgivable was the frequent serving of rancid butter and fish, sour bread without salt, and black joints of lamb. Meat was said to come "direct from the shambles to the spit."[14] Ham or rice or potatoes would appear at meal after meal in the same form, while turnip greens in season would be almost as permanently present as pepper and salt.

The lack of variety was partly inevitable, but partly a lack of cooking imagination. Costly transportation and primitive preserving processes limited the common menu. Meat could be only salted or dried and eggs packed in limewater. Onions could be kept in a cold, dry room, and some vegetables, such as turnips and carrots, could be buried in sand. Jellies could be kept because of the sugar, and catsup because of the spices. Other preserving was largely impossible; hence the diet was narrowly limited for a good part of the year. But too many people, particularly in the South and West, lived on corn bread and sowbelly ("corn bread and common fixings") the year round. The epicure bemoaned particularly the failure to exploit such distinctive and delicious delicacies as tomatoes, eggplant, corn on the cob, Virginia fried chicken, and New England clam or fish chowder. As one of them said, "For many years I have never undergone such gastronomical privations, as in the western parts of America."[15]

Most distressing was the American penchant for grease, in which everything seemed to swim. Visitors protested bitterly "the national propensity for grease. . . . It enters largely into the composition of

---

[13] Hamilton, *Men and Manners*, 210–11.
[14] *Ibid.*
[15] Saxe-Weimar, *Travels*, II, 128.

every dish, and constitutes the sole ingredient of many. The very bread is, generally, not only impregnated with some unctious substance, but when sent up to the breakfast table, is seen to float in . . . oleaginous matter."[16]

Since most housewives learned their cooking from their mothers, and since the mothers seemed to prefer grease and monotony, progress was slow. Even the current cookbooks were of little help, since their references to a hot oven, a pinch of mustard, salt to taste, or butter the size of an egg were fairly useless to anyone but an expert cook. Some of the recipes sound incredible. The *House-Keeper's Book* of 1838[17] advised a quarter-pound of coffee for each three people; the coffee should be added gradually to boiling water and allowed to simmer gently for an hour, after which it should be permitted to settle and then be decanted. Whether the resulting brew was drunk or eaten was not stated, but the aversion of many foreigners to American coffee is understandable.

Not the least of the hurdles for the fastidious diner was his immediate surroundings. Many Americans ate everything from oysters to peas with a knife, swallowing half of the knife with each bite, to the awed amazement of the uninitiated. Even at home napkins were rare, and tablecloths seldom spotless. Americans were sloppy eaters, so that by the end of a meal the table was strewn with spots from everything on the menu, together with scraps of discarded food. At this point each man plied his toothpick—possibly a sliver of wood, but perhaps a penknife or silver toothpick for the more aristocratic. Then he inserted a fresh cud and looked for a spitting box, which he generally missed.

Whether a meal was in the poorest home or the most gorgeous hotel, people grabbed the food within reach, and gulped it in what would have been silence had it not been for the champing of jaws. Within fifteen minutes, even a large hotel crowd would be back in the lobby, leaving only a few scraps to be gummed by those with bad teeth. " 'I'll be d—d,' said one man, 'if ever I saw a Yankee that didn't bolt his food whole like a Boa Constrictor. How the devil can you expect to digest food, that you neither take the trouble to

[16] Hamilton, *Men and Manners*, 210–11.
[17] (Philadelphia, W. Marshall and Company, 1838), 110–11.

Feminine fashions in the 1830's
From *The Lady's Book*, January, 1832

dissect, nor time to masticate? It's no wonder that you lose your teeth, for you never use them; nor your digestion, for you overload it; nor your saliva, for you expend it on the carpets, instead of your food. It's disgusting, it's beastly.' "[18] A deliberate eater brought the surprised American comment that you "eat as if you actually enjoyed your food!"[19]

Celerity of eating can be blamed only partly on the lack of attractiveness of the food. Americans really felt themselves in a hurry, for there was so much to be done and so little time. Of more immediate importance was the fact that all the food was put on the table at once, which meant that the great advantage lay with the first arrival, particularly if he had long arms and a big bite.

Meals were served at stated hours, but these hours varied from class to class and from region to region. Working people had breakfast and supper fixed by their hours of labor; the big meal of the day, dinner, came about noon. People of more leisurely pursuits had breakfast between 7:00 and 8:00, dinner between 1:00 and 4:00, and supper between 6:00 and 10:00. In general the Northeast ate toward the ends of these periods, while the South and West approached the earlier limits. A few ultrafashionable folk had dinner as late as 5:00 or 6:00, while New Englanders sometimes had tea around 6:00—a custom considered effete by the rest of the country. Frequently the times for meals were changed on Sunday. With the noon dinner, the dinner guest could hardly stay for the evening, although he sometimes remained for tea. An evening party usually included the serving of supper.

Meat was the staple of every American meal, except for the faddish vegetarians. Animal food was generally considered most digestible and charged with greater energy. Religious Americans also argued that God must have created animals for some useful purpose, and that His pleasure was indicated when He gave the Israelites animal food. Very rare was the meal—such as the New Orleans breakfast of coffee, French bread, radishes, and strawberries—which contained no meat.

Common breakfast dishes were potatoes, hung beef, eggs, coffee

[18] T. C. Haliburton, The *Clockmaker* (New York, Leviathan Press, 1927), 61.
[19] Combe, *Notes*, II, 82–83.

or tea, and toast, hot biscuits, or hot cakes, with corn bread in the South and West. Eggs were usually soft-boiled and then turned out into wine glasses. The more elaborate breakfaster might have anything the larder contained. Supper duplicated breakfast, except that porridge was common. When eaten fashionably late, this meal included more choice delicacies and large quantities of wine. "Tea" might include coffee and tea, ices, creams and jellies, preserves, pickled oysters, cakes, candies, fruits, and various wines.

The big meal of the day embraced everything the locality afforded, the family purse could encompass, and the housekeeper's imagination could reach, although soup was generally ignored. The ideal dinner afforded half a dozen meats, which might include ham, pork, beef roast, beef steak, mutton chops, bacon, chicken, turkey, duck, and fresh and pickled fish. Vegetables came with the season— asparagus, lettuce, white potatoes, spinach, turnips, radishes, cabbage, corn on the cob, pumpkins, and celery. Such items as cheese, pickles, and oysters might or might not be served as a separate course. Desserts might include pie or other pastry, rice or bread or other pudding, custards, fruits, blanc-mange, and ice cream, the last a particularly favored dish. Often the final course was fruit—not only the common domestic varieties but also such exotic delicacies as pineapples and oranges. Of course the poor family had only a limited number of these foods at any one time.

Poorly cooked food, swimming in grease and gulped in haste, required copious amounts of liquids—not only water, tea, coffee, cocoa, and chocolate, but also stronger and more virile concoctions. Water was taken ordinarily from the rivers and tasted of mud. Tea and coffee were both expensive and poor, while whiskey was comparatively cheap and made the diner forget the lack of tastiness of his food.

People drank liquor not only to wash down their meals, but also to promote business deals, to demonstrate friendship, for their stomach's sake, and just because they enjoyed drinking. Liquor was the easy escape for men harassed by business worries. Bottled optimism made every business succeed—at least until the morning after. The bar, with its vast array of bottles, its warmth, its hum of conversation, and its jovial atmosphere of good cheer, was the center of male conviviality. Each patron usually drank a little more than he should—partly because of the American tradition of "treating."

Apparently the American also did some of his serious drinking at home. "An American, instead of going in a leisure hour to dance merrily at some place of public resort, as the fellows of his class continue to do throughout the greater part of Europe, shuts himself up at home to drink. He thus enjoys two pleasures; he can go on thinking of his business, and can get drunk decently by his own fireside."[20] This comment undoubtedly overemphasizes the frequency of solitary drinking.

The distinctive American drink was whiskey, especially in the South and West, where the annual per capita consumption was said to be five gallons. A distillery soon appeared in each new community, since whiskey was relatively easier to ship than the grain from which it was made. The usual western price of twenty-five cents a gallon kept it within reach of the average family, which could serve it at all meals, and keep a jug and tin cup just inside the door to warm and solace the casual visitor. Real festivities, such as huskings, house raisings, and funerals, brought an easily induced overindulgence.

The favorite American mixed drink was the mint julep, which at this time did not necessarily include whiskey. One recipe called for a dozen sprigs of mint, a spoon of sugar, a third of a glass of peach and common brandy, and fine-cut ice to fill the glass, with a suggestion of pineapple along the edge. The resulting drink may well have been a princely tipple, but it hardly merited the description of a "mild and refreshing draught,"[21] particularly when served, in accordance with the old Virginia custom, to each guest before breakfast.

There were many other drinks. Brandy was distilled from native fruits and sold for about twice as much as whiskey. Gin had wide but small sales, cognac was available, and West Indies rum was popular in New England. Beer, porter, and ale, frequently adulterated and sometimes iced, were widely available. Cider, either soft or hard, seemed to be losing popularity.

[20] Tocqueville, *Democracy*, II, 271.
[21] Hoffman, *Winter in West*, II, 266.

The preferred dinner wines were Madeira and then claret, both reported good. Sherry was less popular, and port was rare; in fact, port was drunk ordinarily as a medicine, and was reported poor in quality. The sourer Rhenish and Moselle wines were just rising into favor. Champagne corks popped at many a dinner party, and a New Jersey substitute of turnip juice, brandy, and honey was declared quite palatable. A large dinner party included several wines, and was ended with brandy or another cordial, which in the South was drunk by the men after the women had left the table. As sobriety lessened, the vigor of the conversation increased.

Tobacco was the frequent companion of liquor. The "segar" was the common male smoke, with here and there a woman trying one of the smaller sizes. Most cigars came from Cuba, and included such well-known brands as Pelion, Silva, and Dosamygos. Cigarets had not yet arrived from the Spanish Southwest. Pipe smoking was but moderately popular, although it could be seen among the older women of rural areas. Some of the old-timers still used snuff, but the snuffbox was definitely on the way to becoming an antique.

The well-nigh universal male use of tobacco was for chewing, for "the air of heaven is not in more general use among the men of America than chewing tobacco."[22] Every store sold it, every male cheek contained its cud, and rumor held that each southern belle carried a "pigtail" in colored paper to refresh her swain if his own supply failed. The chewing would have been more endurable if the men had been even moderately considerate in dispensing with their surplus saliva and tobacco juice. They sprayed it over bars, restaurants, stores, hotels, streets, railway carriages, canal boats, legislative halls, parlors, and churches. Even the neat and cleanly Shakers had "spitting boxes" which the chewers missed with the greatest regularity, while a ministerial convention might ruin the ladies' best carpets.

Spitting was particularly objectionable at a mixed social gathering, where "the gentlemen spit, talk of elections and the price of produce, and spit again."[23] Even a tolerant lady might have been re-

[22] F. Trollope, *Domestic Manners of the Americans* (2 vols., London, Whittaker, Treacher and Company, 1832), I, 161.

sentful when her waltzing partner spat directly in front of her, so that the juice trickled down over the flounces of her floor-length dress. A crowded stagecoach was likewise an unfortunate place for the tobacco chewer; "being generally drunk, he spat right and left in the coach, and especially after dark, discharged volleys of saliva, utterly reckless of consequences."[24]

Americans who objected to the use of tobacco seldom mentioned the spitting evil. They argued most vigorously on the proposition that tobacco dulled the senses and sapped physical vigor. Typical was the story of the two students who tried to see how much they could smoke; after eighteen pipefuls, one of them fell dead. Or the perennial story of the vigorous young man who fell a slave to tobacco, dwindled to a shadow, and finally committed suicide.

Earnest young men formed antitobacco societies, signed pledges, and worked to save others. They wanted government prohibition, at least of the use of tobacco on the public streets. A typical pledge read: "We, the subscribers, believing that the habitual use of tobacco is not only useless, but greatly injurious, do hereby pledge ourselves that we will not use the same in smoking, chewing, or snuffing (except when recommended by a physician), and that in all suitable ways we will discourage the use of the same in the community."[25] Equally earnest young women passed resolutions against "this vile and poisonous weed,"[26] and pledged themselves to refuse their company to men who used it.

> 'Tis a curse to the soil, 'tis a worm to the purse;
> For the breath it is bad—for the character, worse;—
> Abjure it,—or live among barbarous tribes,
> That Beauty abhors and that Fashion proscribes.[27]

[23] *Ibid.* (1912 edition), III, 523.

[24] Hamilton, *Men and Manners*, 291.

[25] *Western Christian Advocate* (Cincinnati), October 10, 1834, p. 94.

[26] *American Magazine of Useful and Entertaining Knowledge*, Vol. I (July, 1835), 496, quoted in Mott, *Magazines*, 474.

[27] Holbrook, *Sketches*, 315.

13. Women

"AMERICAN WOMEN are the prettiest in the whole world"[1] rhapsodized a long succession of devotees to female beauty, but not without dissenters who reported pasty faces, sloping shoulders, "their busts not sufficiently developed,"[2] and "Devilish Big Feet."[3] Only the most churlish curmudgeon could denounce them as "*All* deformed & unhealthy looking."[4] Such male observations were based presumably on only the upper tier of the feminine form, since prevailing fashions shrouded the lower two-thirds in almost complete mystery.

The ideal of womanly beauty was youth, freshness, pallor, and languor. Most poetically beautiful to the age was a young and innocent maiden who faded into an early consumptive grave before experience had robbed her of her innocence. Languid pallor indicated little sun and less exercise. A true lady might make beds and sweep floors, but other bodily activity should be little more than a short, unhurried stroll. The most vigorous sport permitted a woman "conformably with the preservation of her feminine character for grace and delicacy"[5] was horseback riding, and even in this sport several New York women almost caused a riot by riding without corsets. Youth and freshness meant an age of less than thirty, since lack of exercise, overwork, frequent childbearing, and improper food and clothing caused women to become drawn and haggard early, quite different from the interesting delicacy considered so attractive in young girls.

[1] Marryat, *Diary*, 39.

[2] Lieber, *Stranger*, 80.

[3] Armstrong, *Five Generations*, 343.

[4] Smith, *Journal*, 10.

[5] I. G. Rosenstein, *Theory and Practice of Homeopathy* (Louisville, Hinkle and Logan, 1840), 178.

Women's clothes were designed for beauty rather than for comfort or health. The prime mark of gentility was the small waist produced by the current armor of cloth and whalebone. A favorite technique was for the lady to tie her corset strings to a bedpost, expel her breath, and walk as far away as possible. The results were considered esthetically pleasing, but were anathema to a legion of reformers, who fulminated against these "libels upon the great Creator's most wonderful contrivance, the human frame."[6] Scathing denunciations were widely printed, being particularly virulent in the medical and educational journals; the women's magazines raised more feeble outcry. Anticorset societies dotted the country and even the poets broke into print:

Song of the Corset[7]

The beautiful girls, with their sunbright curls,
Submit to my pressure sly,
Till the hectic streak and the sunken cheek
Proclaim the destroyer nigh! ...
Oh, she soon will feel that my suicide steel
Must stifle her panting breath!
That the sable pall must o'ershadow all
In CONSUMPTION and pain and death!

The corset crusade met trouble when it appeared in lectures, for there was grave doubt about the propriety of public discussion of feminine undergarments and bodily functions. The sedate *Boston Medical Journal* held that such lectures presented to a mixed audience were "so revolting to any one not wholly lost to a sense of delicacy and common propriety, that for the honor of the medical character we hope that there will never be a repetition of these popular lectures on the evils of tight lacing."[8] Whether the lectures impaired the morals of the auditors is uncertain, but they had no visible effect on the evil they denounced.

[6] Kemble, *Later Life*, 23.
[7] *Mirror*, Vol. XI (October 5, 1833), 111, quoted in Mott, *Magazines*, 477.
[8] *The Boston Medical and Surgical Journal*, Vol. XII (July 1, 1835), 337.

An American woman was well dressed—whether the leisured rich or the Irish maid on her day off. Silks, up-to-the-minute hats, fine gloves, elegant parasols, and lace veils were exclusive to no one class. Parisian styles were watched eagerly by city dressmakers, who were copied by country seamstresses and by women who made their own clothes, for "the French mode dominates in the United States."[9]

A formal evening dress aped the hourglass. It might be made of any rich material such as silk, crepe, satin, or fine muslin, and be any color of the rainbow. Above the constricted waist was a tight bodice which displayed large areas of the "neck"—a modest description of the part of the anatomy which necessarily emerged plentifully for public inspection. Necklines might be square or V-shaped or straight, so that the entire shoulders emerged. Early in the decade, sleeves were leg-of-mutton, flared with whalebone, buckram, or even down pillows. Later the tight French sleeves made the wearer of an old dress uncomfortably aware of the inflated bags on her arms.

Compensating the abbreviated bodice was a voluminous skirt which hung between the shoetops and the floor. The slight bustle used late in the decade was practically lost in the draperies. The material saved in the bodice appeared in skirt decorations—flounces, ruffles, fringes, painted figures, and embroidery. Most striking were the velvet bands in contrasting colors and decorated with yards of embroidery. And then there was the "Lace—lace—lace, wherever it can be stuck on. The gowns have lace trimmings and falls—spencers, shawls, caps, bonnets, handkerchiefs; all have lace."[10]

Milady's dress needed little foundation above the waist and a great deal below. Underwear consisted of vest and drawers of fine cambric, muslin, or wool. Then, of course, came the corset and corset cover, followed by flocks of petticoats—flannel in the winter and muslin or other lighter cloth in the summer. Stockings were of wool, cotton, or open-work silk in any color, but white was preferred. They were visible only with a strong wind, a high coach step, or some unfortunate accident. Everyday shoes were of black leather and high, but a party brought forth low-heeled slippers or sandals, often

[9] Pierson, *Tocqueville*, 364.
[10] *Godey's Lady's Book* (Philadelphia), September, 1839, 141.

fastened with ribbons across the ankles. The color was optional, but was usually black or white, and the common materials were satin, morocco, or kid. High-heeled shoes came into vogue late in the decade.

A hat was a massive affair with a coal-scuttle effect both fore and aft. If not of straw, it was a silk- or satin-covered frame. Elaborate trimmings included varicolored ribbons, bunches of flowers, feathers, or whatever other bright material the milliner or wearer could imagine. Late in the decade the small Victorian bonnet began to gain favor.

Cold weather might find the lady decked in a pelisse; very smart was a white merino pelisse trimmed with chinchilla, with a cap to match. Or she might sport a long coat, possibly with collar and cuffs faced with heavily embroidered velvet. With such a coat she would probably wear a tippet and carry a large muff—ermine if she were wealthy. If the weather were wet, India-rubber–coated shoes or overshoes, a rubber-covered coat, and the very popular umbrella were necessities. In the summer she carried a small lined parasol, decorated with checks or figures, more for appearance than for shade.

Hairdressing was a real problem unless a woman could afford a male or female hairdresser the afternoon before a party. The hair was generally piled high—some said to expose the higher phrenological characteristics in the front of the head and to conceal the animal passions in the rear. Cascades of curls decorated the sides and occasionally the top, while surplus back hair was sometimes caught in a net. Missing hair could be supplied by detachable bunches, curls, top pieces, or even complete wigs. Gray hair—premature, of course —could be dyed with a hair "restorer" under a trade name such as Essence of Tyre, or Kimball's Komegan or Generative Curling Fluid; the only recorded effects were bad. A final decorative touch could be feathers, feather flowers, plumes, flowers, combs, jewels, ribbons, gold and silver hair bands, or sprigs with ruby, emerald, pearl, or turquoise decorations.

Accessories were plentiful. Handkerchiefs might be cambric, crepe, or silk, embroidered in various colors. Gloves were colored kid, silk, or thread, with white kid most popular. Black silk mitts were supposed to make the hands looks smaller. Rings, necklaces, earrings, or serpent bracelets might be supplemented by a gold pencil on a gold chain, eyeglasses, smelling-salts bottle, or a jeweled bouquet holder attached to a finger ring by a gold chain. The general glitter might be made more dazzling by the prodigal strewing of steel spangles and cuttings of quills or tortoise shell more or less promiscuously over the dress.

An infinite array of cosmetics put the final bloom on the rose. Perfumes, which sometimes apparently substituted for bathing, included rose water, oil of amber, cinnamon, orris, peppermint, vanilla, and other common odors, but also dozens of trade-name preparations which are now unidentifiable. Patent remedies promised to make chapped hands and lips smooth, remove freckles, eliminate dandruff, eradicate superfluous hair, and produce lustrous eyebrows or shiny fingernails. Complexions could be glorified with face powder, rouge, and lip salve.

A lady's ordinary daytime dress was a simpler edition of her evening finery. Necks were higher and sleeves longer. Materials were ordinarily gingham, prints, organdy, calico, or muslin. Decorations were slightly less lavish, but included small capes, lace, velvet, berthas, fichus, and flounces. Shawls were popular—camel's hair or cashmere, or possibly velvet or satin, wadded, lined with colored silk, and trimmed with lace. Ornate aprons were very fashionable. Small patches of silk, satin, or cashmere were trimmed freely with black lace and given pockets formed like scallop shells. Best of all was an embroidered muslin apron, lined with pink, blue, lilac, or pale yellow silk, with a lace border.

Lower in the economic scale, party clothes were similar to those of the wealthy, but common garments were much more utilitarian. A farmer's wife with seven children hardly wore an organdy dress and an embroidered silk apron for making tallow candles and scrubbing the floor. Homemade linsey-woolsey garments might be deficient in style, but they were long on wear; while shoes, stockings, and other accessories might be omitted most of the year. At the very bottom of the economic scale, the Negro slave wore the poorest possible material made like a long bag, open at each end and tied in the middle.

Less exciting than female finery was the apparel of the lady's male escort. The men's fashion center was London. Tailors advertised their familiarity with Bond Street and Saville Row, while poor men's wives copied as best they could. In general, men's clothes were very similar to those of today. Only the very elderly and conservative clung to Revolutionary costumes, and when a religious convention in New York in 1835 produced a few men "in black small clothes and shoes, and one or two even with cocked hats,"[11] the occasion merited comment.

A man seldom wore coat, waistcoat, and trousers of the same material. Most coats were broadcloth, in black, blue, or olive or dark green. Summer coats might be linen or gingham in white and brown. The broadcloth frock coat was the proper costume for such formal occasions as weddings and funerals; it was generally, but not always, black. Imagination boggles at the description of a flowered chintz frock coat and a pea-green frock coat with velvet collar—and any coat might be embellished with gold or other ornamental buttons.

Pantaloons were usually cassimere, but might be cord, kersey, satinet, lasting, nankeen, drilling, or ribbed velvet, and were supported by suspenders. If not black, they were generally very light in color. Ordinarily the legs were tight, and strapped under the boots. The fop used whalebone stays to get a perfect fit, and might have his trousers flare a trifle at the bottom.

Waistcoats in satin, silk, velvet, and wool were every color of the spectrum, with green very popular, and they were made resplendent by designs in bright colors. Stocks remained in style, but late in the decade the shirt and cravat were introduced; the collar button was said to be the invention of a distracted wife. False bosoms and collars were cheap substitutes. Underwear was shirt and drawers of unbleached cotton, flannel, or wool, depending on the weather. Shoes seldom fit, whether the ordinary calf, goat, or cowskin brogans or pointed sealskin or morocco pumps. Waterproof mixtures and India-rubber shoes protected against wet weather.

Overcoats, topcoats, surtouts, and pea jackets were made ordinarily of a heavy woolen material such as pilot cloth. White or black beaver hats were giving way slowly to the cheaper silk hat. Straw

[11] Nevins, *Hone Diary*, 1, 159.

hats were either white or a dark mixed color. Handkerchiefs were cotton or linen. Gloves of wool or buckskin protected from the cold, with doeskin worn only for appearance. Currently popular were rings, watch guards, and breast pins as large as half-dollars. The dandy carried a cane with an ivory head. Rainy weather evoked rubber-finished coats and umbrellas, a good umbrella being possibly of blue silk with white stripes, with a handle carved like a dog's head.

The average man of 1830 was smooth shaven, having shaved himself with a straight-edge razor. His hair had been cut by his sister or his wife, since barbershops were only available in the larger towns:

> *To all who have hair or beard to crop*
> *I recommend my shaving shop:*
> *Cheap and luxuriously I trim*
> *The roughest beard on any man's chin.*
> *I cut hair on the newest plan*
> *And charge less than any other man.*[12]

Young blades created a furor with mustaches or long ear locks, which may have had some influence in the revival of whiskers toward the end of the decade after a century of oblivion. Like women, men could obtain "remedies" for baldness, dandruff, and gray hair, but they had the exclusive prerogative of buying products like Pommade Noir, advertised to promote the growth of whiskers and to make them jet black.

A girl was impressed with her female distinctiveness from birth. A little girl was cautioned not to be as boisterous as a little boy, but to be sober and sedate and helpful. She received special training, pursued special occupations, and wore feminine clothes. Although physical sex differences were not mentioned in polite society and lectures and books on sex were considered indecent, the average girl did not need her mother or a doctor to give her a long-delayed statement of the "facts of life." As a member of a large family and surrounded by

[12] *Lynchburg Virginian*, September 2, 1832.

farm animals, she was not dependent on vague and flowery references to bees and flowers, or on the leering remarks of dubious friends. She not only knew how life was produced, but had witnessed the process.

The girl's first half-dozen years were spent at home learning the necessary household arts. Then, if her father could spare the money, she went to school—possibly more than her brothers, since her work at home was less necessary. At twelve to fourteen she finished her common-school education, and then helped her mother or got a job until she was married. A few girls from prosperous families went to finishing school or seminary to absorb French, music, deportment, fancy sewing, painting, and other aids to social success and to luring a husband. After marriage, a young lady might use these accomplishments—perhaps—to amuse herself and her friends.

Americans believed overwhelmingly that coeducation was morally dangerous and that the male mysteries of the classics and mathematics could not be undertaken by women without injury to their delicate natures. The traditionalists insisted that "making puddings and nursing babies . . . must be attended by one sex or the other, and of what use can algebra and other abstruse matters be to a woman in her present state?"[13] The opposition countered by asking the utility of French and of painting on china, but without making many conversions to its radical doctrine.

The most thrilling period of a girl's life was the late teens, when "the sex is most alluring, because we know it to be the most innocent."[14] Formal schooling was past, and the troubles of marriage were in the future. She was young, vigorous, and frequently beautiful. She was comparatively free from the careful chaperonage of contemporary Europe, and received the current American adulation given the pure and ignorant.

American society had a minimum of stilted formality; in fact, some foreigners felt people were overly friendly and "stinking with national conceit."[15] The ruling, self-conscious middle class of the

---

[13] Marryat, *Diary*, 38.
[14] Cooper, *Notions*, 1, 25.
[15] Pierson, *Tocqueville*, 68.

age of Jackson resented any assumption of superiority. President Jackson himself set the tempo with his receptions, which included everyone from the formally clad aristocrat to the roughly dressed farmer who clambered on a gilt chair to view the crowd before helping to mob the refreshments.

Yet the United States had a plethora of pseudo-colonels, judges, and generals, and foreign titles were given exaggerated respect. Even the unprepossessing Joseph Bonaparte was the social lion of Philadelphia, while the biggest party of the decade honored the nineteen-year-old Prince de Joinville, third son of King Louis Philippe; guests were taken by specially chartered steamship from New York to Newport, where Delmonico served the food, and where the entertainment was climaxed by a sham naval battle.

Society with a capital S was confined largely to the cities. The formal dinner party occurred in midafternoon and was followed ordinarily by music or conversation—although intelligent conversation seems doubtful in view of the elaborate menus. The evening party included supper and possibly dancing. A large ceremonial dinner, as for a visiting celebrity, embraced mountainous piles of food followed by an almost endless succession of toasts, each accompanied by a glass of wine, until the latter part of the evening disappeared in a hazy glow of good fellowship.

Very attractive to the young people was the ball—an evening dancing party with supper, often involving fancy dress. The most-awaited New York affair was the annual Bachelors' Ball, at which eligible New York men paid back their social obligations. The one of February 14, 1832, for example, was a fancy-dress affair held at the City Hotel. The ballroom was decorated with grottos, bowers, evergreens, pilasters, sofas, and mirrors. The ceiling was hidden by checked drapery, and the floor was painted various colors. Every girl who attended treasured her memories until she was an old lady. Such a party started fairly early, about 8:00 P.M., and seldom lasted later than 1:00 A.M., since these old-fashioned folk still held the notion that the night was designed for sleep.

Middle-class society copied the events of the elite—dinners, evening parties with supper, and balls, but seldom teas. Almost never were card games included, since many persons considered them immoral. There was much calling back and forth. Sewing circles gave an excuse of charity for intensive gossip. Church suppers stirred the smaller towns. Singing schools gave vocal relief and romantic opportunities. Candy-pulling parties occasioned riots of noise and laughter.

In the rural districts, especially in the West, there were house raisings, quilting parties, husking bees, weddings, funerals, and other community activities which gave opportunities for eating, drinking, and dancing to excess. Jokes tended to be of the practical or horseplay variety, except that a wedding inspired the suggestive leer—in spite of the well-advertised modesty of the period.

Social gatherings tended to be decorous, if not dull. After a copious meal the women gathered in one corner to talk clothes, recipes, and babies, while the men moved elsewhere to discuss politics, crops, and business. Rougher elements of the community put more emphasis on liquids than on solids, and differences of opinion, exaggerated by alcohol, led at times to fist fights, gouging matches, shootings, and stabbing affrays.

Many Americans were convinced that dancing was worldly and immoral, and some ministers would leave a room in which dancing started; one of them asserted that "Dancing is associated . . . with balls; and this is one of the worst forms of social pleasure."[16] Moral dangers were supplemented by the physical. Dancing meant for a woman active exercise in too few and too tight clothes; hence she perspired freely and cooled too rapidly. The late hours, the excitement, the lack of sleep, and the expense were all bad.

The bad repute of dancing was partly due to the abuses of public balls. Profit-making dances by hall proprietors, or dancing masters, or by such organizations as the Firemen, Boat Club, Odd Fellows, or National Guard, were open to anyone who could pay the customary price of one dollar for a man and two ladies. Subsidiary businesses were plied by pickpockets, prostitutes, and the inevitable adjoining bar. Conditions became so bad that the popular masked ball of a previous day had to be eliminated as at least a mild gesture toward morality.

[16] W. E. Channing, *An Address on Temperance* (Boston, Weeks, Jordan and Company, 1837), 55.

The very nature of dancing made the conservatives shudder with horror as the cotillion, quadrille, and reel were being replaced by the waltz, mazurka, and gallopade. Worst of all—and most popular—was the waltz. Here the partners clasped each other in their arms and rotated in a manner to rouse the lowest passions; the man could peer into the exposed bosom of his partner, while other predatory males could ogle her ankles as the whirl of the dance raised her skirts. Quite obviously a female would soon lose the crowning virtue of modesty, while the violent exercise was actually dangerous—witness the man who waltzed, became faint, called for water, and then died. Husbands ordered their wives not to waltz, and wives, their daughters. Many pious communities barred the waltz. But in spite of—or because of—this outcry, the waltz was soon accepted, whereupon the naughty dance was the polka. Flaming youth.

Most energetic of all dancing was by the Negroes. "It is impossible for words to describe the things these people did with their bodies, and, above all, with their faces, the whites of their eyes, and the whites of their teeth, and certain outlines which either naturally and by the grace of heaven, or by the practice of some peculiar artistic dexterity, they bring into prominent and most ludicrous display. . . . It is only wonderful to me that we were not made ill by the double effort not to laugh, and, if possible, not to breathe."[17] Later generations stopped laughing and started to copy.

No young miss, whether at home with her mother, working in a Lowell mill, or embracing the social whirl, forgot that her main business was the acquisition of a husband. By accepted fiction man was the pursuer, but in fact woman utilized every feminine wile to encourage pursuit and to expedite capture. A girl unmarried by her mid-twenties was well advanced toward an unlovely spinsterhood in which she soon lost her looks, her social importance, and her economic security.

Every girl believed romantically in love at first sight for the "one man," but probably the usual fact was an almost imperceptible ripening of a long friendship. "I found myself clinging to his in-

[17] Kemble, *Journal*, 96–97.

FRUITS

OF PHILOSOPHY:

OR

THE PRIVATE COMPANION

OF

YOUNG MARRIED PEOPLE.

BY CHARLES KNOWLTON, M. D.,
Author of "Modern Materialism."

"Knowledge is Wealth."
Old Saying.

SECOND EDITION, WITH ADDITIONS.

BOSTON:
1833.

Title page of one of the earliest known copies of
a pioneer book on birth control

terests, distressed by his long absences. I found on analyzing my re-gard for him that I loved him."[18] And then the long and deep con-versations: "He has made an exposition of his character to me. So simple. So pure. So just what Jesus loved. We talk little of heaven, but are already deep in schemes for our future independence and comfort."[19] Then the long letters and the appeals for still longer: "Let me follow you some day, from the moment you open your eyes ... till sleep closes the eyes I love so well."[20]

Ideally, young love was confined to deep conversations, long letters, or the treasuring of a scented glove or a precious lock of hair. In actual fact, hugging, kissing, and other caresses expressed strong inward urges, and seemed unobjectionable to all but the most pru-dish. Not infrequently, however, youthful ardor exceeded the most tolerant standards, and the young lady found herself on the road to maternity—whereupon her young man usually did the "right thing" and married her. Cynics noted that an unreasonably large propor-tion of "premature" babies were the first born.

The more religious and conscientious lover was greatly per-turbed lest human love replace or supersede the love of God and therefore be sinful. A very able man declared his love thus: "I know it will surprise and even amaze you, Angelina, when I say to you as I now do, that for a long time, *you have had my whole heart.*" But then conscience forced him to add: "*Not supremely.* Grace has re-strained me from that extreme. I *do* love the Lord our righteousness *better* than I love *you.* And it is *because* I love Him *better* that I love you *as* I do."[21]

Angelina proved not surprised by the declaration and returned the love, but she had her own religious troubles: "One thing I want to ask you, My Dear Brother. Ought God to be *all in all* to us *on earth?* I tho't so, and am frightened to find *He is not,* that is, I feel something else is necessary to my happiness. I laid awake thinking why it was that my heart longed and panted and reached after you

[18] H. W. Morrow, *The Father of Little Women* (Boston, Little, Brown and Company, 1927), 67.

[19] *Ibid.*

[20] P. G. and E. Q. Wright, *Elizur Wright* (Chicago, University of Chicago Press, 1937), 29.

[21] Barnes, *Weld Letters,* II, 533.

as it does. Why my Saviour and my God is not enough to *satisfy* me. Am I sinning, am I ungrateful, *am I an* IDOLATOR?"[22]

An engagement ended normally in either a church or a home wedding, where the word "obey" was frequently omitted from the bride's vows. The usual wedding was celebrated in the evening and followed by a reception or a supper. Then the happy pair might take a wedding trip, although more frequently the bride and groom went directly to their new home, where, after a reasonable period for settling down, they received their friends.

Once married, the girl put aside the frivolity of youth, "just as if she entered a convent, except however that it is not taken ill that she have children."[23] Gaiety and charm were presumably turned to common sense, self-control, industry, economy, piety, affection, and love for home. The wife was merged in her husband, a change symbolized by the taking of his name. He acquired her property, had exclusive use of her person, and could inflict moderate physical chastisement.

The wife was expected to love, cherish, counsel, and obey her husband. "As the vine which has long twisted its graceful foliage around the oak, and been lifted by it into sunshine, will, when the hardy plant has been rifted by the thunderbolt, cling around it with its caressing tendrils, and bind up its shattered bough; so it is beautifully ordered by Providence, that woman who is the mere dependent and ornament of man in his happier hours, should be his stay and solace when smitten with sudden calamity, winding herself into the rugged recesses of his nature, tenderly supporting the drooping head, and binding up the broken heart."[24]

The wife should be completely absorbed in her husband. "Even when exhausted nature sinks to brief repose, forgetfulness is denied. Even in sleep she seems awake to the one great object of her care. She starts and rises from her slumbers, raises her drooping head, watches with dreamy eyes the face she loves, then sinks again to rest,

[22] *Ibid.*, II, 553–54.

[23] Pierson, *Tocqueville*, 144.

[24] *The New England Farmer and Horticultural Journal* (Boston), Vol. XVI (October 4, 1837), 99.

to start with every chime or clock, or distant sound, that formerly had passed unheard, or only served as lullaby to her sweet sleep."[25]

The theory that a wife obeyed her husband, honored him, bore his children, and ministered to all his wants, was not always in accord with the facts. Sometimes she was a bad cook, a poor housekeeper, and an empty-headed fool. Sometimes it was the husband who did the pampering, with the wife domineering and shrewish, or dissatisfied and querulous. At other times the couple lived in a hotel or rooming house to avoid the very duties that the wife supposedly gloried in performing. In other words, husbands and wives acted quite humanly and naturally.

Sex conduct inside marriage must remain partly shrouded in mystery. The double bed, the nightgown and nightshirt, and the cold room seem to suggest frequent sex expression. But there were several deterrents. Both husband and wife worked hard, and dropped into bed dead tired. Furthermore, they had been impressed that frequent intercourse was not only sinful but physically debilitating; the healthiest man or woman was presumably the virgin. And, of course, such an ecstatic pleasure must obviously be a sin.

Marriage should be consummated, according to the moralists, with a sense of piety and responsibility rather than with those "innumerable, horrible, unspeakable, earthly, sensual and devilish distortions of married life."[26] Ideal marriage was the mating of immortal souls and should be far above the earthy degradation of physical passion. But by this time the purist had overshot his mark, so he backed down to the extent of admitting intercourse to be proper for the begetting of children, which presumably meant not over once a year. He was slightly consoled by the belief that sex relations would not be so attractive to married people as to unmarried, since excitement was much greater if a stranger were involved.

Marital intercourse was also limited by the deeply rooted conviction that no nice woman had strong physical desires. She was merely the receptacle for male passion, and wife and husband would both have been shocked if the wife had shown exuberance. Such demonstrations were reserved for prostitutes. This attitude must

[25] *Arkansas Advocate*, May 11, 1831.
[26] Barnes, *Weld Letters*, II, 640.

have damped sexual displays. Then, too, the husband felt it was both sinful and physically dangerous if he made demands on his wife during pregnancy or shortly after parturition. The average wife was almost always in one or the other condition.

A final hazard was the frequency with which marital relations ended in pregnancy. Many a couple tried to limit its progeny by abstaining from intercourse—frequently a losing fight which produced only mental and physical tension. Contraceptives were little known, of dubious effectiveness, and anathematized by religious and medical leaders as "conjugal onanism." Their use brought a heavy feeling of guilt which was unalleviated by success.

Sex morals apparently were not good, even though adultery was rare. Prostitution was commonplace, and nonprofessional moral lapses had the eloquent testimony of the number of unmarried mothers. Rape was frequent, if the newspapers are to be believed. Masturbation seems to have been widespread in spite of the shock and horror tactics used to combat it; people tried, somewhat unsuccessfully, to believe that it was rare among boys and nonexistent among girls. Homosexuality was not mentioned publicly, but consider the writer (male) who bemoans the stiffness and formality of his correspondent (also male): "And often when the gushings of my soul have prompted me to throw my arms around your neck and kiss you, I have violently quelled these impulses and affected a *manly bearing*." However, he continues, in imagination "your stern voice startles me from my maiden dreams!"[27] Other abnormalities sometimes emerged, as when a Brooklyn pastor in 1844 admitted fondling ten young girls too intimately and showing them his sex organs; of course, he blamed the devil.

Almost as important to the wife as her husband were her children, whom she often bore so regularly that her spouse became "somewhat restiff under these multiplying blessings."[28] The only trial worse than having too many children was having none, which provoked jests about the vigor of the couple, particularly the virility of the man.

Young children, according to the storybooks, learned their basic

[27] *Ibid.*, II, 642.
[28] Kennedy, *Swallow Barn*, I, 36.

religious and philosophic truths at their mother's knee. "Our moral and political institutions depend, for their purity and permanence, on that simplicity and singleness of purpose, which are generally imbibed at the mother's knee."[29] Actually, the young finishing-school product, married at sixteen and a mother by seventeen, was hardly qualified for such instruction, while the harassed mother of half a dozen had her hands full in feeding and clothing her offspring. There were flaws in the current conviction of the sanctity and divine inspiration of motherhood.

Children were worked hard—at least from the modern stand-point—since the father insisted on his legal right to their earnings until they came of age. But many contemporary viewers-with-alarm bemoaned the disappearance of the hardships and strict discipline of a past generation. "I am afraid that the next generation . . . will be a poor, weak, inefficient & selfish race, as parents will listen to all their whims & indulge them in sloth & petulance."[30]

Few marriages ended in divorce, regardless of their success. Now and then a husband or wife deserted. A missing husband doubled the wife's labors. A missing wife brought a newspaper notice:

Elopement

Whereas, Nancy, my wife, has left my bed and board without any provocation, this is to forbid all persons from harbouring or trusting her on my account from this date, for I shall pay no debts of her contracting.

Daniel Collins.[31]

Legally, divorce was difficult. The acceptable pleas were usually adultery, desertion, extreme cruelty, or impotence, and a few states insisted on an act of the legislature. More important, however, was the general disapproval, based on moral, economic, and social grounds. Farming needed both husband and wife, as did the rear-

[29] *The Discussion: or the Character, Education, Prerogatives and Moral Influence of Woman* (Boston, C. C. Little and James Brown, 1837), 15.

[30] E. N. Vanderpoel (comp.), *Chronicles of a Pioneer School* (Cambridge, Harvard University Press, 1903), 314–15.

[31] *Niles Gazette and Advertiser*, February 6, 1836.

ing of children. Few husbands and wives, no matter how unhappy, were willing to risk universal condemnation.

Woman's place in society was related to her physical disabilities. She was smaller and weaker, even though men sometimes forgot this fact in hiring laundresses and scrub women. She was subject to special ills, including pregnancy, parturition, and lactation, which occupied a large proportion of a married woman's time. The obvious corollary was that she should have duties that could be performed in the home, and this standard was maintained even when the woman was not married. She was expected to accept these limitations with resignation, since they had resulted from Eve's sin in leading Adam astray.

Physical sex differences implied to most people equivalent mental differences, even though a small but vocal minority insisted that the sexes were inherently equal in ability, and that apparent inequalities represented only differences in training. The usual dogma was that women's minds were inferior. "The intellect of woman bears the same relation to that of man as her physical organization; —it is inferior in power, and different in kind."[32]

Arguments concerning total brain power implied no disagreement in what was held to be the obvious truth, that women inherently had distinctive mental and emotional traits. These were stated many times, with variations. "Man is strong, woman is beautiful; man is daring and confident, woman is diffident and unassuming; man is great in action, woman in suffering; man shines abroad, woman at home; man talks to convince, woman to persuade and please; man has a rugged heart, woman a soft and tender one; man prevents misery, woman relieves it; man has science, woman taste; man has judgment, woman sensibility; man is a being of justice, woman of mercy."[33]

Prime virtues for a woman were faith, simplicity, goodness, and self-sacrifice. She should be tender, affectionate, frail, sentimental, pious, loving, humanitarian, decorous, meek, gentle, submissive,

[32] A. Jameson, *Characteristics of Women* (New York, Saunders and Otley, 1837), 39.
[33] *Galena Advertiser*, March 7, 1835.

humble, and pure: "By a glance she will draw a deep and just conclusion. . . . While she trusts her instinct she is seldom deceived, and she is generally lost when she begins to reason."[34] Above all, the woman should love, trust, and honor God—even more than she did her husband—since "religion with them is a sentiment, which like love, rejects all doubt, and suffers no analyzing process to disturb and cool its confiding faith."[35]

Woman's crowning virtue—supposedly innate—was her modesty. This modesty included not only personal fastidiousness but also a withdrawal from the hurly-burly, rough contacts of the market place. "Retired within the sacred precincts of her own abode, she is preserved from the destroying taint of excessive intercourse with the world. . . . and her heart is untainted by the dire temptations of strife with her fellows."[36]

Intense modesty could be called prudery, and one lady remarked: "I hope the charge will always remain a true one."[37] In polite company, no undergarment was ever mentioned, although this prohibition did not extend to the printed page or even to the lecture. Delicate females hesitated to discuss their symptoms with their doctors. Medical handbooks suggested the doctor cut short any visit to a lady's bedroom, make any intimate suggestions through a nurse or elderly female relative, and make a real examination only in case of great necessity, and then under a sheet in a darkened room. A proposal to dissect a female body was considered improper, and in the South would have brought a challenge from the nearest male relative. Even a phrenological examination of the head was considered a trifle indelicate, and ladies were praised for refusing to thus compromise their modesty.

For some reason the female form was considered increasingly immoral as one moved south. Polite society referred to the neck when it meant the breast, and to the breast when it meant the abdomen—a stomachache was thereupon a pain in the breast. Sea bathing was suspect because, even with woolen dresses and petticoats, the

[34] *Public Ledger* (Philadelphia), May 18, 1836.
[35] Hale, *Notes*, 40.
[36] Cooper, *Notions*, I, 105.
[37] D. L. Child, *The History of the Condition of Women* (2 vols., Boston, Otis, Broaders and Company, 1843), II, 267.

wet clothes outlined the lower extremities. No one spoke openly of a "leg," which was the most taboo word in the language. "If you are not ashamed of having legs you ought to be—at least, we are in this country, and never mention or give the slightest token of having such things, except by wearing very short petticoats, which we don't consider objectionable."[38] The leg complex was carried to inanimate objects, as "a square piano-forte with four *limbs*."[39] Rumor had it that the most refined female academies covered such "limbs" with little trousers ending in lace frills.

Exaggerated modesty had its anomalies. Décolletés were very low. Advertising was rather frank. Physical-education lectures, with skeletons and antomical drawings, were delivered to mixed audiences. A gentleman caller finding the lady sewing on a chemise would make sly remarks which would receive polite evasions, but no one was fooled. Both sexes knew the "facts of life," and each knew that the other knew.

Immuration within the sanctity of the home did not imply that women should have no influence on the world of affairs. Quite the contrary. In quiet and subtle ways they moved toward truth, justice, and beauty as they elevated the more hardened male and wrote on the clean, new pages of childhood. "How much is society indebted to their influence; how large a proportion of our intelligence, as well as our virtue, do we owe to them as individuals! What would our country be if they were allowed less influence in society?"[40]

Americans boasted complacently of the exaggerated respect given to women. The few protestors were a scattering of women who insisted that excessive courtesy implied male dominance and sensuality, and visitors who considered American women spoiled. But even this apple had its worm. In many cities a woman was unsafe on the streets, especially at night. The kindest explanation is that the majority of sex attacks were made by a few degenerate males who could not distinguish in the dark a pure and chaste female from her erring sister.

[38] Kemble, *Girlhood*, 563.

[39] Marryat, *Diary*, 154.

[40] *Things As They Are: or, Notes of a Traveller Through Some of the Middle and Northern States* (New York, Harper and Brothers, 1834), 122.

American women, it must be admitted sadly, did not always embody the ideals which the philosophers of both sexes praised. Complete daintiness, with a strong mixture of religious contemplation, was hardly possible for the average wife with half a dozen children under foot as she slaved at cooking, cleaning, sewing, and tending a garden. When the father came home, she was hardly prepared to radiate peace, sympathy, and loving kindness. Her nearest approach to the ideal came on Sunday, when she dressed in her best and took the children to church. Her unmarried sister, caring for someone else's children, should at least have acquired Christian fortitude; actually, she tended to become waspish.

Even herculean efforts to attain the proper feminine virtues did not always bring praise. When a diligent woman carried needlebook, thread, thimble, and pincushion with her in making a call, she was berated over "the slavery to which fashion has reduced them."[41] When she went to church, she was accused of primary interest in showing her new clothes, which was vanity, or of overidealizing her minister, which was derogatory to her husband. When she joined a society to evangelize the Chinese, reform prostitutes, or furnish clothes for paupers, she was told that her real purpose was gossip. When she held the inevitable ladies' charity fair, she was told that she was blackmailing men into paying fancy prices for useless knickknacks.

Almost no secular amusement was free from criticism. Even the simplest party generated undesirable excitement and late hours. The theater presented displays of illicit passions and crimes to the degradation of the pure female. Novel reading was at least wasteful of time, and probably dangerous morally. Lectures and debates were doubtful amusements for impressionable womanhood, with even the galleries of Congress suspect. No matter what women did, or failed to do, someone was displeased.

The husbandless woman faced even greater difficulties, for where could an occupation be found that would not unduly tax her lesser intellect and delicate physique? Where could she preserve her sensitive nature from the dulling contacts of competitive business, and her modesty from the rude and even lewd remarks of the sterner

[41] Hale, *Notes*, 85.

sex? Certainly not in an executive job, any kind of selling, or any occupation in which men and women must work side by side. Yet even women had to eat fairly regularly. They could do laundry or scrubbing, work as seamstresses, dressmakers, milliners, or boardinghouse keepers. All these occupations called for long hours, hard work, and small pay. In industry, woman could traditionally enter printing, textiles, shoes, food, and tobacco products, even though they worked beside men. In justification it was pleaded that these had been home industries earlier—a plea not entirely true. The truth was that men were not sufficiently entrenched in these industries to repel the feminine invasion.

If women worked, then current ideology insisted that conditions approach those of the home, where feminine virtues flourished best. Girl textile workers were herded into synthetic homes. Home industries, such as making stockings, shirts, hats, trousers, and dresses, were widely approved in spite of starvation wages. An abortive effort was made to discover other similar jobs which would not injure feminine delicacy. The radical suggestion to raise the wages of women was rejected because of the supposed operation of some vague but powerful natural law which would then end the occupations and leave the women penniless.

Hard work and low pay encouraged many women to adopt their oldest profession, prostitution. But thereby good theory was endangered, for "No woman ever voluntarily surrendered the blessings of a fair name. The sensitive plant shrinks not more instinctively from the touch, than the nature of woman from defilement."[42] The obvious conclusion was that a prostitute had originally been seduced, raped, or tricked into a fraudulent marriage—probably through youthful innocence.

Estimates of the number of prostitutes varied, with New York being credited with anywhere from one to ten thousand. The existence of many brothels was made evident by their prodigal output of shootings and stabbings. Most publicized was the case of the prostitute, Helen Jewett, who was found beaten to death in April, 1836. Bloody tracks led over a back fence, and a known visitor of the previ-

[42] *The Advocate of Moral Reform* (New York), Vol. I (January, 1835), 3.

ous night, R. P. Robinson, had whitewash on his coat, and owned the murder axe. At the trial, the defendant proved to be a good-looking and well-connected lad of nineteen, while the witnesses for the prosecution were prostitutes. Robinson never took the stand, and the jury pronounced him "not guilty" within fifteen minutes.

The clientele of a brothel consisted mainly of bachelors, particularly sailors and young bloods of fashion, but one spot check showed at least one-third to be married men. Such patrons may have had sick or absent wives, but there is also the possibility that a repressed wife with a feeling of sin could not compete with the sophisticated prostitute. The fact that many men frequented brothels was an open secret—but still a secret, since men did not boast of their amours.

Prostitution was often considered a necessary evil that provided an outlet for men's passions, so that they would not contaminate pure womanhood; the "bad" woman preserved the virtue of the "good." Laws against prostitution were unenforced, and the police undoubtedly received protection money. Periodically a few madams and girls were haled into court to keep them impressed with police power. In New York they were charged as vagrants and confined with other females in large rooms at "the college of vice at Bellevue,"[43] where they did effective missionary work.

The evil of prostitution attracted its due proportion of reformers, who curiously enough exhibited no interest in the economic condition of women or in modifying current moral concepts. Prostitutes were approached with moral exhortation. Men were urged to be more "pure"—to avoid late hours, fashionable parties, plays, novels, and other titillating excitements—to work hard, and to live simply. "Good" women were implored to shun libertines and to eschew such evils as low-necked dresses and waltzing, which aroused men's lowest passions and inspired them to visit prostitutes.

Female moral-reform societies often did little more than provide opportunities for ladies to discuss subjects that otherwise were taboo. The following extract from one annual report suggests that the ladies rolled sex over their tongues with lingering relish: "Though we have not been called upon to mourn the fall of any members of our society, yet some circumstances lead us to appre-

[43] J. R. McDowall, *Magdalen Facts* (New York, Author, 1832), cover.

hend that there have been recent outrages upon the cause of moral purity within the bounds of our congregation."[44]

The usual method of attack in fighting prostitution was to enlist the aid of a male Magdalen Society, whose members preached to the fallen women and sometimes established homes for those desiring regeneration. The theory was that the unfortunate women were more sinned against than sinning, and that innate female purity would respond joyously to a religious appeal if the process of degeneration had not gone too far. Unfortunately the results were slight. Few answered the appeals, and the majority who entered homes eventually lapsed again into their old ways.

Best known of the Magdalen societies was that of New York, sponsored by that outstanding philanthropist, Arthur Tappan. Its agent was the young Presbyterian divine, John Robert McDowall, whose hectic career included marriage to a woman twice his age, unorthodox handling of society funds, and excommunication by his church. Dissension rent the organization, and it soon split into a men's group "to convert these abandoned people to God by preaching,"[45] and a women's group to assist "females who show signs of repentance,"[46] which in turn soon gave way to a successor.

McDowall's first report was considered so shocking that the city was rocked to its core, and mob action threatened the author. The objection was not that the report was untrue, but that it was indecent, as witness its pirating by the ungodly in the search for pornography. The later *McDowall's Journal* was also diverted from its purpose by the unregenerate, who reputedly used it as a "whore-house directory." The immediate effects of McDowall's work were small, but he may be credited with doing something to force public recognition of the magnitude of the evil against which he battled.

In spite of the general agreement on the proper place of women in society, changes were coming. A few men and women were conscious rebels from the traditional standards, but more important

[44] Quoted in E. E. Calkins, *They Broke the Prairie* (New York, Charles Scribner's Sons, 1937), 167.

[45] Barnes, *Weld Letters*, I, 130.

[46] *Third Annual Report of the New York Female Benevolent Society* (New York, Osborn and Buckingham, 1836), 7.

were the contributions of thousands of women who had no conscious desire for change. A girl working in a textile mill accepted whole-heartedly the ideal of woman as a wife and mother, functioning in the sanctity of her home, and yet she was a symbol of a changing economy that was making the old ideas obsolete.

The general process of change was well illustrated in the field of politics. Almost everyone agreed that "there can be no excuse for a female deserting her allotted privacy and volunteering to en-counter gladiators in the political arena."[47] Women should be pro-tected "from the strife of parties, and the fierce struggle of political controversies" to "give a tone to . . . domestic happiness."[48] The clinching argument was historical—that "it seems indisputable that the experiments hitherto made in the way of female government have been signally unfortunate."[49]

Most women agreed that political activity would be desexing and that even the right of suffrage would be demoralizing. They agreed that equal political rights "would tend to the total disor-ganization of the family institution, . . . dissolve the family ties, and destroy all that makes woman efficient as a moral helpmate of man,"[50] and raised the cry "from pine-clad Maine to the farthest Louisiana bayou. 'Let the men take care of politics, we will take care of our children!' "[51] Even private political conversations were some-times held too fatiguing for the mind of woman: "The female char-acter in America is yet too gentle and delicate a thing for this British fashion."[52]

Women might generally accept their exclusion from politics and still enter the forbidden room by the back door or a window. A wom-an quite properly conversed of clothes and food, but might slide into politics when she talked of the money to obtain them. Her proper

[47] *The New York Mirror, and Ladies' Literary Gazette*, Vol. VIII (September 25, 1830), 95.

[48] Cooper, *American Democrat*, 38.

[49] A. Jameson, *Memoirs of Celebrated Female Sovereigns* (2 vols., New York, Harper and Brothers, 1840), Introduction, 19.

[50] A. J. Graves, *Woman in America* (New York, Harper and Brothers, 1843), 168.

[51] *The Ladies Companion* (New York), Vol. IX (October, 1838), 296. Quoted in Mott, *Magazines*, 484.

[52] *Niles Register*, Vol. XXXIV (April 5, 1828), 100.

interest in babies might inspire an active mind to consider the militia system lying in wait for the babies. Or she might enjoy reading or writing literature, and, excluding the few who deplored the immodesty of a lady's permitting her name to appear in print, most people admitted that "poetry, fiction, and the lighter branches of the sciences are woman's appropriate sphere, as much as the flower-garden, the drawing-room and the nursery."[53] But here again, unless she were a Felicia Hemans or a Lydia Sigourney, she might skid into a male subject such as business or government.

Women were welcome in religious and moral reform movements, and furnished a high proportion of the workers for such worthy causes as missions, abolition, and temperance, but once more troubles arose. The ladies began, immodestly, to be interested in holding offices in the movements. Furthermore, they soon realized that political action was vital, as in the abolition movement, and that to be effective, they could not work entirely through their husbands and brothers. Consequently they began to speak publicly—at first to audiences of their own sex and then to mixed audiences.

Women on the lecture platform stung the traditionalists into full cry, since these "female exhibitions in publick"[54] violated all current ideas of woman as a modest and retiring creature, confined to the sanctity of her home. A group of Massachusetts ministers expressed the widespread horror when they excoriated "the mistaken conduct of those who encouraged females to bear an obtrusive and ostentatious part in measures of reform, and countenance any of that sex who so far forget themselves as to itinerate in the character of public lecturers or teachers."[55] The height of horror was reserved for Fanny Wright as she presented sexual and religious radicalism to mixed audiences; such conduct was practically blasphemy.

Some women even attempted to invade the pulpit to give their messages. "A woman properly educated, and with feelings suitable to her sex, would as soon be caught pitching quoits or engaged in a game of nine-pins, as be seen in the pulpit; and womanhood is as

[53] *Portland Magazine*, Vol. I (October, 1834), 1, quoted in Mott, *Magazines*, 485.

[54] G. T. Chapman, *Sermons* (Burlington, Vt., Chauncey Goodrich, 1832), 18.

[55] Quoted in F. J. Hosford, *Father Shepherd's Magna Charta* (Boston, Marshall Jones Company, 1937), 82.

lovely in one place as the other."[56] The force of this magnificent sarcasm is somewhat lost on a later generation that accepts both female speaking and female sports.

The slashing criticism received by women for overstepping masculine prerogatives in their crusade for moral reform served to make some of them unpleasantly conscious of their inferior status. Able abolition leaders such as Sarah and Angelina Grimké and Abby Kelly became sex conscious and began to fight for women's rights. Again one heard of taxation without representation, and that governments derive their just powers only from the consent of the governed. Women objected to being classified with children, Negroes, the insane, and the criminal, and even questioned the omniscience of the male sex. Treason was abroad in the land as the females held they were not properly represented by husbands, brothers, and sons. The Women's Seneca Falls Declaration of Independence was less than a decade away.

Feministic radicals left most Americans with conflicting emotions of irritation, amusement, and bewilderment, for did not a woman already have all the best of life—a protected existence, a better seat at the theater, and the adoration of men? A woman solved the paradox neatly: "Many silly things have been written, and are now written, concerning the equality of the sexes, but that true and perfect companionship, which gives both man and woman complete freedom *in* their places, without a reckless desire to go out of them, is as yet imperfectly understood. 'In the future' it will be perceived that all this discussion about relative superiority, is as idle as a controversy to determine which is most important to the world, the light of the sun, or the warmth of the sun."[57]

Arguments over the place of women immediately involved the marital relationship, since obviously not all marriages had been made in Heaven. The conservatives talked of human failures in effort. The liberals supported more rights for wives, such as control over their own property. The radicals talked of easier divorce. Theophilos R. Gates wanted complete freedom of divorce, while Abner Kneeland added state care for children. John Humphrey

[56] *Morning Courier*, June 27, 1835.
[57] Child, *History of Women*, II, 211.

Noyes experimented with "male continence" and group marriage. Joseph Smith Jr. embraced polygamy for the Mormons.

One of the radicals, Robert Dale Owen, who aimed at complete sex equality with institutional care for children, insisted that current sex practices were the core of the troubles. He wrote: "Nothing short of control over the reproductive, it appears to me, can relieve women from sexual slavery. If they must be, on all occasions, nuns or mothers—mothers, too, perhaps of a dozen children—they are & will remain slaves; they suffer and will suffer, grievously, both physically & mentally. I cannot conceive equality between the sexes, except with the recommendation contained in the M. P. as a foundation stone."[58]

The "M. P." to which Owen referred was his little book *Moral Physiology, or, a Brief and Plain Treatise on the Population Question* (1830), which had the distinction—dubious at the time—of being the first American book to describe and approve contraceptive methods, and the second in the world. The English-born Owen was a man of varied interests, which may explain why the book was hastily done and inadequate. Of the three contraceptive methods described, preference was given the poorest—that mentioned in Genesis. Owen argued the sex act as normal and desirable, holding that people not only would not and could not refrain, but should not. Only by contraceptives could the overly large family, with its strain on the pocketbook of the father and the health of the mother, be averted. The advantages claimed were largely personal.

Owen's book might have been more significant if it had not been overshadowed by another, *Fruits of Philosophy, or, the private companion of young married people*, written by a young American doctor, Charles Knowlton. Knowlton's interest was a direct result of his background as hypochondriacal boy, penniless medical student, doctor with few patients, and husband with a growing family and no funds. Seeking to solve his own troubles, he investigated contraceptives, and then wrote down his results; a few patients were enthusiastic over the manuscript, so in 1832 he had it published.

Knowlton argued for contraceptives on both personal and social

[58] L. M. Sears, "Some Correspondence of Robert Dale Owen," in *Mississippi Valley Historical Review*, Vol. X (December, 1925), 313.

grounds. In social terms, contraception would avoid the overcrowding envisaged by Malthus, and hence avert the necessity of vice, war, famine, and disease on a large scale. In personal terms, the proper spacing of children would improve the wife's health and the family's finances. The alternative of abstention was both physically undesirable and practically impossible, leading only to the evils of masturbation and the resort to prostitutes. With knowledge of contraceptives, young lovers could marry, and thus enhance the happiness and morality of the community. Knowlton then described the sex organs and their functions, although with some errors, and gave instruction in several contraceptive methods.

These two books were greeted with profound silence by the American press, which probably was shocked. The one exception was a comment by the *Boston Medical Journal* on the Knowlton book: "We think . . . the less that is known about it by the public at large, the better it will be for the morals of the community."[59] Knowlton got into jail, but Owen did not. Probably the objections and prosecutions would have been greater if the books had appeared a few years later, after Victorian morality had become really dominant.

The distribution of the books is difficult to estimate. Possibly fifteen to twenty thousand were sold within the decade, but the number of readers was undoubtedly greater. One can imagine a wife reading surreptitiously at night after the children were in bed, hiding the book behind the mantel clock, and then next day slipping it under her apron to carry to her next-door neighbor. Possibly constant circulation is the reason few copies of either book remain. Of course an alternate possibility is that a later generation considered the matter too vile to be allowed to exist.

The influence of the books is also difficult to estimate. The American birth rate fell throughout the nineteenth century, with a specially large drop between 1840 and 1850, if the census figures are reliable. After a period of obscurity, both books were revived in the late eighteen seventies, and there seems to have been an exceptionally large decline in the birth rate between 1880 and 1890. These juxtapositions may have been entirely accidental, but they certainly were at least a remarkable coincidence.

[59] *Boston Medical Journal*, Vol. XXVII (November, 1842), 256.

The family, as one of the most basic of human institutions, changes slowly and reluctantly. A ten-year period is too short for even a minor revolution, and yet the American family was obviously in a period of transition between 1830 and 1840. Its functions were declining. The activities of the old self-sufficient farming family were being eroded by the tide of manufacturing and transportation. The single-product factory helped produce the single-product farm, with its increased dependence on the outside world, as well as more city families in which the father worked outside the home and the mother acted more and more as a purchasing agent.

Women became increasingly independent as their labors became less and as greater opportunity beckoned from the new mills. Each feminine mill worker was one more woman who could survive without male support, no matter how little she desired her new independence. Inevitably women came to be drawn into social, religious, literary, and political activities, and here they began to feel the impress of their inferior status and to become more interested in their "rights."

These changes were all accentuated by the increasing use of contraceptives. Smaller families were less fitted for diversified farming. Homes could be smaller, and apartments became practical. Fewer children meant more time for each child, and less financial strain; also, it meant easier divorce. Fewer children also brought more free time to the wife, with hours and energy for new play and work; increasingly she could leave the house to shop and to gossip, to hear lectures, to attend plays, and to participate in meetings to advance abolition, suffrage, and other reforms. The family was in the throes of a revolution. A brave new world was being born.

14. Schools

EDUCATION was a favorite theme for patriotic orators and for writers of polemics. "No nation, when the majority of the people is well educated, can remain enslaved."[1] Education should produce diligence, honesty, and morality. It should prevent crime, pauperism, and demagoguery. It should promote patriotism by telling of past heroes. "There can be no fear of our institutions as long as education is cherished."[2]

Fulsome praise of education did not imply universal schooling. Education was at private expense, and usually came when the family could least afford it. Many a father decided that his son was more valuable plowing than studying, or that a new barn was more necessary than his children's schooling. Such decisions were often approved by the wealthier, for if everyone were educated, who would perform the manual labor? The result was that even in favored New England, which boasted 90 per cent of its eligible children enrolled in common schools, less than half would be present any given day, while the South and the West had poorer records. In New England, however, almost every child attended school at some time— "I have lived more than forty years in New England, and have not . . . met with ten individuals . . . who could not read and write."[3]

If the father could not or would not pay to educate his children, the obvious answer was for Papa Government to do the job, and various reformers raised the battle cry of free public education. They did not go so far as compulsion, but they had visions of a democracy where the phrase "all men are created equal" would be more than a platitude of the Independence Day orator.

[1] *The American Quarterly Review* (Philadelphia), Vol. VI (September, 1829), 145.

[2] Schoolcraft, *Memoirs*, 585.

[3] Hall, *Letters*, 30.

Free public education was not received with open arms. Increased taxes were always painful, and even propertyless persons feared their effects on business and employment, while many of the richer men deplored the socialistic trend: "It would be a compulsory application of the means of the richer, for the direct use of the poorer classes; and so far an arbitrary division of property among them."[4] The results were expected to be less education for the wealthy, dissatisfaction of the poor, and deterioration of educational standards as private competition was replaced by the inevitable political manipulations of government. Moreover, since most states already provided free education for the poverty-stricken inhabitants, it carried the stigma of need, so that a self-respecting family hesitated to lower itself in the eyes of its neighbors by sending its children to a free school.

Elementary education was the province of the local school district, which usually had no power of taxation. A local committee hired the teacher and theoretically supervised the school, but actually often ignored it. Costs were paid grudgingly by the parents. Nearly every state contributed through a school fund, which ordinarily was collected from such special incomes as land sales, canal charges, and bank-charter fees. The infinitesimal sums were usually divided on a dollar-matching basis, but with the joker that there was seldom more supervision than a request for an annual report.

Friends of better education worked frequently through the states, with the thought that state supervision, made potent by the bludgeon of state funds, would offer the greatest hope for improvement. Most important were the state boards set up by Massachusetts in 1837 and by Connecticut the following year. In each case the secretary was an exceedingly able man, respectively Horace Mann and Henry Barnard. These men were less interested in compulsion than in inspiration. Each edited a magazine, spoke widely, and held teachers' conventions. They sponsored the most progressive educational practices, and were of great importance in advancing the cause of American education.

Schools needed desperately a public sympathy and financial sup-

[4] *Philadelphia National Gazette*, August 19, 1830, quoted in Commons, *Documentary History*, V, 110.

port that they did not receive. The average community felt satisfied with itself if it provided any school at all, almost regardless of the qualifications of the master, the nature of the building and equipment, and the length of the term. State after state had no more than a three months' term, and parents seemed to feel a glow of pride in holding down costs to, say, a dollar a year per child.

The most obvious way to save money was in the teacher's salary. A master might receive ten to twenty-five dollars a month and be "boarded around"; he was paid only for the time he worked. Quite obviously the cost per child declined as the number of children increased. If the average class of thirty or forty was expanded to one hundred, costs would be halved. Imagination boggles at even fifty boys and girls ranging in age from six to sixteen, in ability from moron to genius, and in grade from beginner to advanced student— all in one small schoolroom.

Teaching costs could be further reduced by the monitorial (Lancastrian) system. The teacher worked only with the more advanced students, who in turn heard the daily lessons of the youngsters. This procedure might even be expanded to a sort of circuit system in which the master supervised several schools. The supporting argument was that monitors were more sympathetic with their charges and used more effective illustrations—a sad commentary on the average teacher. Most people, however, wanted their money's worth of the teacher's time for their children, and the Lancastrian system was on the wane.

The simplest way of all to save money was to replace male teachers with female, at half the price. Some difficulties arose when the older boys were rowdy, but not as many as were expected. Since teaching was traditionally a man's job, a new theory had to be devised, but the philosophers were competent: "I am convinced that the best form of school, is that in which the arrangement of Providence in regard to families is imitated; the principal being male, and the assistants female."[5]

Low pay for teachers implied lack of community prestige in a society devoted to economic gain. A master was hired quite casually,

[5] *American Annals of Education and Instruction* (Boston), Vol. VIII (March, 1838), 142.

with the main eye on the lowness of his pay and his physical ability to handle the larger boys. He was expected, incidentally, to be able to read and write. He was largely left to his own devices unless he performed some outrageous act like crippling a student or encouraging boys to catch mice to illustrate the effects of carbonic acid gas. Then he was discharged. As one sympathetic observer commented: "They are hired at the lowest possible wages that will support life . . . but what is worse, they have no sympathy, no encouragement from any one."[6]

Since teaching was unattractive with its low pay, hard work, insecurity, and lack of prestige, it could hardly attract able people. One pedagogical manual remarked: "It is well known that many who are employed to teach our primary schools, are deficient in almost every necessary qualification."[7] Teaching was attractive mainly to unemployed farmers and storekeepers, to college boys on their long winter vacations, and to young ladies waiting for Prince Charming. Any proposal to improve education ran immediately into the almost unanswerable question of "who shall teach the schoolmaster?"[8]

Educational reformers attacked the problem by insisting on better-trained teachers as the prerequisite for higher pay and better schools. They insisted that teaching was a skilled profession and that a teacher should not only have real mastery of his subject matter, but should understand such erudite mysteries as child psychology and pedagogy, and even try his hand at practice teaching. Here and there officials in secondary schools and colleges began to talk of specific preparations for teaching, with Samuel Reed Hall opening a school in 1823 at Concord, Vermont, entirely for teacher training. New York became the first state to appropriate money regularly to promote the training of teachers. A law of 1827 gave aid to particular secondary schools for this purpose, and eight years later the program was widened.

The greatest single stride toward better-trained teachers came with the establishment of the first American "normal" school at

[6] Richards, *Howe*, II, 102.

[7] S. R. Hall, *Hall's Lectures on School-Keeping* (Hanover, Dartmouth Press, 1929), Preface, 3–4.

[8] Hamilton, *Men and Manners*, 123.

Lexington, Massachusetts, in 1839, as the first step in a larger state program. Only girls were admitted, and the curriculum included elementary and advanced subjects, child physiology and psychology, principles and methods of teaching, and practice teaching. The new pedagogical subjects were labeled "moonshine"[9] by hard-headed realists, who were sure the ability to teach was innate, like red hair, and that in any case it was foolish to give elaborate training for a poorly paid and part-time job. A long and discouraging search for a principal for the new Lexington school finally unearthed a reluctant Unitarian minister who included janitor work among his multiple duties, and who was skeptical of what he considered the frivolity of his students. Of the thirty odd girls who enrolled, only a few finished the course. Yet Lexington was the symbol of a new day for the American teacher.

Improved teacher training was but a small dipper of water on the desert of American teaching ignorance, for most teachers remained untrained and isolated, and yet it showed a distinct trend. Men such as Mann and Barnard traveled widely to explain new methods and materials, and, even more important, to bolster the self-respect of the profession. Improved morale became evident as the teachers formed societies to learn about and discuss common problems.

Increasing educational interest brought a growing flood of publications, with the periodicals of Mann and Barnard in the van. A deluge of pedagogical treatises start with *Hall's Lectures* (G. R. Hall) of 1829, and informed the alert teacher on everything from the proper ventilation of the classroom to the psychology of a child of six. Educational literature was undoubtedly helpful, but many a young teacher must have wavered between tears and laughter as he or she read of the virtues of patience and reason and light when the immediately pressing problem was the curbing of three overgrown rowdies who fancied themselves the village wags.

The elementary teacher's first view of the scene of his labors was seldom inspiring. The school was a crude, one-room shack, possibly eighteen feet square, which might hold thirty to eighty students,

[9] *The Christian Review* (Boston), Vol. VI (March, 1841), 29.

thus providing less air than a penitentiary. The average value of a Massachusetts school in 1838 was estimated at two hundred dollars, with the city institution only slightly better than the country.

A school ordinarily occupied the poorest farming land of the district, which meant that the yard was a patch of much-trampled earth spotted with stones and a few anemic and maltreated shrubs. Rarely did a town school have a gymnasium, and then only in the face of the hostility of many parents who felt that strength should be saved for farming, housework, or some other useful occupation. Toilet facilities might be a cornfield. Sanitation and ventilation were generally lacking, and no one suggested a doctor to check colds and other common ailments.

The equipment was limited to bare necessities. Backless seats forced the gawky sixteen-year-old to fold his legs uncomfortably, while the six-year-old could not touch the floor. Desks might be long tables, with possibly a separate table for the master. Coats might be thrown on the floor. Heat was furnished by a stove at one end of the room. Blackboards were rare novelties. Writing materials were un-ruled paper and homemade quill pens and ink—no pencils. Maps, charts, and pictures were unusual. Books were scarce despite several cheap series designed particularly for the common school.

A teacher's first job was to subdue the older boys. Sometimes he thrashed them in a fist fight, and not unknown was the threat implied by a brace of pistols. For ordinary discipline the ubiquitous birch rod was sanctioned by tradition, by Holy Writ, and by the *American Annals of Education.* An ingenious master might use a ruler on the palms, or force the pupil to hold a book at arm's length or to kneel on the floor with body erect, or might tie his big toes to the rod of the stove so that the feet cleared the ground. Less drastic was a system of merits and demerits, keeping after school, a fool's cap, or public and private admonitions.

Discipline, as described by the latest books of pedagogy, should be kindly, with punishments infrequent. The teacher should keep his temper, be impartial, explain his actions, and obtain the good will of the natural leaders. He should make friends with his students and keep them occupied with interesting work. Competition as an incentive was argued vigorously. Some felt that it was the way of the world and hence should be encouraged. Others thought it produced undesirable emotions, and favored appeals based on the usefulness of knowledge and the love of approbation.

Traditional instruction stressed memorizing, as of the alphabet, lists of words to be spelled, rules of grammar and arithmetic, parts of speech, and names of rivers and state capitals. The expected result was the acquiring of important information, but even more that the child would "be excited to habits of mental activity."[10] Such methods were almost unavoidable for the poorly trained master with half a hundred children in an ungraded school.

Rote memory was commonly stimulated by studying aloud: "We find the whole swarm running over their long, tough syllables, in a high concert pitch, with their elbows upon the desks, their hands covering their ears, and their naked heels beating time against the benches. . . . And, high above this din, the master's note is sounded in a lordly key, like the occasional touch of the horn in an orchestra."[11]

Elementary schools stressed spelling, reading, writing, arithmetic, geography, and composition, all interlarded with religious piety. The Bible was read regularly, while the children might be asked each day to check a long list of virtues such as faith, resignation, repentance, industry, and charity, to see where they had sinned. Almost equally vital was American history, depicting the blessings enjoyed by a free people, and in itself a religious exercise, since "a good history is an index forever pointing to the throne of God."[12] More progressive schools added such subjects as elocution, French, surveying, bookkeeping, and natural philosophy (science), with a few radicals talking of civics and of agricultural or manual training.

Textbooks were one of the plagues of a teacher's life. A child might appear with his father's dog-eared, fly-specked speller and his mother's carefully preserved geography, both poorly printed and illustrated. The teacher could not demand uniform texts, and might be forced to use half a dozen authors in various editions. The

[10] Quoted in J. Mulhern, *A History of Secondary Education in Pennsylvania* (Lancaster, Pa., Science Press Printing Company, 1933), 321.

[11] Kennedy, *Swallow Barn*, I, 67.

[12] *The Quarterly Register and Journal of the American Education Society* (Andover), Vol. IV (May, 1832), 272.

one amelioration was that certain authors appeared with considerable frequency.

The springboard for all elementary education was the "speller," where Noah Webster ruled unchallenged. His book had sold fifteen million copies by 1837, and ultimately sold seven times that number. His program was logical but uninspired—the alphabet, two-letter syllables, three-letter syllables, words, and then moral precepts and other elevating dogmatisms. His greatest contributions were the modernizing, stabilizing, and Americanizing of the English language.

The idea of a separate "reader" was still new, and the field highly competitive. The revolutionary graded readers attained maximum popularity with the five William Holmes McGuffey books published between 1836 and 1841. McGuffey, an Ohio college president and professor of classics, ultimately had sales of 122,000,000. His reputation came neither from originating the idea nor from his own writing—in fact, he settled a plagiarism suit out of court—but from his excellent typography, illustrations, and selection of stories. Many of the tales are still readable, unless one gags at large doses of morality and piety. Several of the selections, such as "Twinkle, Twinkle, Little Star" and "Mary's Little Lamb," have become embedded in American folklore.

Grammars, led by the Englishman Lindley Murray's eighteenth-century production, were all atrocious. Children memorized parts of speech and rules of syntax and punctuation, and then parsed sentences until they could draw diagrams in their sleep. The only subjects not taught were how to write and speak effectively.

The traditional plan in geographies, such as those of Woodbridge and Olney, was to start with the major divisions of the earth and work down. Now came S. G. Goodrich, writing under the name of "Peter Parley," who had the brilliant inspiration to present geography as the story of a boy visiting various parts of the world. The first was *The Tales of Peter Parley About America* (1827), a simply told story with good illustrations, including questions to be used by the uninspired teacher. The idea was immediately popular, and some seven million copies were sold in the succeeding thirty years.

There were many other texts. Arithmetic was dominated by Duboll, although Emerson (1838) produced the first really modern text. American history was the domain of Rev. C. A. Goodrich, who followed tradition by centering his accounts on the perfection of our Revolutionary heroes. The best elementary science texts were those of Almira Phelps, but their clientele was small.

The great day of the school year was the final exercise, to which the parents and the school board were invited. The master examined his charges with questions carefully designed to show their progress. Little Mary and John recited elevating poetry or prose, and then the local minister closed the ceremony with a few uplifting remarks and a prayer.

The traditional school had a number of critics who had been influenced by the teachings of Pestalozzi and Froebel. They asserted that "the province of the instructor should be simple, awakening, invigorating, directing, rather than forcing of the child's faculties upon prescribed and exclusive courses of thought."[13] They talked of the folly of teaching the spelling of unusual words, of repeating rules of syntax without learning to write, and of learning remote and useless geographical facts. They held that memorized facts and rules were useless unless applied—that the child should learn by doing. Here and there a teacher tried to apply these precepts.

Radical educators pushed all sorts of "crazy" innovations—that geography should begin with the student's home neighborhood, that maps should be homemade, that history should be recounted by the student in his own words, that reading should precede the learning of the alphabet, that spelling and writing should not be taught separately, and that parsing should be de-emphasized. A few teachers applied these ideas, but unless a master had a private experimental school of his own, he stood an excellent chance of being discharged by an irate school board, incited by indignant—and conservative—parents.

The real educational novelty was the "infant school" for children between eighteen months and five years old. Ordinarily it was

[13] Odell Shepard (ed.), *The Journals of Bronson Alcott* (Boston, Little, Brown and Company, 1938), 12.

a charity venture "for the children of the poor who have not attained the age at which they can be received into other schools."[14] A few were private and profit making, catering to women who could afford to pay someone else for taking care of their children. Now and then one specialized in the hothouse forcing of infant prodigies —that is, prodigies of memory.

The infant school broke with traditional education by discarding spellers, readers, and stiff benches in favor of toys and games, amusingly patterned wallpaper, and colored pictures and engravings. Even the most ardent disciplinarian could not expect a child of three to sit long and quietly with a book. The philosopher of the movement insisted that "play is the appointed dispensation of childhood," even though he then added quickly that "beneficent wisdom consists in turning this to its designed purpose."[15]

The great prophet of the infant school was Bronson Alcott, a Connecticut schoolmaster who did most of his work in Boston. Alcott held that "instruction drawn from common circumstances and objects, assumes all the freedom and simplicity of domestic conversation; and so far as consistent with common order and discipline, follows the unpremeditated thoughts and feelings of every child."[16] In sober fact, Alcott's New England training produced strict order and regular routine, while his "conversations"[17] with the children were little more than the children's repeating his teachings. He opposed corporal punishment, but actually used it at times—possibly by getting the naughty child to fix his own punishment. Yet Alcott individualized instruction to a revolutionary extent and encouraged at least a modicum of student government. He used stories, pictures, and maps extensively, presented his material simply and interestingly, and soft-pedaled rote memory in favor of imagination and originality.

Alcott failed—but his failure is more to his credit than his successes are. The inevitable criticisms of any new idea rose in volume

[14] *Ladies' Magazine* (Boston), Vol. II (January, 1829), 41.

[15] A. B. Alcott, *Observations on the Principles and Methods of Infant Instruction* (Boston, Carter and Hendee, 1830), 5.

[16] *Ibid.*, 11–12.

[17] A. B. Alcott, *Conversations with Children on the Gospels* (2 vols., Boston, James Munroe and Company, 1836).

when Alcott published his *Conversations on the Gospels,* which many called "indecent and obscene" in dealing with "subjects which are universally excluded from promiscuous companies of men and women."[18] A climax came when Alcott admitted a Negro child; all but his personal friends withdrew their children, and the school collapsed. Alcott then tried simplicity and vegetarianism in a communal living experiment at Fruitlands, almost ruining the health of his wife.

The worst fault of the infant schools was that they insisted too strongly on religious and moral training. Teachers were serious men with high ideals—admirable traits in moderation. Religious philosophy dominated child psychology. The child as an immortal soul to be saved overshadowed the child as a young animal to be exercised and as a young brain to be developed. Efforts at dispassionate objectivity foundered on the reefs of sentiment and religion. Alcott himself tried to make scientific observations of his own children— first Anna, and then Louisa May and Elizabeth. When he includes such an observation as "Behold the babe! It is a flame of light!"[19] he makes apparent the dominance of religious emotionalism over scientific objectivity.

Education for the average American boy or girl began and ended in the elementary schools. For each one hundred primary students of 1840 there were ten in secondary schools and one in college. Advanced education was not felt to be economically valuable; hence it was reserved largely for potential ministers.

A secondary school was generally considered the proper preparation for college, although a boy might be tutored by his minister, or enroll in a college-preparatory department. The thousand private academies that dotted the country favored the classics and mathematics, completing their curricula with rhetoric, philosophy, logic, chemistry, botany, and mineralogy, with sometimes such options as French and music. Students memorized a text and regurgitated it upon request. Maps, books, and scientific apparatus were scanty.

[18] Odell Shepard, *Pedlar's Progress* (Boston, Little, Brown and Company, 1937), 193–94.
[19] *Ibid.,* 143.

The discipline of an academy was strict, for the school was presumably acting as a parent. In fact, some schools were military academies; the latest and possibly the best was Virginia Military Institute (V.M.I.), founded in 1839. The cost per year was possibly two hundred dollars, including board and room. Since this fee was too high for many potential students, some of the schools reduced costs by having the boys work on an academy farm or in a shop for two or three hours a day. This plan of manual labor became so popular that it was extended to such colleges as Bowdoin, Middlebury, Western Reserve, and Wabash.

Academies or seminaries for girls were rarer, since they filled no real functions except as way-stations between the common schools and matrimony. They presented such feminine subjects as making wax flowers, painting in water colors, weaving tapestry, embroidering, and bead and lace work. Specialties such as French and music were encouraged—at a slight additional fee. Presumably the girl was being trained to catch her man, but apparently no attention was devoted to holding him, as by learning household management, cooking, and the care of children. At the end of a seminary course a girl might receive a certificate or a medal, or she might palpitate to such a degree as M. P. L.—Mistress of Polite Literature.

A seminary girl had every minute of her day planned, even her letters home being required work that called for correction. Physical exercise was usually limited to short and sedate walks with a chaperone, although a few schools offered dainty calisthenics. Clothes were simple. Deportment was watched closely to promote neatness, politeness, and grace. Frivolous conversations, including gossip and giggling on the streets, were theoretically eliminated. Sundays were observed scrupulously and dully.

A few of the girls' schools did not follow the general pattern. Some, like Wheaton and Mt. Holyoke, taught sciences, history, government, psychology, philosophy, and even the traditional male classics and mathematics. In a few cases boys and girls took identical subjects in the same or neighboring schools, while here and there a school advertised the equivalent of a college education.

Most Americans looked askance at teaching girls the same subjects as boys, for girls "are human beings under a weaker structure, and in a peculiar form."[20] Exposing them to the classics and mathematics would undermine their bodily and mental health, and produce the very objectionable "learned female." Sneers greeted the young ladies who "emerge from the portico of the seminary full of algebra, equality, and the theory of the constitution."[21] Worst of all was coeducation, which added moral dangers to intellectual and physical ones.

Here and there an iconoclast argued that women were capable of learning male subjects, even stating that "there exists an aptitude in the female mind and a capacity for mathematical learning equal to ours."[22] Such radicals held that Latin and Greek were at least as useful as painting on velvet. Some even supported coeducation, asserting that "it would tend to excite emulation, to soften the manners of both sexes, and to change that kind of attachment which savors rather of appetite than esteem, into rational and durable friendship."[23]

Outstanding among the most advanced of the girls' schools were the Troy Female Seminary, under Mrs. Emma Willard and later Mrs. Almira Hart Lincoln Phelps, and the Hartford Female Seminary of Miss Catherine Beecher. The curricula paralleled those of the men's schools. Both presented sciences which included laboratory work, and both had systems of student self-government. Miss Beecher also developed visual education, including the magic lantern, limited each teacher to one subject, stressed small classes, and encouraged the student to advance as fast as her abilities permitted.

The academy's young and vigorous rival was the public high school, which had the obvious advantage that it took the older children and hence permitted the common schools to cut costs by hiring women teachers. The high school had other more revolutionary effects. It was sensitive to the demand for "practical" subjects such as bookkeeping, surveying, and mensuration. It provided more equal treatment for girls and greater opportunity for poorer students of

[20] *The New England Magazine* (Boston), Vol. III (October, 1832), 280.

[21] Marryat, *Diary*, 37.

[22] Quoted in E. L. Bolzau, *Almira Hart Lincoln Phelps* (Philadelphia, Science Press Printing Company, 1936), 106.

[23] *Ibid.*, 74.

both sexes to obtain a secondary education. The high school was an important force toward the democratization of education.

Colleges were "nurseries of piety,"[24] with many, like Amherst, feeling their highest mission to educate "indigent young men of promising talents and hopeful piety . . . with the sole view to the Christian ministry."[25] Practically every college president and professor was a minister, while many a college boasted that the majority of its graduates were in the same profession.

A college worked prodigiously to guard and nurture the piety of its students. Conduct was supervised closely, with unmarried faculty members policing the dormitories; admonitions and prayers were buttressed if necessary by disciplinary action. Compulsory chapel twice a day, church services twice on Sunday, midweek prayer meetings, and sometimes even prayer at the beginning and end of each class should have softened the heart of even the most hardened sinner.

Piety was by no means forced upon unwilling students. Most of the boys were headed for the ministry, and carried the prayers of their God-fearing farmer fathers who had consecrated them to their holy mission. One cynical observer insisted—one hopes erroneously—that "the sagacious farmer keeps at home his strong and well formed offspring, to walk between the handles of the plow, and whistle in the furrow; but his children less indebted to nature he sends to Dartmouth."[26] But regardless of the method of selection, college boys were intensely devout, prayed fervently, and formed spontaneous prayer meetings, mission clubs, temperance societies, and self-criticism groups. Large numbers testified publicly to their conversion in the periodic waves of religious revivalism that flooded the colleges.

The various religious denominations were of overwhelming importance in college education. Harvard was Unitarian, Princeton was Presbyterian, Yale and Dartmouth were Congregational, Columbia and William and Mary were Episcopalian, Brown was Bap-

[24] *Western Christian Advocate*, Vol. I (May 2, 1834), 2.

[25] Quoted in P. Hibben, *Henry Ward Beecher* (New York, G. H. Doran and Company, 1927), 41.

[26] Holbrook, *Sketches*, 73.

"Dartmouth College," from a lithograph by Stodart & Currier,
published by G. B. O. Tyler *ca.* 1835

Courtesy of Dartmouth College

Founder's Hall, Girard College, Philadelphia;
Thomas V. Walter, architect, 1833

Courtesy of Wayne Andrews

tist, Georgetown was Catholic, and Rutgers was Dutch Reformed. Graduates of these and similar schools, inspired by religious sentiments, were influenced in founding new southern and western schools. The Methodists were most active in the production of new colleges, since they had been but recently converted to the importance of an educated ministry; their key institution was Connecticut Wesleyan (1831). Other faiths, such as the Baptist, Episcopalian, and Catholic, were only slightly less energetic.

While a good half of the fifty or more colleges established during the eighteen thirties were religious in inspiration, there were also examples of other motives. Lafayette expressed the civic pride of Easton. Marietta planned to train teachers. Charleston College was a pioneer city institution. New York University expressed a revolt against the exclusiveness and classicism of Columbia. The universities of Alabama, Missouri, and Michigan were state projects, the last embodying the most ambitious educational scheme of the day.

A new college was even more hard pressed for funds than its older sister, and every college president spent most of his time begging for money. Possible donors received appeals to local pride, piety, morality, and self-interest. Most ingenious was New York University, which arranged rewards for any degree of generosity. Twenty-five dollars gave free use of the library and reduced tuition for one student. The benefits increased with the size of the gift, until ten thousand dollars permitted the establishment of a professorship and the naming of its occupant during the lifetime of the donor.

Maximum college enrollments came just before the depression of 1837, when about ten thousand students were spread over more than one hundred colleges. The schools claiming two hundred or more undergraduates, and arranged in order of size, were Yale, Dartmouth, Princeton, University of Virginia, Harvard, and Union. No faculty had more than thirty members, including the president. The catalogues showed about one professor to each twelve students, but actually a good many professors were little more than window dressing, for example, the local minister or doctor, or someone appointed who never arrived.

The average college had one important building which the catalogues described as "spacious and elegant" but which in fact was a dilapidated three- or four-story monstrosity containing both classrooms and quarters for the students. Equipment was limited to a few blackboards, a box of dusty mineral specimens, and a few moth-eaten stuffed animals. The library could often be moved in a wheelbarrow. Only sixteen schools claimed as many as ten thousand volumes, while Harvard's fifty thousand was unrivaled. One room contained all the books, arranged by size. Once a day the custodian would unlock the door and regretfully part with a book or two, entering the name of the borrower in a ledger. Many a student never entered the library. Possibly the most attractive feature of the college was its low cost—say thirty dollars for tuition and about one dollar a week for room and board.

The college curriculum was as dependable as the tides. In the dominating position were such standard classics as Horace, Tacitus, and Graeca Majora. Only slightly less important was higher mathematics, particularly geometry, trigonometry, and calculus. Much lower in the scale were such subjects as the sciences, mental philosophy, logic, rhetoric, political economy, and the law of nations. Sometimes there were such frills as romance languages, belles-lettres, and bookkeeping. During his last year the student took the inevitable "evidences of Christianity" course under the president. The curriculum was almost completely prescribed, with each class taking the same subject at the same time.

Even the calm and cloistered traditionalism of the college curriculum had its exceptions. A few schools introduced laboratory science, which the conservatives insisted merely pandered to the boy who liked to mess around with stinks, to cut up dead cats, or to take walks to look at rocks. Rensselaer was highly important as our first technical school which applied its work practically. Among other novel subjects were romance languages and English literature. The University of Virginia had provided the first chair of history in 1822, but most people shrugged it off by asking what you could expect of a school that offered stenography. Elective systems were sometimes advertised as bait to credulous students.

The greatest shock to academicians was the serious criticism of the classics, as poor in style, lacking in utility, not helpful for mental discipline, and full of errors. After the first incredulous gasp of shocked horror, the mass of college presidents and faculty rose in righteous indignation; as the president of Columbia said: "When the floods of innovation threaten to destroy the foundations of learning, the strongest barriers must be opposed to their progress."[27] A few schools backslid enough to give a degree without the classics, but salved their consciences by awarding a degree other than the B.A.

A college professor was seldom a specialist. Rather, he was a drillmaster for large elementary classes. His pay seldom reached one thousand dollars a year, and usually was no greater than that of a skilled artisan. His arduous duties included not only long hours of teaching, but also the coaching of oratory, preaching, pleading for money, admonishing erring students, and policing the dormitory. Somewhat amazingly, he frequently had sufficient extra energy to fight vigorously with his colleagues, with the president, or with both.

Teaching was dull, pedantic, and uninspired. The professor might do a little lecturing, but generally he stuck to obvious questions from such standard texts as the Legendre *Geometry* or the Paley *Evidences of Christianity*. In answer, the student parroted the text. Examinations were infrequent and oral and open to the public. One result of this system was a complete lack of understanding between student and professor. Students were "prone to consider the *Faculty*, as, of course, an adverse body, needlessly strict, and even tyrranical, and leagued against their pleasures."[28]

Evidences of revolt existed as certain men asserted that "our colleges are but little more than machines that grind out a Bachelor of Arts in four years."[29] A young and inspired teacher such as Mark Hopkins insisted that "having a mass of facts . . . without the discipline which the investigation or ascertaining of these facts is calculated to give the mind, does not amount to much,"[30] but such men were in a small minority.

[27] Nevins, *Hone Diary*, I, 61–62.

[28] S. Miller, *Letters from a Father to His Sons in College* (Philadelphia, Grigg and Elliot, 1843), 35.

[29] *Knickerbocker*, Vol. V (May, 1835), 422–24, quoted in Mott, *Magazines*, 472.

[30] *Early Letters of Mark Hopkins*, 220.

Since colleges were small and financially destitute, they were eager for students, admitting them as young as thirteen or fourteen. The applicant had to pass an examination, generally not very exacting, on the classics and mathematics, and present a character testimonial, written usually by his local minister.

Each college day was planned in detail from chapel at daybreak until the last study period at night. The college provided rooms which the student furnished, but usually permitted off-campus residence. The college also provided board, normally compulsory, and by well-established tradition every student generation protested at the food; at Yale a "bread-and-butter" rebellion led to some hundred students quitting college. The college year had two terms, with a long winter vacation to permit needy students to teach. Commencement came usually in late August and was similar to the modern exercises.

Students were generally well behaved and decorous, for they came from pious and God-fearing homes. The mother wrote long admonitions to "watch and pray," to "set your face as a flint against every sin, especially pride;"[31] to avoid getting wet, smoking, late hours and expensive fads like football; and to cultivate religion. Son in turn recorded in his letters and diary his exemplary conduct and his detestation of intemperance, vanity, idleness, and immorality— all in highly religious language. Letters might be signed "Yours in the Lord." Quite truly was he absorbed with the health of his soul.

Yet these were vigorous young men, with physical energy that was but meagerly expended on ball games, ninepins, walking, and tussling; and few schools followed the lead of Williams in having regular gymnastic work. The result was sporadic drinking, gambling, and fighting, which appear with monotonous regularity in the college records. "Travellers, in passing through *Princeton,* have been, more than once, prejudiced against our college, by happening to see several students hanging about the tavern doors; swaggering with an air of vulgar and insolent importance; smoking, and, perhaps, using profane language."[32]

Many of the student escapades were but youthful pranks re-

[31] Wright, *Wright,* 17.
[32] Miller, *Letters,* 34.

sulting from high spirits. A bed that collapsed, missing windowpanes on a cold night, a door locked on burning tobacco and asafetida were considered humorous in a day of horseplay. Overturning carriages, stealing chapel bells, bobbing the tails of faculty horses, or tearing down fences might be interpreted similarly. But tolerance wears thin when students appeared with pistols and dirks, engaged in pitched battles with the town boys, set fire to the college buildings, destroyed the property of unpopular faculty members, and even physically maltreated some unfortunate professors. Certainly such actions could hardly be excused as mischievous pranks.

Much of the trouble came from the faculty hostility to almost any form of amusement as a departure from the high purposes of the college. No organized sports distracted young men from the study of Greek verbs, and no stadia dominated the landscape. Dramatics were taboo. Bands, singing groups, temperance and mission societies, college newspapers, Phi Beta Kappa, and other scholastic organizations were tolerated. Greek-letter fraternities were viewed with deep suspicion, and sometimes outlawed.

The one social group encouraged by the college was the literary society boasting some such name as Philomathean or United Brothers. The entire student body was ordinarily divided between two rival societies, each sporting the customary mysterious initiation ceremony and complex ritual. Meetings in college rooms featured the reading of papers and the debating of such profound topics as whether pride is essential to happiness and whether a thief or a liar is more degraded. Probably no one was influenced to change his mind, but the students enjoyed themselves and the college was happy in the thought that spare moments were being spent educationally.

The really radical innovation in college education was the admission of women as candidates for the sacred B. A. degree. For some time several schools such as Amherst had permitted girls in their classes, but without awarding a degree, while a number of girls' schools had proclaimed they were teaching college subjects— which they probably were not. Now the struggling little western school of Oberlin began "the elevation of female character by bringing within the reach of the misjudged and neglected sex all the instructive privileges which hitherto have unreasonably distinguished the leading sex from theirs."[33] One educational journal exulted ecstatically: "Woman is to be free. The hour of her emancipation is at hand. Daughters of America, rejoice!"[34]

Oberlin admitted women more by necessity than from choice. Overshadowed by the near-by Western Reserve, it had been on the point of dissolution when a secession from Lane Theological Seminary threw it a life line. In desperation it had invited the seceders to Oberlin, even though the invitation must include Negroes. Apparently the admission of Negroes was such a sad concession that the inviting of women was but a minor blow. Not until 1837, however, were the girls permitted to aspire to degrees. They then had complete equality, except that their commencement essays in 1841 on such subjects as "A Lady's Apology" and "True Heroism" were read by the faculty; apparently speechmaking on a public platform was not quite ladylike even for educated females.

The Oberlin experiment allayed certain ancient fears at least a trifle. The immorality of coeducation failed to materialize except in the minds of the most prurient, although possibly the test was not very searching since Oberlin men contained a significant proportion of highly moral theological students. Also the girls obviously were not ruined either mentally or physically by the classics and mathematics, in spite of the "discouragements with which we met in our first year."[35] Finally, higher education did not de-sex the girls and make them unattractive; all four of the first entering class married Oberlin men, with one halting her college career for that purpose.

Colleges preoccupied with the preparation of prospective ministers naturally fed the theological schools, many of which were connected with the undergraduate colleges. Every important sect except the Methodists had one or more theological schools, and the total number of students was about thirteen hundred. Among the best known were Andover (Congregational), Princeton (Presbyte-

[33] Hosford, *Father Shepherd's Magna Charta*, 5.
[34] *American Annals*, Vol. VIII (October, 1838), 477.
[35] Hosford, *Father Shepherd's Magna Charta*, 77.

rian), General Theological Seminary (Episcopal), and Yale (Congregational). Yale was becoming liberal to the extent that Professor Taylor even denied the total corruption of human nature; the conservatives were horrified, and Professor Bennet Tyler in consequence led a secession.

Best known of the western seminaries was Lane (Presbyterian) at Cincinnati, galvanized into life by Lyman Beecher to save the West from Popery and paganism, which were twin evils in his mind: "if we gain the West, all is safe; if we lose it, all is lost."[36] Beecher's main fight came actually not with the devil but with his own students, who so lacked tact that they supported immediate Negro emancipation—to the shocked horror of Cincinnati citizens, of the trustees, and of Beecher himself, who favored colonization. A Lane secession then gave Oberlin the breath of life, as previously related.

The ideal theological training was given by Andover, the largest and possibly the best school of its type. Andover was unusual in requiring a B. A. for entrance. Its first-year work was Biblical literature and languages, its second, theology, and its third, homiletics. With this arrangement three or four professors could handle the entire curriculum. Andover had unusually high standards, for the average theological school clutched at anyone who offered himself, even if he had inadequate training, and ran him through the mill quickly and cheaply. The poor boy might receive aid from the American Education Society.

The hopeful legal genius ordinarily read his Coke and Blackstone and Kent in a lawyer's office and then passed an easy examination. A popular lawyer might draw many students, but the famous Litchfield office of the late Tapping Reeve, who had pioneered in the case method, was declining in favor. A few colleges had law schools which presented lectures on such matters as torts and crimes, but, all told, they probably attracted less than four hundred students.

The aspiring medico was also trained in the office of an older practitioner. For the states licensing doctors, the usual requirement was three years in a doctor's office, during which time the candidate should leave long enough to audit two courses of lectures, take an

[36] C. Beecher, *Autobiography . . . of Lyman Beecher* (2 vols., New York, Harper and Brothers, 1864–65), II, 224.

examination, and write a thesis. These requirements helped to inspire some thirty medical colleges, of which the University of Pennsylvania drew best in the East, and Transylvania in the West.

Medical curricula were fairly standard, with four professors handling (1) theory and practice of medicine; (2) chemistry and materia medica, including pharmacy; (3) anatomy and surgery; and (4) obstetrics. Here and there were variations, including frequent courses in medical jurisprudence. Apparently the doctors were poor lecturers, which may explain the curious custom of having the student repeat identical studies in his two terms. A professor was paid by receiving part of his students' fees. Actual experimentation was extremely rare, with dissections infrequent because of a lack of cadavers. Rare hospital visits were the student's only contact with reality, and no school but the University of Pennsylvania had any regular provision for internship.

Medical professors were marked by extraordinary pugnaciousness. They hurled the grossest insults at their colleagues, at their presidents, and even at more or less innocent bystanders. School after school was rent by internal dissension, with the minority seceding to form a new school, which in turn was split until some of the faculty ended in private practice.

Education should not be limited to the book learning acquired by young people in school. These same children probably received their best training on the farm, in the home, or in the shop. Older people learned through their contacts with other people, their reading of newspapers, books, and magazines, and their attendance at church, at public lectures, or at the very popular museums.

The greatest single project for adult education was the lyceum, which expanded so rapidly that within five years of its birth it needed a national co-ordinating body, the American Lyceum (1831), with its own magazine, the *Annals of Education*. A local lyceum society frequently had its own library and assembly rooms, where its members might read or discuss such pressing issues as capital punishment, the education of women, or possible war with France.

The greatest activity of the lyceum was the presentation of lectures. Thousands gathered to hear science talks, as on phrenology, or geology, or anatomy, often with papier-mâché models. History, travel, religion, literature, and dozens of other themes appealed because of their combination of information and amusement—a combination later to be exploited by Chautauqua. One very popular program was a speech by General Gaines on "National Defense," followed by one by his wife on "The Horrors of War." Other lyceum speakers included such big names as J. Q. Adams, Webster, Emerson, Barnard, Choate, Cushing, Everett, and Rembrandt Peale.

The lyceum gave evidence of the desire of Americans to be informed, provided the information was not too difficult to attain, too costly, or too demanding in time. The same characterization might well be applied to formal education in school. People believed in it, even though they were not always willing to spend the necessary time and money.

The surprise about education should probably be not that in many respects it was grossly inadequate, but rather that it was so good. The United States was growing rapidly, and might have been expected to have very little energy to spend on educational matters. Actually the number of schools at all levels was increasing rapidly, with educational experiments that ranged from college education for women to play schools and student self-government. Very few of the educational ideas of the next century were not found at least in embryo in the eighteen thirties. Education was one of the many phases of life in which the innovations of the thirties forecast the trend of the future.

15. Churches

THE UNITED STATES was deeply religious. The mother writing to her son in college, the Lowell girl to her parents, or a man to his beloved, included inquiries about the soul. The family had morning and evening prayers and long graces at meals. Schools stressed religious instruction. A casually met cattle drover or tavern keeper might plead for one's salvation. "Grog parties commence with prayer, and terminate with benediction. Devout smokers say grace over a cigar, and chewers of the Nicotean weed insert a fresh quid with an expression of pious gratitude"[1]— but here possibly exaggeration entered.

Life after death was a perpetual and nagging concern. "For a fit of ambition, go into the church-yard and read the grave stones. They will tell you the end of ambition. The grave will soon be your bed-chamber, the earth will soon be your pillow, and the worm your mother and sister."[2] A rather somber and depressing point of view, in spite of its well-meant aim to focus attention on the eternal verities.

Sunday was the great day of religious celebration. Most people attended church, even though ministers bewailed the small and predominantly feminine congregations—and church meant two long sessions on hard seats in a poorly heated building. New York and Philadelphia stopped traffic during church services by placing chains across the streets. Labor on the Sabbath was limited to acts of mercy and to necessary chores such as milking. No food should be cooked. The day should be spent in meditation and prayer. Anything exciting was wrong; as Hawthorne commented, a certain Sabbath "wore away largely, and therefore wickedly."[3]

[1] Hamilton, *Men and Manners*, 406.
[2] *Western Christian Advocate*, April 29, 1836, p. 3.
[3] Nathaniel Hawthorne, *Passages from the American Note-Books of Nathaniel Hawthorne* (Boston, Houghton Mifflin Company, 1868), 171.

Unfortunately, all the sheep were not snow white. In fact, the contention was made that "We are a nation of Sabbath-breakers!"[4] Even a widespread plot was discerned: "A powerful, systematic, and simultaneous effort is making by the forces of the ungodly, to blot out the Christian Sabbath, and thereby, with one stroke, exterminate the whole system of revealed religion."[5] Particularly in the West one could find stores and saloons open, and even theaters and dance halls. Railroads and steamships ran excursions. Sunday papers were delivered. Mill machinery was repaired. Thousands protested the Sunday carrying of the mail, only to be overruled by tens of thousands who wanted their letters on Monday morning.

Sunday might be "desecrated" by even reading or writing letters. One young lady wrung her hands in anguish over a letter from her fiancé: "Perhaps I ought not to have read it until Monday, but I could not help it, and I don't know but I should have committed as much sin thinking of it as in reading"—but then she added honestly: "though for that matter it did not keep me from thinking of you. . . . I think of you even in church."[6] One might even profane the Sabbath by doing nothing: "The Sabbath was profaned by the young, in idly sauntering about our pleasant hills and fields, forgetful of Him who created the world, and man to praise Him; while, to their parents, the day was one of slothful inaction, or spiritual darkness."[7]

The more pious viewed with shuddering horror the inevitable results of Sabbath violation. "To husbands, fathers, and brothers . . . would you have the marriage covenant maintained inviolate? Do you value chastity, sobriety, intelligence, industry, cleanliness, and domestic enjoyment? . . . Wives, daughters, sisters, if you would not be the slaves of idle, dissipated, unfeeling men . . . if you would not be put in circumstances, where you would consider it not only a duty but a virtue, to take the life of your infant, throw away your chastity, submit to all the horrors of paganism, and to death itself, without the hope of immortality . . . we beseech you come *without*

---

[4] *Ibid.*, 18.
[5] H. Kingsbury, *The Sabbath* (New York, Robert Carter, 1840), 290–91.
[6] Wright, *Wright*, 30.
[7] Bolzau, *Phelps*, 59.

delay, and lend your efficient influence to do away the sin of Sabbath-breaking."[8]

The religion of America was overwhelmingly Protestant Christianity. The only non-Christian religion of any significance was that of the Jews. In general, non-Christian religions were lumped into the one term "paganism," and dubbed with the combined worst qualities of all. Furthermore, the majority sentiment feared and disliked the Roman Catholics, who were grouped with infidels and pagans as headed for perdition, and appeared to many to be worse than atheists.

A sprinkling of "freethinkers" questioned some of the Christian dogmas, such as that of the verbal inspiration of the Bible. The average American made no fine-drawn distinction between deism, agnosticism, and atheism. Delightful shivers ran up and down his spine when adherents of them were castigated in the religious press: "Infidelity with cloven foot, is going about seeking whom he may devour, scattering seeds of death, corrupting the press, and poisoning the fountains of knowledge."[9] This well-publicized menace, when brought from under the magnifying glass, proved to be a handful of uninfluential men who edited a few little papers and formed a few societies, of which the national one was the American Liberal Tract and Education Society, organized in 1836. Their biggest day of the year was Thomas Paine's birthday, which they celebrated in almost complete seclusion.

The average American could hardly avoid the basic religious truths with which he was overwhelmed from birth to death. Home, school, pulpit, and press all united in one mighty paean to traditional beliefs. Methodists might fight Episcopalians, Baptists might look suspiciously on Presbyterians, and all Protestants might hate Catholics, but all agreed on certain issues—that a literally inspired Bible was the final authority on all subjects, that the beautiful organization of nature showed God's handiwork, and that the truth of Christ's teachings were attested by the unpleasant life of pagans and the rapid spread of Christianity.

Under such conditions the boast of the orator that "We enjoy

[8] Kingsbury, *Sabbath,* 300.
[9] *Annual Report of the Maine Missionary Society* (Portland, 1833), 7.

perfect civil and religious freedom"[10] was an exaggeration, even though the last state church was disestablished in Massachusetts in 1833. Peculiar religious ideas were opposed vigorously, and their possessors could not hope for social acceptance, much less for political or economic advancement. In fact, they might well land in jail, as did the elderly Abner Kneeland, who received sixty days for blasphemy, whereupon he printed in his paper a tombstone with the inscription "Here lies Liberty of Opinion and Freedom of Speech and the Press."[11] As for the atheist—"If there *really* is such a thing as an atheist we hold it right that his testimony should be rejected, as would that of a person notoriously *insane*."[12]

Possibly the most ominous problem for religion was the potential conflict between science and religion. Geologists were expanding man's background beyond the Usher chronology, other scientists were finding more species of plants and animals than could be contained by the largest Ark, and a few ingenious souls were talking of an evolutionary process in plants and animals. For the immediate present the conflict was delayed by the position of devoutly religious scientists who asserted that their discoveries only enlarged man's knowledge of the plan of the Deity, and illustrated anew Divine benevolence.

Many Easterners looked upon the West as religious problem number one, holding that "the religious and political destiny of our nation is to be decided in the West."[13] Obviously the West lacked churches and ministers, and was addicted to blasphemy and Sabbath breaking. "*Mormonism* is there to delude them. *Popery* is there to ensnare them. *Infidelity* is there to corrupt and debase them. And *Atheism* is there, to take away their God as they go on to the grave, and to blot out every ray of hope that may beam on them from beyond."[14] In fact, "here is to be the battle field of the world. Here Satans seat is. A mighty effort must be made to dislodge him *soon*,

[10] *The National Preacher* (New York), Vol. V (August, 1830), 41.

[11] *Boston Investigator*, June 22, 1838.

[12] *Niles Register*, Vol. XXXIII (February 2, 1828), 374.

[13] L. Beecher, *A Plea for the West* (Cincinnati, Truman and Smith, 1835), 11.

[14] *Fifteenth Annual Report of the American Home Missionary Society* (New York, 1841), 73.

or the West is undone."[15] If the battle were not won, "they will roll back upon us as a tide of vice and irreligion."[16] The conscientious Easterner was urged to use his money to save the nation from the Devil, the Pope, and "Joe" Smith.

Of course the fear of western irreligion was largely unjustified. Migrants carried their religion along with their other household possessions. The Bible had a place of honor in the average log cabin, religious papers were devoured avidly, and few doubts were cast on revealed religion. It was true that customs of Sabbath observance were different and blasphemy was prevalent, but the lack of churches and ministers reflected only the sparseness and poverty of the population. The growth of Catholicism was bad only from the standpoint of doctrinaire Protestants. The West was basically as religious as the East, even though formal expression was different and not so frequent.

Americans were predominantly Protestant, but not therefore completely uniform. The Bible permitted varying interpretations, and with the lessening of the authority of the priesthood, the individual had considerable choice. That eminent divine William Ellery Channing held that "Whenever doctrines are taught from the Christian records, opposing any clear conviction of reason and conscience, be assured, that it is not the teaching of Christ which you hear. Some rash human expounder is substituting his own weak, discordant tones for the voice of God."[17] Rather incredibly, from the Channing standpoint, consciences did not seem always to agree. The result was a diversity of Protestant sects, with the number tending perpetually to increase.

Most aggressive and expanding of the Protestant sects were the Methodists and the Baptists, each claiming some half-million communicants. Each held optimistically that the individual might be saved from sin through his own efforts. Each preferred eloquence and moral fervor above education for its ministry. Each favored religious emotionalism and participated enthusiastically in western

[15] Barnes, *Weld Letters*, I, 67–68.

[16] *The First Report of the American Home Missionary Society* (New York, 1827), 55.

[17] W. E. Channing, *Discourses* (Boston, Charles Bowen, 1832), 173.

camp meetings. Each had a system for serving sparse western populations, and the Methodist circuit rider was frequently the only contact of a Westerner with the rest of the world.

The Baptists had just been riven by dissension. Alexander Campbell had been the latest exponent of uniting all believers—excluding,
of course, Roman Catholics—under the simple forms of the New
Testament. The actual result was not union but further division,
with the addition of the "Campbellites" or "Christians," who were
strongest in the Ohio Valley.

The Presbyterians were sterner and more gloomy. In general
they supported an educated ministry and opposed religious emotionalism, although one of their number, Charles G. Finney, was the
greatest revivalist of his day. A "New School" was dominant for the
first third of the century, and established Union Theological Seminary to offset the conservatism of Princeton. The "Old School,"
which opposed both doctrinal innovations and co-operation with the
Congregationalists, came into power in 1837, and acted drastically
by ejecting 533 churches with 100,000 members, mostly in central
New York. A new split over slavery was just around the corner.

Congregationalists were fewer in number, but dominated New
England. As in all sects, there were doctrinal disputes between the
liberals and the conservatives. The modern age raised doubts about
such Calvinistic dogmas as the inherent depravity of man, infant
damnation, and the doctrine of election. Dr. Nathaniel Taylor of
the Yale Divinity School even went so far as to assert that although
a baby was born with an unyielding determination to sin, it was actually guiltless at birth. Such doctrines seemed heretical to the
Reverend Bennet Tyler, and led him to dissociate himself from such
unsound ideas and to establish his own more orthodox school.

Congregationalism failed to expand satisfactorily. Co-operating
with the Presbyterians under the Plan of Union of 1801, western
churches were established jointly, with the result that the Presbyterian form of organization was usually adopted; even Lane Seminary was Presbyterian. Hence the ending of the Plan of Union when
the "Old School" returned to power. Moreover, the Congregationalists found trouble in rivaling the emotional appeals of the Methodists and the Baptists, who invaded even New England. Lyman

Beecher wrote about Finney: "I'll meet you at the state line . . . and fight every inch of the way to Boston, and then I'll fight you there."[18] Other Puritan divines were tempted to fight fire with fire; as one said: "It is sometimes desirable to increase the distress of the awakened sinner . . . by throwing the anxious and unhumbled rebel into the hands of an angry God, who will kill him or spare him alive, save or destroy him, as seemeth good in his sight."[19]

The Unitarians represented a split from the Congregationalists, and were important through wealth and the control of Harvard, rather than through numbers. Outstanding was the "extremely delicate"[20] William Ellery Channing, but the man of the future was Theodore Parker. Many held the Unitarian church "Christian only in name,"[21] partly because it required "the sacrifice of so little personal gratification."[22] Even more condemnatory was the description: "With music and feasting and dancing they drive all religion away during the week, and then they go to meeting to thank God that they are not bigoted, superstitious fanatics."[23]

Less numerous were the Lutherans, who arrived with the German migration. The Episcopalians flourished, particularly among the socially elect of New York City; they split between high- and low-church adherents. A handful of Universalists under the active Hosea Ballou went farthest in denying the supernatural and in insisting upon the universal possibility of salvation. The Quakers were generally approved for their simplicity, industry, and probity, but even the Quakers were split by dissension; Elias Hicks during the late twenties had led a secession on the proposition that Christ was human rather than a divine part of the Trinity.

The religious scene was further complicated by dozens of minor sects. Most picturesque were German pietist groups such as the Moravian and Amish, but there were also other German, Dutch, Welsh, and French sects, to say nothing of the independent Negro

[18] Beecher, *Autobiography*, II, 101.
[19] Quoted in S. Fleming, *Children and Puritanism* (New Haven, Yale University Press, 1933), 39.
[20] Kemble, *Girlhood*, 576.
[21] Pierson, *Tocqueville*, 156.
[22] *Early Letters of Mark Hopkins*, 201.
[23] Wright, *Wright*, 24.

"The Dance," as performed in Shaker religious ceremonies

churches. Only the theological specialist could describe the distinctive beliefs of the Restorationist, Bible Christian, Mount Zion, Primitive Christian, New Jerusalem, American Seventh Day, Primitive Methodist, Associate Church, and "Two-seeders." The last of these believed that the Devil sired Cain and hence doomed his children, while Abel's children were the elect. Most erudite and mystic were the Swedenborgians, who were incomprehensible to all outsiders. Swedenborgianism was enriched by mesmerism and clairvoyance in the teachings of that unique medium, Andrew Jackson Davis.

American absorption with religion, plus American ingenuity, naturally encouraged new faiths, some distinctive to the United States. One William Miller, a New England Baptist, immersed himself in the more abstruse portions of Holy Writ, to emerge with the startling conclusion that the end of the world and the day of judgment would arrive on March 21, 1843. For over a decade he aroused Americans to their peril, having ever greater success as the critical day approached. Some said his believers reached one million. To their intense mortification the only end of the world was a picture in the New York *Sun*. New estimates produced a later date, which again proved wrong. The most faithful of the Second Adventists then held a little more vaguely that the fatal day was close at hand, but a good many backslid.

Most resplendent of the religious eccentrics was Robert Matthews, commonly called "Matthias," who rejected religious formalism and considered himself the spirit of truth. Cutting his hair to resemble pictures of Christ, he liked to roam the streets of New York, followed by a crowd of curious small boys, and to preach to drunkards and harlots. Rumor held that he had a wardrobe embroidered in gold and silver, that he planned to occupy a golden throne in the center of an immense temple in the New Jerusalem, that he owned golden keys to fit the golden gate, that he had a six-foot rule to measure lots for the faithful, and even that he claimed to be God and to have written the Bible.

Matthias attracted rich "angels," but in time some became skeptical and haled the master into court on charges of theft, assault, and poisoning. Matthias took the stand in a green silk frock coat lined with pinkish silk and decorated with a silver sun and stars; around his waist was a crimson sash. His evidence was in general a rarified and elaborate nothingness, but on two points he was extremely pertinent and lucid—the legal title to his property and his innocence of any crime. The court finally imposed a sentence of four months for assault and for contempt of court, after which Matthias receded into obscurity.

More appealing was the shy, gawky, red-haired Vermonter John Humphrey Noyes. Conscience-ridden and timid, he confided to his diary: "I could face a battery of cannon with less trepidation than I could a room full of ladies with whom I was unacquainted."[24] Graduation from Dartmouth was followed by conversion, which in turn led to Andover, where intensive self-contemplation brought the bitter repenting of everything he had done before, and the decision to attend a stricter school—Yale. Licensed to preach in 1833, he took his first small church near Peekskill, New York.

Noyes did not long remain a small-town minister. After a year of mental turmoil he announced to his startled friends that he had attained perfection and that no one with sin could be called a Christian. Many of his friends were outraged, and his preaching license was canceled in spite of his explanation that he meant only purity of heart and not of external action. With this declaration he largely isolated himself, not even having much contact with other "perfectionists" of the time.

Sex proved to be almost as great a problem to Noyes as religion. Ultimately he found a solution—ascetic celibacy for himself, but complete freedom for everyone else; marriage should be a feast with "every dish free to every guest."[25] The shocked horror which came from this announcement was intensified by the actions of certain disciples. Two married couples apparently became unsettled about who was married to whom. Two girls tested the power of the spirit over the flesh by visiting a male friend late at night—and the flesh won. One of the girls and a friend decided their home town was to be destroyed, and ran to a neighboring hill to pray, shedding

[24] G. W. Noyes (ed.), *Religious Experiences of John Humphrey Noyes* (New York, Macmillan Company, 1923), 20.

[25] Quoted in R. A. Parker, *A Yankee Saint* (New York, G. P. Putnam's Sons, 1935), 44.

their clothes as they ran. The town was more shocked by the nudity than thankful for its salvation.

To cap the climax, Noyes himself fell in love. After wrestling with his conscience, he decided that God would release him from his vows, and wrote Harriet seven reasons why God would approve their union; from some oversight he did not mention Harriet's money. But he remained consistent by insisting that "we can enter into no engagements with each other which shall limit the range of our affections,"[26] to which proviso Harriet agreed.

After his marriage (1838) Noyes and his most devoted followers lived together in his rambling house at Putney, Vermont. Here it was that he discovered his "male continence" which permitted cohabitation without fear of the continual pregnancies which had made the life of his wife burdensome. Here also it was that he announced that "The Kingdom of Heaven Has Come,"[27] which meant the end of private property and of marriage, on the authority of the Bible. The end of marriage did not imply the end of sexual intercourse, for Noyes stressed the Biblical injunction to love one another. He insisted that love should find an expression quite universal, but without licentious passion. Also he distinguished carefully between sex expressions for love only and those designed for propagation.

Group marriage was the most advertised development at Putney. As Noyes described it, "We gave each other full liberty"[28] only after lengthy prayer and soul searching. Any member having sex relations was subject to stern reprimands if he admitted to lascivious thoughts. But consciousness of rectitude did not save the group from the bitter displeasure of their more earth-bound Vermont neighbors, who feared for the morals of their impressionable daughters. Ultimately Noyes recognized the desirability of removing his colony to the comparative peace of Oneida, New York.

The linking of unusual sexual practices and communal property was by no means peculiar to Noyes. A simple example was that of George Rapp, formerly at New Harmony, Indiana, and now at Economy, Pennsylvania. The combination of celibacy and com-

[26] *Ibid.*, 59.   [27] *Ibid.*, 121.
[28] Noyes, *Noyes*, 202.

munism worked successfully under the domineering and slightly crotchety Rapp. Later the colony experienced secessions, while the celibacy made it self-liquidating.

Best known of the communistic and celibate groups were the Shakers, who held that man had fallen because of sexual intercourse and could be regenerated only by its cessation. They drew the ideals of chastity, poverty, and communism from the New Testament, and the praise of God by singing and dancing, from the Old. They frowned on all display and ornamentation and may have been the only people in the world to accord women full equality.

The convert to the Shaker faith did not at first give up his property and family life. Only after his faith had become stronger and he entered the third stage of his initiation did he embrace these ideas. Then he went to live in an artificial family, controlled by an equal number of men and women. The men and women ate at different tables, and their work was divided along traditional sex lines. Clothes were simple, uniform, and unadorned; the men wore brown homespun suits, while the women wore gray gowns that were so skimpy as to be called "disgusting."[29]

The Shakers had twenty to thirty communities in the North and West, the most-visited one being the central community at Niskayuna (Watervliet). Everything was clean and well tended. Farms were cultivated intensively, and manufacturing included the famous Shaker sweaters. Every visitor attended the religious services, where the sexes were separated but where both helped to conduct the meeting. The usual singing and preaching were supplemented by religious dancing, which meant advancing and retreating rhythmically, with arms outstretched and hands in motion. Greater emotional elation brought jumping and running.

Visitors to the Shaker communities were almost entirely hostile, and while they were forced to admit the obvious cleanliness and prosperity, they questioned the intelligence and even the sanity of the inhabitants. They were certain that new members came "from among the ignorant and weak-minded,"[30] and that Shaker communities were composed of "disappointed maidens and withered

[29] Martineau, *Society*, I, 313.
[30] *A Northern Tour* (Philadelphia, 1825), 249.

batchelors,—of all, in short, who, having survived the age of passion, were content to make a merit of resigning pleasures in which they could no longer participate."[31] Such charges, as well as that of ill health, may have been inspired by the unflattering costumes. Rumors of sexual irregularity were probably inevitable. Neighbors resented the peculiarities, the clannishness, the common voting, and the prosperity of the Shakers, who were but slightly protected by the well-advertised religious freedom of the United States.

Most important of the sects that combined communal living with unusual sex views was the Mormon. The story of the prophet Joseph Smith, of his Vermont birth, his New York boyhood, his visions, his recovery of the lost books of Mormon, his miraculous translation, and his founding of the new faith has often been told. Likewise has there often been recounted the troubles in New York, the unsuccessful venture at Kirtland, Ohio, the tribulations in the effort to establish a New Zion in Missouri, and the settlement at Nauvoo, Illinois. The end of the decade found the Mormons still in Nauvoo, with no thought of moving.

The Mormons were above all industrious. At each new home they built an imposing city which included a magnificent temple, and labored to produce well-tilled farms, wide city streets, grass, flowers, drainage, sanitation, and schools. Superficially they were desirable neighbors, but actually the Gentiles disliked their religious ideals, envied their prosperity, and feared their political power. And the Mormon population continued to grow, with large families and a continual flow of converts, many of whom were recruited abroad by such missionaries as Brigham Young.

The central problem of Mormonism was the character of Joseph Smith. Obviously he was big and handsome and strong—filled with the zest of living. But was he a charlatan, a self-deluded fanatic, or an inspired man? Mormons held him a true prophet, favored by God, but non-Mormons called him ignorant, boastful, profane, drunken, untruthful, avaricious, and lascivious—a "very illiterate and impudent desperado in morals, but . . . [with] a vast fund of low cunning."[32] Polygamy was as yet only a matter of rumor. Smith

---

[31] Hamilton, *Men and Manners,* 354.
[32] P. Cartwright, *Autobiography* (New York, Hunt and Eaton, 1856), 341.

claimed later that he received his first revelation in 1831, but he denied the practice in 1835, and it was never admitted publicly until the Mormons had moved to Utah.

These were but the larger among a great number of experiments in communal living. At Zoar Community in Ohio men and women lived simply and communistically; family life was normal except that children were removed from the home for education between the ages of six and twelve. Ararat was a Niagara River island used for a Jewish colony, which included Indians as members of a lost tribe of Israel. Hopedale (1841) was religious but not sectarian, and accepted all such current reforms as prohibition, abolition, women's rights, and nonresistance. Well known nonreligious communities such as New Harmony, Icaria, Fruitlands, and Brook Farm came either earlier or later than the eighteen thirties.

Contrasting sharply with the diversity and bickering of the Protestant sects was the calm stability of the Roman Catholic church, which had its American center in the great domed cathedral at Baltimore, where the Provincial Council met. Many of the new immigrants were Catholic; they congregated in the seaboard cities, but also crossed the mountains into the Ohio and Mississippi valleys. Certain western towns such as St. Louis and New Orleans had long been Catholic. Now the church organization spread as far west as the Diocese of California, while the sacred orders were active in education and charity. Even a certain number of Protestants were attracted by the peace and confidence of the Catholic church. The half-million Catholics of 1830 doubled within the decade.

Catholic growth was viewed by the Protestants with a dislike that easily shaded into hatred. Many Americans were certain that Catholics took orders from the Pope, who was leagued with the Austrian emperor and the Irish to overthrow the Union. Even the less extreme held Catholicism to be "the main stay of the battle against republican institutions,"[33] and asserted that "in all countries where Romanism has the ascendancy, neither religious nor civil liberty can have any permanent existence."[34] Widely accepted were tales that

[33] Beecher, *Plea for the West*, 85–86.
[34] *Annual Report Maine Missionary Society*, (1833), 10.

all Catholics voted as their priests told them, that young priests commonly had sex relations with attractive parishioners under the cloak of the confessional, and that convent walls concealed the wildest of sex orgies.

For once the Protestants found themselves united in common action. The American Home Missionary Society issued the clarion call: "The most formidable foe to the universal spread of the Gospel is, doubtless, to be found in the Roman apostacy; and to meet and overcome this foe, will be among the most arduous and illustrious victories of the people of God. If, then, in the arrangements of Providence, we are permitted to wage this warfare on our own ground, let the conflict come."[35]

The first attack was a barrage of words by the ministers, backed ably by the laymen. The religious press, credited with furnishing three-quarters of American reading, was filled with diatribes against the Catholics. The lay press followed suit. Catholic replies received scanty circulation, while several Protestant-Catholic debates did little but reinforce the prejudices on both sides.

Scurrility reached a maximum in pamphlets and books with titles such as *A Foreign Conspiracy, The Master Key to Popery, Female Convents,* and *Jesuit Juggling.* The convent stories were particularly popular. Rebecca Reed's *Six Months in a Convent* (1835) sold so well that a sequel was profitable. *Maria Monk's Awful Disclosures* probably deserved its title; the "awful disclosures" ultimately proved not to be the contents of the book but the fact that a publishing concern should print the lascivious imaginings of a common prostitute with a police record and that the book had been ghostwritten by a nephew of the president of Yale.

Diatribe and pornography paved the way for more direct action. When a Protestant minister nightly knelt and prayed before a Catholic church that it go bankrupt, trouble was in the air. Mobs, as at Boston, New York, and Philadelphia, burned churches, destroyed Catholic homes and property, and mistreated individual Catholics. In some cases the mobs were as much anti-Irish, and sometimes anti-Negro, as they were anti-Catholic.

The crowning anti-Catholic outrage was the burning of the

[35] *Sixteenth Annual Report of the American Home Missionary Society,* 84.

Ursuline Convent at Charlestown, Massachusetts, in 1834. The convent had a girls' school, one of the students of which was the emotionally unstable Rebecca Reed. When Rebecca left school, she told lurid tales of conditions there; and as she found people credulous, her inventions became ever more fantastic. These incendiary sparks were fanned to a white heat by Lyman Beecher, who should have known better, and soon a mob stormed and burned the convent; the church was saved only by police action. Even worse, most Americans seemed to approve the work of the mob; only a few were brought to trial, and these were acquitted. Few Americans thought of anti-Catholic agitation as any denial of the freedom of religion guaranteed by the Constitution.

A church building might be anything from the great city edifice, with stained-glass windows, a fine organ, and a robed choir, to a western barn from which the cows had been removed for the day. It was used only for religious exercises, including Sunday School, weddings, and funerals. The northern church had a stove at one end, but the foresighted parishioner brought a box of charcoal embers for his feet.

Church pews were seldom free. When they were auctioned at the opening of the church, a mercenary communicant might speculate on a favorable location. On occasion he might blackmail the minister by threatening to keep pigs in his pew or to sell to Negroes. Pew rent replaced the modern voluntary collection. A growing agitation that "Free Grace and Free Seats ought to go together"[36] had produced little more than a few inferior pews for poor people, visitors, and Negroes.

The minister was the key figure of any church, but apparently in many cases he was stupid, ill prepared, and bad mannered. The church press pleaded that it was "the immediate duty of the Christian church"[37] to encourage more capable boys to embrace the ministry, but with disappointing results. In the West it was observed that "nine tenths of the ministers . . . are second or third rate men in

[36] *Western Christian Advocate*, Vol. I (May 2, 1834), 1.
[37] *Norfolk Auxiliary Society for the Education of Pious Youth for the Gospel Ministry* (1836), 10.

every particular."[38] Well-wishers advised the minister not to make his toilet in public, pick his nose, get drunk, or spit tobacco juice on the carpet. One basis of judgment of the minister was his salary, which extended from the excellent four thousand dollars of the rich city churches to the one hundred dollars plus gifts common in the West.

The minister was above all a preacher, and to this end collected quotations and illustrations assiduously. Frequently he wrote out his sermons so they could be used again, although many a young eastern theological-school product found his beautifully prepared discourse going very flat for a southern or western audience that preferred extemporaneous oratory. The usual churchgoer desired his emotions to be either stirred or soothed, and viewed new ideas with resentment. Hence the average minister stuck conservatively to such unobjectionable topics as Devotion, Prayer, Christian Love, Death, A Good Wife, or Debts, picking his illustrations to avoid offense.

The young minister was taught that he was responsible only to God, and that he should at once make this fact clear to the people who paid his salary. "THE SACRED MINISTRY is no experiment suggested by the wisdom of man; it is a positive institution of the Lord Jesus Christ."[39] This ideal was accepted in theory by most people, but in fact the usual minister either accorded with the views of his parishioners or found that greater peace was possible if he did not stress any differences in opinion.

The influence of the ministry on American life is doubtful. The minister was accorded much respect and was an essential at any public event. On the other hand, he was criticized frequently—for dry sermons, long prayers, undue officiousness on canal boats and steamboats, and even for excessive drunkenness and for too great intimacy with the female lambs he was shepherding. Any discussion of current problems brought the accusation of "polluting the pulpit by preaching political sermons on the *Sabbath* day"[40]—possibly from those who disagreed with him. Except for a few men such as Beecher, Fisk, and Wayland in the East, and Dow, Cartwright, and Finney

[38] Barnes, *Weld Letters*, I, 67.

[39] *Fourteenth Annual Report American Home Missionary Society*, 71.

[40] Baltimore *Republican*, quoted in New York *Standard and Statesman*, April 29, 1834.

in the West, most ministers probably only reinforced traditional morality. They followed rather than led.

The supreme revivalist of the age was Charles Grandison Finney, who overwhelmed even Philadelphia, New York, and Boston before teaching at Oberlin (1835), which he made an outstanding theological center. Finney was not only deeply devout but also intensely practical, using emotional appeals as consciously as an organist pulls the stops on his organ. Theodore Weld, another noted divine, feared that revivals "are fast becoming with you a sort of trade, to be worked at so many hours every day, and then laid aside."[41] Efficient in his trade, Finney introduced the protracted meeting, the "holy band" of converts acting as assistants, the "anxious seat" for repentant sinners, and public prayers by women. With his feet on the ground, he recognized clearly that conversion was only the beginning and not the end of religious experience.

Finney was but the outstanding practitioner of religious emotionalism. The agents of the Home Missionary Society were particularly enthusiastic over revivals, since they produced many conversions and the figures sounded well in their reports; time after time they reported how "a deep and awful solemnity spread over our worshipping assemblies."[42] The "burnt-over district" of central New York seemed especially susceptible, but any correlation with economic conditions or social classes is difficult. Colleges were affected with particular virulence, with each class experiencing at least one "general freshening of the soul"—encouraged by the faculty. The emotional involvement was almost incredible: "At a meeting this morning in one of the rooms of College the students were nearly all together, and quite a number were in tears."[43]

A revival was almost as standardized as a church service. The stage was set by prayers, hymns, and sermons. Increasing fervor was demonstrated by a scattering of "Hallelujahs" and "Praise the Lords." The minister increased the pressure by a sepulchral description of the ghastliness of death, the dissolution of the body, and the unmitigated horrors of hell; Heaven was treated lightly as not

[41] Barnes, *Weld Letters*, I, 15.
[42] *First Annual Report American Home Missionary Society*, 91.
[43] *Early Letters of Mark Hopkins*, 120.

so impressive. Continually came the refrain: "May our Lord and Saviour have mercy for you poor sinners."[44] Mass hysteria approached the breaking point. Men and women sang, shouted, and prayed aloud. Repentent sinners confessed their transgressions. Even casual visitors were caught in the morbid excitement, which was continued day after day until all the susceptible had succumbed.

Translated into the western idiom, the revival became the camp meeting—a tent city to which the surrounding countryside gravitated to talk politics and gossip as well as to be saved. Women made a census of new babies, young people did their courting, rowdies collected at saloons on the edge of the clearing, and everyone came to see the fun. Each day had three general convocations, together with family prayers and smaller extra meetings. Evening services were most impressive as the dark forest frowned on the tense faces illuminated by flaring pine torches. People jumped, jerked, swayed, screamed, wept, barked like dogs, yelled for joy, foamed at the mouth, spoke in unknown tongues, and lapsed into unconsciousness. The greater the reaction, the better. The minister felt boastful when "one gay lady . . . was so overwhelmed as to be unable to stand or even to sit up without being held."[45]

Not everyone approved of religious revivals. Even Finney admitted physical bad effects. Drunkenness, selfishness, superstition, and other distressing concomitants appeared. And worse, "it is questionable whether even gross licentiousness is not at least equally encouraged by the excitement of passionate religious emotions,"[46] and many people, including ministers, did not differentiate between human and divine love. All too frequently revival services produced a crop of illegitimate babies. Even strict policing of the meetings was not quite effective.

Cynics contended that the usual conversion was of either a young boy or a young girl in no great need of reform, or of a confirmed sinner who was re-saved by each new minister. The unique James Jesse Strang described a meeting thus: "The revival lasted a fortnight or more. Some dozen or twenty were converted, principally

---

[44] *Morning Courier*, May 11, 1830.
[45] Barnes, *Weld Letters*, I, 10-11.
[46] Martineau, *Society*, II, 344.

271

small boys and very young ladies. Nearly half allready returned to their wallowing again."[47] And yet one cannot read the lives of ministers and missionaries without realizing that many a conversion at such a meeting was lasting and significant.

Religious impulses were not limited to the luxury of an egoistic concern with personal salvation. The truly religious man felt a strong urge to help others, especially those who did not want help. Being socially minded and having the American passion for organization, he joined with his fellows to form a multitude of religious societies—each with its constitution, bylaws, and officers. Many were interdenominational, and all were always hard pressed for funds to meet their ever expanding budgets. In certain ways they were big business. Twenty-two spent some nine million dollars in 1834. The directorates were frequently interlocked, and the great philanthropic tycoons were the New York merchant brothers, Lewis and Arthur Tappan.

Each worthy cause could boast at least one reformatory society —to improve asylums and prisons, to free or colonize the Negroes, to promote temperance, to bring world peace, to help fallen women, to stop Sunday mail, to eliminate corsets or tobacco, for life-saving, to suppress profanity, or to do anything else that the ingenious philanthropist could imagine. The outer limit was the Friends of Universal Reform, who gave blanket approval to all reforms.

Some reform groups were so active that even the most remote backwoodsman had heard of them. The American Bible Society aimed toward a Bible in every home, and printed millions in a score of languages, giving them free if the family were poor. It included all sects but the Episcopalian, which had its own organization. The American Education Society helped hundreds of poor boys to become ministers through "loans" that were never called. It, too, was interdenominational, although several churches had independent organizations.

The American Tract Society, interdenominational but with parallel denominational organizations, flooded the country with reli-

[47] Quoted in M. M. Quaife, *The Kingdom of Saint James* (New Haven, Yale University Press, 1930), 195.

gious tracts. Dozens of agents strewed the nation with millions of badly printed and highly moralistic tracts, which today would produce immediate nausea; luckily most of them have disappeared. The society also published several sets of religious books and the widely read *Christian Messenger*.

The Sunday School was a major philanthropic effort. Early in the decade it claimed almost a half-million students, and the number increased rapidly. The emphasis tended to be placed entirely on the study of the Bible. Red and blue tickets and tracts were the rewards for memorizing the Scriptures, and child prodigies in memorizing were highly touted. The American Sunday School Union, which represented most denominations, issued a graded series of lessons and questions, dictionaries, commentaries, manuals, lesson helps, magazines, tracts, periodicals, and a "Select Library." Its dozens of agents crisscrossed the country to organize new schools, and were particularly active in the West, where intensive work had started in 1829.

Of top religious priority was mission work, both home and foreign. Largest of the home missionary organizations was the American Home Missionary Society, supported by the Presbyterians, Congregationalists, and Dutch Reformed; other sects had independent groups. The A. H. M. S. avowed rather grandiloquently that "the destiny of this nation . . . is to christianize the land, from the mouth of the Oregon to the Gulf of St. Lawrence. Its missions should spread over every part of it, its missionaries throng every hill and valley; until the school-house and the church should be found on every hill top, side by side."[48]

The objectives of the A. H. M. S. seem to imply major efforts in the West. Actually, an analysis of the figures shows that three-quarters of the aided churches were in New England and New York, mainly in the rural areas. The society believed that each church should help itself as much as possible, so seldom gave more than part of the necessary funds, and tried to withdraw as fast as possible. It undoubtedly saved the lives of many small, struggling churches.

Poor communities were not always enthusiastic about being the

[48] *Fifteenth Annual Report*, 101–102.

objects of charity. They thought they detected an air of patronage, and resented the control that went along with the money. As for the agents of the society, they might be described as "these little college-bred chaps and theological scavengers" who go "prowling and skulking about through our country . . . making proselytes and begging money."[49] No region enjoyed being considered a field for missionary work.

More dramatic and appealing was the foreign mission. Oregon Indians were more thrilling than Vermont farmers, and Chinese were more romantic than Indiana backwoodsmen. The leading society was the American Board of Commissioners for Foreign Missions, which was Presbyterian, Congregational, and Dutch Reformed; other sects had their own groups. The American Board spent a quarter of a million dollars on 440 white workers at seventy-nine stations in the peak year of 1837. In 1830, three-quarters of the missionaries served the American Indians, particularly the Five Civilized Tribes; the remainder manned stations in India, Ceylon, Malta, China, and the Sandwich Islands. A decade later only a quarter of the missionaries served the Indians, while the overseas work had been extended to such intriguing places as Turkey, Persia, Siam, Singapore, and Borneo.

The typical Protestant mission station was headed by a missionary and his wife, assisted by a male and a female teacher, a doctor, and a farmer. About one station in four had a printer and a printing press. Missionaries were ordinarily men of piety, vigor, and fair education, who had as their object the transmission of a complete culture and not only a religion. They began their missions in a fever of optimism, certain that the pagans were all a-twitter to hear the "good news" from a "superior" civilization.

The basic difficulty of the average missionary was that he knew nothing of the language or culture of the people to whom he was going. He had only the conviction that all heathen were "addicted to every *abomination* that ever came into the heart of man to do, and which renders human society like that of the *infernal regions. Ignorant, sensual, grovelling,* they live and die like the brute."

[49] Quoted in E. M. Coulter, *William G. Brownlow* (Chapel Hill, University of North Carolina Press, 1937), 33.

Obviously "the whole system of idolatry . . . must be destroyed."[50] It required at least a year for a man with these convictions to discover that he might be mistaken, and some men never really understood another culture.

Not all of the missionaries were men of intelligence and judgment, while even the best worked too long and hard with people whom they did not treat as equals. Selfishness, dogmatism, dictatorialness, and tactlessness were all too frequently the results. Tired missionaries found difficulties upsetting, and fought with their colleagues and with the members of other missions, while all Protestants united to belabor the Catholics—not the best possible advertisement for the Christian peace and brotherly love they were teaching. Little wonder that the number of their conversions was disappointing.

All the usual missionary troubles were well illustrated by the best-known enterprise of its day—the mission to the Oregon Indians. Four Indians had visited St. Louis in 1831, possibly in part to investigate Catholicism. They were publicized incorrectly as representatives of many natives who thirsted for Christianity. The first response was a Methodist group that did almost no work with the Indians. The American Board after some hesitation sent the elderly and sickly Parker, who missed the annual caravan across the Plains. Joined by the middle-aged and ailing Whitman, he started next year, but neither man did missionary work at that time. Still another year, and Whitman was joined by Spalding, a man "not remarkable"[51] for common sense. Also in the party were a new and pregnant Mrs. Whitman, and Mrs. Spalding, who had not recovered from the effects of a stillbirth. It was not a promising group, particularly when Spalding was still resentful that Mrs. Whitman had earlier turned down his offer of marriage.

Work in Oregon proved disappointing, for the Indians were by no means eager for Christianity. Not only did conversions lag, but the natives objected even to such obvious cultural advantages as pants, Mother Hubbards, farming, and monogamy. In fact, they were so recalcitrant that the missionaries had to learn their language.

[50] *Norfolk Auxiliary Society* (1832), 6.
[51] Hulbert, *Oregon Crusade*, 285.

As for the missionaries themselves, overwork, too close association, and a lack of humor brought inevitable frictions. From time to time they met, confessed their errors, and promised a reformation which proved short lived. Everyone wrote long letters of self-justification to the American Board. They insisted, in letters that ranged from pathetic begging to dictatorial demands, that success depended on more men and materials. Actually, as the Board suspected, additional recruits did not improve the situation perceptibly, and the Board considered seriously the abandonment of the entire enterprise.

The failure of the Oregon mission enterprise is understandable, even though it was manned by men and women of energy, piety, self-sacrifice, and high Christian ideals, and even though these consecrated people labored mightily under adverse conditions. Like so many others in various parts of the world, they spent their lives in what essentially was a losing fight. Whether they are to be admired or blamed, their experiences were typical of the missionary movement of the eighteen thirties.

Religion was the twin of democratic institutions in the minds of Americans of the time. Soon to be combined in the phrase "manifest destiny," they were expected to sweep the world. Each American felt an individual responsibility to spread the doctrines which he was certain were the supreme will of the Lord. "How important that in such an eventful era as this in which we live, we should be up and doing all that is in our power to forward the glorious work of man's redemption."[52]

Not only was God's eternal purpose certain, but the ultimate goal could be achieved within the next generation if men would only put their shoulders to the wheel. As Samuel Parker said: "These western fields are white, or whitening, for the harvest. What is wanted is labourers, self-denying, pious labourers. Will not pious young men, and the churches, hear and obey the last command of our Saviour."[53] The world could be transformed into a copy of Protestant America if only men shouldered their burdens. The millenium was at hand. The vision was clear.

[52] Quoted in Hosford, *Father Shepherd's Magna Charta*, 79.
[53] Hulbert, *Whitman*, I, 83.

16. Reformers

ARELIGIOUS AND NATIONALISTIC AMERICA, convinced of the perfectibility of human institutions within a generation, did not overlook domestic distress and imperfections. The busy housewife and the hard-pressed businessman were solicited continuously for funds to promote temperance, educate missionaries, help wayward girls, assist needy seamen, or give support to any one of the thousand other worthy causes that man's mind could imagine. Charity and reform were considered proper spheres for private benevolence, and only here and there did the government lend a hand.

The relief of poverty was largely in the Lady Bountiful tradition, with an occasional basket of food to a needy family and outworn clothes to the seamstress. Private groups, such as the Association for Relief of Respectable Aged Indigent Females, or the Society for the Relief of Poor Widows with Small Children, handled specialized cases. Now and then there was a clearinghouse of information to avoid duplication of effort in some city.

Private charity never quite did the whole job, and consequently the government was forced to take a hand. Sometimes a town or county made money payments—never a satisfactory system, as the aid was eroded by private avarice. The larger town or county frequently supported an almshouse, sometimes with state aid. The sick and insane were quite commonly admitted, and the overcrowded dormitories were breeding grounds for disease. Many a superintendent grafted on food and supplies. The inmates supposedly worked at farming or making textiles, but often were in fact idle.

Government aid to the poverty stricken was not accepted by everyone with equanimity. Close readers of the Bible argued that Holy Writ said we would always have the poor with us, and that most of the poor were either lazy or improvident, or were being punished justly for their sins. Part were immigrants, who it was rumored came to America with an eye to entering such a "Pauper Palace"[1] as that at Philadelphia. The panic of 1837 made public relief more necessary, for even a good American could write that "we are come to such a pass in our country that a portion . . . of our population can get no work."[2]

While many paupers were elderly people whose lives were nearly over, the same thing could not be said of orphans, who were obviously salvageable material. The smaller community depended on relatives and friends, but the larger town frequently had an orphan asylum. Unfortunately the asylum was modeled altogether too much on a prison, with strict discipline and a no-talking rule. The boys were taught farming and the girls housework. A modicum of education averted illiteracy, and a dash of recreation made the entire dish edible if not palatable. Ultimately the boy was apprenticed to a farmer and the girl to a housewife. The results were no better than poor, since many of the orphans graduated into jail. The orphan asylum de luxe, as provided by the two-million-dollar Girard will, was as yet only a marble building and a long presidential report.

Education of the deaf and dumb was in private hands, although most states paid for a few needy scholars. Oldest and reputedly the best of the schools was the American Asylum at Hartford, Connecticut, under Rev. T. H. Galludet; its methods were copied widely. Only students under twenty-five were admitted. Rooms were clean and food good. Talking was with one hand, for Galludet rejected the European innovation of articulation. Handling simple objects, playing games, and hearing stories were replaced in time by more complicated expressions of abstract thought. By the end of the course (four to seven years) the girl had learned housework and the boy a trade.

Education of the blind was introduced to the United States by the almost simultaneous opening of schools at Boston, New York,

[1] Combe, *Notes*, I, 241.
[2] *Democratic Review*, Vol. XIII (July, 1843), 23, quoted in Mott, *Magazines*, 470.

and Philadelphia in 1832–33. Best known was the Boston School, which in time came to be called the Perkins Institution. Its head, but not originator, was that flaming champion of the underdog and the underprivileged, Samuel Gridley Howe. Howe had been dissatisfied with the medical career for which he had been trained, and had fought for Greek independence, after which he was persuaded to undertake work with the blind.

Howe was above all a popularizer. In general he used prevalent European methods of raised letters in metal frames and raised geographical designs. He added greatly to the literature for the blind, including a complete Braille Bible from plates furnished by the American Bible Society. He toured the country arousing interest and support. He had the idea of the ladies' "fair" to raise money. He exhibited his children so successfully that he could write that many women are "so interested in the blind that I am afraid some mammas will put their children's eyes out."[3] He failed, however, to persuade Congress to establish a central library for the blind.

Howe's most famous student was Laura Bridgman, the first blind deaf-mute to be taught the use of language. Howe himself journeyed to Hanover, New Hampshire, to get this bright little seven-year-old girl, and trained her in his own home. The first progress was slow since all ordinary avenues of communication were closed. Tags with raised letters were attached to common objects such as keys and spoons; then the article and tag were separated, for Laura to reconnect. Next the letters of each word were scrambled for Laura to reassemble. By 1841 Laura could carry on simple manual conversations, and in time she could do such things as knit and sew. She was never taught to speak. Her case aroused tremendous interest which brought additional help for other unfortunates.

The feeble-minded and mildly insane ordinarily roamed the streets as the butts for the jokes of the village loafers. If objectionable or dangerous, they were locked in unheated garrets or sheds by embarrassed relatives and allowed to exist precariously on crusts and in filth. Many a town took the lowest bid for the support of the

[3] Richards, *Howe*, II, 118.

pauper insane—a system with appalling abuses. The census of 1840 contended optimistically that one in six of the insane had institutional care, but the usual institution was a hospital, prison, or almshouse, and the usual care consisted of chains and frequent punishments. In many institutions, these unfortunates were not even segregated.

Of the twenty-five to thirty insane asylums, the largest and best known was the Massachusetts State Lunatic Hospital (Worcester), headed by Dr. G. B. Woodward. Also well considered were the Hartford (Connecticut) Retreat and the Bloomingdale (New York) Asylum. Most such institutions were private, and provided all the luxuries for which relatives or friends would pay. State institutions accepted paupers free, but charged everyone else.

Doctors held that "insanity is generally a curable disease. . . . Its pathology is now well understood,"[4] but this optimism was far from justified. Even in classification the doctors were hopelessly at sea. Worcester (1838) labeled its patients, in order of frequency, as cases of mania, melancholia, dementia, or idiocy, but Dr. Woodward hastened to deny confidence in the classification. The Friends' Retreat (1836) reported partial insanity, dementia, moral insanity, mania, and idiocy. The modern student can only guess at the types.

Causes of insanity were also uncertain. The Worcester staff dogmatized that "insanity arises from diseases of the brain. . . . The causes may be moral, mental or physical."[5] Most asylums gave high ratings to ill health and intemperance, but one rejected intemperance entirely. Masturbation was much favored, even though amputating the clitoris was a disappointing treatment. Most doctors gave prominence to disappointments, particularly financial and amorous, while religious excitement was given some blame. In fact, every human trouble from parturition to attending a sick friend received credit, while even then some cases had to be tagged with cause "unknown."

The basic trouble of the doctor, in classification or in treatment,

[4] *Lunatic Asylum of South Carolina Report* (Columbia, S. C., I. C. Morgan, 1842), 11.

[5] *Eighth Annual Report of the Trustees of the State Lunatic Hospital at Worcester* (Boston, Dutton and Wentworth, 1841), 64.

was whether the trouble were mental or physical. Should one treat the body or the mind? Older practice, stemming from Rush and Cullen, blamed the body, holding that the human engine had too great a head of steam, which should be reduced by cathartics, emetics, and bleeding. Such treatment weakened the patient and of course reduced frenzy.

The up-to-date practitioner rejected the debilitating treatment with scorn. "It is one of the chief glories of our age, that this barbarous system has, in a great measure, been abolished throughout the civilized world, and for it has been substituted, what may be emphatically called, the *rational* treatment."[6] The progressive asylum advertised rest, moderate exercise, and pleasant surroundings. Farms and shops, games, a library, and church services were to occupy the mind. Warm and cold baths soothed the patient, with cold showers for the more violent. One school of thought placed much reliance on large doses of narcotics.

The actuality was more drab than the advertising. Work was never sufficient for everyone, while living conditions were seldom ideal and often terrible. "Rational" treatment all too frequently gave way to the older chains, padded cells, straps, mittens, muffs, and straight jackets.

Every asylum claimed an impressive proportion of cures. Ordinarily the figure was given at about 50 per cent, with possibly 80 to 90 per cent of cases received in their first year. Presumably many patients were discharged in temporary spells of sanity or because they improved somewhat. The doctor wanted to believe the best, and did not follow up cases to discover whether his patients remained "cured."

The experts of the thirties may have been far from the perfection they claimed, but they made real and important advances. They recognized that many forms of insanity were curable, that debilitating measures were not good, and that proper surroundings and occupations had therapeutic values. The later work of Dorothea Dix was not that of a person crying in the wilderness, but rather the effort of one who desired to expand the best practices of her time.

The criminal was another object of solicitude for philanthropic

[6] *Lunatic Asylum of South Carolina,* 5.

persons, for even in favored America perverted personalities violated the laws created by free men. Tocqueville, who was surveying American penology, asserted that in America "no one renders obedience to man, but to justice and law,"[7] but apparently the truth of his statement lay largely in its implication of a lack of police officers. Americans themselves had no delusions: "The frequency of crime in this country is startling! There seems to be a complete disorganization of society—a laxness of morals prevailing everywhere—a recklessness on the part of the criminal."[8]

Theft was prominent in a materialistic society—from the "rolling" of drunks to stealing horses and holdups. Personal violence started with fist fights and climaxed in homicide. Counterfeiting was so common that each storekeeper provided himself with a book listing the common frauds. City slums were rabbit warrens of petty criminals such as drunkards, prostitutes, pickpockets, and pimps. Gangs of hoodlums and criminals terrorized the larger cities, attacking pedestrians, insulting and assaulting women, destroying property, doing petty pilfering, and engaging in the protection racket. Slum boys were trained in juvenile gangs and then graduated into the senior organizations.

Dueling was on the wane, but the South and the West still maintained their code of honor; St. Louis had its Bloody Island and New Orleans boasted an average of two dueling deaths a week. Antidueling sentiment increased remarkably because of several notable duels of the thirties. In one, a brother of Nicholas Biddle and a member-elect of Congress were both killed at a distance of five feet. In another, two members of Congress used rifles at eighty yards; one of the men died.

Imprisonment for debt was decreasing, but as late as 1828 New York had one thousand prisoners whose debts averaged twenty-five dollars apiece. The paradox of placing a debtor where he could never pay his debt was being recognized by state after state. Imprisonment for debt was being abolished completely for women, but the new state laws still permitted jailing men for large debts, where fraud was involved, or where the debt was a court fine.

[7] Tocqueville, *Democracy*, I, 118.
[8] *Public Ledger*, April 28, 1836.

Convicted criminals were relatively few, partly because such actions as speeding and spitting on the sidewalk had not yet been termed offenses, and partly because the laws were not well enforced. Even in the large cities, the police were neither many nor active. Anywhere in the nation an injured and irate citizen thought of his own fists before policemen and courts. On a larger scale, mobs lynched Negroes and abolitionists, burned mail and convents, rioted against the bank, attacked actors, ejected gamblers and prostitutes, or accomplished other ends that they considered good.

The unfortunate man who was arrested for a crime which he may or may not have committed was held in jail pending trial unless he could afford bail. At the trial he was represented by a lawyer who favored the rotund and florid type of oratory. Visitors noted that lawyers were highly regarded—"the real aristocracy of America"[9] —which was a tremendous change of opinion from their disrepute during the Revolutionary period.

The judge might be a man of dignity and learning, but all too frequently he was a political appointee who might remove his coat and shoes, tip back in a rocking chair, put his stockinged feet on the bench, and spit tobacco juice in the general direction of the spittoon, meantime deciding cases without benefit of Coke and Blackstone, or even of the statutes. The *Journal of Law* advised the judge to "draw your learning out of your books, not out of your brains."[10] The judgment might be made on technicalities, but better technicalities than the "common sense" of a stupid judge.

Conviction on a minor charge brought a fine or imprisonment, or both, with whipping becoming rare. Imprisonment was in a city or county jail. The usual jail had several conglomerate rooms which held a mixture of drunkards, petty thieves, prostitutes, debtors, insane, and people awaiting trial. Infrequently a city jail classified its prisoners and gave them work. The only ordinary classification was the segregation of women—not a vast improvement, since the women still experienced the necessity of propitiating the guards.

Conditions in the average local jail were bad almost beyond belief. The prisoner was often chained to the wall, with no bed, and

[9] Marryat, *Diary*, 230.
[10] *The Journal of Law* (Philadelphia), Vol. I (July 7, 1830), 5.

possibly two dirty blankets. He was embedded in filth, both human and otherwise. Baths were limited to an infrequent few spoonfuls of cold water. The prisoner might be almost naked, since clothing was not provided. Work was seldom more than occasional hemp picking. The mortality rate was frightful. Appeals to the guards brought only flogging or incarceration in a damp and lightless dungeon with bread and water. The great positive contribution of the local jail was instruction in crime; the prisoner graduated to the state prison.

A man convicted of a major crime might be sentenced to hang. A hanging was a public event, presumably designed to intimidate other potential criminals. Actually it was something of an amusement, and hundreds of families brought their lunches and their children to enjoy the spectacle. The chief figure of the ceremony often capitalized his brief moment of glory before the trap was sprung by either proclaiming anew his innocence or advising his auditors to be warned by his sad fate.

A man sentenced to state prison usually had hopes of escape or pardon—"nothing is so common, when first a prisoner is conducted to prison, as the bold expression and confident expectation of speedy enlargement."[11] Such optimism was not justified by the figures, and there is also considerable question whether the right men were pardoned.

A state prison merited the faint praise that it was superior to the usual local jail. Poorest was the old type which retained conglomerate rooms, no work, and vile living conditions; it lingered in the South and West. Most progressive was the Pennsylvania system, as developed at Philadelphia and Allegheny. After the usual hair cropping and outfitting in prison clothes, the prisoner was placed in a cell 11 feet, 9 inches by 7 feet, 6 inches, to which was attached an exercise yard about twice as large. Here he stayed continuously until his release. For several days he was left in complete solitude and inaction, so that he might repent. Then the boon of work was provided. For such work he received pay, from which the cost of his keep was deducted. The great advantage of the Pennsylvania sys-

[11] D. L. Dix, *Remarks on Prisons and Prison Discipline in the United States* (Philadelphia, Joseph Kite and Company, 1845), 28.

tem was that the prisoner was not further contaminated by contact with other prisoners.

The great and bitter rival of the Pennsylvania system was the Auburn (New York) plan. Lengthy and complicated contrasts were made, but the simple truth was that the Auburn plan was cheaper, and therefore appealed to most state legislatures. Under the Auburn plan the prisoner was isolated at night in a cell so small (7 feet by 3 feet, 6 inches) that it could contain only a cot and a stool, under the supposition that such isolation should decrease homosexuality and the contamination of first offenders. During the day the men moved in lockstep to dining hall and workshop. Universal silence, tagged the "Hush-Hush"[12] system, was the rule, but was commonly evaded to a greater or less degree.

Even the best penitentiary was no bed of roses. No ventilation was provided. Stoves in the corridors were more for the guards than for the inmates, and even when the prisoner slept in all his clothes and under the usual two flimsy cotton blankets, he might suffer from frost-bite. A little cold water sufficed for bathing, with warm water every two or three months being considered sybaritic. Medical care ordinarily consisted of haphazard ministrations by a part-time and poor practitioner. A hospital was an unequipped room attended by an untrained prisoner. Sickness was suspected to be shamming to avoid work, and could be proved only by dying, which was not rare.

Food stressed the institutional standbys of porridge, which was cheap, and soup, which could utilize otherwise inedible scraps. The average meal was insufficient in quantity, badly prepared, and often spoiled. An economical legislature paid the warden five to ten cents a day per man, and then the warden grafted what he could, with the assurance that no investigator would take a criminal's word in opposition to his own.

Prison work, designed to show a profit, was always a problem. If the warden acted only as a supervisor, he pocketed what he could; if he made a flat payment to the state, he mistreated the men. The newest idea was to use an outside contractor, but experience soon showed that the profit motive linked to absolute powers of life and death produced inhumanly cruel taskmasters. Incidentally, outside

[12] Lieber, *Stranger*, 170.

workmen objected to prison production, regardless of the method of control.

Never was the prisoner allowed to forget that he was a social outcast. His head was shaved, or worse, only half-shaved. His coarse, cheap clothes might be distinguished by alternate black and white stripes, by half-red and half-blue, or by blue with red stripes along the seams, or marked with red initials on breast and waist. Letters were censored. Church services were optional, but there was no escape from the self-constituted religious counselor who made periodic visits to inquire about the health of his soul. The only usual reading was the Bible. Some few prisons had small libraries and even classes in reading and writing for the illiterate, but ordinarily there was no education or recreation, for were not these men in prison for punishment? A choir at Charlestown, Massachusetts, was a radical innovation.

The disciplinary ideal was to "be pitiless and just."[13] Seldom did a warden try kindness—as the rare soul who gave each female prisoner a bouquet on the Fourth of July. Leg irons, frequently with an iron ball, were common. Refractory prisoners were chained at night. Punishments were assessed for poor work, stealing, talking, insolence, and spoiling work. Sometimes an uncontrolled guard might be sadistic, or express personal antagonism, or practice blackmail. Six to eighty or ninety lashes with either the cat or a strap was the preferred punishment, although a paddle with holes was said to be an exquisitely painful alternative. Whipping was approved since the man could immediately be put back to work, and then the process repeated if necessary.

Other punishments varied with the ingenuity of the warden and guards. Commonly included were iron gags, straight jackets, cold showers, and strapping the prisoner rigidly to a chair. Every prison had its solitary cells—usually below ground, dark, damp, and filthy —where a man might be broken both physically and mentally. A diet of bread and water which omitted the water was really punishing. Many wardens and guards had reputations for cruelty, which were real achievements under the circumstances. The job of warden was usually a political plum, while a guard supplemented his inadequate pay by selling favors to the prisoners.

Prison sentences were considered the just retribution by society, and were expected to prevent crime through fear. The obvious fact, that many prisoners committed later crimes, was laid to the too great attractiveness of prisons or considered the evidence of a depraved nature which could be changed only by moral suasion or divine intervention. Rarely was the comment made that bad prison conditions might produce crime. One of the few penetrating comments was made by a phrenologist: "Each is confined on account of some erroneous training of the mental faculties which require to be corrected & each should be treated as a *moral patient* with kindness & not suspicion."[14]

The most important penal improvement was a trend toward the classification of prisoners. Women had been segregated earlier. Now the insane were being removed to asylums, and juveniles were being placed in separate institutions. The juvenile House of Refuge or Reformation took boys under twenty-one and girls under eighteen— not only convicted criminals but also refractory children suggested by a police officer or other responsible person. The first three reformatories of this kind were at New York (1825), Philadelphia (1826), and Boston (1826); all three were founded privately but soon became public.

The juvenile reformatory followed a modified Auburn system, with separate night cells, congregate workshops, and fairly strict discipline. But each child was given physical and mental education, and the boy ultimately apprenticed. A distinct novelty was the indeterminate sentence, although each child attained freedom when he came of age. Good conduct was rewarded by special privileges, such as swimming or a trip to town. Bad conduct was punished by withdrawing such rights as talking and playing games; corporal punishment was rare. Two of the schools had jury systems by the inmates, and one refused to accept the word of an informer, trusting entirely to the honesty of the children. Here were ideas that were later to be tried in senior institutions.

Penal reform should have been advanced rapidly by two very active reforming groups, the Pennsylvania Prison Society and the

[13] Pierson, *Tocqueville*, 208.
[14] Smith, *Journal*, 12.

Boston Discipline Society, but unfortunately they devoted their major energy to supporting respectively the Pennsylvania system and the Auburn system, with little time for such possibilities as the indeterminate sentence and parole. Great fields of reform remained available to Dorothea Dix as she started her work in the early forties.

The emotional peak of reforming zeal was attained in the drive against liquor. An elderly and feeble temperance movement was galvanized into activity by six sermons preached by Lyman Beecher in 1825. The following year there appeared the American Society for the Promotion of Temperance. It soon had the enthusiastic assistance of state and local societies, which appeared even in the colleges, at army posts, and in Congress. The American Society may have been optimistic in estimating one million members in 1834 but the vigor of the movement was unquestioned.

The temperance movement was strongly religious in content. Agents of the American Home Missionary Society were urged to "save a free people from that raging fire which feeds its flames with the bodies and souls of men."[15] Local societies were frequently affiliated with churches, and their magazines, pamphlets, and books were strongly moralistic. The stronger ones paid agents to found new societies and persuade men to sign the pledge.

Temperance speakers, both lay and professional, overran the nation. Top billing went to reformed drunkards, of whom the star performer was the English-born John B. Gough. Gough had been on the stage as an accordion player and had been addicted to strong drink. After he took the pledge, he and his accordion went into the temperance movement. Very distressingly he was later (1845) discovered drunk in a New York brothel; his unconvincing explanation was that his soda water had been drugged.

Temperance propaganda took the form of speeches, books, pamphlets, legislative petitions, and mass conventions. Books were sometimes collections of poetry or songs. Magazines included the famous *Genius of Temperance* and the impressively titled *Rum-Seller's Mirror and Drunkard's Looking-Glass*. Of the sermons, Rev. Eli Merrill's "ox sermon" reputedly sold two million copies in a single

[15] *Third Annual Report American Home Missionary Society*, 61.

year, while Rev. G. B. Cheever achieved success with his *Deacon Giles' Distillery*—partly because it got him jailed and hence made him a martyr.

Once a year, from 1833, the temperance workers held immense, simultaneous meetings throughout the United States, Canada, and England. At such a gathering on February 28, 1837, the massed school children of Boston sang the following effusion to the tune of Peterborough:

> " 'Tis but a drop," the father said,
>   And gave it to his son;
> But little did he think a work
>   Of death was then begun.
> The "drop" that lured him, when the babe
>   Scarce lisped his father's name,
> Planted a fatal appetite,
>   Deep in his infant frame.
>
> "'Tis but a drop," the comrades cried,
>   In truant schoolboy tone;
> "It did not hurt us in our robes—
>   It will not, now we're grown."
> And so they drank the mixture up,
>   That reeling, youthful band.
> For each had learned to love the taste,
>   From his own father's hand.
>
> "'Tis but a drop,—I need it now"—
>   The staggering drunkard said;
> "It was my food in infancy—
>   My meat, and drink and bread.
> A drop—a drop—oh let me have,
>   'Twill so refresh my soul!"
> He took it—trembled—drank and died,
>   Grasping the fatal bowl.[16]

[16] Channing, *Temperance*, 95.

Liquor was accused by the temperance people of most of the ills of the world. It was credited with accelerating the pulse and encouraging consumption, fevers, cholera, apoplexy, and poor vision; every autopsy showing alcoholism and every adverse doctor's statement was publicized. Drink was given responsibility for 200,000 unhappy families, for nine-tenths of the almshouse residents, for over half of mental ailments, for half of minor crimes, and for many of the major crimes. The grog shop was described not as the poor man's club but as the resort for criminals, gamblers, and prostitutes.

Temperance people were religious minded, and Beecher went so far as to hold that "drunkenness is a sin which excludes from heaven."[17] Unfortunately, however, the Bible did not prove a good temperance tract. The best that could be done was to emphasize social costs and moral degradation, and every reader of temperance literature knew the steps of descent—a small convivial glass, drunkenness, poverty, wife beating, crime, and death in delirium tremens.

The frequent emotional appeals often took the form of more or less hypothetical cases. "I have seen a lovely young female, who had been reared in the arms of parental tenderness, her heart swelling with the delusive hopes of inexperience, led forward into connubial life, with prospects as bright and promising as the unclouded morning sun. Again I have marked the fitful melancholy, the fading cheek, and the anxious look, which told that agonizing suspicions as to him in whom centered all her hopes and affections, were busy at her heart; until the fatal truth burst upon her, as she found herself fettered to pollution, and clasped in the arms of living death, embodied in a *drunken husband*. And she struggled against cruel disappointment, and degradation, and anguish; until a kindly consumption led her from her earthly suffering into a premature grave."[18]

All this ammunition was bound to hit some targets. Certain farmers stopped furnishing liquor at harvest time, the Baltimore and Ohio refused to hire liquor users, the army stopped liquor rations,

[17] L. Beecher, *Six Sermons on the Nature, Occasions, Signs, Evils, and Remedy of Intemperance* (Boston, T. R. Marvin, 1827), 81.

[18] *Fourth Annual Report of the New York State Society for the Promotion of Temperance* (Albany, Packard and Van Benthuysen, 1833), 15.

unmarried girls refused drinking escorts, housewives boycotted stores selling liquor, and young men urged farmers to stop feeding distillers' swill to their cows. Temperance hotels appeared all over the country, and even in Kentucky a visitor might not be offered a drink. One million people signed the pledge, and the A. T. S. claimed twenty thousand saved from drunkenness—a somewhat vague statement since salvation apparently had come to only five thousand drunkards.

The temperance people had real hopes that "this drunken world of ours"[19] might be remade so that "drunkenness may no more be heard of in the earth."[20] In fact, some of them actually held that "drinking is rapidly going out of fashion."[21] Their elation was premature—probably as a result of looking through the wrong end of the telescope. Figures showing reduced production are at least suspect, while imports did not drop until the depression. Probably the drinking habits of the average American were not greatly changed.

Part of the agitation was in the direction of legal enactments. Several states and cities responded with restrictive legislation, although no state went so far as outright prohibition. Most publicized was the Massachusetts law that the smallest sale to a single customer must be fifteen gallons, except on a doctor's orders. Violation was widespread, such as allowing a customer to pay to see a "striped pig," after which he received his liquor free. Efforts at enforcement brought threats of mob action, and juries would not convict. The law was repealed within a year by an almost unanimous legislature.

The greatest troubles of the temperance movement came not from the natural opposition of the liquor interests, but from internal schism. The first great fight was of moderation versus abstinence, with the abstinence people the more vigorous—"*moderate drinking* and *intoxication* are criminal. Intemperance is a disease."[22] Total abstinence won. Then the question arose whether abstinence applied only to distilled liquors or also to wines and malt beverages. Again the radicals were more outspoken—"It is not the *abuse* of intoxicat-

---

[19] *American Quarterly Temperance Magazine* (Albany), February, 1833, 93.

[20] *Norfolk Auxiliary Society* (1832), 8.

[21] Althea Bass, *Cherokee Messenger* (Norman, University of Oklahoma Press, 1936), 87.

[22] S. B. Woodward, *Essay on Asylums for Inebriates* (n.p., n.d.), 19.

ing drinks which makes men drunkards. *It is the use of them at all;* for, if men drank only water; there would be no drunkards."[23] The A. T. S. vacillated on the problem and lost strength during the mid-thirties, only then to be hurt further by the depression.

Agitation was revived about 1840 by the Washingtonian Society, which was organized by and for drunkards. The female equivalent was the Martha Washington Society. Total abstinence was the goal. The Washingtonian movement favored experience meetings climaxed by stirring emotional appeals. It sponsored big parades, with the favorite float showing a reformed drunkard surrounded by his kneeling and grateful wife and children. The upward surge of the movement was soon to produce the first state prohibition law in Maine.

The reformers who were the most hopeful martyrs, and who in the long run produced the greatest troubles and the most drastic changes, were the abolitionists. While no real reformer was a diplomat, the opponents of slavery seemed to have a deeper and more moving conviction, and to have been less willing to compromise, than other religious and moral zealots.

Slavery had long been opposed by many Americans from both North and South. Its elimination was delayed largely by the value of slaves in cotton culture and by the presumed hazard of freeing millions of blacks who were not far removed from savagery. Bitterness came only when the English antislavery movement of the eighteen twenties was reproduced in the United States by such men as the Quaker Benjamin Lundy. Slaveholders and their sympathizers resented being pictured as immoral and inhuman fiends, and began to fight back with ever more extreme arguments. Instead of holding that slavery was a necessary evil, they began to support it as a positive good. "But it is no evil. On the contrary, I believe it to be the greatest of all the great blessings which a kind Providence has bestowed upon our glorious region."[24]

Proslavery arguments had become standardized by the eighteen

[23] C. Yale, *The Temperance Reader* (Boston, Hilliard, Gray and Company, 1835), 10.
[24] Quoted in W. S. Jenkins, *Pro-Slavery Thought in the Old South* (Chapel Hill, University of North Carolina Press, 1935), 79.

Eastern State Penitentiary, Philadelphia;
John Haviland, architect, 1821–29. Typical of
an architectural trend in the period

thirties. Their continued repetition brought conviction, at least to the South. The Negro was held different in body and inferior in mind. The structure of the body, shape of the head, weight of the brain, and insensitivity of the nervous system all indicated an inferiority which was demonstrated by stupidity, timidity, dependence, and lack of initiative. The Negro had never exhibited ability which would justify anything more than a slave status, in which he received at least better food, clothing, and care than the northern unskilled laborer.

A second great line of argument was that all important civilizations of the past, including those of the Bible, were built upon slavery. As for the South, prosperity and a high culture were possible only because of slave labor. Without slavery the Negro's natural indolence would bring poverty and degradation. Savagery would reassert itself, and Negro mobs would seize white property and rape white women.

The venerated Declaration of Independence, with its statement that "all men are created equal," with "certain unalienable rights," was a real problem. The simplest solution was to deny that the Negro was a man, but some Southerners were willing to go further and question the Declaration. "We talk a great deal of nonsense about the rights of man. We say that man is born free, and equal to every other man. Nothing can be more untrue: no human being ever was, nor is or ever will be born free. Where is the freedom of an infant in swaddling clothes? No two men were ever born equal or ever will be. Are they equally strong, equally talented, born to equal pretensions and chances? If nature has ordained inferiority, that inferiority will tell its own story through life, and such is the fact."[25]

But not all Southerners were entirely convinced by their own arguments. Many doubted that Old Testament conditions were a proper model for nineteenth-century America, that Christ's teaching countenanced slavery, and that Negroes were excluded from the "all men" who were "created free and equal." Then they hedged, holding that slavery might well be best at the moment in the South; ministers preached humility and obedience to God's will.

[25] *Southern Literary Messenger*, quoted in Jenkins, *Pro-Slavery Thought in the Old South*, 125.

Southerners might well differ among themselves over slavery, but increasingly they would not tolerate outside criticism. Antislavery tracts and other objectionable literature was seized by vigilance committees and burned. Persons were threatened. Southerners became sensitive about their "peculiar" institution and even saw slurs where they were not intended. Hotheads injected the slavery issue into every public and private question and even predicted the failure of the Union. For example a South Carolina editorial of 1829 read: "If the discussion of the acquisition of Texas brings on the agitation of the slave question, as we are sure that it will, a rupture with the northern states will become almost inevitable."[26]

The one reform that could still obtain a general hearing was the establishment of a colony for the Negroes at some place outside the United States. The American Society for the Colonization of the Free People of Color of the United States, with loosely affiliated societies all over the nation, was subsidized by Congress. It sponsored the state of Liberia, which by 1835 had a population of three thousand. Most Liberians were free Negroes who migrated through preference, but a few had been freed for the purpose. Even with missionary aid their condition was poor, and, curiously enough, they owned slaves.

Colonization was losing support as obviously an inadequate solution. More extreme Northerners and Southerners swung toward thoroughgoing proposals. The moderates gave some support to the American Union for the Relief and Improvement of the Colored Races, founded at Boston in 1835 to ameliorate the condition of the slaves, but it came a generation too late to be important.

Southern arguments had been developed in part to answer northern charges, which were becoming ever more extreme. The calm, unhurried, Quaker-inspired agitation was being replaced by the more drastic proposals of men who believed in "abolition *immediate universal.*"[27] Those versatile reformers, Lewis and Arthur Tappan, headed the new movement and attracted an able group which included Theodore Weld, George Bourne, Joshua Leavitt, and Wil-

[26] Columbia (S. C.) *Telescope*, quoted in *Niles Register*, Vol. XXXVII (November 28, 1829), 213.

[27] Barnes, *Weld Letters*, I, 99.

liam Goodell. While their aims sounded drastic, their actual first moves were moderate, being centered largely on a Negro school at New Haven.

The moderate Tappan plans were blasted wide open with the explosive force of William Lloyd Garrison, who founded *The Liberator* at Boston in 1831. His opening declaration was a battle cry: "I *will* be as harsh as truth, and as uncompromising as justice. On this subject, I do not wish to think, or speak, or write, with moderation. I am in earnest—I will not equivocate—I will not retreat a single inch —and I will be heard."[28] This bumptious young man was unquestionably in earnest, and even his greatest enemies admitted that he made himself extremely audible.

Garrison seemed to have been born to trouble. On one early occasion he had been saved from jail by Arthur Tappan's money— an expenditure which Tappan later may have regretted. For Garrison became more notorious, and was indicted, burned in effigy, and almost lynched—but always he was heard. His vitriolic and vituperative paper was frequently excoriated and at times burned, but it, too, was heard. Garrison considered himself the most important American abolitionist. He persuaded his pet New England Anti-Slavery Society to provide the funds to visit England, where he was accepted on his own valuation. When he returned to America—on borrowed money—he had the idea of a national starring vehicle.

The Tappans and their friends were greatly embarrassed by Garrison. They had planned a national society, but had postponed it partly because Garrison's inflammatory speeches had antagonized so many moderates. Now Garrison forced their hand, for if they did not act, he would. They formed the New York Anti-Slavery Society (October, 1833), which compromised moderate and radical positions in the incomprehensible formula, "immediate emancipation which is gradually accomplished."[29] Then they invited hand-picked delegates to a "national convention" at Philadelphia; each delegate was instructed: "To avoid interruption in our meetings,

[28] Quoted in E. D. Adams, *The Power of Ideals in American History* (New Haven, Yale University Press, 1913), 37.

[29] G. H. Barnes, *The Anti-Slavery Impulse 1830–1844* (New York, D. Appleton-Century Company, 1933), 49.

we wish this to be considered confidential."[30] Arthur Tappan was
the logical president, and his magazine, *The Emancipator*, the official organ. A gesture was made toward Garrison by giving him a
minor office and a leading voice in the resolutions and by the purchase of some of his pamphlets.

The abolition movement centered to some extent in the classroom of C. G. Finney at Oberlin. Indeed this college had been
bludgeoned by Tappan money and Lane secessionists into admitting
Negroes. Finney was an abolitionist, but a moderate. He insisted
that for his students salvation should be the central theme and not
abolition, lest we "become embroiled in one common infernal squab-
ble that will roll a wave of blood over the land."[31] Finney's friend
Theodore Weld was one of the most effective of abolition workers
until his voice failed; and Weld in turn converted James Gillespie
Birney, who was invaluable as a reformed slaveowner with legislative experience; Birney ran for President in 1840 and 1844.

The Anti-Slavery Society claimed to have acquired 2,000 local
societies and 175,000 members by 1840, but the figures are exaggerated. Many of the societies lived but briefly, and most of them
contributed only spasmodically. The national group circulated books
and pamphlets, with Weld's *Slavery As It Is* the basic text late in
the decade. It subsidized magazines such as *The Liberator* and *The
Emancipator*. It encouraged speakers. It paid agents to tour and
organize new societies. It circulated antislavery petitions.

The arguments of the abolitionists in time became commonplace.
As religious people they stressed the supposed moral degradation
of both master and slave, and then, because slavery existed in Biblical times, they were driven into the delicate position of denying that
the Bible was always a rule of conduct. Additional arguments were
based on natural rights, the bad psychological effects on both slave
and master, and economic retardation. The inferiority of the Negro
was explained by his environment. Accounts of sadistic beatings and
rape had dramatic effectiveness, especially when accompanied by
pictures, but were not used as often as might have been expected.

Abolitionists expected to meet southern hate, which rose perceptibly during the mid-thirties. The South was indignant at this

[30] Barnes, *Weld Letters*, I, 119.   [31] *Ibid.*, I, 319.

blatant attack on property rights guaranteed by the Constitution. "The abolitionists . . . have by their intemperance, united the whole South against them as one."[32] No longer was mild argument the proper reply—"No! Fellow Citizens! wait not, slumber not, sleep not! Wherever you see the danger, seize and trample on it, and do not merely 'scotch the snake,' but kill it."[33] State legislatures penalized "incendiary" publications such as *The Liberator*. Mobs burned antislavery literature until the post office stopped deliveries. Known abolitionists risked lynching. Presidents Jackson and Van Buren objected—not to southern mob actions but to the abolition propaganda that gave it rise.

Southern hostility was, if anything, beneficial to the cause of abolition, and the abolitionists were much more concerned over northern apathy. Most Northerners were just not interested, with the result that money was hard to raise. No collections were taken at meetings lest the audiences be scared away. The Anti-Slavery Society found difficulty in raising its five-thousand-dollar annual budget, and depended primarily on a few rich contributors. Its magazines showed a heavy deficit since over a third of the subscribers forgot to remit. Its agents received only pittances; the best of them, Weld, was paid eight dollars a week and expenses.

Many Northerners were outright hostile. Some may have depended on southern business, while others resented any kind of radical change. Many were really concerned that abolition could "have no other effect than to render more oppressive the condition of the slave, and which, if not abandoned, there is great reason to fear, will prove the rock on which the Union will split."[34] There was real objection to "the miserable fanaticism that has commenced to walk abroad in our land."[35] Possibly some of the ultimate trouble came from hoodlums who were glad to take excitement wherever they found it.

Abolitionists perforce—and sometimes gladly—became martyrs. Lewis Tappan's home was gutted, and his office saved only by armed

[32] R. H. Shryock (ed.), *Letters of Richard D. Arnold* (Durham, N. C., Duke University Press, 1929), 14.

[33] St. Louis *Commercial Bulletin*, September 2, 1835.

[34] Frothingham, *Everett*, 132.

[35] *Morning Courier*, October 1, 1833.

clerks, police, and militia. Garrison had a Faneuil Hall meeting disrupted, and was paraded through the streets with a halter around his neck; the police jailed him for his own protection. Whittier was pelted with mud. Weld meetings were interrupted by mud, lampblack, eggs, and other missiles; he himself was twice hit by stones, once being knocked unconscious. His reaction was that "Blessed are they who die in the harness and are buried on the field or bleach there."[36] Abolition halls and churches were destroyed, agents mobbed and burned in effigy, and printing presses wrecked. Reverend Elijah Lovejoy, an Illinois abolitionist editor, was murdered, and members of the mob were freed by a jury. Cases of violence were almost endless.

Mob violence seemed justifiable to many Southerners who felt that abolitionists talked "treason against the lives and property of the citizens of the slave states,"[37] but for many Northerners it resulted in martyrdom, and brought sympathy. As for the Anti-Slavery Society, it changed its policy in 1836 to one that seemed more effective and less hazardous. Emphasis went to direct speeches rather than to written material. More stress was placed on specific and short-run objectives, such as the end of the slave trade in the District of Columbia and no expansion of slavery in the territories. More work was done with local groups, particularly in the small towns and in the country—not spectacular, but ultimately effective.

Petitions were used extensively from 1834, and with ever increasing effectiveness. A nationwide organization was co-ordinated by the New York office of the Anti-Slavery Society, which then turned the petitions over to friendly congressmen such as John Quincy Adams. The ordinary petition was short, with a title describing the contents, and was concerned with some matter such as slavery in the District of Columbia, the annexation of Texas, the interstate slave trade, slavery in the territories, or the admission of Florida without slavery.

The very volume of these petitions endangered other Congressional business, and in self-defense Congress passed a "gag" rule that petitions should be laid on the table after reading only the titles.

[36] Barnes, *Weld Letters*, I, 310.
[37] St. Louis *Commercial Bulletin*, August 12, 1835.

This action was legally proper but politically mistaken. Adams harassed the House with hundreds of petitions on abstractions such as liberty, the human race, and the principles of the Declaration, summaries of the contents of which were in the titles. Abolitionists shouted that their right of petition was being violated, and thereby attracted additional sympathy.

The abolition movement found both strength and weakness in its appeal to the feminine part of the population. The Grimké sisters, Sarah and Angelina, were a fine illustration. Born in a slave-holding South Carolina family, which they later said was a part of "circles of dissipation and folly,"[38] they early wept co-operatively over Negro troubles. Moving to Philadelphia, they became Quakers, and sat with the Negroes in the back of the church to protest segregation. As time passed, they became more active in writing and speaking—at first only to their own sex and then to mixed audiences. Angelina was coached by no less a person than Theodore Weld, and became so successful that a New England speaking trip turned into a triumphal tour.

The Grimkés, like other women reformers, became increasingly disturbed by the opposition they received merely because they were women. As a result they began to talk feminism even more than abolition—a development that was encouraged by Garrison. Weld accepted the feminism but insisted that it should not imperil the abolition movement. He was not particularly successful forensically, but attained a measure of practical success by marrying Angelina; housekeeping and maternity decreased her active interest in feminism.

At the same time that the Anti-Slavery Society was becoming more conservative, Garrison was becoming more radical. He issued dicta on religious truths, rights of women, education, morals, land disposal, or any other subject that occurred to him. When his intemperate diatribes led many churches to close their pulpits to him, he thundered against all church people. When he failed to obtain desired legislation, he repudiated governments and held constitutions to be sinful.

[38] C. H. Birney, *Sarah and Angelina Grimké* (Boston, Lee and Shepard, 1885), 18.

The panic of 1837 almost killed the antislavery movement. Arthur Tappan went bankrupt. Contributions dropped. Central control collapsed. Important members, such as J. Q. Adams, withdrew. Worst of all, Garrison captured the national convention of 1840, and the Tappan forces seceded to create a rival American and Foreign Anti-Slavery Society. A prominent abolitionist moaned in 1840: "Like yourself, I can go neither the Old nor New Anti-Slavery Organization *at the present*. I am sick, heart sick, of the quarrels of abolitionists between themselves."[39] When Birney ran for President on the Liberty party ticket in 1840, he polled only seven thousand votes. Great powers of prophecy would have been necessary to estimate properly the importance that abolition was to attain within the next two decades.

Of all American reform movements, the most magnificently and romantically unrealistic was the one supporting international peace. Its supporters were never numerous, partly because Americans were by no means pacifist but rather aggressively expansionist, and partly because a major war seemed a remote possibility. No such war threatened in Europe, and there were no aggressive neighbors in America. Any American foreign-looking interests were generally to fulfill a messianic complex to save the rest of the world along American lines.

American thinking about war was extraordinarily unrealistic. In spite of expansionist policies, the army numbered only some six thousand men, mostly riffraff, slovenly in dress and lacking in discipline; about 15 per cent deserted each year. It was employed largely on the frontier. Its officers were often West Pointers, but the pay was so low that many of them resigned. The navy was utterly unimpressive, with some fifty men-of-war, and an unsympathetic national administration which gave no hope for improvement.

In view of American expansionism, the main reliance in the militia was almost incredible. Theoretically some 1,500,000 males between the ages of eighteen and forty-five would spring to arms if trouble came, but actually these men were almost entirely untrained; militia musters were going out of fashion and survived

[39] Barnes, *Weld Letters*, II, 849.

only as sprees for the boisterous. The only hopeful sign was that the people against whom any such army might be used were much less numerous and often even less prepared.

Head of the American peace movement was the American Peace Society, formed in 1828; its prime mover was William Ladd. Its arguments against war have long since become commonplace; the stress was on economic losses, the appeal thought to be strongest for Americans. Its speakers and writers favored such measures as disarmament, the outlawry of war, a Court of Nations to codify international law, and a Congress of Nations to promote international amity and good will. The great internal argument was whether a defensive war was ever justified. Until 1837 the American Peace Society approved such a war, but in that year it decided that "all national wars are inconsistent with Christianity, including those supposed or alleged to be defensive."[40] The new position may have been consistent, but it was not popular with the majority of Americans.

Dissent from the ideals of the American Peace Society came from both conservatives and radicals. The conservatives saw the virtues of force under certain circumstances. The radicals, such as the members of the New England Non-Resistance Society (1838), opposed not only war but all use of force, including that of the government to preserve law and order. When Edmund Quincy refused a commission as justice of the peace from Governor Everett of Massachusetts, he proclaimed: "I do, therefore, in the presence of Almighty God, and before you, as Chief Magistrate of this Commonwealth, hereby abjure and renounce all allegiance which I may have acknowledged myself at any time to owe to any government of man's institution. And I call upon Heaven and you to witness that I have put away from myself this iniquity forever!"[41]

American reformers were always intensely in earnest, and almost always strongly religious. They did not question the value of their proposals in producing a perfect world. Only rarely did they possess humor, for moral reform was a serious matter which should

[40] *Tenth Annual Report, American Peace Society* (1838), 2.
[41] Quoted in M. A. D. Howe, *Causes and Their Champions* (Boston, Little, Brown and Company, 1926), 281.

not be degraded by levity. Charged with high religious and moral ferver, the reformers could break but not bend—any compromise or retreat was sin. The result was that they created frequent trouble, now and then ending in martyrdom.

Some of the reforms were either undesirable, or at least untimely, while others were futile wastes of time. But practicality was not a proper test for a true reformer, since he was a man of principle who followed conscience in the search for an ideal, no matter how remote. Some of the reforms were ultimately accepted, and their proponents have consequently been labeled as brave men of great vision, who are to be congratulated on their self-sacrifice for a better world of the future. Only a cynic comments that in many cases the same results would probably have been attained anyway—maybe a little more slowly, but with less friction and unhappiness along the way. Even if reformers should be respected as commanding historical figures, they frequently made very uncomfortable friends.

Reform movements illustrated the abundant vitality of the young republic, but, much more important, their existence proved a diversity of American interests that is frequently overlooked. Religious and moral utopias dominated the lives of hundreds of men who might otherwise have been making their fortunes in shipping or manufacturing. They took millions of dollars that might have built railroads and iron foundries. Obviously the American did not think exclusively in economic terms. Material prosperity was but one of the traits of the perfect civilization that was coming into being in the United States. And utopia was not far distant, but could be attained within a generation if each man only did his part. Change meant progress, and progress would culminate in perfection in the near future.

17. Doctors

AN AMERICA OF HARD WORK, of food drowned in grease and bolted in haste, and of intense suspicion of exercise and fresh air, was a happy hunting ground for the doctor. Even in the supposedly healthy West, fevers and ague chased each other merrily. A national death rate of thirty to thirty-five per thousand was about three times the modern figure. Half the deaths were those of boys and girls under twenty, and one in five was from a lung ailment, thus giving factual backing for the frequent literary concept of the innocent girl fading into an early consumptive grave.

The high American death rate was only slightly affected by the poorly trained doctors. One American doctor asserted that the boy to go into medicine was the son too weak or too lazy for farm or shop, too stupid for the bar, and too immoral for the pulpit. The description is harsh but not entirely wrong. Most doctors learned their trade through being apprenticed to a practicing physician; they swept floors, rolled pills, read a book or two, watched their monitor, and ultimately hung out their shingles. A minority took two courses of medical lectures, but usually without seeing a dissection or even a real patient. A few studied abroad. The average doctor started practice at the age of nineteen or twenty.

Most states had licensing laws, but they were decreasing in effectiveness, so that by 1845 only three states made any effort at enforcement. The average law denied the unlicensed doctor access to the courts to collect his bills; in a few states, fines were levied for unlicensed practice. Licenses were usually granted by a state board appointed by a local medical society. Examinations were cursory. In general, anyone who wanted to practice merely hung out his shingle.

The many medical societies were little more than self-admiration clubs. Periodically the members dined and listened to speeches which lauded their work and castigated "quacks"—that is, anyone outside the charmed circle. The societies collected libraries, set prize essays and sometimes published periodicals. A few adopted codes of ethics, usually following the Englishman Thomas Percival. Sometimes price schedules were set up, but seldom was anyone disciplined for violations. An effort to form a national organization proved abortive.

Medical literature was bulky, but of little value. Medical journals had as high a mortality rate as their subscribers' patients, since the average doctor was no more punctual in meeting his own bills than were his debtors. Such magazines depended heavily on articles clipped from foreign publications, often without credit. They were bombastically nationalistic, boasting grandiloquently of the accomplishments of American medicine. Medical books were mostly foreign, being reprinted without royalties, but books by such Americans as Chapman, Gibson, Dewees, Eberle, Duglison, Bigelow, and Gross were increasing in popularity. A scattering of monographs had varying merit.

The acid test of the position of the doctor was his income, which was not large. A popular city doctor might receive upwards of eight thousand dollars a year, but the average medical man called five hundred dollars satisfactory. Individual charges were fairly high: one dollar for an office call and more for home or night calls. Obstetrical care cost from four to fifty dollars, a major operation from fifty to one hundred dollars. The trouble was that patients paid their doctor last. Many a doctor compounded his own pills and medicines, took pupils, or even did other work to buttress his income.

Doctors had small prestige primarily because of their own inadequacies. Contradictory diagnoses and treatments, lack of proper professional standards, and their eternal bickerings and intemperate language all decreased their reputation. Even the uninformed layman had his doubts of the efficacy of the professional, except in cases where confidence was more important than medicine:

Belief is half the cure—to doubt, obstructs
The free secretion of the spongy ducts—[1]

[1] Hale, *Notes,* 176.

The state of American medicine was easily apparent to anyone who glanced at any of the lists of deaths. The cause of death was stated in hundreds of cases as "unknown," a term which was just about as informative as other published causes, including the padded "fever" and "inflammation" groups; "child-bed fever," for example, presumably meant only the absence of any identifiable ailment. Most mysterious were such entries as fits, decay, sudden death, mortification, gout in the stomach, hip complaint, and drinking cold water. One doctor complained to the *Boston Medical and Surgical Journal* about mortality figures and terms: "The names are all new, and for all the knowledge I get of 'em the diseases might just as well be new too."[2]

Fevers were among the more important matters of uncertainty. Excluding such oddities as "lake fever," they were ordinarily described as "continual," lasting more or less continuously; "remittent," rising and falling; or "intermittent" (or "ague"), alternating with chills. They were also classified as "inflammatory," indicating high blood pressure, or the reverse. The term "bilious fever" might include yellow fever, dysentery, typhoid, acute endocarditis, pyemia, and septicemia. Malaria might be classified as intermittent, remittent, bilious, congestive, malarial, or typho-malarial fever.

The favored explanation of fever was decayed vegetable matter, particularly from marshy areas; these "miasmata exert their principal malignity in the first hours of the evening."[3] Alternate suggestions were moisture, a chemical substance not yet isolated, soil, climate, bad water, the state of a river, mountain water under ground, rare air, or comets. One of the best medical journals posited an invisible fluid, analogous to caloric or electricity. With such uncertainty, epidemics were particularly depressing, since even quarantine and sanitation measures were of doubtful efficacy.

Treatments followed the maxim that "Mildness of medical treatment is a real cruelty."[4] A powerful calming or depressing influence,

[2] *Boston Medical Journal*, Vol. I (1828), 799, quoted in H. B. Shafer, *The American Medical Profession, 1783 to 1850* (New York, Columbia University Press, 1936), 19.

[3] *Boston Medical Journal*, Vol. II (February 17, 1829), 6.

[4] A. A. Benezet, *The Family Physician* (Cincinnati, W. H. Woodward, 1826), 8.

if not fatal to the patient, was followed by a tonic when the fever abated. Bloodletting was the ordinary calming agent, being accomplished by leeching, cupping, or cutting a vein or even an artery. It was advised for all fevers and inflammations, and also for gastritis, softening of the brain, dysentery, bronchitis, rheumatism, smallpox, measles, piles, consumption, epilepsy, tetanus, angina pectoris, diabetes, jaundice, insanity, or what have you? The texts advised letting some ten to twelve ounces at a time, but many doctors were more generous. One doctor made some sort of record by removing six hundred ounces in two months; the average human body contains about two hundred ounces.

Next to bloodletting "mercurial cathartics are the dependence, the indispensable remedy,"[5] and this meant calomel, which was given in tremendous doses.

> *Howe'er their patients do complain*
> *Of head, or heart, or nerve, or vein,*
> *Of fever, thirst, or temper fell,*
> *The Medicine still, is* Calomel.[6]

Depletion was further advanced by other laxatives, purgatives, and cathartics, such as castor oil, sulphur, and rhubarb. Then came emetics, as ipecac or tobacco; mustard and other plasters; drugs to induce sweating, urination, menstruation, or salivation. If the patient survived both fever and treatment, he was then given baths and massages, and invigorated with such tonics as iron, arsenic, quinine, and citrus fruits.

The one disease really being eliminated was smallpox. Each outbreak saw masses of people rushing to be vaccinated, and the cowpox serum was introduced during the thirties. The only epidemic was late in the decade among the Indians of the upper Mississippi Valley; some tribes, such as the Mandans, practically disappeared.

Other fevers were frequently epidemic. Malaria (ague) was considered an inevitable trial to be borne with all possible fortitude.

[5] J. E. Cooke, *Essays on the Autumnal and Winter Epidemics* (Lexington, Ky., Transylvania Press, 1829), 68.

[6] Quoted from *Richmond Enquirer* in R. H. Shryock, *The Development of Modern Medicine* (Philadelphia, 1936), 246.

Scarlet fever, scarlatina, and measles were not distinguished, and the lack of knowledge of cause and treatment led to the analysis that they are "under no fixed laws." One doctor, who observed that the usual bleeding and calomel were frequently fatal, came to the startling conclusion that scarlet fever was "purely nervous"[7] and should be treated with stimulants.

Yellow fever was epidemic every two or three years, especially in southern cities like New Orleans, where rumor had it that twenty to thirty graves were always kept open and ready. Causes, diagnosis, and treatment were the same as for other fevers, with no attention given the annoying "moschetos." The most satisfactory way to avoid yellow fever was to go north in the summer.

The great epidemic of the decade was cholera. Coming from Europe in 1832 to Quebec and Montreal, it spread down the Champlain and Hudson valleys to New York City, which was scared sick. During July and August twenty thousand people deserted the city, parties were canceled, business slowed, the streets were almost deserted, and public buildings were converted into hospitals. About half of the six thousand cases ended fatally. From New York the cholera spread up and down the coast; crossing the mountains, it swept west to St. Louis and south to the Gulf. Overtaking troops headed for the Black Hawk outbreak, it killed more soldiers than the war. Mississippi steamboats stopped periodically to bury their dead—"the firemen just dig a hole and throw them in."[8]

Cold weather reduced the epidemic, but a revival the following summer was particularly virulent in the West. Kentucky was hard hit, with stricken people collapsing on the boats, on the streets, and in the hotels. Observers claimed that the state lost 10 per cent of its population, and that some towns lost up to 50 per cent. Later outbreaks were only sporadic, and ended by the close of 1835.

Cholera was investigated and discussed by the doctors at great length, but the only factual result was a description of the progress of the disease. Investigations showed greater incidence among the

[7] *The Maryland Medical and Surgical Journal* (Baltimore), (October, 1839), I, 13.

[8] J. T. P. Evan, "Mrs. Caroline Phelps' Diary," in *Journal of the Illinois State Historical Society*, Vol. XXIII (July, 1930), 216.

old, intemperate, black, poor, ill fed, and badly clothed, but cleanliness and good food did not stop the disease. Most doctors doubted that it was contagious because of the ineffectiveness of quarantine. Miasmic theories were favored, but alternatives were the influence of sun, moon, comet, gas from the earth, animalcules, bad food, night air, heat, or intemperance. Some approval attached to the opinion that "after the drunkards die off it will not be more formidable than Scarlitena."[9] Most honest was the president of the Medical Society of New York, who admitted in his presidential address that "The first and moving cause of this, and all widespread epidemics, is known alone to Him, who has established these general laws by which universal nature is governed."[10]

The most accurate statement about the treatment of cholera was that "The Doctors do not understand the disease, and very opposite treatments have their strenuous advocates."[11] Bleeding and calomel were common, with one authority talking of a single dose of 240 grains of calomel. Opium was used frequently. Special diets were common. One doctor favored warm and irritating rubbing, as with cayenne or mustard. Another preferred ice water internally, including ice suppositories and anal ice-water douches. Thomsonians swore by steam baths and lobelia. Most people wore flannel next to the skin, carried sacks of camphor, and put chloride of lime everywhere. One person's guess was as good as another's, and recovery was a tribute to the patient's constitution.

Human ignorance led to speculations about the Divinity. Many a devout man held that God was angry with the world's enmities, carnal spirit, backsliding, whoredom, drunkenness, Sabbath breaking, and other enormities, and would end his punishments only when the world was cleansed both morally and physically. A doctor asserted that "The present crisis appears to us . . . appropriate . . . for public petitions to the only power which can, under all and any circumstances, afford us entire security."[12] And who can assert that prayer was not as effective as the current medicines?

[9] *New Hampshire Medical Society Records 1791–1854*, 257.

[10] *Transactions of the Medical Society of New York*, Vol. I (1833), 220.

[11] J. F. Cooper (ed.), *Correspondence of James Fenimore-Cooper* (2 vols., New Haven, Yale University Press, 1922), I, 303.

[12] *Boston Medical Journal*, Vol. V (September 20, 1831), 98.

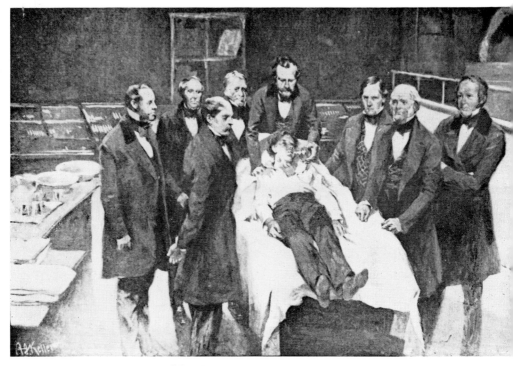

The Discovery of Anaesthesia; first public
demonstration at Boston, October 16, 1846

Typhus and typhoid were first differentiated by Dr. William W. Gerhard of Philadelphia in 1837, but the discovery was then useless because no one knew the cause or proper treatment of either. Some credited typhoid to youth, new residence, time of the year, locality, or sex; most thought it noncontagious. The treatment was disputed, particularly bloodletting, which "has been alternately praised as of indispensable utility, and rejected as pernicious in the extreme"; the doctor then added that "its efficacy appears now to be indisputably established."[13] One eminent doctor, however, sprinkled cold water on the patient and then let Nature do her work, while another gave a laxative and then prayed.

Other diseases might be listed, but the listing becomes monotonous with the inevitable comments that the causes were unknown and that the treatment usually consisted of bleeding and calomel. The greatest single exception was tuberculosis, because most doctors had observed that depleting treatments were so universally fatal that they stuck to fresh air and exercise.

Obstetrics was a profitable part of a doctor's practice, in spite of the competition of midwives. Regardless of his experience and the many articles in the medical journals, the doctor lacked much elementary knowledge. For example, various authorities held that the fully developed microscopic child came entirely from the father, that it was entirely the product of the ovum, or that it was a mixture. Such confusions were due in great part to a lack of proper examinations, even post mortem.

A pregnant woman was generally advised to be moderate in eating and exercising, to keep a calm temper and use no excessive alcohol. Only a rare doctor advised her to eat for two. Prenatal influence was accepted by a few doctors and most laymen, but the more advanced of the profession were impatient: "I had hoped this absurd notion had long since been exploded, or that it was confined to the weak minded and illiterate."[14]

The gynecologist had a special problem in that the current conception of modesty deterred a lady from consulting a physician until

[13] *Transactions of the Medical Society of New York*, Vol. II (1835), 118.
[14] *Boston Medical Journal*, Vol. XVI (July 5, 1837), 347.

it was absolutely necessary, and then to draw back from liberties with her person. Medical treatises advised various techniques which were designed more to protect the lady's modesty than to be efficient. One described the use of a speculum thus: "No practitioner, whose mind is properly constituted, will propose the examination unless he conceives it absolutely necessary; and, when proposed, if executed in the way recommended by Dr. Warrington . . . the most fastidious could scarcely object."[15] The method was for the doctor to put one hand through a hole in the covers, to separate the labia.

The actual delivery usually took place at home, which at least avoided the contagious and infectious diseases spread by the hospitals. Actually, however, the doctor himself carried infections—a fact stated by Dr. Oliver Wendell Holmes in 1843, but unimportant until the introduction of antiseptics. The prospective mother braced her feet on the foot of the bed and pulled a towel attached to a bed post. The doctor performed such functions as bandaging and giving an opiate. In abnormal cases he used forceps or vectis (kind of lever). The child was encouraged to breathe by closing one nostril and using a small bellows in the other. The mother was given a special diet for a few days and encouraged to give breast feeding. If the child were lucky and stayed alive, he was weaned at eighteen months to two years. Incidentally, it should be noted that there were many good books on child care.

Not every pregnant woman looked upon motherhood with joy. In fact, some of them were unmarried. The result was a flourishing market for such abortives as Dr. Relfe's Aromatic Pills, which were advertised widely. Professional abortionists blossomed vigorously; the famous Madame Restell was becoming a New York institution. Now and then an abortionist was haled into court or mobbed, but generally the business was unchecked. The alternative to abortion was infanticide, which apparently was not rare.

Venereal disease was common. Theories of its origin varied, some doctors holding it was not contagious, but generated spontaneously, as by cohabiting too soon after a wife's delivery. Hospitals had special wards for it, and some doctors specialized. Every doctor had his

[15] *The American Medical Intelligencer* (Philadelphia), Vol. I (April 15, 1837), 33.

own remedy, usually a mercury compound, but the honest doctor admitted that his specific was not very effective. Most sufferers probably preferred patent nostrums such as Minerva Pills, The Unfortunate's Friend, or Levison's Red Drops—"the only absolute Specific that has ever been discovered for the cure of the most dangerous disease bad company is the cause of."[16]

Doctors apparently deplored sex except within marriage to produce babies that would be delivered by the profession. Particularly was the doctor horrified at masturbation, which he called onanism. It was held to produce an almost unlimited list of ills, including dry hair, bloodshot eyes and poor vision, timidity, headache, stomachache, feebleness, costiveness or diarrhea, neuralgia, consumption, and loss of memory. Frequently it led to idiocy and insanity: "It is not only most certain in its activity, but above all other kinds of insanity, it stamps its victims with every abhorrent and loathsome stigma of degradation."[17]

Self-respecting citizens assumed that only the most depraved members of society, such as criminals and the insane, had formed the degrading habit of masturbation. Imagine their horror when a well-known hygiene lecturer, Mrs. Mary S. Gove, insisted convincingly that the practice was widespread, among women as well as men. The final revelation was that not only masturbation but homosexuality existed in such places as factories and boarding schools. Outraged indignation pleaded for prayers to bring greater self-control.

The most outstanding American medical work of the decade was that of William Beaumont, a Yankee army doctor. While stationed at Mackinac, Beaumont was called to attend Alexis St. Martin, a nineteen-year-old French Canadian boy who had been seriously wounded by gunshot. Alexis fought his way back to health, but his stomach remained visible through an unhealed hole in his side. Moreover, the stomach could be entered by a small loose flap, but would retain food.

Beaumont in time got the inspiration of using Alexis as a walking

[16] *Public Ledger*, April 9, 1836.
[17] *Sixth Annual Report of the State Lunatic Hospital at Worcester*, 9.

laboratory to investigate the process of digestion. He even took advantage of Alexis' uncertain temper by noting the effects of anger on the action of the stomach. Finally, he took a year's furlough to go East for chemical tests, to consult other men, and to read the available literature.

Beaumont's conclusions were published in 1833. The active digestive force was identified as a gastric juice containing hydrochloric acid, and was found to be secreted only when food arrived. The digestibility of various foods was analyzed, thus laying the basis for modern dietetics. Later research elaborated the Beaumont findings, but did not replace them. Unfortunately, the good doctor never did any later work of importance. As for Alexis, he married and had children; when he died in 1881, he was over eighty years old.

Various doctors made interesting efforts to relate disease to other factors of life. One man used the army climatic records to try to connect disease and climate. Another tried to make correlations with the various trades. Still another investigated the relations between disease and religion. Such work was inconclusive because it was based on inadequate information, but it was at least suggestive.

Many doctors observed the close connection between the mind and the body, and argued the ethics of taking cases they considered nonfunctional. They speculated on the possible effectiveness of mesmeric and other magical cures, and when confronted by what they considered hypochondria, might give imaginary treatments such as bread pills. One doctor recorded a case in which the patient insisted he had a snake in his stomach; the doctor made an incision and produced a snake. In this, as in other similar cases, the permanence of the cure may be doubted. Hysteria was considered to be basically nervous, but since it was usually exhibited by women, it was held to be connected with some disturbance of the uterus.

Most sick Americans probably never consulted doctors. Each family had its own favorite remedies, with the wife ministering to ailments from a sprained ankle to childbirth. Some cures had value and others were based entirely on superstition, as "June water" for "a never failing remedy for disorders arising from the use of ardent spirits."[18] A seventh son of a seventh son was believed to have unusual powers of healing. Various magazines and books were designed to make each man his own doctor. Some of their "cures" should be immortalized; for example, if one had diabetes, "Strong decoctions of the Stinging Nettle, drank freely, will, in most cases, effectively cure."[19]

Hopeful self-medicators provided a splendid market for patent nostrums, hundreds of which were sold at every drug and grocery store, and peddled from door to door. Often they were labeled "panaceas." They boasted impressive names, such as "Dr. Leidy's Vegetable Febrile Elixir"; the "doctor" of the label might be one in name only, or his name might have been used without his consent. Testimonials were commonly fraudulent. Rumor had it that certain "doctors" set up business with a roomful of patent medicines, which they prescribed according to the labels.

Patent medicines were advertised freely, and manufacturers expected editorial blurbs. Claims were limited by neither law nor morality. Typical was Goelicke's Matchless Sanative, which claimed "Uncommon Excitement in Boston! Trembling among the American Physicians!!!" The trembling was produced by Mr. Goelicke's discovery, after a lifetime of work, that consumption was "a disease occasioned by a disordered state of the Vis Vitæ (or Life Principle) of the human body."[20] Moreover, he had discovered a cure, which he had labeled with his name, and which he had used effectively in many cases (testimonials printed). If the buyer did not have consumption, the Sanative also was effective in such troubles as palsy, gout, dropsy, insanity, indigestion, diabetes, jaundice, spine complaint, ague, delirium tremens, headache, eye trouble, leprosy, and sickness in pregnancy.

The maker of a patent medicine spent little on the contents of the bottle or box. His large costs were packaging, publicity, and commissions. The results seemed entirely satisfactory to the manufacturers, who made large profits from large sales. The popular

[18] Hale, *Notes*, 99.

[19] T. Monroe, *The American Botanist, and Family Physician* (Wheelock, Vt., Jonathan Morrison, 1824), 129.

[20] Galena *Advertiser*, September 28, 1839.

Brandreth's Vegetable Universal Pills, with a plant employing sixty-three men, were reputed to sell five thousand boxes a day in 1836. The company published its own monthly "Brandrethian."

Irate doctors investigated the contents of some of these remedies. Brandreth's Pills were discovered to contain colycinth, aloes, gamboge, soap, peppermint, and cinnamon. The popular Swaim's Panacea was composed of sarsaparilla, marsh grass, borage flowers, senna, rose leaves, sugar, honey, and wintergreen, plus at times varying amounts of mercury and arsenic. Bateman's Pectoral Drops, used widely to quiet fretful children, contained between 7.5 and 106 grains of opium per pint; little wonder that it quieted a child.

The drug situation was far from satisfactory. Druggists learned through apprenticeship, and many were incompetent. The drugs were frequently impure and often adulterated. The first American pharmacopoeia had appeared in 1820, but rival groups sponsored two successors in 1830, so that not until 1840 was there again a single official book. A few pharmaceutical schools had only a handful of students, since there were no legal restrictions. The best pharmaceutical magazine was the *American Journal of Pharmacy*. Several important drugs were being introduced, although not all were recent discoveries. Possibly most significant was quinine (quinine sulphate) for malarial fevers, which was popularized by Dr. Sappington's Vegetable Febrifuge and Ague Pills. Iodine was being used for goiters, tumors, venereal ulcers, and uterine difficulties. Nitrous oxide had some application for asthma. Silver nitrate was being introduced as a caustic. Other drugs coming into use included aconotine, ether, arnica (used internally), chlorine, codeine (discovered in 1832), nux vomica, morphine, croton oil, and strychnine.

Decorating the fringes of medical practice were myriads of new therapeutic systems. Many were honest efforts to promote human welfare, but others were the schemes of get-rich-quick charlatans. The regular doctor made no effort to distinguish between the honest and the fraudulent, calling them all "frauds" run by "quacks," thus discarding the baby with the bath. Equal scorn was heaped on the homeopath, the mesmerist, and the Indian doctor, although luckily not always with fatal results. The layman was often completely cynical about the whole affair; "Medicine slays its thousands and quackery its tens of thousands."[21]

Medical curiosities existed on every hand. The faith doctor healed by the laying on of hands or by blowing in the face. The Uroscopian made all diagnoses through the urine. Hydropathy deluged the patient with water both internally and externally. For some the vapor bath was a cure-all, while others favored the sulphur bath, with sulphur burned in a tight box. Chrono-Thermalism had a unitary theory of disease causation, and trusted electric energy for most recoveries. Natural Bonesetters created health by massage and manipulation to restore the bones to their proper positions.

Best known of the irregular medical systems was that of the elderly Samuel Thomson, who as a sickly New Hampshire farm boy had discovered the cause and cure of disease. Now he helped mankind by selling his entire knowledge as part of a membership in his Thomsonian Friendly Botanic Society. His theory was that the life force ("Vis Vitalis") is an all-pervading electric fluid, which manifests itself most commonly as heat. Heat (caloric) increases life, its diminution means disease, and its absence is death. Consequently fever is a friend to be encouraged, while bloodletting and mineral medicines are enemies. Disease should be treated by removing all obstructions and permitting Nature to take her course.

Despite the simplicity of the theory, Thomson used some seventy herbs combined in six numbered medicines and several special preparations; his stand-bys, however, were the steam bath and lobelia (an emetic). The Thomsonian received a book of instructions and bought a battery of medicines. When his little boy caught chickenpox or measles—and the treatment was the same for both— he thumbed his book and read he should give an emetic, the composition or infant drops, a little of #6, and an enema. For insanity he used the nerve powder, then #4 and #1, meanwhile diverting the mind of the patient. Any contingency could be met if only the amateur doctor could recognize the disease when he saw it.

Thomsonian medicine swept the land almost as rapidly as the cholera. Hundreds of agents sold thousands of gallons of medicine. Societies bloomed everywhere, infirmaries dotted the nation, some

[21] *Godey's Lady's Book*, September, 1839, 130.

forty magazines and a number of books proclaimed the gospel, colleges were founded, and a national convention assembled in 1832. Printed testimonials indicated victory over every human ill from gout to parturition. Thomson himself estimated (1839) that 100,-000 families had rights to his medicines and that 3,000,000 people used them.

Regular doctors fulminated against the "steam doctor" or "quack," whereupon the Thomsonian retorted "mineral poison doctor" or "fashionable doctor." Thomsonian failures were pilloried and the Thomsonians replied in kind. The regulars had the advantage, however, of legal support. Now and then a Thomsonian was fined for unlicensed practicing, and one regular collected fifty dollars for being called a fraud. Several Thomsonians were charged with manslaughter, but in the one recorded conviction the regulars disagreed on the disease, the proper treatment, and the effect of the lobelia that was administered.

More heart-rending to Thomson than external attack was internal dissension. Agents refused to pay their commissions. Disaffected groups split away. Rivals were established. Thomson was distressed both by the loss of revenue and by the lack of respect for the father of botanic medicine. Not until after his death (1845) did the Thomsonians merge with their two chief rivals to form the American Eclectic Medical Association.

Thomsonians may have been abysmally ignorant of medicine and overwhelmingly interested in the profits of their line of medicines. Yet they spearheaded a healthy revolt against the excessive bloodletting and calomel of the regular practitioner, thus performing a service of real merit.

A better-founded reaction against excessive bleeding and drugging was the homeopathy of Samuel C. F. Hahnemann, a well-trained German who lived until 1843. Hahnemann had observed that a drug given to a healthy person frequently produced symptoms of the disease for which that drug was the remedy; for example, cinchona bark produced intermittent fever. Hahnemann generalized that a correct drug was the one producing the symptoms to be treated, and that the effect was somewhat like rubbing snow on a freezing person. Less understandably, he advocated minute doses.

In addition, he insisted on thorough examinations, including inquiries on the patient's sex life. He opposed any liquids but water, heavily spiced foods, hot apartments, lack of exercise, night amusements, and obscene books.

Homeopathy expanded in the United States in spite of the hostility of most doctors, including Dr. Holmes, who wrote a book on *Homeopathy and its Kindred Delusions*. Members of the profession insisted that Hahnemann was treating only symptoms, not recognizing that they were doing the same thing. They ridiculed infinitesimal doses of a drug that created the symptoms to be cured. They accused homeopathy of resembling witchcraft. They explained the obviously low homeopathic death rate by saying that dosages were so small they did no harm—itself a bad admission for the man wedded to the existing allopathy.

The two major medical journals presented the usual reactions. One of them thundered against the "tissue of absurdities, such as Hahnemann has attempted to palm upon the world," but doubted that intelligent refutation would be valuable, and insisted that "Ridicule, and not argument, is the remedy best adapted to their case."[22] The other was more concise, labeling homeopathy "the greatest of all modern medical moonshine."[23]

The first important public-health movement was sponsored by one Sylvester Graham, a temperance worker who made no pretense to medical expertness. Graham decided that people would be healthier not only if they abstained from liquor, but if they ate carefully and moderately, and in general lived regular, temperate, and useful lives. Working particularly on diet, he opposed all meats except fresh-water fish and birds that lived on seeds, fruit, and grass. He discarded butter, cheese, and milk, but permitted cream and well-cooked eggs. He recommended fruits and vegetables, and rye, corn, barley or oat bread, with greatest favor going to whole-wheat bread—"Graham bread." Almost all food should be eaten raw so that it would be chewed thoroughly. Such advice may have been extreme, but it was valuable in view of current American eating habits.

[22] *The American Journal of the Medical Sciences* (Philadelphia), Vol. XVII (November, 1835), 154.

[23] *Boston Medical Journal*, Vol. XIII (September 16, 1835), 95.

Graham toured the country, attracting large audiences to his dozen "lectures on bran biscuits and saw dust tarts."[24] Sometimes he talked to ladies only, or even to just married ladies, and wild rumors circulated that he treated sexual intercourse and exhibited nude women—or at least pictures of them. A Boston mob of 1837 had to be dispersed by the police. The lectures were in fact highly moral, dealing primarily with diet, dress, and exercise.

Graham inspired many other "priests of starvation,"[25] including Mary Gove Nichols of somewhat questionable fame. Several propaganda magazines were established, including Graham's *Journal of Health and Longevity*. Boardinghouses on the Graham principles were opened—the Graham diet, regular hours, no feather beds, a cold sponge bath every morning, and regular exercise. The absence of meat and liquor must have been a real test of the faith of the true believer.

As in the case of many new ideas, the medical profession was skeptical. Doctors scoffed at the "fanatic absolutism in dietetics." They accused Graham that "your pretended science of life is chiefly the science of your own idiosyncrasies," and that "the insolence of self-esteem, and the intoxication of vanity, are but poor qualifications for the search after truth."[26] Furthermore, Grahamism was "atheistical in its tendencies, and destructive in its operation." The humorous Sam Slick called it "tarnation nonsense."[27] Such opposition seems almost incredible in view of the general desirability of the program and of Graham's modest disclaimers to having discovered any panacea.

The great pride of American medicine was surgery, with the doctors claiming that "The idea of presenting anything altogether new in surgery, at this period, is preposterous."[28] This claim seems today itself preposterous, since there was then no knowledge of either anesthetics or antiseptics, and many of the operations were of the rough and ready variety, particularly in the West. The suture

---

[24] *Morning Courier*, November 25, 1836.
[25] Rosenstein, *Homeopathy*, 181.
[26] *Boston Medical Journal*, Vol. XIV (February 17, 1836), 29.
[27] Haliburton, *Clockmaker*, 156.
[28] *Boston Medical Journal*, Vol. XX (February 27, 1839), 48.

of a deep gash might be performed with a sewing needle and thread. An amputation might be performed with a butcher knife, a meat saw, and a hot iron. No gloves were ever used and the only cleansing agent was water. Strangely enough, some of the patients survived.

The knowledge of anatomy was somewhat better than might have been expected in view of the difficulty of obtaining bodies for dissection. "Resurrections" were viewed with general loathing, for how could a dissected body be raised on judgment day? Bodies were obtained in various surreptitious ways, but many a young doctor never performed a dissection. State laws were being relaxed to permit the dissection of the unclaimed bodies of paupers and criminals, but the situation was still not favorable for the prospective surgeon.

Surgery was limited in general by the lack of knowledge of antiseptics to surface operations such as the removal of tumors or the setting of fractures. Even an amputation at shoulder or hip or the excision of ribs was unusual, while the opening of the abdominal cavity increased the chance of infection almost to a certainty; even if an operation of this kind was "successful," the patient usually died.

The absence of anesthetics was also a major handicap for both patient and doctor. No patient ever forgot a major operation—if he lived; luckily most of them fainted, but many a leg was removed or a jaw excised without the patient's losing consciousness. The doctor was hampered by the muscular contractions and twistings of his patient, even when the unfortunate soul was strapped to the operating table. Furthermore, he was torn by the human sympathy that experience might blunt but not destroy. The result was that an outstanding operator was noted as much for speed as for delicacy and accuracy.

Several painkillers had limited effectiveness. Bleeding or a tight strap above the incision helped a trifle. Opium, laudanum, nightshade, henbane, or other drugs lost effectiveness with severe pain, as did whiskey. Hypnotism was a possibility that was little used. The appeals of patients confronted with torture, and the answers of the doctors, were among the most pathetically hopeless of human documents. "I told her these sufferings were the visitation of Supreme Goodness, and ought not to be met with impatience, but a full confidence in his goodness, and a resignation to his decrees. To this she appeared fully to assent."[29] This particular patient died in intense agony.

The greatest tragedy of all was that the means to relieve pain were at hand and known, only no one thought of applying them. Nitrous oxide was the toy of traveling showmen. Ether had been known for some time. Chloroform was discovered in 1831 by three different men, one an American, but was described only as a diffusable stimulant. All three were put to use as anesthetics in the eighteen forties.

The best-known surgeons were Valentine Mott of New York and John C. Warren of Boston. Mott performed some noteworthy amputations, but was particularly famed for his ligation of the large arteries; while he proved the technical possibility of this operation, the advantage to the patient was negligible, since he almost always died from infection. Warren, too, was noted for his bold amputations, but also for the removal of tumors and cataracts, with the latter operation becoming popular because of his work; he was credited with being the first American to operate for a strangulated hernia.

Among the common operations of the thirties was the tonsillectomy; in the case of children, a tight silver wire stopped the circulation and the tonsils rotted off, while for adults a knife was used. Division of the Achilles tendon was common for club foot. Trepanning was performed several times, usually for epilepsy. Appendectomy was nonexistent, and hernia was usually treated with a truss. Facial surgery was not unknown, as the transferring of the skin of the arm to form a new eyelid or an artificial nose. Diseased eyes were removed, and their glass replacements were described as looking very natural. Philadelphia produced the first American ground-glass lens to correct myopic astigmatism.

The really spectacular operations were those which opened the abdominal cavity—usually with fatal results. A generation earlier had come the first successful ovariotomy, possibly the most amazing operation ever performed. During the thirties, Dr. J. M. Sims was beginning his work on verico-vaginal fistula. A cancer of the uterus

[29] Quoted in E. Warren, *The Life of John Collins Warren, M. D.* (2 vols., Boston, Ticknor and Fields, 1860), I, 184.

was excised at Boston in 1829, but the woman died from hemor-rhages.

Often discussed but seldom tried was the Caesarean section. Its first American use has been disputed, but the best authenticated case was that of Dr. John L. Richmond, who was more a minister than a doctor. Called to a Negro shack in rural Ohio in 1827, and having exhausted every other expedient, he performed the dimly remem-bered Caesarean by candlelight with his pocket instruments—of course without anesthetics. The baby died, but the mother recovered. His published report emboldened other doctors, and while the usual result was two deaths, now and then both mother and child survived.

Never to be forgotten in these female cases was the very real hazard of feminine modesty. The point becomes vivid as we read a doctor's description of a new method of lithotomy: "to keep a fe-male in the unpleasant posture necessary for the use of a lithontrip-ter, so long as necessary for removing a large calculus, is exceedingly annoying to her delicacy; by the present operation the exposure is almost momentary; it is but little more painful and equally safe in its performance."[30] The preference for more modesty at the cost of greater pain seems more than a century removed in thought.

Hospitals numbered possibly two hundred. They were general-ly avoided because they were obvious breeding grounds for such troubles as erysipelas or typhoid or puerperal fever. Even the most modest sanitary measures, such as changing and sterilizing bed linen, were unknown. The bedpan was used and enemas were in-creasing in popularity, but the clinical thermometer and the stomach pump were novelties. Nurses had no regular training, and were ordinarily incompetent and headstrong, frequently disobeying the doctors. Incidentally, Clara Barton was receiving her training in this period.

The average hospital was a charitable agency designed primarily to care for the indigent, although it also accepted paying patients. It was assumed that a person who could afford home care would prefer it. Many hospitals accepted the insane. Probably the Massachusetts General Hospital, opened in 1828, was America's best. It boasted

[30] *Maryland Medical Journal*, Vol. I (July, 1840), 293.

attractive nurses and able doctors who gave clinical lectures for students, but even these excellencies did not attract patients, for half its hundred beds were usually unoccupied.

Various other benevolent medical institutions were common. Several cities had free dispensaries that provided diagnosis and medicine, but no hospital facilities; the doctors donated their services. Free eye and ear infirmaries were available. The notable Wills Hospital for the Relief of the Indigent Blind and Lame was opened in 1834, and Boston had a lung infirmary. A common institution was the Lying-In Hospital, reserved for "indigent and respectable females."[31] The better-to-do had their babies at home, but the disposition of the poor, unmarried mother remains vague.

Dentistry was frequently a part-time occupation for a minister or banker or storekeeper or wig maker with time on his hands. It might be practiced rather lackadasically by a regular doctor, who cleaned and pulled teeth, and sometimes filled them, as a side line. In the cities there were a few men who specialized in dentistry exclusively; sometimes they advertised themselves as painless, which could imply nothing short of hitting the patient over the head with a sandbag. Since no medical school taught dentistry, the practitioner either learned by apprenticeship or just experimented for himself; rarely he had some medical background.

American teeth were bad. Apparently most people did not brush their teeth, and the others had only toothpastes that were abrasive. When a tooth ached, the sufferer could take an opiate or endure the rough and ready dentistry that combined a rusty forceps with a strong pull. If he lived where he could visit a full-time dentist, he could have his teeth cleaned, filled, or extracted—all with hand tools. After the dentist had his fun, the patient could get false teeth.

The professionals were proud of their fillings because they held they removed more decay than did their European contemporaries. Various filling materials included wood, which expanded with dampness but also rotted in the mouth; lead, which oxidized; tin; and mercury compounds, which made the teeth black. Preference generally went to gold and platinum, although various enamels had

[31] New York *Evening Post*, January 15, 1831.

the virtue of more nearly matching the color of the teeth. If the teeth were too close together, the defect was corrected with a file.

The making and insertion of false teeth was the greatest challenge to the ingenuity of the dentist. Most false teeth were porcelain, although the loot from grave robbing still had some currency. A single tooth could be attached to its neighbors. A plate was fastened to the unremoved stumps of teeth, sometimes with wooden pegs driven into the stumps. At other times the new teeth were set in a gold plate and soldered to the stumps. producing much pain, discoloration, unpleasant taste, and foul odor. The introduction of anesthetics was a product of dentists' trying to remove stumps of teeth without unbearable pain. Apparently dentists were more kind-hearted than doctors.

Ambitious and intelligent dentists were working hard to improve the standards of their profession. The *American Journal of Dental Science* was established in 1839. During the same year two Baltimore dentists tried unsuccessfully to persuade the University of Maryland to give a course in dentistry, and upon their failure founded the Baltimore College of Dental Surgery, the first such school in the world. The procedure was like that of the medical school; each student took two courses of lectures and an examination, after which he could boast the title of doctor of dental surgery. The American Society of Dental Surgeons was organized in 1841, and Alabama passed a first regulatory law the following year. Dentistry was obviously on the upgrade, regardless of its continuing inadequacies.

American medicine of the eighteen thirties was one of the many fields about which the modern commentator may either laugh or weep. He may laugh at the pathetic practices and the grandiloquent claims, and he may weep at the many obvious failures which made life shorter and less happy than it should have been. Yet he cannot overlook American strivings and hopes that were in time to produce a really learned and able profession.

18. Scientists

AMERICAN INTEREST IN SCIENCE was demonstrated by the scattering of magazine articles, the popular lectures, the museum collections, the school and college courses, and the various national scientific societies. The Smithsonian Institution was in embryo, with money available whenever Congress should act. Philadelphia was the national scientific capital—the home of the American Philosophical Society, top scientific organization, and of the Franklin Institution, devoted to practical inventions.

Achievements in pure science were naturally limited by the youth of the country. Money and leisure were both rare. The only people who could afford lives of science were the talented amateurs who had sufficient wealth to stay away from business, and the college professors who sandwiched a little research between the pressing duties of busy days. Outstanding was Benjamin Silliman of Yale— a versatile, self-made scientist who edited *Silliman's Journal,* possibly the best scientific publication of its day. Silliman was primarily a geologist, but did not limit himself to that field.

Silliman was typical of most American scientists in not sticking to any single branch of science. Geologists, for example, were almost always mineralogists and often chemists; the first alum plant in the United States was developed by a geologist. But variations were much wider than this. That catholic and eccentric genius, Constantine S. Rafinesque, wrote about animals, plants, fish, shells, birds, electricity, astronomy, chemistry, and geology, but also about archaeology, architecture, psychology, navigation, history, poetry, and religion. Not only did he write, but most of the writing was good.

American sciences were largely in the collecting and classifying stage, since the new varieties of American animals, plants, and rocks had not yet been exhausted. Outstanding work was done with plants

(Gray and Torrey), conchology (Thomas Say), entomology (Say), ornithology (J. J. Audubon), herpetology (Holbrook), botany (J. J. Bigelow). Nathaniel Bowditch, whose older work on navigation was standard, died in 1838. His successor was Matthew Fontaine Maury, with his *A New Theoretical and Practical Treatise on Navigation* (1836). Practically no work was done in zoology or in physics, except with electricity.

Most popular of the sciences was geology, which ordinarily connected with mineralogy. At least nineteen states provided for geological surveys, which incidentally considered birds, animals, soils, and other matters. Any important exploring party, such as that of Wilkes in the polar regions, usually included a geologist. Most geology consisted primarily of collecting and classifying, which implied the development of an American nomenclature. The most important trend was the increasing use of fossils to fix the relative ages of rock strata.

Chemistry was largely inorganic, but both quantitative and qualitative. Attention was paid the applications to agriculture. The known elements of 1830 were fifty-five, including all the common ones but argon. The most original work of the decade was done on atomic weights, but as was often true in chemical matters, the results ultimately proved valueless because of impure materials and inexact methods.

Astronomy had many devotees, including young people in love. Accomplishments were limited by poor equipment; the only observatories were those at the University of North Carolina and at Williams. The appearance of Halley's comet in 1835 and several large displays of shooting stars reinforced the current expectation of the imminent end of the world. Most fascinating was the Symmes' theory that the earth was composed of at least five hollow concentric spheres, each inhabited on both the concave and the convex sides; Symmes wanted to lead an expedition to find the entrances at the poles.

Science was expected to praise God by showing ever more clearly the wonders of His universe. No one questioned the proposition that the facts of nature agreed with the statements of the revealed word of God. Any apparent disagreement must mean either that science was in error or that the Bible had been misinterpreted. Individuals varied from merely scoffing at any inconvenient scientific finding, to making elaborate Biblical interpretations to get around apparent discrepancies.

Considerable ingenuity was often necessary to make geology and Genesis agree, particularly when geologists were using fossils of great antiquity, while the accepted Usher chronology of the world went back only to 4004 B. C. And then how about such matters as the flood? Silliman realized that no downpour would do the job, and so argued that the water must have come from inside the earth at the rate of a foot every two minutes to have covered the highest mountains in forty days and forty nights. Many minds were simpler and more direct. Rev. Samuel Parker, in a common-sense way, concluded that erosion could not account for the channel of the Columbia, but "that God had with his finger drawn a channel."[1]

Greater troubles were in the offing with the discovery of thousands of new species of plants and animals, which would have overcrowded the largest Ark. Several scientists such as Rafinesque speculated about the probability of the evolution of plants and animals from simpler to more complex forms. Here and there someone applied such ideas to man, and talked of a "intermediate link between man and the Brute creation."[2] Darwin later gave an American, William Charles Wells, much of the credit for originating the idea of evolution through natural selection. One of the first practical applications of such theories was to justify slavery by holding the Negro as not quite a man. Later they were the basis of a furious argument between science and religion.

More consistent with the American pattern of life than work in abstract science was the utilization of science in practical mechanical gadgets. As late as 1833 the chief of the patent office resigned because of lack of work, but even as he resigned, the flood of inventions was rising with tremendous rapidity. Six years later Philip Hone could exclaim upon the introduction of Daguerre's photo-

---

[1] Quoted in G. P. Merrill, *The First One Hundred Years of American Geology* (New Haven, Yale University Press, 1924), 183.
[2] Sullivan, *Travels of Jedediah Smith*, 72.

graphic machine: "How greatly ashamed of their ignorance the by-gone generations of mankind ought to be!"[3]

The very volume of important inventions overwhelms any investigator. Agricultural machines ran from well-drilling machinery and the reaper to a sausage-filling machine and a lactometer. The home received new stoves, refrigerators, and dishwashing machines. The Colt revolver was revolutionary—a bad pun. A tide-harnessing machine was invented by the architect Robert Mills. The suspension bridge was made practical by John Roebling's wire rope. Diving suits were expected to replace the diving bell, and a submarine telescope was invented, while Fulton's submarine was available. Various flying machines were patented—usually a balloon with wings like a bird's. An Illinois pioneer tried to fly a monoplane with wings which were flapped by a crank; he failed.

Business practices received their quota of aid. An "Ever-pointed pencil" resembled the modern mechanical pencil. Various short-hand systems were developed. An adding machine reputedly added, subtracted, multiplied, and divided. The world's first typewriter (1829) was the invention of a Milwaukee genius who was also responsible for the solar compass. There even was a "Phreno-Mnemo-tehny" (memory) system. Americans were at least ingenious.

Inventive ability did not imply that Americans were not naïve as well as ingenious in scientific matters. Many inventions were completely impossible and useless. Thousands of people believed that hair snakes came from human hair, that hazel rods could divine water, that rain might be produced by large fires or by the explosion of cannon. Americans were a queer combination of acquisitiveness and inquisitiveness, practicability and credulity—even as their descendants.

No scientific work was more pregnant of the future than that with electricity. Typically American was the fact that the three outstanding experimenters were a college professor, a back-country blacksmith, and an eminent painter. The college professor was Joseph Henry, who developed the electromagnet and hence provided the basic necessity of the telegraph—a way to transmit signals

[3] Nevins, *Hone Diary*, I, 435.

for a long distance over wires without diminishing their intensity. The blacksmith was Thomas Davenport of Brandon, Vermont, who in 1834 built the first electric motor, which he used on a model railroad and to run a printing press. It was entirely practical except that batteries were not a satisfactory source of power.

The eminent painter was Samuel F. B. Morse. To what extent Morse, rather than Henry and others, can be credited with the invention of the telegraph is still disputed, but there is no question that Morse invented a telegraph code and was responsible for the practical development of telegraphy. His final model was completed, tested, and patented in 1837, but private capital was skeptical: "I do not think that . . . there is sufficient demand for telegraphic communication to warrant the cost of his apparatus."[4] Ultimately Congress provided a line between Washington and Baltimore, which was opened in 1844 with the famous query "What hath God wrought?" Proved practical, the telegraph was adopted by private interests with amazing celerity and prodigious profits.

Electrical experimentation did not rest on any understanding of the nature of electricity. Most people thought it a fluid, and there was considerable speculation upon its proper uses. Certain doctors decided that it was a panacea for disease and claimed to use it effectively for the cure of anything from neuralgia to cholera.

The great electric fad of the decade was animal magnetism or mesmerism, even though this "science" had no real relation to electricity. Hypnotism, to use the modern name, was a very old phenomenon, but it did not obtain wide American interest until the late eighteen thirties, when it was popularized by a young Frenchman, Charles Poyen. Starting with his tour, the idea spread as rapidly as the cholera.

Hypnotic sleep was produced ordinarily by passing the open hands over the subject from head to foot, sometimes touching the body and sometimes not. Less frequently an operator stared into his subject's eyes, meantime passing his palms before the subject's face. Now and then suggestion alone was used, with no physical passes. To avoid differences in susceptibility, the professional usually clung to a regular subject, preferably a boy, but often a young lady. Local

[4] Armstrong, *Five Generations*, 259.

wags allowed that there was nothing strange when a young lady had peculiar feelings after a man passed his hands up and down her body.

The commonly accepted theory was that magnetism was some sort of invisible fluid which ordinarily passed from operator to subject, but which might be acquired in other ways, as when a lady was magnetized by an electrical storm and followed a piece of iron around the room. The most important scientific advancement came when James Braid (English) and Phineas P. Quimby (American) arrived independently at the conclusion that all hypnotism was basically self-hypnotism. This point of view, however, took many years to obtain any general acceptance.

Hypnotism had certain obvious virtues as a source of amusement, but was even more exciting, for its medical possibilities. As an anesthetic before the introduction of ether, it permitted the painless removal of teeth and tumors, or even of arms and legs. The greatest difficulty in using it in surgical work was its uncertainty.

As the craze for mesmerism expanded, hundreds of "authentic" claims were soon advanced. In some of them, such as cures for loss of voice, hysteria, cramps, stammering, sleeplessness, and headaches, the claims may have been justified. But cures of rheumatism, epilepsy, tumor, ague, and dozens of other ailments seem incredible unless the diagnoses were worse than seems humanly possible. Just as incredible was the use of hypnotism for diagnosis. The hypnotized subject looked into the patient's body and told the doctor what was wrong, whereupon he prescribed the proper remedy.

The medical applications of hypnotism actually led to the effective work of Dr. Quimby. In time he discovered that his treatments were just as effective regardless of the medicine, which might be nothing but bread pills or plain water. The conclusion was that hypnotism was self-induced and that the important results came through autosuggestion.

The crowning wonder claimed for mesmerism was that in his somnambulistic sleep the patient could see through locked doors, read sealed messages, describe places he had never seen, understand strange languages, and even forecast the future. Some subjects even communed with Christ and His angels. Clairvoyance was an accepted part of the new science for most believers.

Reactions to hypnotism were varied. Many people accepted it as they accepted religious teachings—because they wanted to believe, and hence to feel happier. Some of the believers were educated men, like President Wayland of Brown. Others were doctors, like Charles Caldwell. A few of these believers did intelligent work, but most of them were no more penetrating than the opponents.

The skeptical outnumbered the credulous. The phenomena were frequently "exposed" to the satisfaction of the exposer. The usual opposition to this "most philosophical of all impostures"[5] was that the phenomena were not real, but due to "the influence of the imagination." Apparently almost no one realized that this "influence of the imagination" was real, and was at least as important as any other truth.

The hypnotists quite properly received greatest discredit because of their claims of supernatural power. Wags suggested that the new science would permit the secretary of state to listen to foreign conversations, a father to watch his son sow wild oats, a scientist to get results without experimentation, and a wife to keep an eye on an unfaithful husband. More serious commentators likened the mesmeristic mania to the witchcraft delusion of Salem. "We may then . . . look upon Animal Magnetism as one of those temptations of the Evil One, which . . . is allowed by God to try this age."[6] Even more bluntly—"mesmerism is sorcery . . . its real phenomena are performed by the dark powers of Satan himself."[7] Thus was it included with astrology, palmistry, chiromancy, spiritism, and necromancy.

Doctors and other scientists could hardly be blamed for their almost universal skepticism of the claims of mesmerism, but they could be criticized for making almost no real investigations, with an effort to find what if any truth existed. Most of the inquiry was prosecuted by untrained amateurs with inquiring minds. Mental therapy might have advanced much more rapidly if scientists had been willing to investigate intelligently what seemed to them improbable.

[5] *American Quarterly Review*, Vol. IV (December, 1828), 427.

[6] *Southern Literary Messenger*, Vol. V (May, 1839), 325.

[7] H. Jones, *Mesmerism Examined and Repudiated* (New York, J. S. Redfield, 1846), 9.

The other important current scientific fad was phrenology, which led hypnotism in both time and interest. Whereas hypnotism seemed the plaything of charlatans, phrenology impressed itself as a science based upon diligent medical research. The European originator, F. J. Gall, and his chief disciple and coworker, J. G. Spurzheim, were both doctors, who had worked experimentally and who had presented their evidence and conclusions in long, dry, and technical volumes.

Through phrenology, the practitioner attempted to determine temperament, intelligence, and aptitudes from a person's exterior. Attention was devoted to the general configuration and coloring of the body, but even more to the shape of the head. The brain was described as a bundle of various traits, each of which could be estimated from the outside of the skull. To the charge that a soft brain could not change the shape of a hard skull, the phrenologist answered that facts were facts, regardless of speculation. He had examined thousands of heads and considered such phenomena as dreams, somnambulism, visions, insanity, split personality, and brain injuries. The results were inescapable.

The phrenologist gave descriptive names to the various organs of the brain, and located them precisely. Properly marked skulls soon dotted the country. Amativeness and other animal passions were in the lower back of the head; destructiveness, acquisitiveness, and similar unpraisworthy traits were near the ears; moral and religious sentiments were in the upper top; reasoning faculties were behind the upper forehead; and so on through the long list. The phrenologist recognized the interrelation of these traits, and that one might alter or neutralize another.

The real popularity of phrenology dated from the arrival of Spurzheim in 1832. He was received enthusiastically, especially by the doctors, who attended special lectures and dissections. The *Boston Medical Journal* expressed the opinion that "Dr. S. will form among us a new era in education, and open, to the minds of the most intelligent, new and correct views of their moral and intellectual powers, and the best means of cultivating them all."[8] Upon his untimely death, the president of Harvard presided at the funeral serv-

[8] *Boston Medical Journal*, Vol. VII (October 17, 1832), 162.

ices, Dr. Follen gave the oration, the Boston Medical Association attended in a body, and the *American Journal of the Medical Sciences* intoned: "The prophet is gone, but his mantle is upon us."[9]

Other lecturers followed Spurzheim and drew large audiences. Phrenological societies overran the land, each with its collection of skulls (casts). Special magazines were established. The roster of converts included a host of outstanding men in all fields—such as Dr. Charles Caldwell ("the Spurzheim of America"), Dr. J. C. Warren, Samuel Gridley Howe, Henry Ward Beecher, Horace Mann, Nicholas Biddle, Timothy Flint, Robert Dale Owen, and Lydia Maria Child. Sarah Grimké felt phrenology to be "perfectly consistent with the other works of God and with enlightened reason and religion."[10] Every important man, including Black Hawk, had a phrenological reading, and a mild furor was created by the head of the murderer William Miller.

Even such a widely accepted science had its detractors, who ranged from the humorous to the vindictive. Most obvious was the semihumorous account of some ludicrous phrenological mistake—a prominent citizen being analyzed as a criminal or vica versa—which might conceivably have been the mistake of society and not of the phrenologist; or the perennial boy whose peculiar analysis was really due to "pumphandletiveness." The supreme master Spurzheim was himself not free from humorous digs:

> *Great man of skulls! I must let loose*
> *My pen against you;—more's the pity,*
> *For surely you have played the deuce*
> *Among the noodles of the city.*
> *I wo'n't malignantly assail*
> *Your fame, and say you mean to joke us;*
> *But faith, I can't make head or tail*
> *Of all this mystic hocus pocus.*[11]

Scientific criticisms were rare, but Dr. Sewall asserted that anatomy showed no divisions of the brain, that brain changes would not

---

[9] *American Journal of Medical Sciences*, Vol. XII (August, 1833), 473-77.
[10] Barnes, *Weld Letters*, II, 529.
[11] *New England Magazine*, Vol. III (November, 1832), 397.

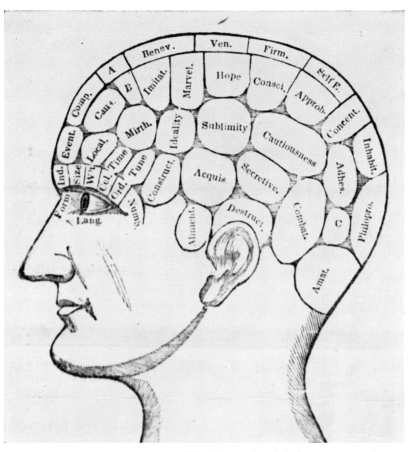

The Phrenological Organs of the Brain
From P. L. Buell and N. Sizer, *A Guide to Phrenology*

affect the outside of the skull, and that head injuries did not always affect the faculty supposed to reside at the point of injury. These assertions were poorly buttressed by fact and accompanied by unpleasant invective, but gained dignity when they were labeled by the outstanding American phrenologist, Dr. Caldwell, as "a mass of falsehood, spurious pretension, and studied artifice, thrown together for selfish and other unbecoming purposes . . . a bloated aggregation of garbled and perverted matter, assorted and arranged without either judgment or genius, tact or scholarship."[12]

Many religious persons had misgivings about the new science, which seemed to them materialistic, and to deny the direct control of God over human affairs. They writhed when "this carnal philosophy, with its limited conceptions, its gray truisms, its purblind theories, its withering conclusions, and its weary dogmatism, is to supplant the lofty faith of antiquity, and the sublime philosophy of the Bible, and to sit in judgment on the Infinite and Eternal!" God was to be eliminated in favor "of little lumps of flesh." "Behold here the true nature and the full dimensions of the human soul!"[13]

Actually, phrenology was injured more by its friends than by its enemies. "Practical phrenologists" seized the doctrines as a basis for money making, and toured the country giving lectures as the "come-on" for private readings at fifty cents or one dollar a head. One woman practitioner was regretted as making the science "the instrument of a petty income to an ignorant, presuming, flippant-tongued female."[14] Practitioners of this stripe degraded the subject and tended to connect it in the public mind with palmistry and astrology.

The later practitioners did little of the kind of detailed research upon which phrenology had originally been based. Rather, they accepted the gospel and then refined it by adding dozens of new organs which they discovered without proper evidence. Possibly inevitable was the linking of phrenology with the other current fad of mesmerism to obtain "phreno-magnetism." A good showman mesmerized

[12] C. Caldwell, *Phrenology Vindicated, and Anti-Phrenology Unmasked* (New York, S. Colman, 1838), 14.

[13] Boston *Christian Examiner*, November, 1834, quoted in R. W. Haskins, *History and Progress of Phrenology* (Buffalo, Steele and Peck, 1839), 155-56.

[14] *Boston Medical Journal*, Vol. XXV (September 1, 1841), 69.

his subject and then touched various organs in the head; the organ of order led the subject to arrange books, the organ of combativeness brought a fight, and so on. Sometimes the combination of phrenology and hypnotism was called Phrenopathy.

More ingenious souls elaborated increasingly complex systems. Andronomy was bad enough, but it was expanded into Magneto-Physiognomico-Craniology. Another man boosted Psychography (mental telepathy), which he considered the basis for mesmerism. J. S. Grimes invented the theory to end all theories—Etherology. An imaginary "etherium" transmitted light, heat, electricity, gravitation, and emotion from one body to another; it accounted for mesmerism, neurology, pathetism, catalepsy, somnambulism, clairvoyance, and other phenomena too numerous to mention. This "etherium" was produced "by the decomposition of the blood in the capillaries of the brain."[15]

Phrenology was by no means an unreasonable belief in its day, and its effects on contemporary thinking were almost entirely good. It discarded such metaphysical ideas as original sin, total depravity, and divine intervention, to substitute the concept of a natural organism which developed according to surrounding conditions. The mind was no longer something mysteriously divine, but a proper subject for human investigation and control.

Every phrenologist believed that sickness, pain, cruelty, bad temper, and other undesirable human characteristics were the results of natural forces and not of the visitations of God, and that they could be modified or altered by proper environment and training. The effect of beliefs of this sort on child training, on the treatment of criminals and the insane, and on other human problems are obvious. Proper hygiene and play for children, less lacing and more exercise for women, and better ventilation for everyone were among the many desirable and specific suggestions. The phrenologists further insisted that the laws of the universe could not conflict with any proper religious beliefs, and that therefore it was man's duty to search for the truth. This spur to the seeking of scientific truth was itself a virtue, even though one of its results was the discrediting of phrenology.

[15] J. S. Grimes, *Etherology* (New York, Saxton and Mills, 1845), 2–38.

The contrast between phrenology and hypnotism was one of the remarkable situations of the eighteen thirties. Phrenology was received with enthusiastic acceptance by the best-informed intelligence of its day; later it was to be considered worthless. Hypnotism was greeted with widespread skepticism; later its basic truth was accepted, and it led to the opening of the field of psychiatry. Apparently there may be errors in the contemporary reactions to new ideas.

Most Americans of the eighteen thirties found little time for pure science, which was reserved largely as the toy for the dilettante or the abstract mental discipline of the pedagogue. The idea of devoting large amounts of time and money to investigations that were not expected to produce immediately practical results seemed ludicrous when time and money were at such a premium. The only surprise is at the amount of work done, particularly in collecting and classifying, and not in the many things that were not done.

Practical applications of science appealed very much to Americans. The isolation of oxygen was possibly an amusing stunt, but the invention of a diving suit might actually bring returns in dollars and cents. Of what good was knowledge for its own sake? All human discoveries were of advantage only in so far as they made man more comfortable, more moral, or more religious. The purpose of life was simple and clear—to improve the special American civilization which God considered as His supreme accomplishment on earth. Science was good and desirable only as it contributed toward this end.

PART IV : AT PLAY

19. Sports

THE UNITED STATES was intensely serious about earning its living and in trying to convince the rest of the world of the superiority of the free institutions of a young and vigorous people, but not even Americans could work at these jobs twenty-four hours a day. The godly devoted their spare moments to conversing on elevating subjects and reading improving literature, but the less devout overcame their qualms and indulged in such frivolous amusements as dinners, dancing, and the theater.

Amusements avoided the moral questioning of the strait-laced if they were combined with work, as in husking or quilting bees, house raisings, or harvestings. Group competitions added to both the fun and the accomplishments, without lessening perceptibly the trips to the stone whiskey jug. Kissing games added spice, and only the prudish objected when the lucky finder of a red ear of corn gave an unusually enthusiastic salute to the girl of his choice. After the work was completed, then came feasting and dancing.

Whittling was also in the twilight zone between work and play. Most notorious of the whittlers were the Yankees, but the accusation that a New England boy waiting for his girl friend to primp might whittle half through the mantel, was probably an exaggeration. Likewise to be taken with caution was the rumor that the careful wife saved her furniture by providing each male guest with a stick of wood.

Whether business itself should be classified as a major sport may be argued, but politics unquestionably provided amusement in its speeches, private discussions, parades, and banquets. A politician needed the constitution of an ox and the digestion of a goat to withstand the continual banquets, each with prodigious quantities of food and equally prodigious quantities of oratory, together with unend-

339

ing toasts that made the last speeches fade into an alcoholic haze. Election day brought general good fellowship climaxed by the victory parade of the successful party.

A Presidential trip was the perfect excuse for celebration. When President Jackson passed through New York in 1833 on his way to a New England tour, the city produced its biggest welcome since the arrival of Lafayette. Ships were drowned in bunting, guns roared, city officials intoned a welcome, and a cheering crowd lined the route of the parade to City Hall. Multiply this reception by every city and town visited by the Presidential party, and it is apparent why Jackson's health gave out by the time he reached Concord, New Hampshire.

Since Americans were above all patriotic, the year's biggest celebration came on Independence Day, the Fourth of July. From daybreak until midnight the nation was one grand hubbub of bells, firecrackers, fireworks, pistol shots, and cannon fire. Streets were lined with stands: some for roast pig, oysters, pineapples, gingerbread, sugarplums and other comestibles; others "where everything drinkable is to be had but water."[1] Intoxicants were so common that by evening many of the gentlemen and a few of the ladies wobbled perceptibly.

The high point of any Fourth of July celebration was its monster parade, in which aged Revolutionary soldiers were given the place of honor. The body of the parade included the militia, civic officers, doctors, lawyers, actors, mechanics, reform societies, fire companies, and all other civic organizations. After the parade came prayer, the reading of the Declaration of Independence, and several orations "fruitful in those sonorous periods and stereotyped patriotics indispensable on such occasions."[2]

Following the parade and speeches came a big public dinner, succeeded by the inevitable and numerous toasts—to the Constitution, Liberty, Lafayette, the mother of Washington, and the rest—each filled with ringing oratorical phrases. Then came the real oratory of the day, which was apt to be a little hazy because of the many

[1] Nevins, *Hone Diary*, 1, 15.
[2] Edmund Flagg, *The Far West*, Vols. XXVI and XXVII of R. G. Thwaites (ed.), *Early Western Travels* (30 vols., Glendale, A. H. Clark Company, 1904–1907), XXVI, 226.

SPORTS

toasts drunk. The celebration finally ended with fireworks—sea serpents, giant rockets, Bengal lights, Chinese fire, fairy bowers, crowns of Jupiter, Turkish temples, stars of Columbia, and magic circles.

There were many other celebrations, which often had patriotic cannotations—the anniversaries of Lexington and Concord, Forefathers' Day at Plymouth, Thanksgiving in New England, the opening of the Erie Canal, the beginning of work on the Baltimore and Ohio, the dedication of Bunker Hill Monument, and others. Each boasted its parade and its orations painting gloriously the past, present, and future of the United States. A New York parade of 1830 commemorating the death of Lafayette was particularly intriguing; included were "butchers on horseback, or drawn in a sort of rustic arbor or shambles, tastefully festooned with sausages. Tailors, with cockades and breastknots of riband, pacing to music, with banners representative of various garments, waving proudly in the wind. Caravans of cobblers most seductively appareled, and working at their trade on a locomotive platform, which displayed their persons to the best advantage."[3]

The New Year was honored by parades and noise-making. In New York each lady stayed at home to receive male callers, and later boasted of the number; the gentleman bragged of the number of glasses he had drunk before he became unconscious and was poured into a cab. Christmas was less boisterously observed, although the stores closed and everyone ate himself into a stupor; Christmas presents included the usual pictures, work bags, fans, vases, dolls, games, jewelry, card cases, and candies. April Fool's Day was utilized for practical jokes. St. Patrick's Day was observed in Irish communities. May Day suggested a flower-picking party which started early enough to see the sun rise. St. Valentine's Day was increasing in favor, with both lace-edged greetings from Cupid and comic screeds.

No amusement had more general popularity than travel, which could be justified as educational. A potential traveler might be limited to walking on Broadway or the Battery in New York, but usually he could at least steam up the Hudson, Delaware, or Poto-

[3] Hamilton, *Men and Manners*, 40.

341

mac, or enjoy a short railroad excursion. Frequently he picnicked; New Yorkers preferred Long Island or Hoboken, and other cities had their own picnic spots. Most exciting was the big Hoboken amusement ground called Elysian Fields, made seductive with shaded walks, garden benches, and lanterns.

Popular seaside resorts were located near the large cities for reasons of transportation. The great exception was Newport, which was becoming the fashionable summering place for the wealthy of New York and Boston. Less opulent Bostonians visited the two-mile-long Nahant Peninsula, which was lined with cottages and tipped by an immense hotel. The common pleasures of eating, sleeping, and gossiping were interrupted infrequently by walking, riding, fishing, and playing games; for sea bathing, the ladies could preserve their modesty in a rock-bound cove.

New Yorkers were enthusiastic about Rockaway, where the Marine Pavilion could feed four hundred persons at the same time. Visitors gawked at the expensively gowned ladies "flirting over the backgammon-board, tripping affectedly across the room, languishing with a seventy dollar cambric handkerchief, starting up in ecstasy at the entrance of a baby."[4] Trotting matches, champagne suppers, and balls entertained the sporting. Sea bathers were hauled to the beach in an omnibus, but some of the ladies termed their common bathhouse "intolerable,"[5] while the more modest deplored the inevitable revelation of the female figure as the women returned in their wet bathing suits—which incidentally were complete outfits, often including corsets.

The most popular Jersey resorts were Long Branch and Cape May. The former drew boardinghouse trade from both New York and Philadelphia, while the latter was Philadelphia's favorite. Inland resorts, like Schooley's Mountain near Easton, were less visited than the coast towns.

America's most popular resort town was Saratoga Springs, with its twenty thousand visitors a year. Rumor had it that the fashionable trade was declining, but Saratoga continued to have no trouble in filling its top-notch hotels, which charged up to ten dollars a week

[4] Martineau, *Society*, II, 216.
[5] Kemble, *Later Life*, 98.

for room and board. Newest, largest, and most impressive was the four-story brick "United States," which could accommodate four hundred guests.

The Saratoga visitor felt a moral obligation to drink the water even if he did not bathe in it. By performing that duty in the morning, he had the rest of the day for sitting, promenading, and gossiping. For active exercise the man might smoke a cigar and the woman net a purse. The more sporting could fish, ride, play cards, shoot billiards, or dance, for there was a ball every evening. The ever present gambling was mainly on horses and cards.

Some of the northern travelers went to resorts such as Clifton, Avon, or Ballston. Many visited Lake George and the falls of the Hudson. A few brave souls went to the White Mountains, where they possibly climbed Mount Washington, and a handful even ventured into Canada.

The crowning glory of northern travel was a visit to Niagara Falls, usually by way of the Erie Canal. Reams of paper recorded the rhapsodies of visitors. They exclaimed in awe at the view from the platform on Goat Island. The adventuresome climbed down one of the two stairways, donned rubber coats, and went behind the falls —for which they received certificates. The hotelkeepers tried to gild the lily by blowing off large hunks of rock, but the resulting splashes were unimpressive. The sending of a steamer loaded with animals over the falls, however, drew an estimated thirty thousand spectators, including the usual pickpockets.

Southern planters escaping the summer heat and yellow fever flocked to the northern resorts, visiting enroute such wonders as the Natural Bridge and Mammoth Cave; at the cave there was a large hotel, and guides were furnished at a dollar a head. Many of the Southerners also visited southern watering places, particularly those of the present West Virginia.

The great Virginia attraction for the socially elite was White Sulphur Springs. Here the guests occupied individual cabins of one to four rooms, some individually owned but most rented from the hotel and receiving hotel service. All meals were eaten in a central dining room, which frequently was filled to its capacity of six hundred. Such accommodations cost about twelve dollars a week. The life was much like that at Saratoga, and centered around the drinking of or bathing in the spring water.

Other southern mountain spring resorts were available for those who could not afford White Sulphur prices. Most were in Virginia, but some were in Pennsylvania and Kentucky, and North Carolina had Warm Springs, with a hotel that could cater to eight hundred guests at once. Practically all these resorts copied the White Sulphur system of independent cottages, although some also had hotel rooms.

The greatest possible travel glory came from a trip to Europe—in part because it was the most expensive. The fashionable young man might visit London, Paris, and Rome before settling down to business. A certain social prestige resulted from the ability to boast that at least part of one's wild oats had been sown in Paris.

Americans took their amusements somewhat surreptitiously, often disguising them as education. Travel, the lyceum, libraries, and art galleries could thus be defended against the most rigorous conscience. Also generally approved was the private museum, which prospered mightily on its usual admission price of twenty-five cents. The museum was pre-eminently moral, so that a man might take his wife and children without fear that they or he would be embarrassed.

The museum was devoted to curiosities. Almost always it exhibited mammoth bones, an Egyptian mummy, animals, snakes, shells, minerals, plants, Indian relics, and portraits which certainly included one of General Jackson. Possibly there was a French cuirass from Waterloo, a lamb with two heads and six legs, and part of the boiler of the ill-fated *Moselle*. Always there were wax figures—of Washington, Napoleon, Black Hawk, the Siamese twins, a duel, a Chinese lady, the sleeping beauty, and others; most popular were criminals committing their dastardly deeds, with a quantity of synthetic gore. A good museum also presented variety acts, such as trained animals, singers, dancers, human curiosities, magicians, and acrobats. Possibly there was a menagerie, which might be as small as one anaconda or boa constrictor.

America's outstanding museums were those of the Peale family at Baltimore, Philadelphia, and New York. Baltimore boasted fine collections of American birds, animals, and insects. Philadelphia was noted for Indian relics and its mastodon skeleton. New York specialized in living attractions, for example, a magician who made an egg dance, fried a pancake in a clean hat, and turned wine into roses. Fancy glass blowing was demonstrated. Two live cannibals vied with the Siamese twins, who appeared in the flesh. Mr. Candeerbeck played twelve instruments—in fact, six at one time—and could imitate anything from a bird's warble to church vespers.

Peale's chief New York competitor was Scudder's American Museum, later to be glorified by Barnum. Scudder emphasized size. Five rooms, each one hundred feet long and lighted by gas, were credited with 150,000 curiosities. Special attractions were dioramas and cosmoramas, including the eruptions of Etna and Vesuvius and the conflagration at Moscow.

Most famous museum of the hinterland was that of Dorfeuille at Cincinnati, which boasted a fountain and a German band. The climactic exhibit was a representation of Hell, with figures by Hiram Powers and lighting effects by Samuel Colt. Entering a darkened room, the visitor was confronted by caverns and molten lakes, growling bears with mens heads, snakes darting and hissing, a murdered man with the knife protruding, a suicide hanging by the neck, skeletons walking in shrouds, a man with a boar's head, dwarfs that grew into giants, imps of ebony with eyes of flame, reptiles devouring youth and beauty, cakes of fire, and mountains of ice. Originally the surrounding railing had been electrified, but the effects were so disastrous that the practice was discontinued. This entire spectacle was advertised, of course, as a moral education for youth.

More specialized museums dealt with a single subject each; for example, Chinese curiosities or wax figures or the Masonic ritual. An Anatomical Museum gave weekly lectures on the dangers of tight lacing. Pictorial exhibitions, as of the Indian pictures of George Catlin, were not unusual. The Diorama and Arcana of Useful and Recreative Science included such attractions as a picture of New York, a revolving coal stove, a prismatic machine, and an optical machine which showed part of Broadway in miniature.

The magic lantern and its variants were popular. The phantasmagoria used an opaque background to produce a luminous figure; a picture of skulls, accompanied by the rattling of chains and bones, made the timid spectators shudder. If the machine were moved back and forth on a track, the figure would advance and recede. Pictures could be melted into each other, as Franklin to a skull, by substituting during a bad focus. A living person might be reflected on the screen through complicated mirrors and lenses—a process called Catadioptrical Phantasmagoria.

Another variety of picture machine was the cosmorama. The spectator peered through a magnifying glass into a dark box to view pictures that seemed larger and more lifelike therein. The "periphanoscope" or "zoetrope" or "wheel of life" gave the illusion of motion as the observer looked through a slit at a series of pictures rotated on a disk.

Painting exhibitions seemed to be popular in proportion to the size of the canvas. A large painting was called a panorama; if it needed rollers, it achieved the title of diorama—although the terms "diorama" and "cosmorama" were sometimes confused in practice. William Dunlap, eminent author and artist, drew big crowds for his "Eidosphusicon or Moving Diorama" of the Hudson Valley, which was rolled past the audience to give an illusion of motion. Niblo's Garden claimed a 50,000-square-foot masterpiece in 1836, and there were many others. Some portrayed quiet scenes, such as Jerusalem, Niagara Falls, or Athens. Others were more dramatic, such as the departure of the Israelites, the battle of Austerlitz, the Thames tunnel, the ejection of the Vicksburg gamblers, the destruction of Sodom and Gomorrah, and the burning of Moscow.

The revolutionary development in pictures was the daguerreotype, a French invention brought to America by Morse in 1839. The camera-obscura method made acceptable prints on copper plates, but the process was difficult and expensive. Furthermore the subject had to be almost impossibly patient, for even with the best methods he had to sit absolutely quiet for about three minutes, which probably accounts for the strained expressions on so many of the early daguerreotypes.

Americans were fascinated by the unusual. Frimbey's living statues, with their machinelike movements, were popular. The "living skeleton," Calvin Edison of Vermont, five feet, two inches tall and weighing sixty pounds, was rumored to have a two-year $40,000 contract which was reduced $500 for each pound he gained. The Siamese twins, joined at the navel, were much admired. Porter, the Kentucky giant, towered seven feet, six inches. The Canadian Modeste Malhoit weighed 619 pounds, and his ankle measured three feet, five inches around. Jugglers, singers, dancers, and magicians shuttled between museums and theaters, but a reputedly well-preserved West Indian mermaid stayed in the museums.

In the realm of automatons, Maelzel had the most popular exhibits. His chief figure was a sitting Turk who played chess with mechanical movements, indicating the wrong move of an opponent by knocking on the table and shaking his head; various explanations were advanced as to how the trick was worked. Maelzel also had an almost life-size trumpeter whom he accompanied on the piano, and small figures that made simple sounds and performed such tricks as walking a slack rope.

Balloon ascensions drew thousands of spectators, and the aviators aimed for height and distance. R. Clayton (1835) started from Cincinnati for the coast, and actually covered 350 miles in nine and one-half hours, landing in Virginia—reputedly the longest flight to date. Since a balloon was filled with hot air, its time of flight was limited by the rapidity of the cooling.

Another popular spectacle was the jump from a great height. Sam Patch was the incomparable master of this stunt until alcohol caught up with him as he jumped the 125-foot Genesee Falls in 1829; it was said that he was dead before he hit the water. Later performers added fancy thrills without obtaining the Patch prestige. Consider a Mr. Scott of Philadelphia, who promised a 200- to 300-foot jump, with two somersaults and the discharge of two pistols before he hit the water. Fame should have been kinder to him.

The menagerie had long toured the country. At its poorest it might include a sad bear, a moth-eaten lion, and a few depressed monkeys. At its best it numbered dozens of rare animals: such as the tiger, lion, leopard, elephant, hyena, panther, zebra, camel, llama, kangaroo, and gnu. The latest additions were the rhinoceros and camelopard (giraffe), which caused startled amazement among the awe-struck yokels.

347

The menagerie alone was somewhat tame for a railroad age. Animal trainers like Isaac Van Amburgh taught monkeys to ride and lions to draw a chariot; now and then he put his head into a lion's mouth. Horses and horsemen, tumblers, acrobats, clowns, singers, and dancers were added; earlier they had toured independently. An American was credited with the first somersault on horseback. A band gave the proper zoom to the street parade that was such an important part of circus ballyhoo. The greatest spur to the business was the arrival in 1836 of Cooke's Royal Circus (English) with the unprecedented total of 130 horsemen and acrobats.

The usual circus toured the country in eight to ten wagons, with an advance agent to post bills. The caravan spruced itself to the utmost before entering a town, and was headed by a clown tooting a horn, shouting, and performing gymnastics. The tent or a canvas wall was erected, seats and a stage placed, and sometimes even gaslights provided. By the end of the decade circuses were touring the country regularly from the Atlantic to the Mississippi, and from Canada to the Gulf; one company boasted of traveling 2,482 miles in 1842. The circus was popular even in New England, where apparently it was considered more moral than Shapespeare.

The great future impresario of the circus was Phineas T. Barnum, who deserted the grocery business in 1835 to exhibited Joyce Heth—aged, toothless, and claiming to have been the nurse of George Washington, whom she referred to as "dear little George." Barnum advertised her as 161 years old; when a post mortem put her age at about 75, he filled the press with moans about how he was defrauded.

After Joyce's death, Barnum managed the juggler Signor Antonio, whom he renamed Vivalla. Business was encouraged by offering a prize to anyone who could duplicate the Vivalla stunts, and then the money was kept in the family by hiring a second juggler. By 1836, Barnum was in the circus business, first as an employee and then as owner of "Barnum's Grand Scientific and Musical Theater." Going broke, he returned to New York to make and sell shoe blacking, cologne, and scented hair grease.

Barnum next collected a troupe headed by the Negro dancer, John Diamond. Business was poor, and by the time the company reached New Orleans only Diamond and a fiddler remained. Fake dancing matches were profitable, but Diamond deserted anyway, and Barnum went to managing canvassers who were selling *Sear's Pictorial Illustrations of the Bible*. The upward road really started in 1841 when Barnum bought Scudder's American Museum, to which he soon added the Peale collections of New York and Philadelphia. His greatest attraction was the dwarf General Tom Thumb, who came under his direction in 1842, and with whom in 1844 he made his first trip to Europe.

Outdoor sports included very little of the baseball and football of a century later. "One old cat" was sometimes elaborated to a square diamond, with the batter midway between first and fourth base; the myth of the Abner Doubleday rules of 1839 had not yet been created. Football was limited to colleges, where a desultory kicking of the ball frequently ended in a free-for-all. This and "other trifling not to say expensive amusements which have exercise as an excuse"[6] were protested as wastes of time and money. Such sports as tennis and golf appeared in the rulebooks, but apparently were not played in the United States.

Less expensive and more popular were ninepins, tenpins (skittles), bowls, and quoits—all outdoor games. Women sometimes risked their femininity in the first two. The ninepins were arranged in a square, with one corner toward the player, twenty-one feet distant; the winner was the person who knocked all the pins down in the fewest tries. Quoits was favored as an after-dinner sport for workmen, who had regular teams; to pitch a two-pound quoit fifty to sixty feet required strength as well as skill. Less popular were handball ("Fines"), squash ("Rackets"), and cricket. Devotees of fencing considered that sport manly and healthful, and playing shuffleboard was a pleasant method of whiling away time on a long ship voyage.

Foot races drew good crowds, even though the track meet was unknown. Thousands went to the Union Race Course on Long Island in 1835 to see nine men try to run ten miles within an hour; only three crossed the finish line, with one having run the course

[6] Wright, *Wright*, 18.

in fifty-nine minutes, forty-four seconds. The best-known walker was Joshua Newsome, who covered one thousand miles in eighteen days in 1830. These records were made with no special equipment and little training; only a few schools, and possibly two public institutions, possessed gymnasiums.

The shove-and-grunt men were particularly popular in the West, where many a community had its local champion wrestler who challenged any other champion within riding distance. The resulting encounter was a combined wrestling exhibition, prize fight, and gouging match with no holds barred, and frequently very unfortunate results for one or both contestants.

Also viciously brutal was boxing, which was little more than street fighting surrounded by a rope. Efforts to make it "gentlemanly" were not impressive, and it was described quite properly as a "fashionable abomination of our loafer-ridden city."[7] The men fought with bare fists, and a round ended when one man went down. The fight ended when one of the battlers lost consciousness—a peaceful conclusion that might require one hundred or more rounds. A big fight attracted hundreds of the riffraff, who sneaked out of the city to some remote spot, thus avoiding the police. If one of the contestants was seriously injured, his opponent was spirited out of the country.

The greatest event of the boxing world was the arrival in 1837 of the English champion Deaf Burke, but no worthy opponent could be found. Later came James ("Yankee") Sullivan, an English-born fugitive from an Australian penal colony, who made hash of several American opponents in 1841 and 1842, and then in turn was pounded to a jelly by the first American champion, Tom Hyer—six feet, three, and two hundred pounds of dynamite.

A pleasant and even idyllic contrast to boxing was the popular and nonstrenuous winter sport of sleighing. The young blade tucked his best girl into a cutter drawn by a fast horse. The larger party crowded into a wagon drawn by two or four horses; rugs, sandbags, and foot stones supplemented the bodily heat of high spirits. Only the least sporting could write: "Set your chair on a springboard out in the porch on Christmas day; put your feet in a pailful of powdered

[7] Nevins, *Hone Diary*, II, 620.

ice; have somebody to jingle a bell in one ear, and somebody else to blow into the other with the bellows, and you will have an exact idea of sleighing."[8]

Good ice drew crowds of both old and young to every stream and lake. The common skate was the Holland type, with wooden toe holds and blade curved well in front of the foot, but the up-to-date skate sported a blade shorter in front and longer behind, and attached with the new mechanical clamps. The really sporting could build a speedy iceboat.

Most water sports were on top of the water, since Americans seemed to hate to get wet, even in a bathtub. The first American swimming school was still a novelty. Boating, however, was really popular, with dozens of competing city boat clubs. The eight-oar shell was rare, and with the four- or six-oar boat a mile in seven minutes was considered very good time. A few scullers made the boatsmen grind their teeth in rage by outracing them.

Most amazing of American sports was archery, which calmly ignored American Indian adeptness so that the well-to-do could ape English habits. The United Bowmen of Philadelphia (1828), including both men and women, was an outstanding organization. The men were picturesque in their green frock coats trimmed with gold and with arrows on the collars, their white pantaloons, their green caps, and their black leather girdles. Their lemonwood bows, strings, arrows, quivers, belts, pouches, and targets all came from England. The target, placed at eighty yards, displayed concentric circles of gold, red, white, black, and light blue (center). A boy waved a silk flag to show the color hit, except that a bulls-eye rated the toot of a trumpet.

Less affluent members of the sporting gentry, particularly in the South and West, congregated to watch battles of gamecocks. Training was a fine art, and the most esoteric practices passed eagerly from mouth to mouth. Steel spurs were sometimes used. The rival owners backed their entries with sizable bets, while most of the spectators likewise showed financial confidence in their favorites.

Fishing and hunting might be considered necessities or pleasures or both. Fishing parties were usually glorified picnics and fishing

[8] Martineau, *Retrospect*, II, 172.

clubs were popular, but only the most zealous fisherman used one of the many artificial flies that were available. Hunters were unlimited by game laws except in the case of deer. Various hunting clubs gave prizes which encouraged competitive slaughter. Real enthusiasts visited the western plains, especially to hunt buffalo. In 1843 the sport was brought East when thirty thousand people watched a buffalo hunt at the Elysian Fields of Hoboken; a stray animal produced a near panic. The most anachronistic hunting was falconry and fox hunting, with red-coated fox hunters particularly in evidence in Virginia and neighboring states. The hunt was above all a social event, and provided topics for many a later discussion over a hot toddy or mint julep.

The hunter was always equipped with a gun and frequently with a dog. In dogs he had almost as great a selection as his great-great-grandson, but guns were not so varied. The old-fashioned muzzle-loading flintlock could still be seen, but most Easterners had adopted the cartridges which Sam Woodcock had introduced in 1826. The really treasured fine gun was an English-made weapon. The Colt revolver was as yet a rare novelty.

Accurate shooting was more important for a Westerner than for an Easterner, which probably accounts for the greater frequency of shooting matches in the West. Most common was shooting at a target—say a paper one and one-half inches square at seventy-five to one hundred yards. Each contestant paid an entrance fee, and the winner had first choice at the quarters of a beef. Many stories were told of wonderful western shooting; for instance, that of Captain Martin Scott, who was greeted by a raccoon in a tree with the remark, "I may just as well come down for I'm a *gone* 'coon."[9] In fact, however, no shooting of the eighteen thirties was good from modern standards.

The sport of sports for all Americans except New Englanders was horse racing. The tracks from New York to Texas were crowded with young and old, rich and poor, fashionable matrons and hired girls. A big race emptied Wall Street and caused the adjournment of the United States Senate. Every available vehicle was comman-

[9] Marryat, *Diary*, 150.

deered. The stands were crowded, and between races the crowd drank, ate pies and apples and even regular meals, played faro and roulette, and consulted quack doctors—provided the pickpockets did not get to their purses too soon.

Meets were so arranged that the best horses could compete in all the good ones. The season opened when spring came to the South, and the horses moved north and returned south with the sun. The hottest months were omitted, with a northern track having its seasons in the spring and fall. Each course was controlled by rules formulated and enforced by a "jockey club."

The usual horse race was open to all comers, with limitation to a particular class such as three-year-olds very rare. Each entrant paid a fee which, together with a purse from the proprietor of the track, went to the winner; seldom was the prize under one hundred dollars and frequently it exceeded one thousand dollars. A trumpet called the horses to the post and the bang of a drum started them. A single race consisted of three heats (sometimes five) of one, two, three, or four miles. Most favored were three heats of four miles each. Now and then a race was handicapped; probably the first steeplechase was in Canada in 1840.

The American four-mile record was held throughout the thirties by American Eclipse, which in 1823 had won its owner twenty thousand dollars by a heat of 7:37. This record fell in 1842, when Fashion covered the same distance in 7:32. Anything under six minutes was excellent for three miles, under four minutes for two, and under two minutes for one. These times were not completely reliable, however, since courses were not always the exact lengths advertised, and judges were sometimes inaccurate even after the introduction of a split-second stop watch in 1829.

The most intense horse-racing enthusiasm was reserved for a contest between a northern and a southern horse, and track owners profited greatly by a long series of such races. The southern horse usually won. Most exciting of the series was a race of 1842 for twenty thousand dollars in owners' bets. In this case the northern horse Fashion won, but only by establishing a new American record, since the southern horse Gibbon also bettered the old time.

Pacing does not seem to have been practiced, but trotting had a measure of popularity, with good clubs at New York and Philadelphia. The horse Edwin Forrest established an American record in 1834 with a 2:31.5 mile. Many of the recorded times for trotting horses were for long distances; for example, Chancellor covered thirty-two miles in 1:58:31.

Public racing enthusiasm plus large prizes inflated the prices of good race horses. Any winner brought at least one thousand dollars, and there was talk of ten times that much; four thousand dollars was refused in 1832 for Terror, a colt by Eclipse out of Lady Lightfoot. Such high-priced property brought an eager demand for competent trainers when the owners did not do their own training, and a frequent arrangement was for the trainer to take part of his pay in a claim on half the horse's winnings. Trainers and owners were so anxious to win that they doped their horses, concealed their names to get more favorable betting odds, and even poisoned their competitors' entries. Cutthroat competition was not confined to the business world.

When the American moved indoors, his choice of games was much more limited. Such traditional amusements as backgammon, chess, and draughts (checkers) had their devotees, while at New Orleans about 1840 there was introduced the novel game of craps. Very popular was billiards, which was a combination of the present carom and pocket varieties. The poolroom loafer was much in evidence at the numerous public halls, but billiards was also a home sport for the better-to-do; President Adams' table in the White House had been practically a national issue.

Card playing was viewed askance by the more religious, and in truth its association with professional gambling gave a reasonable basis for distaste. For those not troubled by religious scruples, whist seemed a highly scientific game; it had a variant called Boston which was much like present-day five hundred. Either game was frequently played for stakes, as was euchre, all fours (high-low-jack-and-the-game), cribbage, *vingt-et-un* (twenty-one), or poker. A variant of poker was brag, in which jacks and nines were wild; naturals were better than "braggers" and no more than three of a kind could be claimed.

Cards gave a great advantage to the professional, and not only because of his greater skill in play. Changing packs, palming, and dealing off the bottom were the rudiments of his art. Specially marked backs were advertised for the professional trade, and trimming the edges was a much-used refinement. Secret drawers, mirrors, and signals by confederates gave nudges to Lady Luck. The professional realized that the average man delighted in betting on a sure thing; for example, that three cards shuffled into a deck would not all come out on top; the impossible then occurred by sleight of hand. He also recognized that the surest bait was to persuade the sucker that he could cheat the professional—which ultimately became a costly lesson in morality for the sucker.

The outstanding gambling games were roulette, faro, and chucker-luck. All three were mathematically profitable to the operator, but were then doctored. Roulette wheels might have concealed brakes. In faro the player picked a number and placed a bet. Cards were drawn from a box (both probably fixed) and placed on alternate piles; if the player's number went on the house side, he lost, and vice versa. In chucker-luck (later chuck-a-luck) the player picked a number between one and six. Three dice were thrown. If his number appeared once, he got his money back; if twice, it was doubled; if three times, it was tripled; loaded dice and palming increased the mathematical odds.

Professional gamblers were attracted by the steamboats, for here were travelers with both leisure and money. Whether the gambler worked alone or with confederates, and whether or not he collaborated with the ship's officers, he always found at least a few unwary passengers with exalted ideas of their own smartness—an egotism for which they often paid dearly.

City gambling houses were both numerous and notorious, with never any more disguise than the transparent claim to be a coffee-house or a billiard parlor. Virtuous citizens hated them, but not primarily because their patrons lost money, which after all was the bad judgment of the customers. The trouble arose in the related vices. Drunken carousing was common. Visitors had their drinks drugged and woke up penniless in the streets. Prostitutes drummed up business. Criminals plotted new outbreaks. In fact the only virtue the solid citizen found in gambling houses was that they were "very good places for recruiting the army and navy."[10]

The most universal type of gambling was the lottery, which ranged from a church raffle to a commercial project offering thousands of dollars in prizes. The big lottery ordinarily issued ten-dollar tickets that were subdivided into as little as tenths. Americans spent millions of dollars each year on lotteries, which were always stacked for the operator and frequently completely fraudulent.

The reformers did not fail to attack "the sin of gambling,"[11] and their societies recounted the social costs and the personal demoralization which might be expected to ensue. The road to degradation started with checkers and whist, and passed with rapid acceleration through poker, faro, horse racing, and prize fighting, to end in drunken debauches and murder. Under the pressure of these arguments antigambling laws were passed, and lotteries were taxed heavily or proscribed. Enforcement was sporadic and ineffectual, however, leading to the cynical charge that the only men punished were those who refused to pay the police for protection.

The most drastic action against gamblers occurred in 1835 at Vicksburg, which was then filled with saloons, gambling houses, and brothels for the river trade. The aroused citizenry ordered the gamblers to leave. When their order was flouted, they smashed the houses and ejected the gamblers—that is, all save five who were left swinging on a single tree as a warning. Other river towns copied this procedure, but with no notable lessening of river gambling. Vicksburg was succeeded as the gambling capital of the river by Natchez and then by other towns.

Most sports were predominantly male, both in participation and in attendance. Women were certainly expected to avoid any strenuous physical activity except washing clothes and scrubbing floors. Even dancing received considerable hostility. Light calisthenics were a radical innovation, and most people thought a short walk more seemly. Riding was proper with a sidesaddle and a voluminous rid-

---

[10] Saxe-Weimar, *Travels*, II, 51.

[11] J. H. Greene, *An Exposure of the Arts and Miseries of Gambling* (Cincinnati, 1843), 11.

"Shooting for the Beef," from a painting
by George Caleb Bingham

"Pitching Quoits," from a painting by George Caleb Bingham

ing habit. Swimming was out of the question, since bathing was done fully clothed and an effort to swim would have brought death by drowning. Women could play dominoes, cards, checkers, or even ninepins and billiards, but with misgivings by many. They could attend horse races and other exhibitions as spectators.

The specially reserved domain of woman was needlework, and she dominated the gossip sessions called tea parties. She also gave the major patronage to palmists, astrologers, and other fortune-tellers. Her current fad was the autograph album, which bore a touching title like "Affection's Gift." She thrust it upon every visitor, and the part of wisdom was to have a trite and flowery sentiment ready for such an emergency. She even invaded the floor of the Senate and the bench of the Supreme Court for victims; a public man signed autograph albums by reflex action.

Games for children, as produced commercially, tended toward the educational, such as The Interrogatory Geographical Game of the World, Zoological Garden, Wonders of Art, Theater of Nature, or dissected scenes and maps. Most toys such as wooden sheep, soldiers, and men came from Germany, but the rubber ball was a product of American ingenuity.

Children had a wide choice of games. They could skip rope, play battledore, spin tops. They could play marbles, leapfrog, or quoits. Many a small boy went hunting, trapping, or fishing while his little sister played house with her dolls. In the winter came snow-balling, skating, and coasting, the latter requiring no more equipment than a board. Indoors there were such amusements as hidden ball, puss-in-the-corner, Mr. Pope and his lady, honeypots, hide-and-seek, blind-man's buff, follow-the-leader, air, earth, and water, word guessing, forfeits, old maid, dominoes, and checkers. Sometimes the game was accompanied by a song:

> *Oranges and lemons*
> *Say the bells of St. Clemens;*
> *Brickdust and tiles,*
> *Say the bells of St. Giles;*
> *Your owe me five farthings,*
> *Say the bells of St. Martin's;*

When will you pay me?
Say the bells of Old Bailey;
When I grow rich,
Say the bells of Shoreditch;
When will that be?
Say the bells of Stepney;
I do not know,
Says the great bell of Bow.

Enigmas had some popularity:

Little Miss Netticoat, with a white petticoat,
And a red nose;
She has no feet nor hands; and the longer she stands
The shorter she grows. (a lighted candle)

And the charade:

My first in your face has a prominent place;
My next in a smile you appear;
A bundle of sweets my whole will complete,
When Flora bedizens the year. (nose-gay)

The conundrum:

Why is a lawyer like a poker?
Because he is so often at the bar.
Why is a proud woman like a music book?
She is full of airs.
What is higher and handsomer with the head off?
A pillow.

And then a rebus, which for a dinner might include a country in the East (turkey), one of the sons of Noah (ham), half a room under ground—a vowel—and a grain omitting the last letter (celery), to be on an equality and to cut short (parsnips), a machine to raise water and a relation (pumpkin), a fruit—the half of a pool of dirty water—and a circle changing the first letter (plum pudding), to chop fine and the last half of a talking bird (mince pie), and so on indefinitely.[12]

American amusements of the thirties were surprisingly varied. In spite of protestations to the contrary, Americans did not spend their few spare moments in reading the Bible and meditating on their sins. Rather amazing is the time they found for recreation with a twelve- to fourteen-hour working day, and consequently there can be little surprise that America in time became the greatest sporting nation of the world.

Recreation showed American traits of character as clearly as did other occupations. Sports tended to be strenuous. They were followed in the company of others, for few Americans found their greatest joy in solitaire. The competitive element ranked high, as it did in other phases of life, the competition being with other men and not with abstract records. Team sports were not as common as individual competitions. And then the moral earnestness of America showed in the continual insistence that recreations have moral and educational values. Sport for its own sake remained under suspicion.

The inevitable presence of gambling reflected not only a basic human urge, but an outstanding characteristic of Americans. Here was no conservative and cringing desire for security, but rather the willingness to gamble for the big monetary rewards that were the chief badges of distinction. For the man who was impatient or who possessed little capital, the turn of the wheel of fortune gave hopes that were unlikely of realization in more ordinary and humdrum business. America was willing to take a chance.

[12] All quoted material on children's games comes from Eliza Leslie, *American Girl's Book or Occupation for Play Hours* (Boston, 1849).

20. The Arts

AMERICA in 1830 was obviously not the art capital of the world, yet it contained a surprising number of men who devoted their lives to swimming against the current. Not only did such iconoclasts exist in the relatively well-populated and wealthy East, but also in the rawness of the West. Actors toured the West. Painters recorded its people and scenes. And some of these artists were native to the country where they worked.

Painting was the most practiced of the fine arts. The older masters such as Gilbert Stuart and Benjamin West were dead, but their mantles had fallen on a bevy of newcomers such as Washington Allston, Chester Harding, Henry Inman, S.F.B. Morse, Rembrandt Peale, Thomas Sully, and John Trumbull. The work of these artists still merits hanging in important art galleries.

The first great hazard for a hopeful American boy in his quest of fame in painting was a lack of instruction. Most Americans were self-taught. A boy with an urge to paint started on his father's barn, graduated to the painting of signs, and might in time become a full-fledged portrait painter. Sometimes he might attain the privilege of working under an established artist like Allston, Trumbull, or Morse. A few hopefuls realized the dream of European training. In an earlier day they had gone to London, where Benjamin West functioned as teacher and godfather, but with West's death in 1826, Rome became the mecca of the hopeful.

The other great hazard for a painter was the difficulty of finding a market. The only potential patrons were hard-headed farmers, bankers, merchants, and sea captains who wanted photographic likenesses of their wives and children, while the artist felt demeaned by doing work of this kind, sneering at it as inferior and of no permanent value. As Dunlap wrote: "I believe the Calvary is very much my best picture, but I have been obliged to paint the portraits of mere every-day folk of the present unholy race; for my saints, though marvelously painted, work no miracles, and could not keep my family from starvation."[1] The candid chronicler must add that neither saints nor "every-day folk" were very good, and that art did not suffer when Dunlap and others stuck to portraits.

The influence of the market brought a tremendous flow of portraits, from men who ranged from the peripatetic five-dollar hack to Thomas Sully, who did some 2,500. Sully is best remembered today because of his strong and vital work and his good flesh tints; his most important commission was to paint the rather uninspiring Queen Victoria. Charles Ingham was probably most popular in his day because his preciseness permitted a lady to recognize even the smallest piece of lace and jewelry.

A special type of portraiture was that of the Indian. Every important exploring party included a painter, and drawings made by these men were later published in significant numbers. Best known was George Catlin, who traveled thousands of miles in the West during the decade, and who is said to have done over five hundred paintings, the majority of which were portraits. Catlin then lectured and exhibited his paintings through the East and Europe. The comment of a visiting Scotch phrenologist on the Catlin pictures was perhaps a proper characterization; he called them "deficient in drawing, perspective, and finish," but then added that the spectator was impressed "with a conviction of their fidelity to nature which gives them an inexpressible charm."[2]

The usual American painter was stopped by current morality from painting nudes. Frequently the artist who had visited Europe desired to paint flesh and muscles rather than flounces and jewels, but the "common-sense" man was certain that only an immoral woman would expose her body to a man, regardless of whether or not he was an artist, and that the ultimate painting would rouse men's lowest passions, irrespective of the theme.

A few painters violated current morality and thereby attained at least notoriety; apparently a good many men liked their lowest

[1] Cooper, *Correspondence*, I, 241-42.
[2] Combe, *Notes*, I, 70.

passions roused. Vanderlyn became known not for his portraits of Madison, Monroe, and Calhoun, but for his nude "Ariadne" as popularized in the engraving by Asher B. Durand. Most exciting were the Otis pictures of the Garden of Eden—"The Temptation," "The Judgment," and "The Expulsion"; only a few tolerant souls noted a general delicacy "that will enable the ladies to participate in the gratification of visiting the exhibition free from any apprehension of a shock to their feelings."[3] A little later, at the height of Victorian modesty, the pictures probably would not even have been shown.

The artist was also limited by the current feeling that certain subjects were not "artistic." The Durand wail, cited earlier, was partly an objection to doing any common people in any situation. Only a few painters such as George Caleb Bingham used such commonplace themes as election speeches and river life; a barnyard or a plowman should certainly not be immortalized on canvas. Even Allston's "Massacre of the Innocents" was criticized by many who held that such a sordid emotion as fear had better be left to literature. Also, there was but minor attention to scenes of nature and still life. Thomas Cole has been dubbed the father of American landscape painting, and the entire group of painters who followed him has been called the "Hudson River School" because several of them painted Hudson River scenes. The landscapes were generally drab, with a meticulous detail and a prevailing brownness.

A properly artistic subject was one that was impressively uplifting, and what could be grander than epic views from the Bible or from history? A scene of this kind required a big canvas, the bigger the better. Every serious artist seeking eternal fame painted at least one of these gargantuan monstrosities, which he then exhibited to win the applause—and small fees—of the knowing.

The most famous of the epic paintings was West's religious allegory, "Death on a Pale Horse," which was exhibited widely and sold for an almost unbelievable $8,000. Allston bid for immortality with several titanic religious scenes, dripping with sublime emotion; for parts of twenty years he worked on his "Belshazzar's Feast," which remained unfinished at his death—probably just as well.

[3] New York *Morning Courier*, April 9, 1835.

Morse did the "House of Representatives," Rembrandt Peale "The Court of Death," and Trumbull "Bunker Hill" and the "Declaration of Independence," while dozens of panoramas of battles and of cities consumed gallons of paint that could have been used more profitably on houses.

If size were admirable, then greater size was even better, and what could surpass the world's greatest river? So reasoned Henry Banvard as he surveyed the Mississippi carefully during the thirties, with a three-mile canvas in mind. Completed in the next decade, it was a somewhat disappointing 440 yards, but delighted audiences paid freely to see it rolled from one wooden roller to another; it grossed $54,000 in seven months in Boston, which was good even for that center of culture. But other artisans of the paintbrush could cover even a greater number of square yards of canvas. The ultimate arrived in 1849 when Henry Lewin completed a 1,325-yard picture of the Mississippi—a panorama to end all panoramas.

Other types of pictorial art were not lacking. Miniatures, including cameos, had wide popularity. Charcoal sketches and caricatures found a small market. Painting on velvet or paper had its devotees. Silhouette artists were in great demand. This art of cutting silhouettes has been credited to Charles Willson Peale, who was also a painter, proprietor of the most famous museum of its day, and the maker of Washington's false teeth; his well-known children were Raphael, Angelica, Rembrandt, Rubens, and Titian.

Preparing pictures for mass production was itself the work of an artist. The woodcut had an ever diminishing currency. Copper engraving was better, and boasted such artists as A. B. Durand, but it was quite expensive. The new, easier, and cheaper process was the lithograph from a stone plate. Its advantages were that it permitted more book illustrations and separate prints of scenery, portraits, race horses, political cartoons, temperance drawings, theatrical scenes, and other popular matter. Widespread distribution was just around the corner when Nathaniel Currier had his first great success with the picture of the burning of the *Lexington* in Long Island Sound in 1840.

Only a few wealthy Americans could afford to buy original paintings, and they generally preferred even a poor foreign reproduction; if they bought domestic products, these were the work of the better-known men. Even the museum and art gallery bowed to foreign judgment, and were proudest of a Rubens, Velásquez, or Tintoretto—advertised as originals, but probably not. The magazines printed only a scattering of articles on artistic subjects, and there was only one real art magazine, the *National Portrait Gallery* (1836), which reproduced American pictures.

The most hopeful trend, just imported from Germany, was the founding of art unions in various cities—not primarily for artists, but for lovers of art. Each member made a small yearly subscription, and the total funds were invested in paintings and engravings. The engravings were distributed to all members, while the pictures went by lot. Here was proof that popularly enjoyed art was not confined to lithographs of race horses and portraits of little Sarah.

Each large American city had an art association. Sometimes it helped young artists. Usually it provided a library and lectures. Always it had a picture gallery and an annual members' exhibition, optimistically designed to sell pictures. These associations seemed rent continually by schisms. The quarrelsome Joshua Shaw led a secession from the Philadelphia Academy, and then a secession from the secession. Morse led a similar revolt (1825) from the New York Academy of Fine Arts to produce the National Academy of Design, which ultimately took over the pictures of its reluctant parent.

The annals of sculpture were pathetically short and meager. The American pioneer was William Rush, who lived until 1833, but inspired few successors; his "Nymph of the Schuylkill" was originally in wood, but now appears in bronze in Fairmount Park, Philadelphia. The carving of stone was almost monopolized by masons who embellished buildings with curlecues and gravestones with cherubs; their reputation was so small that a Scotsman was imported to decorate Girard College.

The two most eminent American sculptors were Horatio Greenough and Hiram Powers. Greenough was Boston born and Italian trained. His "Chanting Cherubs," copied from a Raphael picture, was probably the first sculptured group to be done by an American. Fellow citizens were not enthusiastic about the cherubs, but they felt a glow of pride that a local boy could carve figures in stone; hence when Greenough returned to the United States in the early thirties, he was commissioned to make a statue for the rotunda of the Capitol. The result was George Washington in a toga—an eyesore for years.

Hiram Powers was a completely native product, born in Vermont and maturing in Cincinnati, where his only formal training was a little instruction in modeling. His first big commission was the wax figures for the Dorfeuille museum, but his most famous work was the "Slave Girl," about which one rapt onlooker exclaimed, "I certainly never saw anything more lovely."[4] The "Slave Girl" was done about 1830, and showed a girl in chains—an allegory of the Greek situation. Part of the attraction was that Greece was then much admired, and part that the girl was nude—the nudity probably drew more customers than the beauty. The statue is now in the Corcoran Galleries. Unfortunately for American sculpture, Powers left in 1837 to make his permanent home in Rome.

Architecture was in the throes of a revolution as Georgian colonial gave way to an overmastering Greek trend, inspired partly by American sympathy for the Greeks in their war of independence. Not only houses and churches but even jails and synagogues masqueraded as Greek temples. A New England bank might be reminiscent of ancient Athens if one except the chimney and the covering of snow on the flat roof.

The Greek Revival was not only an effort to capture the Greek spirit, but an exact copying of Greek forms. The usual four-, six-, or eight-columned portico had the proper entablature and pediments, while Girard College had columns all the way around. Here and there a circular house or pavillion was startling. The marble of the Greeks was simulated by flush clapboards, which often were covered with stucco or plaster marked into squares. Where brick was used, it was painted white or gray. Then, all too frequently, the owner could not restrain himself from embellishing his Greek temple with wrought-iron balconies, grilles, and balustrades.

If Greek architecture had only stayed on the outside of the

[4] Nevins, *Hone Diary*, II, 819.

buildings, it would have been at least endurable. But it came inside. Instead of the lovely old wooden mantles, there appeared monstrosities of marble and cement, often decorated with Greek figures. Entablatures embellished the high-ceilinged rooms, which were separated by Greek columns.

The one justification for clemency in judging the Greek fad was that American architecture was very young. Charles Bulfinch, first professional American architect, lived until 1844; in searching for ideas for the reconstruction of the Washington capitol, he emerged with a classical urge, and ended his life as a Greek revivalist. The greatest culprit, however, was Bulfinch's friend Benjamin Latrobe, whose ideas were spread by his two best-known pupils, William Strickland and Robert Mills; the latter's best work was probably the Treasury at Washington. The one hold-out against the Greek influence was Richard Upjohn, who favored the Gothic, and whose best work was Trinity Church, New York.

The rash of pseudo-Greek temples that mottled the American landscape could never dominate the scene. Older houses remained standing. Many people hesitated over the Greek, because of either taste or cost. The alternative, however, was by no means always a thing of beauty. The usual city brownstone house, for example, was even less attractive. The prize monstrosity was Mrs. Trollope's Cincinnati bazaar, which was brick with Gothic windows, Grecian pillars, Turkish dome, and decorative Egyptian figures; in time a coat of whitewash made it somewhat less objectionable.

American patriotism was expressed architecturally in monuments. A memorial for the patriots of Bunker Hill fame was begun with a great flourish in 1825, but then lagged until the women became interested and collected the necessary funds. It was ready for a dedicatory oration by Daniel Webster in 1843.

The greatest monument of that or any other time was the Washington Monument at Washington City, on which work started in 1836. Mill's original plan called for a 600-foot obelisk rising from a circular, colonnaded base. The base was later changed and the top slightly modified, but the stark and impressive simplicity of the Mill's plan was retained. The completion of the project was to be delayed almost half a century.

The accomplishments of American architecture were hardly impressive—a handful of public buildings and monuments, together with a new and worse trend in domestic architecture. But succeeding generations did worse; not until the turn of the century did American architecture provide a fresh, vital, and useful approach.

Music was an art for the masses, even though an American accused his compatriots of being "almost ignorant of the art of music,"[5] while a Frenchman held American music to be "of an unbelievable barbarity."[6] What such people criticized was the quality rather than the quantity of American music, because Americans delighted in making more or less tuneful noises.

Many a girl learned to play the piano as a parlor accomplishment, so that in later life she could entertain, or bore, her friends with "Bright Shines the Moon," "March to the Battlefield," "General Andrew Jackson's Presidential Grand March," or a similar masterpiece. Or she might accompany herself or others in such melodious songs as "'Tis the Last Rose of Summer," "My Gentle Harp," "The Old Oaken Bucket," "Old Dan Tucker," "The Light Canoe," "Good Night," "Comin Through the Rye," and "The Last Link is Broken."

Men preferred the violin and the flute, possibly because music for either could be read from the piano score, and even the rudest community could furnish at least a fiddle for a dance. Both men and women delighted in raising their voices in song, with the "singing school" extremely popular. The master gave out the tune and words bit by bit until they were memorized, while meantime the boys and girls could brush shoulders and lift their voices in what passed for harmony. After the school they walked home—slowly—two by two.

Most people could not read music, hence the "music school" and the "lining out" of hymns. Efforts were made to simplify musical notation by the use of "patent notes," which showed their pitch by their shape. Musical terminology was simplified, so that whereas in 1830 one talked of semibreves and demisemiquavers, one in 1840 could speak of whole and sixteenth notes. A new metronome, better

[5] Cooper, *American Democrat*, 155.
[6] Pierson, *Tocqueville*, 392.

than the old one of Maelzel, made timing more accurate. Unfortunately the nonexistence of a standard pitch made doubtful the same tuning for all instruments.

Instrumental music had the advantage of every modern instrument except the saxophone; even the jew's-harp was popular. New in the early forties was the xylophone—or is that a musical instrument? The rarer instruments such as the oboe, bassoon, viola, and double bass were usually handled by foreign-born players, since there was no instruction in the United States. Pianos by Steinway, Knabe, and Chickering graced middle- and upper-class homes. Early in the decade they were all grands, but in 1837 Chickering patented the first practical frame for an upright, and soon there were such instruments all over the world, including the wilds of Illinois and Missouri.

A pipe organ was exclusively a church instrument, and the richer churches competed for the honor of having the nation's largest. The Second Presbyterian Church of Philadelphia boasted proudly of its 1,890 pipes until the Trinity Church of Boston countered with an $8,000 English importation. Many churches, however, held out against organs, believing them to be irreligious; they might more properly have objected to the loud and expressionless playing that drowned out congregational singing.

Visitors to America commented on "the uncommon partiality our citizens manifest for the noisy part of the orchestra,"[7] particularly the trumpet and the trombone. The most famous musical rivalry of the day was between John T. Norton, a home product who played an old-fashioned trumpet which produced the half-notes by sliding, and Alessandro Gambati, a foreign-born manipulator of a completely valve instrument. Potential fisticuffs between partisans of the two men were averted by a musical duel which drew some 2,500 auditors to the mutual profit of the rivals and also to that of the hall owner, Mr. Niblo, who may have had a hand in encouraging the rivalry. The judges decided for Norton, but the Gambati partisans were sure that their champion had been cheated.

The supreme instrumental event of the period was the tour of

[7] *American Musical Journal* 1834, quoted in F. L. Ritter, *Music in America* (New York, Charles Scribner's Sons, 1883), 214.

the violinist Ole Bull, who arrived in 1843. Bull was simple and unaffected, willing to play even such native gems as "Yankee Doodle," and Americans took him to their hearts to the tune of $400,000 in a little over two years. Incidentally, Bull was succeeded in popular favor by seven Swiss bell ringers (1844), who evoked almost equal enthusiasm.

Native American instrumentalists were few and poor. All New York could not produce enough cellos for the William Tell overture or sufficient talent for an acceptable string quartet. Seldom could as many as fifteen or twenty men be collected even for a symphony, and then some of them sat blankly impotent during parts that they could not play. The best orchestra up to that time was the well-balanced nineteen musicians of the Italian opera company (1832).

Orchestral work was often to accompany singing, as when the New York Sacred Music Society gave "The Messiah" with 186 performers, including 42 in the orchestra—the largest presentation of its type. The usual instrumental group, such as the Euterpean Society or the Musical Fund Society, both of New York, was an amateur organization with a sprinkling of professionals, which gave one or two concerts a year. Significant historically was the professional Philharmonic Society of New York, the inspiration of U. C. Hill, organist, trumpeter, violin teacher, organizer of New York's first string quartet, and director of the Sacred Music Society. The Philharmonic's first concert on December 7, 1842, included Beethoven's "Fifth Symphony," Weber's "Overture to Oberon," Beethoven's "Fidelio," and Mozart's "Belmont and Constantia." The sixty-one players boasted proudly of including two oboes, four celli, five basses, two bassoons, and four horns.

Instrumental music was ordinarily the background for singing, which really appealed to Americans. Published music showed the trend. A little Beethoven, von Weber, and Mozart and a few operatic extracts appealed to the sophisticated. A moderate spicing of marches and waltzes pleased a few. But the overwhelming bulk comprised sentimental ditties like "The Spring Time Is Come," "When Spring Unlocks the Flowers," "O Breathe Not Her Name," and "Peace Within the Grave." Songbooks were common, with some designed to serve the temperance or other causes. All published songs were of unimpeachable morality; children's pieces were advertised as "not only unexceptional, but of good moral tendency."[8] Ribald and obscene songs delighted the ungodly, but they were not published.

The most important new song was "America," an old tune for which the young clergyman Samuel Francis Smith wrote the words, probably in 1832. "Home Sweet Home" was still comparatively new. That stand-by of the bass, "Rocked in the Cradle of the Deep," first rumbled through the air in 1839 from the voice of its composer, Joseph Philip Knight.

Professional singers, often foreign born, toured the country giving something they usually called, rather intimidatingly, "Soiree Musicale." Simple ballads, like "Believe Me If All Those Endearing Young Charms," were the staple, but an operatic aria or two lent dignity and a few humorous songs relieved the strain. A steady diet of "heavy" music, such as piano concertos, always failed. Duets, glees, and even instrumental numbers were sometimes presented; and an occasional brass band appeared with possibly a dozen players. A few wealthy sophisticates entertained their guests with the music of the masters, while, wonder of wonders, an Italian opera company made a successful tour in the middle of the decade.

The urge toward vocal self-expression brought great varieties of results, from the group gathered around the piano of an evening to the large city chorus. Every sizable town had an organization for the presentation of choral music, usually religious. Probably the best was the New York Sacred Music Society, composed of both amateurs and professionals. It was first in the United States to give Handel's "The Messiah" in its entirety (1831). It performed Mendelssohn's "St. Paul" within two years of its world premiere, and was very successful with Neukomm's "David." One of its most notable performances was a native oratorio in 1835—C. E. Horn's "The Remission of Sin," based on Milton's *Paradise Lost*. Its biggest performance was in 1839, when it presented a chorus of one thousand voices.

A concert by the usual local chorus or orchestra was great fun for the participants and their friends, but might well be something

[8] L. Mason and G. J. Webb, *The Juvenile Singing School* (Boston, J. H. Wilkins and R. B. Carter, 1837), Introduction, 2.

less than an artistic triumph. The leader must figuratively have torn his hair as the men missed notes or whole sections or played out of tune, as soloists flatted, as members of the chorus either missed their time or failed to open their mouths, and as chorus and orchestra battled for the right of way. Even kindly local critics felt themselves forced to note these and other musical misadventures.

Local music societies indicated that there was a surprising amount of interest in music, and also that the greatest enthusiasm was for religious works. People involved in choral singing went so far as to organize national conventions, starting in 1829. The results did not seem to include the improvement of congregational singing, but may have helped inspire the thousands of hymns that were composed. No reputable musician failed to write at least one or two, while Thomas Hastings alone could claim over six hundred, including "Rock of Ages Cleft For Me." Many of them, such as "Stand Up, Stand Up for Jesus," and "Just As I Am Without One Plea," have withstood long and hard usage.

Important among American musicians was the Massachusetts-born Lowell Mason, who started a business career as a bank clerk at Savannah. At the age of thirty-four he was drawn back to Boston by an offer of $2,000 a year to play the organ and direct the music of three churches. Doubts about music as a career led him to take a bank job on the side, but his fears proved groundless; in fact, he was the only musician of his day to make a fortune professionally. His greatest profits came from song collections; starting with one in Savannah, he published many works which sold over a million copies. Of his own compositions, best known are "Nearer My God To Thee," "My Faith Looks Up To Thee," and "From Greenland's Icy Mountains."

Mason's greatest importance was as a popularizer of music. His desire to increase musical interest was so intense that his Boston Academy of Music, which he established jointly with G. J. Webb, offered free lessons to any child under seven who would promise to study for at least a year. Instruction was divided into rhythm, melody, and dynamics, with the children immediately beating time and singing simple melodies. A chorus and orchestra provided not only instruction but also incentive. The methods were successful and classes ran into the hundreds. Even more important, the Mason system was standardized for the use of other teachers.

Looking beyond his own pupils, Mason soon dreamed of teaching music to every school child. So eager was he that at first, in 1834, he taught in the Boston schools free of charge; later he received aid from the city. Success was immediate, and other towns copied the idea—the birth of American public-school music.

Another great opportunity lay in work with music teachers, who frequently were badly trained and far from inspired. Mason traveled and spoke widely and encouraged musical conventions. Every summer starting in 1834 the Boston Academy held a session for vocal teachers, who came from as far away as Ohio and Kentucky. There was instruction in musical principles and in individual performances, group discussions, and choral concerts by the class.

The Boston Academy represented one of the efforts to meet the eternal problem of who was to teach the teacher. No college had up till now embraced the opportunity, but starting with the Musical Fund Society of Philadelphia in 1825, various training centers were established, many of them later adopting the Mason methods. Often, like the Musical Fund Society, they expired from financial malnutrition. Outstanding was the Music Vale Seminary (1835) of Salem, Connecticut, which at times enrolled as many as one hundred young ladies learning to sing and play various instruments, and studying theory.

The extent of American musical appreciation received no more eloquent testimony than the existence, even though precarious, of opera. Disregarding minor efforts, American opera really began with the Manuel García Company of eight, which arrived at New York in 1825, opening probably with the *Barber of Seville*. García toured the United States and Mexico with sufficiently encouraging results that a whole series of French, Italian, English, and American companies followed. Far the best was an Italian troupe (1832) of fifty, headed by Giovanni B. Montresor, which included a superior orchestra; the company was too large for American financial support and failed, but it at least inspired an Italian Opera House in New York.

A scattering of Americans displayed what they considered es-

Portrait of Frances Anne Kemble, by Thomas Sully

thetic superiority by acclaiming the opera rapturously, but the majority were skeptical of a play in which the actors sang their lines and in which no word could be understood. Furthermore, the productions were unprepossessing. Soloists were poor in quality and insufficient in number, so that they doubled for several characters; sopranos might sing tenor arias, tenors sometimes broke into falsetto, and difficult passages were cut or rearranged. A chorus was probably no more than a dozen hastily assembled amateurs who could neither act nor sing in time or tune. An orchestra might contain no more than five players, each of whom followed his own fancies, including the omission of difficult parts; the fiddle played every solo part, a trombone might double for a nonexistent cello, and everyone might be out of tune.

Inadequate performers and skeptical audiences led to the streamlining of operas to bring them within the capacities on both sides of the footlights. For example, the better-known Rossini melodies were thrown together to produce the popular *Cinderella*, while the most melodious tunes of several composers were welded into *Rakeby*. Only a few Americans sang in, produced, or wrote operas; most important among them was C. E. Horn, but his success was not great.

The important fact about American opera was not the feebleness of its support, but rather that such a sophisticated musical form could even obtain a paying audience. A city like New York was not a complete musical desert when it supported a fourteen-night run in 1839 of Beethoven's *Fidelio*. America was much more musically inclined than seemed probable for a nation engaged in exploiting a continent. Musical maturity was still in the distant future, but the goal was not hopelessly remote.

> *The Theatre was, from the very first,*
> *The favorite haunt of sin—*
> *From first to last it was an evil place:*
> *And now such things are acted there, as made*
> *The devil blush, and from the neighborhood,*
> *Angels and holy men tremblingly retired.*[9]

[9] *Western Methodist,* May 18, 1834, quoted in D. L. Hunt, *The Nashville Theatre 1830–1840,* Birmingham Southern College *Bulletin,* Vol. XXVIII, No. 3 (May, 1935), 17.

The theater was on the defensive. Clergymen and the religious press thundered against it until the conscientious man or woman hesitated to attend. When two Oberlin teachers were discovered to have attended a New York theater surreptitiously, it was agreed that they had "committed a grievous wrong against God and against the institution";[10] their dismissals were avoided only by heartfelt protestations of repentance.

The surroundings of a theater did little to give it prestige. Located usually in a poor part of a city, it was almost always filthy, with even the pit of the aristocratic Park Theater of New York accused of being the dirtiest place in town—a superlative which was not easily justified. One or more bars lessened critical judgment but increased disorder. Prostitutes improved the shining hours, and rumor had it that the third row of boxes was reserved for them. The Tremont of Boston was probably not the only theater with a connecting brothel.

The theater pit was filled with backless, movable benches occupied by people in various states of dress and undress, who sprawled, ate sandwiches, drank rum, spit tobacco juice, and at times held impromptu fist or knife fights; one critic asserted that she saw a man vomit without attracting particular attention. The gallery was not much better in manners, while even boxholders sometimes put their feet on the rails. Approval of a performance might inspire an ovation that stopped the show. Disapproval brought hisses, catcalls, and overripe fruit. An unpopular actor might need police help to escape from the theater, and several times there were full-scale riots.

The morals of actors and actresses were viewed with suspicion. Actors were only infrequently from the more cultured classes, and were tempted by the hard life, bad hours, exhausting travel, and dirty and drafty theaters, now and then to drink too much. Actresses might individually be considered charming and talented, but collectively they were thought to be little better than prostitutes, with their jobs dependent on bodily favors to the manager.

Most important to moralists, the plays were "disgraced by monstrous distortion of human nature"—"by profaneness, coarseness, indelicacy, low wit, such as no woman, worthy of the name, can hear

[10] Barnes, *Weld Letters*, II, 844-45.

without a blush, and no man can take pleasure without self-degradation"—by "exhibitions of dancing . . . fit only for brothels."[11] Can woman "go where sensuality reigns—where virtue is treated with open scorn, or cover[t] contempt—where the Bibles is caricatured—and where the Savior of the world is crucified afresh, and put to open shame? Can woman do this without injury to her moral nature? No."[12]

These diatribes were not aimed at burlesque shows or striptease acts but at Shakespearean dramas which included scenes of murder and seduction. For example, one theatergoer who saw *Figaro*, in which a woman wore a page boy's costume, commented that "it was apparent that women's nether limbs are much larger in proportion to their size than male's. This was the most indecent thing I saw."[13] Printed dramatic works would advertise the omission of all passages "inconsistent with modern delicacy."[14] This religious prudery was a dampening influence; "pure" plays that satisfied the ministers were so morally platitudinous and innocuous that they died of inanition. One intelligent foreign visitor went so far as to insist that "those who respect dramatic entertainments the most highly, will be the most anxious that the American theaters should be closed."[15]

Most hostile to the theater was New England, where several states forbade it entirely. The Boston of 1830 had two struggling theaters which attempted to make ends meet by also scheduling lectures and church services. One died in the thirties, and the other finally expired in 1843 when Elihu Burritt, "the learned blacksmith," collected sufficient funds to convert it into a church.

The theatrical capital of the United States was New York. Here actors congregated and managers hired their talent. Here were the largest audiences and hence the largest number of theaters. Top billings went to the Park Theater, opposite City Hall, which was

[11] Channing, *Address on Temperance*, 59.

[12] *South Western Christian Advocate*, September 10, 1839, quoted in Hunt, *Nashville Theatre*, 19.

[13] "Diary and Letters of Charles P. Huntington," in *Proceedings, Massachusetts Historical Society*, Vol. LVII (1923–24), 257.

[14] Advertisement in J. Lander, *Journal of an Expedition* (New York, J. and J. Harper, 1832).

[15] Martineau, *Society*, II, 343.

favored by the socially elite after its redecoration in 1834. The Bowery was probably better technically, with its huge stage and gaslights, but suffered from its environment. Some ten additional theaters were opened before 1840, but normally about half of them were dark.

There were theaters of varying impressiveness in many other cities, and there was much competitive boasting of Doric columns, red damask hangings, gaslights, blue domes with white clouds and cherubims, and similar attractive decorations. Philadelphia's three theaters lacked patronage, so that their managers failed with monotonous regularity. St. Louis, Buffalo, and Mobile were particularly proud of their theaters. A tremendous theater that seated 3,500 was opened in 1835 at New Orleans by J. H. Caldwell, whose name bulks large in the history of the southern theater; in the same year Caldwell entered a partnership with the popular comedian, Sol Smith, and for twenty years these men dominated the western stage except for the Ohio Valley domain of N. M. Ludlow. If a town had no regular theater, the traveling players used a barn, store, warehouse, or tent. The floating theater probably originated in 1833 with the Chapman family, of which daughter Caroline was the pet of the audiences.

A theater gave its patrons plenty for their money—at least plenty in bulk. The central attraction was ordinarily a serious play of from three to five acts, but in addition there was a farce for an afterpiece, and sometimes another for an introduction. During intermissions the actors kept the audience amused with popular songs, hornpipes, impersonations, and other variety features. All of this made the evening strenuous for the actors. The usual price for this varied amusement was seventy-five cents for a box seat, fifty cents for the pit, and twenty-five cents for the gallery, although many scales varied from these charges. A real hit sometimes permitted auctioning the seats.

Managing a theater was an extremely hazardous occupation. A city theater cost $30,000 or more, and necessitated upkeep and taxes. A regular company of some fifteen to twenty was paid weekly from $5.00 to $50.00 each. An orchestra cost $10 to $15 a man. A chorus man received about $10—there were no chorus ladies. The one contributor who was paid only sporadically was the author. English plays were free since there was no copyright restriction. An American play was usually bought for not over $500, but the author might receive no more than a benefit performance now and then.

Most depressing to a manager were his payments to visiting stars. While a local company could perform without outside help, audiences demanded the big names of the profession, even as they do today. In consequence the stars toured, playing standard works with various companies and walking off with the lion's share of the receipts. Managers tore their hair, but were helpless. Sometimes a flat rate was specified, but frequently the star received a percentage of all income above an agreed minimum, plus one or more benefits, plus half the manager's benefit. The "benefit" was a performance in which the profits went to a particular actor, and his admirers attended to demonstrate their loyalty.

The star system was highly profitable to the top performers. Five hundred dollars a night was not unusual, although no such sum was possible for a long run. Forrest had a notable eleven days in Boston during which he received over $1,000 a night. Fanny Elssler's $6,390 for eleven nights in Philadelphia left the manager in the red, but by the time she reached New Orleans she reputedly was asking $1,000—which of course included supporting dancers. A manager had the unpleasant choice of facing a deficit or allowing a rival to draw all the business.

Any theater that grossed as much as $500 a night was doing excellently for only an Ellen Tree, an Edwin Forrest, or a Fanny Elssler could draw such houses regularly. Any manager would have been satisfied with a regular $200, for even Forrest had some of the $25 houses that were so common. A benefit might draw $1,000 or more, and curiously enough the top receipts were for dramatists; J. Sheridan Knowles drew an amazing $4,000 house in 1835, while the American John Howard Payne rang the bell in 1832 with an almost incredible gross of $5,000.

Lack of attendance could not be blamed on the press, for an editor never forgot that the theaters advertised regularly. If conscience forbade praise, it at least counseled discreet silence. Nowhere was there important criticism—not even in the rare magazine article or in the few ephemeral theatrical publications.

A tremendous number of plays saw the boards, but certain favorites kept reappearing, partly for the benefit of touring stars. Any company could present a dozen Shakespearean dramas at a moment's notice, for these were the common vehicles for such stars as Kean, Wallach, and Forrest. Particularly favored were *Romeo and Juliet*, *The Merchant of Venice*, *The Taming of the Shrew*, *Hamlet*, *King Lear*, and *Macbeth*. Also standard were the plays of John B. Buckstone—*Damon and Pythias*, *The Pet of the Petticoats*, and *Luke the Laborer*. Sheridan Knowles' *The Hunchback of Notre Dame* was a perennial favorite. Also recurring frequently were *Speed the Plow*, *The Lady of Lyons*, *Young Norval*, and *Raising the Wind*.

A reigning star might limit his repertoire, but the average actor had to provide variety for a limited clientele over a period of months. One woman has been counted in eighty-one parts in a single four-months' season. The member of a small company might assume half a dozen roles in a single evening, and then dance and sing between acts.

For the less sophisticated theatergoer, bloodthirsty melodramas and elaborate spectacles were good lurers of an extra fifty cents. From the raising of the curtain on *The Silent Witness, or a Tale of Blood*, the denizens of the pit were kept on the edges of their hard benches until the villain was finally discomfited and the hero and heroine clasped in each other's arms. In contrast, *The Elephant of Siam or The Fairy Spell* took months to prepare its fancy costumes, trained animals, fires, and earthquakes. Animal acts were popular. The *Mazeppa* smash scene occurred when a man was strapped to a live horse. In *The Lion Lords* the lion tamer Van Ambergh rode a horse up a ramp, a tiger sprang on him, and they wrestled downstage toward the footlights.

American playwrights were for the first time becoming numerous, being encouraged by prizes offered by Forrest and others. Best loved was John Howard Payne, especially for his *Clari, the Maid of Milan* (premiere, 1823), which included the song "Home Sweet Home." Many American plays were on European themes—as N. P. Willis's *Tortesa the Usurer*, R. M. Bird's *The Broker of Bogotá* and *The Gladiator*, and R. P. Smith's *Caius Marius*. Several of these were popularized by Forrest, who, for example, long had the role of Spartacus in *The Gladiator* as a successful item in his repertoire. Other Americans wrote on temperance or similar themes, or dramatized contemporary books. Most frequent, however, were patriotic effusions on Jackson at New Orleans, Molly Pitcher, Columbus, The Green Mountain Boys, Tippecanoe, and the like. The treatment given such themes by aspiring American Shakespeares can easily be imagined.

American dramatic writing served to fix certain stage types almost indelibly. An Indian was either a cruel, despicable, and bloodthirsty savage or a noble and mistreated hero. The latter characterization was that of Stone's *Metamora* (1829), written for Forrest and played by him for many years. The stage Yankee was fixed by Samuel Woodworth in *The Forest Rose, or American Farmer* (1825), popular for a generation. J. S. Jones, in *Solon Shingle or the People's Lawyer* (1839) made classic the villainous banker trying to get the girl by foreclosing the mortgage but outwitted by a simple country boy. By 1840 any theatergoer could predict the dialect and actions of a Hiram Dodge or Deuteronomy Dutiful. A similar trend was occurring for the Westerner as Hackett played Colonel Nimrod Wildfire in *The Lion of the West* (1831), written for him by J. K. Paulding. Incidentally, the descriptive proper names were quite common.

Most actors and actresses were native born, but a high proportion of the stars such as Power, Matthews, Celeste, Kean, Tree, and the Kembles were English, which seems fair enough since most of the plays were English. Whether they were good actors and actresses is difficult to judge. Their acting was usually highly emotional, which can sometimes be labeled ranting and posturing.

The male actor who came nearest to dominating the American stage was the Philadelphia-born Edwin Forrest, who served his apprenticeship under Sol Smith in the West. Once attaining stardom, in 1826, he was the dream of managers, for he seldom played to other than large and enthusiastic audiences. While Shakespeare was a staple, he reputedly spent $20,000 encouraging native writers, and appeared in many American plays.

Forrest was energetic and robust in his acting; he shouted,

379

groaned, yelled, and postured with vast enthusiasm. A few critics talked of uninteresting declamation accompanied by harsh and extravagant gestures, and even called him "a coarse and vulgar actor, without grace, without dignity, with little flexibility of feature, and utterly common-place in his conceptions of character."[16] Most Americans, however, loved him, and flocked to his plays, making him the most popular actor of his day.

Other eminent American actors included James K. Hackett, who specialized in American roles, as a Westerner or a New Englander; his best-known part was Rip Van Winkle. James Wallach was called by Sol Smith the "best *Iago* I ever saw."[17] H. H. ("Yankee") Hill was "all-fired cute"[18] in Yankee roles. "Old Sol" Smith was the favorite comedian of the West. Of English-born tragedians, Charles Kean and Junius Brutus Booth held top rank in spite of the latter's drunken sprees. As the *Courier* said, "Mr. Booth stands on an eminence which no actor of the present day but Kean can pretend to."[19] English comedians included Charles Matthews and Tyrone Power.

The actress who really appealed to American audiences was Fanny Kemble, a member of a prominent English family of actors. Three years after her debut she came to America in 1832 with her actor father to present such plays as *Hamlet, Fazio, Romeo and Juliet,* and the *Hunchback of Notre Dame,* the last of which was written especially for her. Fanny was not unusually beautiful at close range because smallpox had left her features a trifle thickened and her skin slightly pitted, but these defects were compensated for by the excellence of her figure, the brightness of her eyes, and her general animation. Americans immediately took Fanny to their hearts. The press rang her praises, crowds mobbed the theater, and hundreds of admirers followed her train. They proclaimed that she demonstrated "the very perfection of acting"[20] and that she was "the greatest of living actresses."[21]

[16] Hamilton, *Men and Manners,* 35-36.
[17] S. Smith, *Theatrical Management in the West and South for Thirty Years* (New York, Harper and Brothers, 1868), 87.
[18] "Letters of George Sumner 1837-1844" in *Proceedings, Massachusetts Historical Society,* Vol. XLVI (1912-13), 343.
[19] *Morning Courier,* February 11, 1830.
[20] "Huntington Diary," 265.

Lithograph portrait of Fanny Elssler, *ca.* 1840

Fanny herself was at first homesick and confused, and wrote that she would be completely "indifferent to my own success, but that I am working for my livelihood."[22] But a young lady with the theater in her blood could not long remain indifferent, and Fanny soon wrote that "it is a matter of some agreeable edification to me to see the crowds gathering around the doors for hours before they open, and then rushing in, to the imminent peril of life and limb, pushing and pummeling and belaboring one another like madmen."[23] At the very height of her popularity she fell in love with and married Pierce Butler of South Carolina. Her farewell performance was in *The Wedding Day*. Unfortunately the couple did not "live happily ever after." Pierce wanted a domestic wife who would take care of the house and children and entertain. Fanny was interested in writing, and hated the slavery of her husband's plantation. Uultimately there was a divorce, after which Fanny tried unsuccessfully to regain her popularity.

Heir presumptive to the throne vacated by Fanny Kemble was Ellen Tree, another English actress, who in turn married Charles Kean; she was so inspiring as to cause even the reserved John Quincy Adams to break out into a poem about how "fair perfection, all abide in thee."[24] Among the American-born actresses were Josephine Clifton, who toured Europe; Charlotte Cushman, originally a singer; Jane Placide, tragedienne; "lovely Clara" Fisher, "the glory of her sex!"[25]

The American stage was cluttered with child stars, both male and female, who piped through all kinds of dramatic parts, including always that of Young Norval. Best loved was Master Joseph Burke, who arrived in 1830 to tour the country in such roles as Shylock, Young Norval, Sir Abel Handy, Hamlet, and Richard III.

[21] H. Wickoff, *The Reminiscences of An Idler* (New York, Fords, Howard and Hulbert, 1880), 37.

[22] Kemble, *Girlhood*, 542.

[23] *Ibid.*, 574.

[24] Quoted in W. W. Clapp Jr., *A Record of the Boston Stage* (Boston, James Munroe and Company, 1853), 347.

[25] Charleston *Gazette*, quoted in *Niles Register*, Vol. XXXVI (April 25, 1829), 133–34.

Even the reserved Bostonians paid an average of $850 a night to admire him both as an actor and as an intermission violinist. While still a young man, he retired to study the violin.

Music was used freely on the stage, often for no better reason than that the song was admired and some actor thought he could sing it. For example, Mr. and Mrs. Sol Smith both sang, while Charlotte Cushman started her stage career as a vocalist. Mr. and Mrs. Joseph Wood were admired as much for their singing as for their acting, even though Mr. Wood now and then broke into falsetto. Some plays such as *Rob Roy* were really operettas, as were some of the so-called operas. In the musical *High, Low, Jack and the Game*, the actors represented the cards.

Stage dancing was hampered by a deep-seated and widespread conviction that it was immoral. The tights and ballet skirts of the first important French dancing troupe, appearing at the Bowery in 1827, suffused the entire audience in one universal blush; ladies rose and left the boxes. The *mademoiselles* then modestly donned Turkish trousers, but the godly were still shocked, while the ministers thundered denunciations from their pulpits. On the other hand, the publicity attracted every dashing young blade who wanted to feel devilish in peeking at feminine ankles and in hoping for even higher things. In fact, the French dancers became something of a popular rage, with conservatives muttering protestingly about the unhappy deluge of English actors and French dancers.

Ranking high among the dancers was Celine Celeste, who shocked many people pleasantly as she kicked up her heels. In time she learned English and acted in straight drama. Reputedly she earned a yearly $50,000, which one editor remarked sourly was the reward for her immodesty in showing so much of her figure. Presumably he felt that if she danced at all, it should be sedately in whalebone corsets and half a dozen long petticoats.

Unchallenged as queen of the toe dancers was Fanny Elssler, who arrived at New York in 1840. Her opening brought an ovation, as the pit rose en masse, cheered, waved handkerchiefs, and strewed the stage with flowers. For the two years of her American tour such triumphs came in steady succession, uninjured by wails about the immodesty of her dancing and the reputed immorality of her private life. Thousand-dollar houses were commonplace. Managers fought for her services.

Fanny Elssler was described so variously that one suspects the average man had his eyes elsewhere than on her face. Presumably she lacked facial beauty, but when she pirouetted vivaciously in *La Tarantule* or *La Cracovienne,* no one denied her grace and charm. Crowds gathered when she appeared on the streets and besieged her residence. Elssler cuffs, bootjacks, and bread capitalized her popularity. Even the intellectuals were fascinated. After watching her dance, Ralph Waldo Emerson is reported to have said to Margaret Fuller, "Margaret, this is poetry"; to which Margaret responded, "Waldo, this is religion."[26]

A more indigenous art was being developed in blackface minstrelsy. For some years the blackface performers had entertained at the circus or between the acts of plays. George W. Dixon twanged his banjo as he plugged "The Coal Black Rose" and "Zip Coon." The first full-time minstrel act has been credited to the tall, thin, shambling Thomas D. ("Jim Crow") Rice. His "Jim Crow" song was poor in music, words, and rhythm, but it always stopped the show. Rice specialized in coining new verses to fit the particular locality in which he was playing.

The full-length minstrel show bloomed overnight. Heading the parade was E. P. Christy with his four Virginia minstrels, organized probably in 1842; but by the next year three such groups were playing New York. Almost at once the show became as standardized as Fourth of July orations—band, street parade, entrance with end men last, the semicircle of chairs, and the "Gentlemen be seated" as the opening music ended. The audience could rely on the jokes of Sambo and Bones, the dancing, the "Oh, Susannah" type of songs, the banjo and bones, and even that the white interlocutor, usually dressed in white, would be the butt of all jokes.

Specialty acts were infinite in their variety. Many theaters brought the menagerie, circus, or other "horse piece" indoors. A plethora of acrobats was headed by the dozen members of the Ravel family, who also danced, pantomimed, and even acted complete

[26] J. W. Howe, *Reminiscences 1819–1899* (Boston, Houghton Mifflin Company, 1900), 105.

plays; their act was climaxed when Gabriel and his sister walked a rope high above the audience. Also popular was Herr (John) Cline on the tight rope and the Bedouin Arabs performing feats of strength and gymnastics. Living statues were attractive, but ran into the perpetual problem of modesty; one man solved the difficulty by appearing "in a close wrought frame to represent a white Marble Statue, over which the Grecian frock is thrown in such a manner as not to impede the beauty of the attitude, or shock the modesty of the most fastidious."[27]

Among the better-known specialty acts were the Siamese twins Chang and Eng, the Belgian giant Behin, the Beautiful Albiness, and the human skeleton Calvin Edison. Audiences were amused by ventriloquists, magicians, thought readers, jugglers, automatons, and players of musical glasses. Particularly fascinating was the "man fly," Hervio Manco of the withered legs; dressed as a green fly, he climbed over the theater by means of his hands. These acts were not called vaudeville, which was a term used only by Niblo to describe a program of one-act plays, mostly musical.

The American theater was a world of tremendous activity and variety. Eminent actors and actresses strode the boards in everything from Shakespeare to the most lurid melodrama, while specialty acts pleased the most diverse tastes. Acting was first rate—by the only reasonable test of acting, the satisfaction of audiences. Many of the plays were excellent by any standards, and what age can claim more? Scenery, costumes, and lighting were primitive, but they created the fairy world of imagination for which the patron paid, and the highest technical excellence could have done no more. The drama was the most nearly mature of the American arts, with the one possible exception of literature.

[27] St. Louis *Commercial Bulletin*, November 2, 1835.

21. Literature

"IF THE NATIONAL MIND of America be judged of by its legislation, it is of a very high order; ... if the American nation be judged of by its literature, it may be pronounced to have no mind at all."[1] Thus spoke a foreign visitor, but even Americans admitted that "there is a great dearth of good writers at present"[2] and that "A literary man is a sort of a Pariah in our money-making community unless he gets to the comfortable eminence of reputation where Irving and Cooper sit enthroned."[3]

Literary deficiences may have existed, but they were not in quantity. The United States was a literate nation. "The mania for book-making has recently assumed an epidemic character, and, like the late pestilence, unaffected by all changes of weather, save that a murky evening generally aggravates its symptoms, it makes its attacks from quarters the least expected."[4] American presses spawned a good two hundred titles a year, although over half were reprints of foreign works.

Most books were poorly printed, whether the products of small country printers or of such great city houses as Carey, Lea and Blanchard or Harper and Brothers. Economy dictated cheap paper, few illustrations, and small, crowded type. Type was set by hand and locked in galleys; a small edition was printed directly from the type, but a large printing brought "stereotyping" from a metal form which had been made from a plaster cast of the type. Hand presses

[1] Martineau, *Society*, II, 300–301.

[2] Quoted in A. L. Herold, *James Kirke Paulding* (New York, Columbia University Press, 1926), 76.

[3] Quoted in S. T. Williams, *The Life of Washington Irving* (2 vols., New York, Oxford University Press, 1935), II, 31.

[4] *Sketches and Eccentricities of Col. David Crockett of West Tennessee* (New York, J. and J. Harper, 1833), Introduction, 3.

were giving way rapidly to machine presses that could make up to four thousand impressions an hour.

Books were sold most commonly through bookstores, although mail orders and canvassers were not unknown. The bookstores also stocked magazines and writing supplies such as paper, pencils, crayons, sealing wax, ink powder, sand boxes, and even fountain pens. Booksellers were many and important; their New York association held notable annual dinners to which literary celebrities were pleased to be invited. A popular book might sell as many as ten to twenty thousand copies, and even as erudite a production as Prescott's *Conquest of Mexico* sold four thousand at six dollars a copy in one year.

Although a few books sold very well, the average author was wise if he did not depend on his writings for his bed and food. "The efforts of American writers are, for the most part, made in hours of leisure, set aside from business."[5] Americans worked long and hard, and had neither the money nor the leisure to warrant large book purchases; in fact they had a tendency to consider the full-time writer as just a little queer. The best markets were in such metropolitan areas as New York, Philadelphia, Boston, and Cincinnati— in spite of Mrs. Trollope's sarcastic reference to a Cincinnati gentleman who supposed that Pope's "Rape of the Lock" was obscene. In the less populated portions of the South and West the budding literary genius found great difficulty in obtaining a publisher, and the publisher was hard pressed to discover a market.

The majority of American books were reprints of foreign publications, since English authors were popular and there was no international copyright agreement. Poe spoke for his fellow craftsmen when he remarked bitterly that "one might suppose that books, like their authors, improve by travel—their having crossed the sea is, with us, so great a distinction."[6]

Best-selling of the English authors was Scott, whose novels could be found everywhere from eastern drawing rooms to western log cabins; many an American found Scott "too fascinating to be laid aside at the usual hour for repose."[7] But "with the single exception

[5] *New England Magazine*, Vol. IX (December, 1835), 479–80, quoted in Mott, *Magazines*, 494.

[6] E. A. Poe, *Poems* (New York, Columbia University Press, 1936), 16.

[7] Bolzau, *Phelps*, 47.

of Scott, no writer of the present age has occupied the public mind for so long a period, or met so large a measure of applause, as Maria Edgeworth."[8] And with Maria should go the other two of an immortal and saccharine trio, Hannah More and Felicia Hemans. Carlyle had a reasonable following, but Coleridge and Lamb were less read. Dickens became immensely popular late in the decade.

English authors visited the United States in great numbers, even in the thirties, and few could resist the temptation to write of their experiences—often to the distress of their American hosts. Probably most discriminating was Harriet Martineau, who was remarkably active considering her age, sex, and ear trumpet. Americans did not appreciate adverse criticism—indeed they became furious at such a book as Mrs. Trollope's *Domestic Manners* and resented only slightly less such a frank account as Fanny Kemble's *Journal*. They tended then to remember the author as objectionable personally; for example, Captain Marryat was described as "ugly, rough, ill-mannered, and conceited Beyond all bounds."[9]

The bitterest of American disillusionments came from the visit of the immensely popular Dickens in 1842. Upon his arrival at New York he was given a spectacular reception, with Irving in the chair and the mayor making the speech of welcome, and then a triumphal tour followed in which he was lionized everywhere. But Dickens' physique could not withstand American hospitality, and soon he was writing that he was "worn out in mind and body" and that he was feeling "an amount of agony such as I never experienced since my birth."[10] The agony was largely the result of the failure of his mission to obtain an international copyright law. Possibly understandable are the criticisms in his *American Notes* and the fact that his American character Martin Chuzzlewit is not entirely admirable, but Americans felt betrayed—"If the scamp had no regard for his own character, he ought to have had for ours, who made fools of ourselves to do him honor."[11]

[8] *American Monthly Magazine*, Vol. III (May, 1834), 193.

[9] Schoolcraft, *Memoirs*, 562.

[10] "Letters of Charles Dickens, 1842," in *Proceedings, Massachusetts Historical Society*, Vol. LIV (1920–21), 54, 150.

[11] Nevins, *Hone Diary*, II, 673.

Foreign writings other than English had relatively small influence. Most people found the French authors highly objectionable; Hugo and Dumas were held to be characterized "by a degree of extravagance and immorality unparalleled in the preceding history of the drama."[12] German influences were increasing as German stories were reprinted, articles appeared on Goethe and other authors, and Americans such as Everett, Bancroft, Longfellow, and Motley attended German universities. The total effect was small; the first professor of German at Harvard was finding difficulty in obtaining sufficient students to justify his academic existence.

The strength of the English influence did not prevent widespread American variations in the use of words. In the United States every woman was a "lady" and every man a "gentleman." Americans spoke of a "clever" (good) house or meal, of a "fine" (intelligent) woman, of a "slick" play, of a "terribly" handy man. Quite common were words such as "expect," "reckon," "guess," and "calculate." One might feel "ugly" or "bad" or "mean" (ashamed), and "admire to go" to New York. A Virginian admitted that "I'm powerfully weak; but cruel easy."[13]

New England Yankees had their own unique variations. Reputedly an answer of "I don't know" meant no; "I don't know that I shall" expressed doubt; "I don't know but I shall" meant yes. A girl, asked if she had sweethearts, replied: "Well, now, can't exactly say; I bees a sorter courted and a sorter not; reckon more a sorter yes than a sorter no."[14]

The West also had idiocyncrasies. Foreign names were anglicized, as De l'Hotel to Doolittle, Pibaudier to Peabody, Bon Coeur to Bunker, Bon Pas to Bumpus. Common expressions were "corned" (tipsy), "stumped," "make tracks," "clear out," "rise my dander up," "plunder" (baggage), and "strike" (attack). Picturesque similes were frequent: "I wish I had all hell boiled down to a pint, just to pour down your throat."[15]

[12] *American Quarterly Review*, Vol. XIX (March, 1836), 107, quoted in Mott, *Magazines*, 404.

[13] Martineau, *Society*, II, 210.

[14] Marryat, *Diary*, 146.

[15] *Ibid.*, 151.

The Ravel Family, Pantomimists; a popular
form of entertainment in the 1830's

Meade Brothers Daguerreotype Gallery in New York City;
a development in the arts after 1830

Such language variations posed difficult problems for the grammarians, and hence produced a growing demand for a distinctively American dictionary. This desire was finally satisfied by Noah Webster after more than a quarter-century of arduous labor. His two bulky volumes appearing in 1828 contained 70,000 words, and constituted the largest English dictionary as yet published. As later modified, his work has remained standard to the present. It was not only a monument to Webster's industry and perseverance but a real evidence of American scholarship.

Most "thinking Americans" were distressed that the majority of books were novels, which "deluge the country from New York to beyond the Mississippi."[16] Ministers and other moralists were certain that "the habitual use of the stimulus of fiction is always enervating to the intellect, as that of alcohol is to the physical system."[17] They held that novels are "nets to catch young minds in the maze of Satan."[18] Most dangerous would be the effect on a pure, adolescent girl, for "the youthful female mind, requires to be intellectually braced and invigorated by wholesome tonics in the way of study," whereas with novels "the whole mental system becomes enervated."[19] Such admonitions were not always taken to heart. Apparently youth—and also age—was not seriously worried about the sapping of its intellectual and moral stamina.

A novel was no short, light romance for a summer day, but normally a thick two-volume work of complicated plot. The novel of sentiment had been succeeded by the historical romance, and writers ranged history for their material. Moreover, "fine" writing was emphasized. Art must above all be artistic, and a budding author practiced thus: "Oh, had I Jubal's lyre or Miriam's tuneful voice, I should breathe praises of Ocean who approached us in solemn

[16] Martineau, *Society*, II, 250.

[17] *Christian Parlor Magazine*, Vol. I (May, 1840), 21–22, quoted in Mott, *Magazines*, 417.

[18] *Hopkinsonian*, Vol. III (December, 1829), 576, quoted in Mott, *Magazines*, 417.

[19] M. Coxe, *The Young Ladies' Companion* (Columbus, I. N. Whiting, 1839), 69.

dignity, bathing the beach with tears and chanting a requiem in his hollow murmurs."[20]

"Fine" writing was combined with a morbid religious sentimentality to produce overwhelming results. For the man of taste and imagination "the myriad forms of animate creation unite with inanimate nature in one mightly hymn of glory to their Maker, from the hum of the sparkling ephemeroid as he blithely dances away his little life in the beams of a summer sun, and the rustling music of the prairie-weed swept by the winds, to the roar of the shaggy woods upon the mountain-side, and the fierce, wild shriek of the ocean-eagle."[21]

One real accomplishment of the American novel was the increased use of domestic materials, even though the Indian was thereby almost worked to death. Indian life and manners emerged from learned anthropological treatises to appear in every type of fiction. No writer could refrain from producing one or more Indian stories and the poet followed the procession. Any listing of authors who used Indian themes sounds like a Who's Who of American writers. Sometimes the Indian was a hero, but more frequently a villain.

The uncontested dean of American authors was Washington Irving, who wrote with a lightness, a charm, and a carefree tolerance that were as unusual as they were charming. His material was largely American, and he was remarkably free from didacticism. Unfortunately his work of the thirties was not his best. Returning from Europe and his Spanish writings in 1832, he toured the West and then settled in the East. He occupied his pleasant house at Tarrytown from 1835, and there he wrote his western travel books—partly to please his friend Astor. The books were not outstanding, but they remain readable and informative, particularly the *Tour on the Prairies*.

Irving's present place in literature would have shocked and grieved him had he known of it. He dismissed his fictional efforts deprecatingly as "my works of mere imagination"[22] and believed

[20] Morrow, *Alcott*, 69.

[21] Flagg, *The Far West*, Vol. XXVI of Thwaites' *Early Western Travels*, 248–49.

[22] C. L. Penney (ed.), *Washington Irving Diary: Spain 1828–29* (New York, Hispanic Society of America, 1926), 90.

his reputation would rest primarily on his lives of Columbus and Washington, upon which he lavished time and energy. Today his historical works are seldom remembered, while his lighter works of imagination and description delight each new generation.

Second to Irving in popular prestige was James Fenimore Cooper. Cooper was the complete country gentleman, lordly, aristocratic, and genial when approached properly, but otherwise overbearing and pugnacious. His testy temper, sharpened by indigestion, made him see insults wherever he looked, and embroiled him in squabbles that embittered his life. His blunt and often unflattering estimates of his fellow Americans, which he published in several volumes, involved him in endless and acrimonious disputes, including a number of suits for slander which he prosecuted. Between times he lost his temper trying to drive picnickers off his Cooperstown estate. The result during the thirties was such unhappiness that he once decided to stop writing.

A great flood of inferior novels, satires, descriptions, travel, and history flowed from the Cooper pen during the thirties. The only passable book was *The Water Witch*. Ultimately Cooper's reputation rested on the *Leatherstocking Tales*, none of which was published during the thirties. These books sold well, in spite of the publisher's protest in 1827 about the *Mohicans* that the firm "have not made sixpence by it, as yet."[23] Contemporary opinions of Cooper varied. Harriet Martineau said he was "regarded as a much-regretted failure,"[24] but a more common attitude was that "the public read your books and are pleased."[25] In fact, the public was so much pleased that it called Cooper the American Walter Scott—a title which he resented.

Among the other northern novelists, James Kirke Paulding was probably best known. His writings ranged from the humorous skit to the tragic play, but his best work concerned the New York Dutch, with his *The Dutchman's Fireside* remaining attractive in spite of its lack of action. Other authors were relatively less attractive. Hawthorne, for example, was just beginning his work, and his first novel had failed.

[23] Cooper, *Correspondence*, 129–30. [24] Martineau, *Society*, II, 307.
[25] Cooper, *Correspondence*, I, 262.

The great female author of the thirties was Catherine Sedgwick, who was responsible for such sugary masterpieces as *Hope Leslie*. Miss Sedgwick was almost universally admired for her pleasant characters who had such proper and lofty ideals. The nearest to adverse criticism was the mild opinion that maybe a few incidents were forced, but then the critic hastened to add: "but let the incidents be granted, and Miss Sedgwick puts such charming people into them, and makes them talk and act so characteristically, and with such *ideal* propriety, that, in our sympathy with their just and natural feelings, we forget that they are in improbable situations."[26]

Often forgotten is the fact that the South contributed its full share of popular authors. Augustus Longstreet was writing his vivid tales of life in frontier Georgia. Dr. W. A. Caruthers was beginning the idealization of the plantation system. Robert Montgomery Bird's voluminous outpourings included notably *Nick of the Woods, or the Jibbenainosay*, which ran through some twenty editions. The story starts slowly, but very soon Nick (the Jibbenainosay) is laying about him mightily, killing bad Indians by the score, while Roaring Ralph Stackpole furnishes the humor, and a real hero, heroine, and villain provide the drama and love interest. The tale might still be popular if some of the priggishness and stilted language were eliminated.

Important both as a novelist and as an idealizer of the South was the Baltimorean John Pendleton Kennedy, cultured and well-to-do, active in industry and politics as well as in letters. His first and most important book, *Swallow Barn* (1832), is really a connected series of sketches about life on an idealized southern plantation. Here is Frank Meriwether the plantation owner, pompous and opinionated and liking the good things of life; Ned Hazard, the likable spendthrift; Prudence Meriwether, the spinster, who lives on imaginary old flames and real benevolence; Parson Chubb, the schoolmaster, rotund, jolly, and a Latin and Greek scholar. The sketches are charming and well written, more than compensating for the tepid love story in which they are embedded.

Kennedy's *Horse-Shoe Robinson* was one of the most popular novels of its day. Laid in the southern back country during the Revo-

[26] *American Monthly Magazine*, Vol. I, n. s. (January, 1836), 15-25.

lution and coming to a climax at the battle of King's Mountain, its trite and highly patriotic plot concerns a rebel major in love with the daughter of a Tory planter. Galbraith ("Horse-Shoe") Robinson acts as companion and good genius to the hero; he is "an athlete whom the sculptors might have studied to improve the Herculean," but also a man "of shrewd, homely wisdom."[27] To the modern reader the book is tedious, with simple and wooden characters, uncomplicated emotions, and tremendous coincidences. One finds difficulty in accepting a lady who wrings her hands and faints on the least provocation, but then hops out of bed to ride two hundred miles through enemy territory to see Cornwallis.

The typical mawkish writing of the period is well illustrated in the parting of the lovers: "Then it was, and there, that this enthusiastic girl again pledged her unalterable devotion to the man of her waking thoughts and nightly dreams, come weal, come woe, whatever may betide; and the soldier paid back the pledge with new ardor and endearment, in the strong language that came unstudied from the heart, meaning all that he said, and rife with a feeling beyond the reach of words. And after 'many a locked and fond embrace,' full tearfully, and lingeringly, and, in phrase oft repeated, the two bade 'farewell,' and invoked God's blessing each upon the other, and then, not without looking back, and breathing a fresh prayer of blessings, they separated on their dreary way."[28] Since this wild orgy of passion might have seemed immoral to the more prudish readers, Kennedy later admits that the young people had been married all the time.

Measured in reams of output, the outstanding literary figure of the day was William Gilmore Simms, who has been blamed for sixty-five books ranging from history to poetry; in addition he edited at least nine magazines, while his articles, speeches, and pamphlets defy collection. Simms was a poor Charleston boy with social ambitions, who in time found himself a lawyer writing poetry in his spare moments, and then a full-time author. His artistic theory was that the novelist's only object was to interest the reader—not by fine

[27] J. P. Kennedy, *Horse-Shoe Robinson* (New York, American Book Company, 1937), 17–18.
[28] *Ibid.*, 53.

writing but by piling incident on incident and adventure on adventure. In general he followed his theory.

Simms' first elaborate romance, and a very popular book, was *Guy Rivers*, published in 1834. The title was the name of the chief of an outlaw Georgia gang, and "one of the most arrant and arrogant culprits that ever appeared."[29] Exciting adventures are climaxed when the hero is convicted of murder on planted evidence, escapes, is pursued, and finally is exonerated by a death-bed confession, whereupon hero and heroine fall into each other's arms. Comedy relief is furnished by a Connecticut peddler. Long and tedious descriptions interrupt the action. A sprinkling of incongruous French phrases appear in italics. Similes are often incredible, as of a horse that "trod the earth with the firm pace of an elephant, yet with the ease of an antelope."[30] Stilted characters speak mawkishly.

Guy Rivers is at least notable for its unusual sex incidents in a day of prudery. A night conference of a young unmarried girl and a boy in their bedclothes and in his bedroom is at least of questionable propriety. And then the rape scene, with Guy Rivers as the villain:

" 'Hark ye, if ye fear not death, there is something worse than death to so romantic a damsel, which shall teach ye fear. Obey me, girl—report the route taken by this fugitive, or by all that is black in hell or bright in heaven, I—'

"And with a whisper, he hissed the concluding and cruel threat in the ears of the shuddering and shrinking girl. With a husky horror in her voice, she cried out:—

" 'You dare not! monster as you are, you dare not!' then shrieking, at the full height of her voice—'Save me, uncle! save me! save me!' "[31]

Not to keep the reader in unbearable suspense, the uncle arrived in time.

Simms' best and most popular novel was *The Yemassee*, dealing with the South Carolina Indians during the eighteenth century. The Indians were pictured as neither heroes nor villains, but as human beings combining bravery and fear, cruelty and kindheartedness,

---

[29] *American Quarterly Review*, Vol. XVI (December, 1834), 512–19.
[30] W. G. Simms, *Guy Rivers* (New York, Redfield, 1860), 16.
[31] *Ibid.*, 262.

loquaciousness and stoicism. The old chief Sanutee led opposition to the whites because of his love for "the old trees and the shady waters where he was born, and where the bones of the old warriors lie buried."[32] The hero Charles Craven stated the basic red-white conflict: "Until they shall adopt our pursuits, or we theirs, we can never form the one community for which your prayer is sent up; and so long as the hunting lands are abundant, the seductions of that mode of life will always baffle the approach of civilization among the Indians."[33]

Best known of the western novelists were Timothy Flint and James Hall, but Flint's greatest service was in editing western travels and Hall's was in collecting western stories that occupied the twilight zone between history and fiction. A number of amusing books were published over the name of Davy Crockett. A modern literary amusement is to guess the ghost writers and to speculate whether Davy himself contributed anything at all.

Shorter fictional ventures were blossoming under the warm sun of magazine and gift-book encouragement. Usually these were sketches, incidents, or compressed novels rather than short stories. Most oppressively common was the highly sentimental, moral, and religious episode. Typically it concerned a young girl in the purity and innocence of her teens: "a bright and beautiful being, too pure and holy for a sinful world like this. If an angel would have wandered from the skies, and found a dwelling in an earthly form, the beauty of the starry visitor could not have equalled her surpassing loveliness." A pure young man met this paragon, and they fell in love. And then, with literary inevitability, the girl got wet, caught cold, and contracted tuberculosis. "As she grew weaker and weaker, it seemed as if every thought became more holy, until she breathed a language almost divine."[34]

Almost equally popular were the gloomy and macabre tales

[32] W. G. Simms, *The Yemassee* (New York, American Book Company, 1937), 87.

[33] *Ibid.*, 137.

[34] All quotations from *Burton's Gentleman's Magazine and Monthly American Review* (Philadelphia), Vol. VI (May, 1840), 266.

which showed German influence even though they were usually set in France to permit the author to display his stock of French words and phrases. The opening sentence identified the story: "The night was dark and stormy—the rain fell in torrents—." Then conditions became worse—a fine night for murder. Several pages of mounting horror conclude as: "I stood near him on the scaffold—I saw the executioner apply his hand to the cord—the knife, already reeking with blood, fell—and the gory head of the parricide rolled into a basket beneath!"[35]

Nearly every author tried his hand at short stories or incidents. Among the best and most popular were Irving, Paulding, and N. P. Willis. Westerners contributed such characters as Colonel Plug and Mike Fink. W. J. Snelling wrote delightful and understanding sketches of Indian life and incident, with the guiding principle that "the heart of man beats neither slower nor faster under a blanket than beneath a coat and waistcoat."[36] Albert Pike wrote nervous, accurate, and convincing sketches of both whites and Indians, which remain excellent aids to the understanding of the frontier.

Ranking head and shoulders above other short-story writers was that unique and ageless genius, Edgar Allan Poe. His sad and psychotic life—his adoption, the promising start of a career as author and editor, and the end in delirium tremens—has often been described. Some of his tales were worse than mediocre, and he was influenced by the prevailing fashion for French stories with French phrases, but his best stories were highly polished gems, in which every word was chosen carefully to produce the exact emotion about which the story revolved.

Poe was best known in his own day for his poetry and his editing. His collections of short stories sold so poorly that he had difficulty finding publishers. Part of the trouble was that Poe was a poor self-advertiser. As editor of *Burton's Magazine*, he reviewed a collection of his own stories—on the last page—by listing author and title, and then adding "Messieurs L. and B. have just issued twenty-five brief stories, having the above title, which pretty well indicates their

---

[35] *Ibid.*, Vol. VI (January, 1840), 24–26.

[36] J. F. Flanagan (ed.), *William Joseph Snelling's Tales of the Northwest* (Minneapolis, University of Minnesota Press, 1936), 4.

general character."[37] Moreover, the book-buying public expected a two-volume novel, not a thin collection of disconnected tales. As a result many of the Poe stories remained embedded in various magazines and gift books; some of them have probably not even yet been identified.

American humor was scanty—"they laugh mighty little on this side of the Atlantic"[38]—but it existed. Most common was the pun, frequently bad, as when a peddler claimed for his steel buttons: "There is some steel about them, gentlemen, for my brother stole 'em."[39] Crockett asserts that "these Philadelphians are eternally cutting up jokes on words; so I puts a conundrum to them; and says I, 'Can you tell me why the sacking of Jerusalem was like a cider mill?' Well, they all were stumpt, and gave it up. 'Because it made the Jews fly.' Seeing them so much pleased with this, says I, 'Why is a cow like a razor-grinder?' No one could answer. 'Well,' says I, 'I thought you could find that out, for I don't know myself.' "[40]

Even a poor pun was preferable to some of the profound satire. A book such as *The Nosiad; or the Man of Type and the Major Domo* by "Icabod Satiricus" defies modern reading. One breathes a sigh of relief in passing on to a young lady who says to her milk-drinking gentlemen friends: "One would think, gentlemen, you had never been weaned."[41]

The favorite comic character was the Yankee peddler, although lawyers, drunkards, judges, and others had their following. Tales of Yankee shrewdness abounded; for example, the two penniless Yankee youths who were locked in an empty room, traded with each other, and emerged with two dollars apiece. Credit for originating the shrewd Yankee as a literary type usually goes to Seba Smith, editor of the Portland *Courier*, whose widely reprinted Jack Downing letters were excellent political burlesque. Even more

---

[37] *Burton's Magazine*, Vol. VI (January, 1840), 58.

[38] Pierson, *Tocqueville*, 90.

[39] Hawthorne, *Note-Books*, 159.

[40] *The Autobiography of David Crockett* (New York, Charles Scribner's Sons, 1923), 151.

[41] Martineau, *Society*, II, 206.

popular were the various "Sam Slick" books of the Nova Scotian Haliburton.

Most characteristic of the Americans was exaggeration. "When she yawns, you can see right down to her garters," or "he threw everything up, down to his knee-pans."[42] Crockett boasted he was "half-horse, half-alligator, a little touched with the snapping-turtle; can wade the Mississippi, leap the Ohio, ride upon a streak of lightning, and slip without a scratch down a honey locust; can whip my weight in wild cats,—and if any gentleman pleases, for a ten dollar bill, he may throw in a panther."[43] The fantastic tales of "The Big Bear of Arkansas" brought American chuckles, as when the bear stole some corn, but "left a grain or two on the ground, and lay down on them; before morning the corn shot up, and the percussion killed her dead. I don't plant any more; natur intended Arkansaw for a hunting ground, and I go according to natur."[44]

Various situations which seemed hilarious to the man of 1830 have long since become dull. Shouts of laughter do not greet the boy who loses his money at the race track, or the young man embarrassed by disrobing before a strange young lady in a frontier cabin, or the long-winded witness who finally admits that he never saw the object of the suit, or the candidate who steals and re-steals 'coon skins from the bartender to treat his constituents. Moreover, there was no top-notch humorist. The vast majority of books were completely lacking in humor. The spirit of the time called for magnificent enterprise, or for pathos, affection, or religion. Humor was a low emotion to which one did not admit allegiance in public.

Many Americans preferred poetry to prose—an almost incredible choice. Poetry dealt with "poetic" emotions such as love, sorrow, patriotism, and reverence; never was it a simple description of peeling an apple, currying a horse, or attending a museum. Furthermore, the language was "poetic"—which meant that there were many classical and other similes, and a heavy sprinkling of "thous," "ists," "hasts" and other nonprose words.

[42] Capt. Marryat, *Second Series of a Diary in America* (Philadelphia, T. K. and P. G. Collins, 1840), 143.

[43] *Sketches of Crockett*, 164.

[44] F. J. Meine, *Tall Tales of the Southwest* (New York, Knopf, 1930), 15.

Greatest popularity went to the "consumptive school." In the typical effusion a pure young maiden wasted away with tuberculosis through many well-rhymed stanzas, with the last verse finding her lover raining tears on her lonely grave. Equally fitting, and with subject even purer, was the account of the death of an infant or babe —never, of course, a child.

On The Death of An Infant[45]

Mother! that are weeping
Away the midnight hour,
Prayerful thy vigil keeping
Above a broken flower—
Mourn not thou thus deeply
That earth to earth is given;
Take comfort, for thy babe to-night
Is hymning praise to heaven.

Religious sentiment and didactic moralizing were always present.

To Miss A. M.[46]

Oh, mayest thou gentle maid pursue
The path of virtue thou hast trod;
Thy mind's improvement still in view,
Till thou art called to meet thy God.

Under different circumstances, a few of the poets might have had happier fates. Elizabeth Allen's "Resignation," for example, has a certain authentic pathos which is heightened by knowledge of the author's deafness:

Thou, God of all—who holds't my fate,
Dark are thy ways and intricate;
Too deep thy wisdom and designs
For ken of our rebellious minds.[47]

[45] *Burton's Magazine*, Vol. VII (July, 1840), 41.
[46] E. Allen, *The Silent Harp* (Burlington, Vt., Edward Smith, 1832), 53.
[47] *Ibid.*, 75.

All too seldom comes relief from the "pretty" rhymes and cadences that were so nearly universal:

> *God! Fearful majesty is in the sound*
> *Of that dread syllable. The soul bows down*
> *At its enunciation, filled with awe,*
> *Of him who is incomprehensible;*
> *Who fills immensity, whose name is God;*
> *Who is from everlasting, and who knows*
> *Nor past, nor future; living through all time,*
> *In one eternal now.*[48]

The outstanding American poet—and one blushes at the admission—was Lydia H. Sigourney, "the sweet singer of Hartford." Recognized as the best poet of the New World, she strewed the magazines and gift books with her thoughts on immortality, God, and the deaths of innumerable infants and pure maidens. Even Poe gave her "The Ruler's Faith" the place of honor in the magazine he edited, and had his own "Israfel" on an inside page. Modern judgments are vastly different. Her latest biographer says he read some forty-odd volumes of her writings in a futile search for even a passable poem.

Lydia's intensely poetic and moral sentiments were confined carefully to her poems. Married late in life, she forever bickered with her husband. To her publishers she appeared a sharp businesswoman who turned out poems as a cooper would barrels, testing her success by the number of lines and the size of her bank balance. Immensely industrious, she soon exhausted her slender stock of ideas, after which she repeated herself, sometimes even selling the same poem more than once. In fact she was not above selling the use of her name.

Typical Sigourney poems are a dime a dozen, since above all Lydia was always typical. The following effusion was titled "Vice":

> *In vain the heart that goes astray*
> *From virtue's seraph—guarded way,—*

[48] L. J. Peirson, *The Forest Minstrel* (Philadelphia, J. W. Moore, 1846), 125.

May hope that feelings, just and free,
Meek peace,—or firm integrity,—
Or innocence with snowy vest
Will condescend to be its guest.
—As soon within the viper's cell
Might pure and white-wing'd spirits dwell,
As soon the flame of vivid gleam
Glow in the chill and turbid stream;—
For by strong links, a viewless chain
Connects our wanderings with our pain,—
And Heaven ordains it thus, to show,
That bands of vice, are bonds of woe.[49]

Considering Poe next to Sigourney is almost sacrilege, and yet in cold fact, Poe used similar sentiments and meters. The vital difference was that Poe's genius produced poems of pure artistic joy rather than the usual hackneyed tripe. Consider, for example, the theme and form of the following extract from "A Pæan"—and then enjoy its beauty.

How shall the burial rite be read?
The solemn song be sung?
The requiem for the loveliest dead,
That ever died so young?

Her friends are gazing on her,
And on her gaudy bier,
And weep!—oh! to dishonor
Dead beauty with a tear![50]

Poe's poems were all too few, and one regrets the briefness of the poet's life, which closely paralleled the last stanza of "Israfel":

If I did dwell where Israfel
Hath dwelt, and he where I,

---

[49] *Poems by Lydia H. Sigourney* (Philadelphia, Uriah Hunt and Son, 1846), 206.

[50] Poe, *Poems*, 67.

He would not sing one half as well—
One half as passionately,
And a stormier note than this would swell
From my lyre within the sky.[51]

American poetry was not all sorrow and pathos. The principal alternative was the ringing patriotic effusion which often attained great length in keeping with its importance; *The Fredoniad; or Independence Preserved* ran to four volumes. Most favored were epics of Washington, Marion, or some other American figure, but a foreign hero such as Napoleon or Pulaski could have domestic applications for the patriot. Most of these poems were as similar and as standard as automobiles off an assembly line.

In the cypress groves of the broad Santee,
The Swamp Fox had gathered a gallant band,
Who, scorning a tyrant's stern decree,
Had sworn to defend their native land,
And her freedom achieve, or in death to fall—
They were Marion's troopers, "one and all."[52]

Rhymed patriotic bombast was made more oratorical in the flood of poems to dedicate monuments, open theaters, lay cornerstones, and celebrate the Fourth of July. The following typical "Ode" was written by Rufus Dawes for Independence Day:

Let the voice of the Nation go forth!
Let the roar of your cannon proclaim
From the East and the West, from the South and the North,
The pride of Columbia's name!
The chain of Oppression was yours,
And Tyranny marked you her slaves—
But O! while an oak in the forest endures,
Or a pine on the mountain-top waves,
The birth-day of Freedom shall ring round the land,
And millions of hearts shall for Liberty stand.[53]

[51] *Ibid.*, 45.
[52] *Burton's Magazine*, Vol. VI (January, 1840), 32.
[53] R. Dawes, *Geraldine, Athenia of Damascus, and Miscellaneous Poems* (New York, Samuel Colman, 1839), 337.

Very rarely did an American poet descend from his lofty peak to amuse himself with some less pretentious effort, such as the comparatively new "'Twas the Night Before Christmas." Lowell Mason was responsible for encouraging Sarah Hale to write "Mary Had a Little Lamb" (1830) for the children. A century later one feels almost hysterical appreciation for the trifles of such a man as the "mad poet" Macdonald Clarke, who pictures himself:

> *A poet comfortably crazy—*
> *As pliant as a weeping willow—*
> *Loves most everybody's girls; ain't lazy—*
> *Can write a hundred lines an hour,*
> *With a rackety, whackety railroad power.*[54]

To enumerate the poets of the eighteen thirties would be to list almost every literary man, and yet the period was intermediate. Bryant and Halleck had practically completed their work. Whittier's and Lowell's significant pieces were largely in the future, and Longfellow had just started publishing. Holmes was still primarily a doctor, although he had begun his literary work; his "To An Insect" came as early as 1831:

> *I love to hear thine earnest voice*
> *Wherever thou art hid,*
> *Thou testy little dogmatist,*
> *Thou pretty Katydid!*
> *Thou mindest me of gentle folks—*
> *Old gentle folks are they—*
> *Thou sayest an undisputed thing*
> *In such a solemn way.*[55]

America's essayists were also largely in the future, with two important exceptions. Holmes had begun his series starring the autocrat of the breakfast table, while the learned young minister, Emerson, had already retired to Concord to write his philosophical essays. To a few of Emerson's friends he was little short of godlike, but to

---

[54] L. M. Child, *Letters from New York* (New York, 1844), 105.
[55] *New England Magazine*, Vol. I (September, 1831), 235.

most Americans he was only incomprehensible: "We give it up. We cannot analyze one of Mr. Emerson's discourses. He hardly ever has a leading thought, to which all the parts of his discourse are subordinate, which is clearly stated, systematically drawn out, and logically enforced. He is a poet rather than a philosopher—and not always true even to the laws of poetry."[56]

Literature for more serious readers ranged through medicine, law, religion, and economics. Famous criminals and their trials were described for the "salutary lessons"[57] they suggested. Various guides to good manners seemed not to be very effective. Distinctively ladies' books like *The Flower Vase, Containing the Language of Flowers and their Poetic Sentiments* were common. Children's books like *Visit to Grandpa* or *Sophronia and Her Cat Muff* seemed to be designed largely to please parents.

Books of literary criticism are probably today the most humorous productions of the period. Quite common was the ranking of Signourney and Simms at the top, while at the bottom might be such men as Longfellow and Lowell, whom "posterity will not remember."[58] The main objectives of literature seemed to be patriotic and moral—in fact, it should raise no troublesome political, economic, or moral problems. A good cry was much to be desired.

The best nonfiction market was for history, biography, and travel, with the first two often combined. The nation was accused of "biography mania."[59] The popular era for historians was the Revolutionary period, and the prime subject for biography was Washington. Apparently every writer from Irving to John Marshall expected to crown his career by a biography of the Father of his Country.

Historical writing was handicapped by a lack of material and stultified by an intellectual climate of super-patriotism. Libraries were poor. State historical societies were still feeble, even though

[56] *The Boston Quarterly Review*, Vol. II (January, 1839), 4.

[57] *The Western Monthly Review* (Cincinnati), January 5, 1836, 60.

[58] S. M. Fuller, *Papers on Literature and Art* (New York, Wiley and Putnam, 1846), 132.

[59] New York *Mirror*, May 15, 1830, quoted in Mott, *Magazines*, 421.

Interior of the Park Theatre, New York City,
from a painting by John Searle, 1822

increasing rapidly. An American Historical Society was little more than a gesture. The result was that the historical researcher spent most of his time hunting and copying manuscripts. Peter Force started—but never finished—a documentary history of the Revolution. Jared Sparks, Harvard's first history professor, collected voraciously the diplomatic correspondence of the Revolution, and the letters of Ledyard, Morris, Franklin, and Washington. His editing amended their grammar and removed unworthy thoughts, while his biographies proved amazingly dull. Present historians credit him with little more than good intentions.

The first really pretentious history of the United States was that of George Bancroft, a Harvard Phi Beta Kappa who had studied at Göttingen. He collected materials diligently; for example, Schoolcraft, the best Indian authority, tells how Bancroft "came to see me to confer on the character of the Indians."[60] The first volume appeared in 1834, but the completion of the ten volumes was a slow process since it was interrupted by a secretaryship of the navy and a ministry to England. Bancroft was intensely religious and patriotic, and had definite political convictions, but he produced the best American history to date.

The only other outstanding historian was William Hickling Prescott, another New Englander who had a literary approach. Prescott had the tremendous handicaps of near-blindness and poor health, so that he could read and write but briefly, and travel not at all. Relying heavily on a remarkable memory, he did beautiful work that suffered only from the lack of availability of all sources. Prescott never wrote about the United States.

Books of travel were so many and so varied as to defy generalization. Most popular were descriptions of the United States by foreign visitors; these were devoured by sensitive Americans who tore their hair whenever they were not praised sufficiently. Other accounts dealt particularly with the American West, Europe, and Asia, but even such remote areas as Antarctica were described.

The Niagara-like torrent of American books was bought largely by individuals or private groups. The book club circulated its purchases and then allotted them at the end of each year. The many

[60] Schoolcraft, *Memoirs*, 533.

libraries, almost never public, sometimes included pictures and scientific collections or offered lectures or even regular courses of studies. Colleges and historical societies had small collections. Any library with over five thousand volumes was considered large, and only one claimed as many as fifty thousand.

On the border line between book and magazine was the tremendously popular "gift book," which fortunately afflicted only a single generation. As the name implies it was a de luxe product designed as a fitting gift to a friend of either sex of any age. The gift book was built around its expensively beautiful steel, copper, and wood engravings. Next in importance was the binding, possibly silk or velvet, but sometimes embossed leather decorated by inlaid mother-of-pearl floral designs. As for the text, it was chosen to set off the pictures and to capitalize big literary names. Every prominent writer earned a few dollars this way. The price of such a magnificent production might run as high as twenty dollars a volume.

The gift book was designed to be "worthy to be the present of a good man, to a refined, intelligent and pious woman."[61] Pictures might include "Fanny Kemble," "The Orphans," or "The Death of a Stag." A poem by Sigourney might be featured, as "Monody on the Death of the Principal of the Connecticut Retreat for the Insane."[62] The usual short story was a saccharine tale of sweetness and light, but here and there appeared the work of such a man as Poe or Hawthorne or Hall. Humor was almost absent, and sex was treated idyllically, with any sordid domestic triangle avoided. Now and then a short literary essay or article on science crept into the sacred fold.

The best of the gift books were the *Atlantic Souvenir, The Token,* and *The Talisman.* Others included not only such obvious titles as *Affection's Gift* and *Friendship's Offering* but a complete galaxy of flowers and gems, as *Magnolia, Bouquet, Pearl,* and *Amethyst.* Special collections were aimed at children, abolitionists, religious people, political partisans, the humorously inclined, and in fact at every sizable group of the population.

[61] *Ladies' Magazine,* Vol. IX (June, 1836), 62.
[62] *The Token,* 1835.

The flow of gift books was a mere trickle compared to the flood of magazines that poured from American presses. Some five hundred made their public bows during the decade, but their lives were as ephemeral as those of moths. Literary ambition or local pride could produce a nice fresh magazine but could not pay its bills. A subscription list of one thousand, even with many people dilatory in paying their bills, was an editor's dream of opulence. Advertising was but a slender support, since the maximum was probably four or five pages at not over ten cents a line.

Feebly anemic magazines could not afford high-priced contributors. Since English authors could be pirated, and American seldom received more than a dollar or two a page. Many domestic writers neither expected nor wanted payment, and even refused it when offered. Publication was considered by many as a degrading sort of exhibitionism, so many articles were either initialed or unsigned. An editor might receive ten or fifteen dollars a week, with one thousand dollars a year almost fabulous; if he were also owner, he might expect a net deficit.

American magazines copied their European contemporaries, particularly the English reviews. The most prominent space went to the long book review—really an essay inspired by the book supposedly being reviewed. The balance of the magazine was composed of essays, short stories, incidents, poems, and illustrations—"a light and trifling kind of literature, which is hashed up with condiments for weak stomachs."[63] The resulting stodgy or stickily sentimental mess was less vivid and illuminating than the *Congressional Globe*.

Only two magazines could claim really national circulation. The *North American Review* (Boston) attempted to develop an original American literature, but with something less than moderate success. *Niles Register* (Baltimore) was a miscellaneous collection of all kinds of information clipped from other publications; it lost importance after the death of Hezekiah Niles in 1839.

Each progressive American community fostered a succession of periodicals devoted largely to local authors and read by patriotic citizens who desired to encourage home talent. Boston's best was

[63] Schoolcraft, *Memoirs*, 515.

probably the *American Monthly Magazine,* New York's the *Knick-erbocker,* and Philadelphia's the extremely conservative *American Quarterly.* Richmond had the *Southern Literary Messenger,* edited for a time by Poe, and probably the best in the South. Charleston had a long succession of short-lived periodicals edited by Simms. Even the fragrant *Southern Rosebud,* spread its delicate aroma only briefly. The West had Hall's *Western Monthly Magazine,* which discovered Harriet Beecher, later to marry Calvin Stowe, and Flint's *Western Monthly Review.* Both worked hard to obtain western material, but the few western authors seemed to prefer tales of the British peerage.

A legion of special magazines appealed to lawyers, doctors, railroad men, prohibitionists, educators, and other groups. Religious and reform papers were headed by *The Christian Spectator,* but possibly more interesting were such publications as Noyes' *Perfectionist* and the New York *Amulet,* opposing "Intemperance and Infidelity."[64] At the other end of the scale was *Peabody's Parlour Journal,* devoted to chit-chat of the fashionable world. Frankly scandal sheets, such as the New York *Libertine,* did not appear until the early forties, while the *Police Gazette* started publication in 1845. Other magazines were devoted to men, to women, to farmers, to theater lovers, to sports, and to humor. Any special group might have its own paper—and frequently did.

Most important of the class magazines were those designed for feminine readers. Of greatest popularity in 1830 was *The Ladies' Magazine,* called the first American magazine designed exclusively for women. Its editor was Mrs. Sarah Josepha Hale, a New England girl who married late—at twenty-five—and who nine years later was widowed with five small children. Failing to earn a living by millinery, she turned to literature—at first some atrocious poetry, then a best-selling novel, and finally became editor of *The Ladies' Magazine.* The less said about the magazine itself the better.

The Barnum of the women's magazines was Louis A. Godey, a New Yorker who had become affluent by means of Philadelphia newspapers. In 1830 he originated *Godey's Lady's Book,* which aped English female publications to the extent of reprinting their

[64] Advertisement in the Arkansas *Advocate,* June 23, 1830.

material. Half a dozen years later he absorbed Mrs. Hales' publication, taking along Mrs. Hale herself, who remained his editor for forty years. *Godey's* featured the saccharine and piteous literature that tradition said was the preference of the fair sex, and encouraged women authors. It established the custom of departments for education, styles, recipes, fiction, and other feminine interests. The great joy of subscribers and of later collectors were the hand-colored fashion plates. The proof that Godey and Mrs. Hale had estimated women's tastes accurately was their ability to boast of a circulation of 17,500 in 1840.

Godey's was the progenitor of the modern women's magazine, but, more important, it was the discoverer of the formula for magazine success, which permitted better pay for contributors, which in turn brought better contributors. Other magazines, desiring profits, began to cater more to existing taste, with less effort to exhibit American scholarship or elevate public esthetic appreciation and morals.

Most popular of American reading materials was the newspaper, of which the 800 of 1830 became 1,400 by 1840, with circulation tripling. Even the smallest frontier community had its newspaper, while a larger city might claim a dozen or more. About 10 per cent of them were published daily, and the rest almost always weekly.

Modern writers like to recall nostalgically what they call the golden age of American personal journalism, but contemporaries had no such opinion. "As the press of the country now exists, it would seem to be expressly devised by the great agent of mischief, to depress and destroy all that is good, and to elevate and advance all that is evil in the nation."[65] Newspapers were charged with low taste, excessive vituperation, inaccuracy, favoritism, venality, and almost every journalistic sin except the one they really practiced—dullness.

The average paper was not only edited but almost completely written by the editor, who was frequently poorly educated. Often he or his backers established a paper to express definite political convictions, which were written into the news articles. Editors not only indulged in the most vicious printed slander but even descended to

[65] Cooper, *American Democrat*, 126–27.

409

outright fisticuffs. When Webb assaulted Bennett, and Bryant horse-whipped Stone, the encounters included the four most prominent New York editors, and such cases were not exceptional.

Most current newspaper criticisms were aimed toward virtues which were fatal to hundreds of magazines. The critics wanted only sound and elevating items. They reviled articles on social events, boxing, and finance as being in bad taste and of questionable morals. They castigated the "practice of repeating the proceedings of the courts of justice, in order to cater to a vicious appetite for amusement in the public."[66] They practically had paroxysms when New York papers played up the murder of the prostitute Helen Jewett, and when the Philadelphia papers gave space to the trial of Henry Chauncey for murder during an attempted abortion. The truth actually was that the papers treated news conservatively. They had not as yet conceived streamer heads, myriad pictures, strip cartoons, advice to the lovelorn, letters from the doctor, and dramatic and sporting gossip.

The average American paper had difficulty in surviving financially. Even the better papers such as the Cleveland *Whig*, Richmond *Enquirer*, Washington *National Intelligencer*, Louisville *Gazette*, and New Orleans *Picayune* had their troubles. True enough, America was comparatively literate and prosperous, and the government gave cheap postal rates, but a small-town paper had a limited circulation while a large city sheet had a number of vigorous competitors. New York, for example, had forty-seven papers in 1830. Their combined circulation was only 90,000, of which 25,000 belonged to the *Christian Advocate*. The largest daily, the *Morning Courier and Evening Enquirer*, claimed a circulation of only 4,000.

The brilliant idea of lowering prices to increase profits by larger sales, came to the printer Benjamin Day, mainly as a way to advertise his business. His penny *Sun* copied its news from the standard six-cent papers until financial success permitted its own organization. The *Sun* passionately desired a large audience, so spiced the usual political and foreign items by adding such matters as theatrical notes, animal stories, the account of Fanny Kemble's marriage, and the tales of Davy Crockett. When real news was lacking, it manufactured

[66] Cooper, *Notions*, II, 103.

its own, as the circumstantial story of how Sir John Herschel's new telescope saw not only hills, craters, and foliage on the moon, but also birds, animals, and batlike human beings; significant was the fact that the exposure of the hoax did not hurt the *Sun* circulation.

Among the spectacular stories of the *Sun* were the conviction of Manuel Fernández for the murder of a fellow sailor who had paid undue attention to Manuel's mistress—the *Sun* gave much space to Manuel's story as told by himself; the New York fire; and the revelations of Maria Monk, which it then helped vigorously to expose. Its great failure was in the Jewett case, where the choice morsels went to Bennett of the *Herald*—"Bennett, whose only chance of dying an upright man will be that of hanging perpendicularly upon a rope."[67]

The *Sun's* vigor and color brought immediate returns in circulation, so that by 1834 it was probably the largest in New York—"If the daily circulation of the *Sun* be not larger than that of the *Times* and *Courier* both, then may we be hung up by the ears and flogged to death with a rattlesnake skin." When Day sold the paper in 1838, he claimed the world's largest daily circulation of 30,000.

Imitators of the first penny paper soon outdid the original. "An ill-looking squinting man" named James Gordon Bennett was the prize yellow journalist of his day. Born in Scotland, he had had varied newspaper experiences before he started the *Herald*—"one of the penny papers which are hawked about the streets by a gang of troublesome ragged boys, and in which scandal is retailed to all who delight in it at that moderate price."[68] Bennett featured the personal, the vivid, and the exciting. A murder was manna from Heaven, and he was not disturbed when his coverage of the Jewett case brought accusations from rival editors that he was altogether too familiar with brothels.

Bennett's enthusiasm for varied tidbits of information expanded the traditional definition of what was news. Not only were public dinners reported, but also private social events; Bennett gave headlines to his own wedding. By 1840 such good socialites as Mr. and

[67] Quoted in F. M. O'Brien, *The Story of the Sun* (New York, D. Appleton and Company, 1928), 62.
[68] Nevins, *Hone Diary*, 1, 195.

Mrs. Henry Brevoort asked that their dinner be reported. Stock-market news and prices, and business failures, were soon accepted. Religious information brought only brief cries of sacrilege. Pictures and maps were received with immediate favor, as a map of the burned area of New York in 1836 and a "war map" of the Canadian revolt of 1837. Bennett also had excellent news coverage, with correspondents throughout the Americas and Europe. Fast steamer service was achieved by meeting the steamer offshore, so that often the *Herald* was on the streets before the steamer docked. In fact, Bennett has been credited with the original idea of the Associated Press.

The real services of Bennett were generally overlooked at the time. His vigorous reporting and scurrilous writing brought howls of protests from the injured and their friends, who sometimes collected court damages to the benefit of the *Herald* circulation. Personal vengeance was inflicted by such varied characters as an editor, a patent-medicine vendor, an actor, and a broker. One gentleman broke a horsewhip on Bennett, who then picked up the pieces and handed them back. After each attack a semihumorous account appeared in the *Herald* with advantages to sales. "Horse-whip him, and he will bend his back to the lash, and thank you, as every blow is worth so many dollars. Kick him, and he will remove his coat tails, that you may have a better mark, and he courts the application of the toe, while he counts the total of the damages which he may obtain. Spit upon him, and he prizes it as precious ointment, for it brings him the sovereign remedy for his disease, a fever for specie."[69]

Other new penny papers were Horace Greeley's *Tribune*, the Philadelphia *Public Ledger*, the Baltimore *Sun*, the Detroit *Free Press*, the Burlington *Hawkeye*, the Brooklyn *Eagle*, the Cincinnati *Enquirer*, and the Cleveland *Plain Dealer*—a notable set of names. A curious offshoot was the large-size paper measuring as much as four feet in length and reprinting a complete novel in a single issue. First of this kind was the *Brother Jonathan* (1839), established by Day after he sold the *Sun*.

Both the penny press and the elephantine paper were made possible by technical improvements in printing. A new paper-making

[69] Marryat, *Second Series of a Diary*, 58–59.

process cut the price almost in half. New printing presses, particularly those of R. Hoe and Company, claimed a maximum of four thousand impressions an hour. A rotating disk was used, but the type itself was on a flat plate; not until the forties did the revolving cylinder process become practical.

The current craze for speed invaded the editorial offices. Editors became unhappy at even a few hours' delay, and banded together to supplement the regular mail service. Then, led by the *Sun*, they established effective carrier deliveries and pushed street sales. With greater sales came less partisan vituperation, since editors hesitated to antagonize any large segments of a varied clientele.

A new source of revenue was discovered in the Sunday edition, which was first exploited successfully by the New York *Sunday Morning News* in 1835. To lessen religious hostility the *News* declared that "a Sunday Journal, properly conducted, may be not unaptly compared to a Sunday School."[70] The comparison was rejected indignantly by the most pious, but it soothed the consciences of those who liked papers on Sunday.

The cheap and exciting newspaper lured more readers, and increased circulation in turn attracted more advertisers. But now the advertiser had to work harder to compete with the news article for reader attention. No longer could he relax comfortably with a closely printed list of articles and prices, repeated week after week. Now he cut his information in favor of striking headlines, lurid adjectives, more white space, and even pictures.

Most "progressive" of the advertisers were the patent-medicine salesmen, who loved the before-and-after-taking pictures, such as the unattractive bald man transformed into a luxuriantly tressed Adonis. "Real cases" dotted the newspapers—the man who could not stand erect because of backache and was cured in twenty-four hours by Dr. Sherman's plasters; the girl who was desperately injured in a steamboat explosion, but restored to "blooming grace and beauty"[71] by Jones' Beautifying Italian Chemical Soap and Jones' Coral Hair Restorer.

[70] Quoted in A. M. Lee, *The Daily Newspaper in America* (New York, The Macmillan Company, 1937), 391.

[71] Child, *Letters from New York Second Series*, 250.

"Singular Scrap from Sacred History.

"Solomon, it is well known, was celebrated for his wisdom. But it is not so generally known that he invented a powder, highly beautifying to the Queen of Sheba. Such, however, is the fact, according to Mahometan commentaries. With Solomon the secret of the preparation died; but now, singular as it may appear, after the lapse of so many centuries, it has been discovered by Dr. Gouraud, whose Poudre Subtile will effectually remove every appearance of beard from the lips."[72]

Even poetry was not beyond the ability of the inspired ad-writer, as evidenced by the following scrap from a longer effusion praising the virtues of the Pease and Son Compound Hoarhound Candy:

> *Mark the fond, doting mother rapt and wild,*
> *Leaning above the cradle of her child!*
> *Why this ecstatic bliss at midnight hour?*
> *Her child is saved by Pease's potent power.*[73]

Newspapers were but one of a thousand facets of American life, and yet their change mirrored a process that was typical of all society. More and cheaper newspapers, appealing to the mass of citizens, were typical of a democratization that was affecting all phases of life. Not that a few reformers were bringing light and salvation to the downtrodden proletariat, but rather that the common man was becoming literate and vocal, and impressing his taste on all American institutions.

The older man of conservative and even aristocratic tastes deplored this participation of his less cultured fellow citizens in matters which had long been confined to the favored few. He thought of the change as degrading American civilization. The long-run appraisal is not so pessimistic. The rise of the lower classes did not degrade the upper. The so-called "higher" culture continued to exist, and was fertilized and invigorated by the addition of persons and ideas from the hitherto submerged classes.

[72] *Ibid.*, 249.
[73] *Ibid.*, 251.

The United States during the eighteen thirties was well embarked on the novel and even revolutionary project of developing an entire people rather than only a few selected groups. Mistakes and injustices were not lacking, and yet the kaleidoscopic pattern of an adolescent America brought glimpses of a political and social system in which opportunity would go to each man according to his merits. America was youthful, with its simple concepts of right and wrong, its bombastic religious nationalism, its belief in human perfectibility and progress, but along with these simple ideas went an energy and self-confidence that were to produce something that was at least recognizably close to the ideal which was held so dear.

Bibliographical Notes

THE FOLLOWING SUGGESTIONS are designed primarily for scholars who are interested in the literature of the field of this book. Much dependence was placed on contemporary material, which can be classified as follows:

1. Accounts by foreign travelers, who included such well-known persons as Trollope, Martineau, de Tocqueville, Lieber, Hamilton, Chevalier, Marryat, Lyell, Saxe-Weimar, Combe, Latrobe, and Count Arese; many lesser-known people also published their travel accounts.

2. Accounts by American travelers such as Hawthorne, Cooper, Irving, Child, Gregg, Jedediah Smith, Parker, Dwight, Robinson, McKenney, Hoffman, Schoolcraft, and Hall; again there are many lesser-known figures, some of whom are mentioned later in other connections.

3. Guidebooks, gazetteers, city directories, and other compendiums, of which there were many.

4. Letters and reminiscences, including those of Hone, Cartwright, Beecher, J. Q. Adams, Bigelow, Johnson, Caldwell, Peggy Eaton, Sewall, Finney, Pattie, Flint, Mrs. Jason Lee, Kit Carson, Greeley, Gross, Mary A. Holley, Julia W. Howe, Bancroft, Howells, Huntington, Fanny Kemble, Long, Irving, Owen, Macready, McLoughlin, Samuel Gridley Howe, Emerson, Sturtevant, Sumner, Crockett, Prescott, Hopkins, Koerner, Weld, James Fenimore Cooper, Sibley, Payne, Thomas Cooper, Caroline Phelps, and Mrs. Kirkland.

5. Newspapers and magazines. A variety of newspapers were picked to cover the various sections of the country. Many magazines were consulted, including not only the general and the literary but also the specialized—women's, religious, medical, pharmical,

dental, mental disease, phrenological, scientific, farming, sporting, educational, musical, mathematical, peace, abolition, historical, temperance, legal, sociological, and railroad.

6. Official reports of philanthropic societies, insane asylums, reform groups, and many other kinds of organizations.

7. Contemporary pamphlets and books on every conceivable subject from sermons to scientific brochures, cookbooks to schoolbooks, gift books to music books, and veterinarians' manuals to disquisitions on women.

The following bibliographical notes are concerned largely with secondary works. Certain classes of material are excluded since they are well known to all scholars: general histories; regional histories, as of New England, the South, the West, and the Pacific Coast; state histories; river and lake histories; group biographies and biographies of prominent political figures; and histories of the public domain, the latest of which is R. M. Robbins, *Our Landed Heritage* (Princeton, 1941). Magazine articles are seldom included. Mention should be made of a volume, comparable to this book, in the American Life series—C. R. Fish, *The Rise of the Common Man* (New York, 1927)—and of the more recent A. M. Schlesinger, Jr., *The Age of Jackson* (Boston, 1945), largely political. A. F. Tyler, *Freedom's Ferment* (Minneapolis, 1944) is excellent on certain aspects of social history. Merle Curti, *The Growth of American Thought* (New York, 1943) is unique and invaluable for the field it covers, as is Vernon Louis Parrington, *Main Currents in American Thought* (3 vols., New York, 1927–30).

Population

The basic facts of population growth are in the Census; other analyses add little. There are several books on various racial stocks, such as the German, Scotch-Irish, Norwegian, Swedish, and Jewish, but the best single volume on immigration history is W. F. Adams, *Ireland and Irish Immigration* (New Haven, 1932). M. L. Hansen, *The Atlantic Migration* (Cambridge, 1940) deals with the European phases of immigration. Most important of the birth-control books is Charles Knowlton, *Fruits of Philosophy*, which has

417

been reprinted as recently as 1937. Movement to the West is the subject of a large literature—for example, my *America Moves West* (rev. ed., New York, 1947); L. D. Stilwell, *Migration from Vermont* (Montpelier, Vt., 1937) is by far the best book of its type. The many immigrant guides are quite illuminating.

The traditional account of the fur trade is H. M. Chittenden, *The American Fur Trade of the Far West* (3 vols., New York, 1902). Bernard De Voto, *Across the Wide Missouri* (Boston, 1947) is excellent. Stanley Vestal, *Mountain Men* (Boston, 1937) and G. L. Nute, *The Voyageur* (New York, 1931) are both worth while. There are good lives of such trappers as Jim Bridger, Kit Carson, Jim Beckwourth, and James Clymer. John Jacob Astor has been the subject of two good biographies, and there are several histories of the Hudson's Bay Company and biographies of John McLoughlin; the letters of John McLoughlin have been edited by E. E. Rich.

There is no history of the Indians that is entirely satisfactory to the historian, but Flora Seymour, *The Story of the Red Man* (New York, 1929) is probably the most useful. The contemporary works of H. R. Schoolcraft are highly informative—*Algic Researches* (2 vols., New York, 1839) and *Information Respecting the History, Condition, and Prospects of the Indian Tribes of North America* (6 vols., Philadelphia, 1851–57); interesting is George Catlin, *Letters and Notes* (2 vols., New York, 1841). Histories of individual tribes are numerous, with the best on the Five Civilized Tribes—the works of Grant Foreman and Angie Debo are unusually good, while M. L. Starkey, *The Cherokee Nation* (New York, 1946) is excellent. The best account of the overland trail is James Monaghan, *The Overland Trail* (Indianapolis, 1947); and of the Santa Fé Trail, Stanley Vestal, *The Old Santa Fé Trail* (Boston, 1939); Josiah Gregg, *Commerce of the Prairies* (2 vols., New York, 1845) remains a classic. There are several biographies of Sutter. A. Ogden, *The California Sea Otter Trade* (Berkeley, 1942) is definitive. Several accounts exist of individual western forts, such as Hall and Snelling. The writings of Hall J. Kelley have been edited by F. W. Powell, who also has written a life of Kelley. The early Oregon missions have been well covered, particularly in volumes by the late A. B. Hulbert, C. J. Brosman, and C. M. Drury.

Texas has been treated very thoroughly. The best single volume on the eighteen thirties is W. R. Hogan, *The Texas Republic* (Norman, 1946). There are lives of almost all the important figures. Very valuable are E. C. Barker (ed.), *The Austin Papers* (3 vols., Austin, 1927) and A. W. Williams and E. C. Barker (eds.), *The Writings of Sam Houston* (7 vols., Austin, 1938–42). W. C. Binkley, *The Expansionist Movement in Texas* (Berkeley, 1925) may be supplemented by Thomas Falconer, *Letters and Notes on the Texan Santa Fé Expedition, 1841–1842* (New York, 1930). Benjamin Lundy, *The War in Texas* (Philadelphia, 1836) remains an interesting point of view.

Economics

American economic thinking is described in Ernest Teilhac, *Pioneers of American Economic Thought*, translated by E. A. J. Johnson (New York, 1936), and in J. Dorfman, *The Economic Mind* (2 vols., New York, 1946). The works of individuals are available, as well as biographies of such men as Mathew Carey, Henry C. Carey, and Francis Lieber. Lives of individual businessmen, such as Colt, Girard, and Goodyear, are none too complete. R. C. H. Catterall, *The Second Bank of the United States* (Chicago, 1903) is classic, and there are also accounts of some state banks and of the fluctuations of prices and business activity. Very good in their fields are L. H. Jenks, *The Migration of British Capital to 1875* (New York, 1927) and R. C. McGrane, *The Panic of 1837* (Chicago, 1924) and *Foreign Bondholders* (New York, 1935). Industrial histories are not usually very helpful, but exceptions are C. F. Ware, *The Early New England Cotton Manufacture* (Boston, 1931) and the model study by Vera Shlakman, *Economic History of a Factory Town* (Northampton, 1935). Useful in their fields are V. S. Clark, *History of Manufacture* (Washington, 1916); R. M. Tryon, *Household Manufactures* (Chicago, 1917); E. R. Johnson and others, *History of Domestic and Foreign Commerce* (2 vols., Washington, 1915); F. M. Jones, *Middlemen in the Domestic Trade* (Urbana, 1937); and L. E. Atherton, *The Pioneer Merchant in Mid-America* (Columbia, Mo., 1939). Waldemar Kaempffert, *A Popular History of American Invention* (2 vols., New York, 1924) is encyclopedic, while Roger Burlingame, *March of the Iron Men* (New York, 1938) stresses social implications.

Indispensable on labor are the works of John R. Commons. Norman Ware, *The Industrial Worker 1840–1860* (New York, 1924) is valuable. Edith Abbott has several informative articles on the employment of women and children; the Lowell situation has been described a number of times, as in H. A. Miles, *Lowell, As It Was, and As It Is* (Lowell, Mass., 1845). F. E. Haynes, *Social Politics in the United States* (Boston, 1924) gives the political influence of labor, and there are satisfactory biographies of Frances Wright and Robert Dale Owen. Richardson Wright, *Hawkers and Walkers in Early America* (Philadelphia, 1927) tells of peddlers.

Agriculture has no entirely satisfactory history; the best is P. W. Bidwell and J. D. Falconer, *History of Agriculture* (Washington, 1925). H. F. Wilson, *The Hill Country of New England* (New York, 1936) is good for a limited area. Valuable in their particular fields are J. C. Robert, *The Tobacco Kingdom* (Durham, N. C., 1938); C. W. Towne and E. N. Wentworth, *Shepherd's Empire* (Norman, 1945); A. O. Craven, *Soil Exhaustion* (Urbana, 1926); D. M. Ellis, *Landlords and Farmers* (Ithaca, 1946); A. L. Demaree, *The American Agricultural Press* (New York, 1941); and W. T. Hutchinson, *Cyrus Hall McCormick* (New York, 1930).

General histories of transportation are few and poor; B. H. Meyer, *History of Transportation* (New York, 1948) is probably the best. A good regional study is U. B. Phillips, *A History of Transportation in the Eastern Cotton Belt* (New York, 1908). The one satisfactory book on road travel is P. D. Jordan, *The National Road* (Indianapolis, 1948). The best general account of canals is A. F. Harlow, *Old Towpaths* (New York, 1926), and the best account of an individual canal is Christopher Roberts, *The Middlesex Canal* (Cambridge, 1938). There is no satisfactory general railroad history, but there are good accounts of individual roads such as the South Carolina Railroad, New York Central, and Baltimore and Ohio. A model of regional railroad history is E. C. Kirkland, *Men, Cities, and Transportation* (2 vols., Cambridge, 1948). L. H. Haney, *A Congressional History of Railways* (Madison, Wis., 1908) and R. L. Thompson, *Wiring a Continent* (Princeton, 1947) are both good studies. Of the many books on ocean travel and shipping, R. G. Albion, *Square-Riggers on Schedule* (Princeton, 1938) is outstanding. The two top ports have received good accounts—R. G. Albion, *The Rise of New York Port* (New York, 1939) and Harold Sinclair, *The Port of New Orleans* (New York, 1942). The river before the steamboat is well described in L. D. Baldwin, *The Keelboat Age on Western Waters* (Pittsburgh, 1941). Most informative of the various steamboat histories is F. E. Dayton, *Steamboat Days* (New York, 1925). A biography of Henry Shreve is not entirely satisfactory, but there are two good accounts of Commodore Vanderbilt. A special phase of travel is covered interestingly in Jefferson Williamson, *The American Hotel* (New York, 1930).

Social

The discussion of women is unending in the eighteen thirties as at other times. Probably the best history of the family is A. M. Calhoun, *A Social History of the American Family* (3 vols., Cleveland, 1917–19). Costume is covered by A. M. Earle, *Two Centuries of Costume* (New York, 1903). Books advising women and girls how to behave under all conditions are many. A. M. Schlesinger, *Learning How to Behave* (New York, 1946) is interesting. Several outstanding women such as the Grimkés, Lucretia Mott, and Mrs. Phelps have been subjects for biographies. W. W. Sanger, *The History of Prostitution* (New York, 1858) is old, but the best of its kind. A notable amount of literature developed about the work of J. R. McDowell with prostitutes in New York.

Histories of education are anything but exciting, as, for example, P. Monroe, *Founding of the American Public School System* (New York, 1940). Good regional studies are S. L. Jackson, *America's Struggle for Free Schools* (Washington, 1941); E. D. Grizzell, *Origin and Development of the High School in New England before 1865* (New York, 1923); and C. W. Dabney, *Universal Education in the South* (2 vols., Chapel Hill, 1936). Quite suggestive are Merle Curti, *The Social Ideals of American Educators* (New York, 1935) and A. L. Kuhn, *The Mother's Role in Childhood Education* (New Haven, 1947). Outstanding educators such as Horace Mann and Henry Barnard still need complete treatment, but there are reasonable biographies of such people as Bronson Alcott, Amos Eaton, Mark Hopkins, and Catherine Beecher. R. E. Thursfield, *Henry Barnard's American Journal of Education* (Baltimore, 1945) is exhaustive. The contemporary essays of such people as Catherine Beecher and J. G. Carter are useful. The work of A. B. Alcott with children received much attention in his writings and in the records by Elizabeth P. Peabody. A. B. Norton (ed.), *The First State Normal School in America* (Cambridge, 1926) is extremely useful. One of the best of the many manuals for teachers was Alonzo Potter and E. B. Emerson, *The School and the Schoolmaster* (New York, 1843). Schoolbooks of the period are easy to find. Much work has been done with the McGuffey Readers, as H. C. Minnich, *William Holmes McGuffey* (New York, 1936) and R. D. Mosier, *Making the American Mind* (New York, 1947). College histories, to say nothing of other college records, are abundant; among the better are those concerning Amherst, Princeton, Harvard, Oberlin, and Indiana-Asbury. E. M. Coulter, *College Life in the Old South* (New York, 1928) is good. D. G. Tewksbury, *The Founding of American Colleges* (New York, 1932) is informative.

Probably the best general church history is W. W. Sweet, *The Story of Religions in America* (New York, 1930). Every sect has been described in one or more histories. Most useful are the works of W. W. Sweet, largely collections of documents; W. W. Manross, *A History of the American Episcopal Church* (New York, 1935) is especially good. A helpful contemporary survey is Robert Baird, *Religion in the United States* (Glasgow, 1844). Biographies of religious leaders are none too plentiful. Those of the frontiersmen Peter Cartwright and Lorenzo Dow are at least adequate; among the superior works are H. S. Commager, *Theodore Parker* (Boston, 1936); A. M. Schlesinger, Jr., *Orestes A. Brownson* (Boston, 1939); and F. M. Brodie, *No Man Knows My History* (New York, 1945), concerning Joseph Smith. Ministerial writings, as of W. E. Channing, Elias Hicks, G. T. Chapman, and Lyman Beecher are numerous. In connection with the smaller sects, probably most material concerns the Shakers, with the best M. F. Melcher, *The Shaker Adventure* (Princeton, 1941). Most of the writings of John

Humphrey Noyes have been published, and there is a good biography—R. A. Parker, *A Yankee Saint* (New York, 1935). Matthias has only contemporary accounts, as W. E. Drake, *The Prophet!* (1834) and W. L. Stone, *Matthias and His Impostures* (New York, 1835). A favorable account of the Millerites is F. D. Nichol, *The Midnight Cry* (Washington, 1944). Valuable special works are C. R. Keller, *The Second Great Awakening in Connecticut* (New Haven, 1942) and Albert Post, *Popular Freethought in America* (New York, 1943). Anti-Catholic agitation is described in R. A. Billington, *The Protestant Crusade* (New York, 1938); the primary argument over the Rebecca Reed book is large and easy to obtain. The activities of the various philanthropic societies must be followed largely in their own reports, with those of the American Board and of the American Home Missionary Society particularly valuable. C. B. Goodykoontz, *Home Missions on the American Frontier* (Caldwell, Idaho, 1939) and S. L. Gulich, *The Winning of the Far East* (New York, 1924) are useful. H. K. Rowe, *History of Andover Theological Seminary* (Newton, Mass., 1933) is satisfactory. There are many contemporary religious works, as on the observance of the Sabbath, since religion ranks with sex in popular interest.

The best of the various histories of the Negro is J. H. Franklin, *From Slavery to Freedom* (New York, 1947). A number of monographs describe the position of the Negro, both slave and free, while the position of the planter also has received several treatments. Probably the best general account is U. B. Phillips, *Life and Labor in the Old South* (Boston, 1929). F. P. Gaines, *The Southern Plantation* (New York, 1924) traces a tradition. H. Aptheker, *American Negro Slave Revolts* (New York, 1943) is sympathetic. Best on the slave trade are W. E. B. Du Bois, *The Suppression of the African Slave Trade* (New York, 1896) and Frederick Bancroft, *Slave-Trading in the Old South* (Baltimore, 1931). W. H. Stephenson, *Isaac Franklin: Slave Trader* (University, La., 1938) is useful. The literature of the abolition movement is copious. Most influential at its time was T. D. Weld, *American Slavery As It Is* (New York, 1839). The letters of Weld and Birney have been published. R. V. Harlow, *Gerrit Smith* (New York, 1939) is good, and E. L. Fox,

The American Colonization Society (Baltimore, 1919) is satisfactory. The southern point of view is expressed in W. G. Jenkins, *Pro-Slavery Thought in the Old South* (Chapel Hill, 1935) and A. Y. Lloyd, *The Slavery Controversy* (Chapel Hill, 1939). The best over-all picture is G. H. Barnes, *The Anti-Slavery Impulse 1830–1844* (New York, 1933).

Crime and prisons need further treatment. John A. Murrell has been described with doubtful authenticity. Dueling is treated in W. C. Stevens, *Pistols at Ten Paces* (Cambridge, 1940). Contemporary descriptions of prison conditions are probably more useful than even the best histories, such as Blake McKelvey, *American Prisons* (Chicago, 1936) and O. F. Lewis, *The Development of American Prisons* (New York, 1922). N. K. Teeters, *They Were in Prison* (Philadelphia, 1937) concerns prison reform. Dorothea Dix's writings are useful, as well as a recent biography—H. E. Marshall, *Dorothea Dix* (Chapel Hill, 1937). The treatment of insanity and feeblemindedness must be followed largely in contemporary material, although A. Deutsch, *The Mentally Ill in America* (New York, 1937) is passable. Treatment of the blind is best described in L. E. Richards, *Samuel Gridley Howe* (New York, 1935), while M. S. Lamson, *Life and Education of Laura Dewey Bridgman* (Boston, 1879) is very interesting. Temperance material was abundant in the eighteen thirties; the best secondary account is J. A. Krout, *The Origins of Prohibition* (New York, 1925). The peace movement can be followed in the writings of such men as Ladd and Burritt, and in the publications of the American Peace Society. Merle Curti has written on various aspects of the movement; his general account is *Peace or War* (New York, 1936).

The history of science is generally a list of names and accomplishments, of little use to laymen, who include most historians. A few biographies are acceptable, as of Audubon, D. D. Owen, Douglas, Rafinesque, Fontaine, and the Roeblings. The best medical history is R. H. Shryock, *The Development of Modern Medicine* (Philadelphia, 1947). J. T. Flexner, *Doctors on Horseback* (New York, 1937) is very interesting. The last and best of the several accounts of the discovery of anesthetics is H. R. Raper, *Man Against Pain* (New York, 1945). Several biographies, as of Mott, Warren, Drake, and Beaumont, are fair. Most interesting research of its time was William Beaumont, *Experiments and Observations on the Gastric Juice* (Boston, 1833). Among the better special studies are H. B. Shafer, *The American Medical Profession* (New York, 1936); G. Rosen, *Fees and Fee Bills* (Baltimore, 1946); W. F. Norwood, *Medical Education* (Philadelphia, 1944); and W. T. Howard, *Public Health Administration* (Washington, 1924). Such specialties as phrenology and hypnotism were frequently found in contemporary accounts but there are few recent historical descriptions.

Sports are well covered in F. D. Dulles, *America Learns to Play* (New York, 1940); J. A. Krout, *Annals of American Sport* (New Haven, 1929); and Herbert Manchester, *Four Centuries of Sport in America* (New York, 1931). Individual sports have also received book treatment. Quite interesting are the early sporting books and magazines, including editions of the practically eternal Hoyle. The circus is treated in E. C. May, *The Circus* (New York, 1932), while M. R. Werner, *Barnum* (New York, 1923) is good.

The Arts

Basic for a study of American literature is a reading of the writers of the period. There are also many good biographies, of Irving, Longstreet, Simms, Emerson, Cooper, Poe, Legaré, Flint, Paulding, Sigourney, Hall, Thoreau, Pike, Halleck, and others. The outstanding general account is, of course, V. L. Parrington, *The Romantic Revolution* (New York, 1927). Various books of historical humor seem rather dull today. Special studies of particular merit include H. R. Brown, *The Sentimental Novel in America* (Durham, N. C., 1940); Van Wyck Brooks, *The Flowering of New England 1815–1865* (New York, 1936); F. L. Pattee, *The Development of the American Short Story* (New York, 1923); Albert Keiser, *The Indian in American Literature* (New York, 1933); L. L. Hazard, *The Frontier in American Literature* (New York, 1927); and F. W. Faxson, *Literary Annuals and Gift-Books* (Boston, 1912).

The bible for historical work on magazines is F. L. Mott, *A History of American Magazines* (New York, 1930). Various individual magazines, such as *The Southern Literary Messenger*, *Godey's Lady's Book*, and *Niles' Weekly Register*, have adequate accounts. Of the various histories of journalism, possibly A. M. Lee, *The Daily Newspaper in America* (New York, 1937) is best, although others are good. Various papers such as the *Sun, Evening Post,* and *Springfield Republica*n have adequate histories. There are biographies of such men as Greeley, Bennett, Dana, and Kendall.

Histories of the theater tend to be annalistic. Possibly best is A. Hornblow, *A History of the Theater in America* (2 vols., Philadelphia, 1919); and M. G. Mayorga, *A Short History of the American Drama* (New York, 1932) is satisfactory. The same annalistic quality appears in histories of the theater in certain cities, such as New York, Boston, Philadelphia, Nashville, and St. Louis. Lives of actors and actresses are usually poorly done, with honorable exceptions for the two recent lives of Fanny Kemble. Reminiscences by actors and managers, such as W. B. Wood, Sol Smith, N. M. Ludlow, and F. C. Wemyss are illuminating. Valuable special studies include P. I. Reed, *Realistic Presentation of American Characters in Native Plays* (Columbus, 1918); R. H. Ball, *The Amazing Career of Sir Giles Overreach* (Princeton, 1939); and Carl Wittke, *Tambo and Bones* (New York, 1930).

Histories of music are scarce and inadequate, even though a tremendous amount of music has been preserved for the historian; J. T. Howard, *Our American Music* (New York, 1931) does the job as well as any. Julius Mattfeld, *A Hundred Years of Grand Opera in New York* (New York, 1927) is annalistic. John Erskine, *The Philharmonic-Symphony Society* (New York, 1943) is eulogistic. A. L. Rich, *Lowell Mason* (Chapel Hill, 1946) is good.

In architecture, the best general accounts are T. E. Tallmadge, *The Story of Architecture in America* (New York, 1927) and Fiske Kimball, *American Architecture* (Indianapolis, 1928). H. M. P. Gallagher, *Robert Mills* (New York, 1935) is satisfactory. T. Hamlin, *Greek Revival Architecture in America* (New York, 1944) is good.

American painting is covered quite well in I. Isham and R. Cortissoz, *The History of American Painting* (New York, 1927). The most-discussed artist is S. F. B. Morse, largely, however, for his work on the telegraph. J. H. Morgan, *Gilbert Stuart and His Pupils* (New York, 1939) is good. H. T. Peters, *America on Stone*

(Garden City, 1931) concerns lithographs, and there is considerable material by Mr. Peters and others on Currier and Ives.

There is no good history of American sculpture, except as it appears in more general works, such as F. J. Mather, Jr., C. R. Morey, and W. J. Henderson, *The American Spirit in Art* (New Haven, 1923); and Eugen Neuhaus, *The History and Ideals of American Art* (Stanford, 1931). Early sculpturing is described interestingly in A. T. E. Gardner, *Yankee Stonecutters* (New York, 1945).

Index

Abolition: *see* Negro

Acrobats: 384; *see also* circus

Actors: *see* theater *and specific actors*

Adams, Alvin: 177

Adams, J. Q.: 12, 75, 77, 149, 169, 253, 300, 354, 381

Adams Express Company: 178

Agriculture: *see* farming

Alcott, Bronson: 240–41

Allen, Elizabeth: 399

Allen, Ethan: 62

Allston, Washington: 12, 360, 362

American Anti-Slavery Society: 295–97, 298, 299

American Asylum: 278

American Bible Society: 272

American Board of Commissioners for Foreign Missions: 79, 274–76

American Eclectic Medical Association: 316

American Education Society: 272

American Ethnological Society: 65

American Fur Company: 68

American Historical Society: 405

American Home Missionary Society: 267, 270, 273–74, 288

American Journal of Dental Science: 323

American Liberal Tract and Education Society: 256

American Lyceum: 252

American Monthly Magazine: 408

American Peace Society: 301

American Quarterly: 408

American Society for the Colonization of the Free People of Color of the United States: 294

American Society for the Promotion of Temperance: 288, 292

American Society of Dental Surgeons: 323

American Sunday School Union: 53, 273

American Tract Society: 272–73

American Union for the Relief and Improvement of the Colored Races: 294

American and Foreign Anti-Slavery Society: 300

Amherst College: 244, 249

Amulet: 408

Amusements: *see individual entries*

Andover Theological Seminary: 250, 251

Apprentices: *see* labor

Anesthetics: 319–20

Animal Magnetism: *see* hypnotism

Annals of Education: 252

Ararat (Niagara River island): 266

Archery: 351

Architecture: 10, 14, 35, 38, 39, 365–67

Army: 59, 62–63, 67, 69–71, 290, 300

Art: *see specific subjects*

Artisans: *see* labor

Asphaltum: 43

Association for the Relief of Respectable Aged Indigent Females: 277

Astor, J. J.: 67–68

Astor House: 35, 191–92

Astronomy: 325

Atheism: 257

Atlantic Souvenir: 406

Auburn plan (penal system): 285, 288

Audubon, J. J.: 13

Autograph albums: 357

Automatons: 347

Baldwin, Matthias: 176

Balloon ascensions: 347

Ballou, Hosea: 260

Balls: 210

Baltimore: 38, 45, 46, 168, 266, 344

428

433

UNIVERSITY OF OKLAHOMA PRESS

NORMAN